# From
# Sight
# to
# Insight

# From Sight to Insight

## Steps in the Writing Process

### Jeff Rackham

Holt, Rinehart and Winston
New York   Chicago   San Francisco   Atlanta   Dallas
Montreal   Toronto

**Library of Congress Cataloging in Publication Data**

Rackham, Jeff.
From sight to insight.

  Includes index.
  1. English language—Rhetoric.  2. College readers.
I. Title.
PE1408.R13      808′.0427      79-22654

**ISBN 0-03-047566-X**

0  1  2  3      090      9  8  7  6  5  4  3  2

# Preface

*From Sight to Insight* is organized according to the actual process most of us go through when we struggle to put words on the page: (1) perception of subject, (2) recognition of audience, (3) discovery or imitation of form, (4) writing of the first draft, (5) rewriting, and (6) editing. Each of the six steps is repeated, reviewed, and expanded upon in eight separate units. For example, the first chapters on perception of subject ask the student to see and describe specific details about objects, places, and people. In the next unit, introductory chapters on perception require the student to observe and assemble more complex qualities about people (emotions, values, character). Then the emphasis begins a gradual shift from the sensory and imaginative to more objective observations, interviews, and investigations of issues as seen in their relationship to people. By the middle units the act of perception is given increasing structure by demonstrating how some of the traditional models of exposition clarify and organize observations, thoughts, and ideas. The various emotional blocks to reasoning and the dangers of depending solely on personal observation are made clear. Finally, the student is moved through critical analysis and asked to think logically about relationships.

This pattern of growth is repeated for each of the six steps in the writing process. The text leads the student from the personal, imaginative, and concrete to the objective, critical, and abstract; from the senses and emotions to ideas and values. Each step in the writing process is repeated at least five times, often as many as twelve times, but always at a higher level of difficulty.

Because these phases represent a simplification of a process that is, in reality, never identical for any two of us, it seems important to offer the student as many options as possible for discovering his or her own potential at every level. I have, therefore, tried to show how professional writing skills—those of the creative writer, journalist, and essayist—as well as those skills developed through academic and rhetorical models, should be understood as parts of one unified writing process, all of which can be related by an underlying humanistic philosophy.

It was not possible, of course, to avoid some arbitrary decisions about where to locate certain skill developments. In each case, I was guided by a single principle: simple elements should be learned before complex elements. That has led me to divide some traditionally unified concepts into separate but learnable steps. In other texts, for example, documentation is usually reserved for the research paper. The student often feels overwhelmed and inhibited by the massive technicalities. To avoid that, I have introduced informal, in-text documentation at the point where the student first begins to use short excerpts or ideas from written sources and interviews. Documentation requirements then increase gradually throughout the book, reaching the level of formal footnotes and bibliographies only by the end when the student is fully prepared.

In other cases, I have delayed concepts traditionally emphasized at the beginning. No doubt, all instructors want their students to write coherently from the first day as I do. But ten years of experience in using this method of teaching the process have shown that while students are working through the first three or four writing projects on description, narration, and reporting, they have almost no serious difficulty presenting their observations in a naturally related sequence. During those early phases, I find it more valuable to stress other skills. But once students begin to work with abstract ideas, first in Unit 4 and especially in Units 5 and 6, problems with unity and coherence may begin to appear. Thus, a discussion of coherence is postponed until the point when it seems most valuable.

Nine student essays have been included in their entirety. Each was selected because it represented "good" work but not necessarily "outstanding" work. I believe that such a decision is justifiable because the most outstanding work often has about it an originality that literally can't be imitated by someone else. The same principle guided me in selecting fourteen essays by professional writers. The readings collected in best-selling anthologies usually represent the finest examples of thought and style to be found in recent years. I am inevitably impressed. But when I ask myself whether an eighteen-year-old student from the inner city or a midwestern farm can learn to write from such brilliant examples, the answer is no. Students can and do profit from discussing ideas expressed in fine intellectual work (that's why I've not hesitated to include a rather difficult piece by C. S. Lewis in the chapter on Critical Reading). But when it comes to writing, the average freshman needs something more basic and imitable. Thus the professionally written essays included at the end of each unit have been selected not only to illustrate the concepts discussed in the particular unit, but also because they provide models that seem humanly possible to imitate.

Any effective text must also offer both instructor and student the flexibility to meet varying rates of progress. That is why I've provided a "Quick Reference" chart on the inside back cover. It lists skills and techniques that either the instructor or student can locate and make use of at the moment they seem most needed. An *Instructor's Manual* is available. It may be obtained through a local Holt representative or by writing to the English Editor, College Department, Holt, Rinehart and Winston, 383 Madison Avenue, New York, NY 10017.

In preparing this book, I am indebted to many people: to Joseph Sperry for his early encouragement and criticism; to Michael Neuman and Mary Baxter for their support and student examples; to Susan Hopwood and Eric Beversluis for their helpful critiques of specific chapters; to Richard Green of Capital University for providing the time and opportunity; to Robert M. Brown, University of Maryland, College Park; Larry S. Champion, North Carolina State University, Raleigh; David Martin, Monmouth College; Russell J. Meyer, University of Missouri, Columbia; Robert S. Rudolph, University of Toledo; and Thomas L. Warren, Oklahoma State University, Stillwater, for their perceptive criticism of the whole manuscript; to Richard Beal, who repeatedly found the key that solved difficult organizational problems and who encouraged ever higher standards; and, most of all, to my wife, Olivia Bertagnolli, who contributed, criticized, encouraged, and endured. Finally, I want to express my gratitude to Wilson R. Thornley, who taught me that through writing one can discover what it means to be a human being. It is to his spirit, ever alive in all his students, that this book is dedicated.

J.R.

*Columbus, Ohio*

# Contents

*Preface   v*

**INTRODUCTION**
*The Writing Process   1*

**PART ONE   Writing from
Experience   9**

**1 PERCEPTION**
*Exploring the Senses   11*

| | |
|---|---|
| Exercises | *14* |
| Suggested Writing Assignments | *15* |

**2 PERCEPTION**
*Perception and Language   17*

| | |
|---|---|
| Exercises | *21* |
| Suggested Writing Assignments | *22* |

**3 PERCEPTION**
*Being Honest to Your Experience   24*

| | |
|---|---|
| Exercises | *28* |
| Suggested Writing Assignments | *29* |

**4 AUDIENCE**
*Discovering Audience and Voice   31*

| | |
|---|---|
| Exercises | *37* |

**5 FIRST DRAFT**
*Facing the Blank Page   40*

| | |
|---|---|
| Exercises | *44* |

**6 REWRITING**

*Rewriting for Precision and Feeling* **45**

Exercises *50*

**7 EDITING**

*Editing Sentences for Unnecessary Words* **53**

Exercises *59*
Editorial Checklist for Part One *61*

**READINGS**  The Championship Move  *David Hinkle (student essay)* *62*
Being a Boy  *Julius Lester* *64*
Home for Christmas  *Carson McCullers* *67*

**PART TWO**  **Describing People and Places** **71**

**8 PERCEPTION**

*Focusing Perceptions* **73**

Exercises and Suggested Writing Assignments *78*

**9 PERCEPTION**

*Focusing on Character* **81**

Suggested Writing Assignments *87*

**10 FORM AND FIRST DRAFT**

*Creating a Scene* **90**

Exercises *95*
Suggested Writing Assignments *96*

**11 REWRITING AND EDITING**

*Using Strong Verbs* **98**

Exercises *103*
Editorial Checklist for Part Two *105*

**READINGS**  Grandpa and Me  *Sandie Ell (student essay)* *106*
from The Bird and the Machine  *Loren Eiseley* *108*
Remembering Dylan Thomas  *Donald Hall* *111*

## PART THREE Objective Reporting 115

**12 PERCEPTION**
*Perception and Objectivity 117*

Exercises 122
Suggested Writing Assignments 124

**13 PERCEPTION**
*Finding and Selecting Facts 125*

Exercises 131
Suggested Writing Assignments 132

**14 AUDIENCE**
*Context, Purpose, and Voice 133*

Exercises 137

**15 FORM AND FIRST DRAFT**
*Basic Forms in Factual Reporting 139*

Exercises 144

**16 REWRITING**
*Reshaping, Rearranging, Integrating 146*

Exercises 151

**17 EDITING**
*Editing Sentences for Rhythm, Variety, and Emphasis 154*

Exercises 163
Editorial Checklist for Part Three 166

**READINGS** Jazz Studies *Karl Ott (student essay)* 167
Policewomen *Elizabeth Breed Clark* 169
The Poison in Clear Lake *Rachel Carson* 171

# PART FOUR  Factual Investigation  175

**18 PERCEPTION**
*Seeing Beyond the Surface*  177
Exercises                                                          187

**19 PERCEPTION**
*Primary and Secondary Sources*  193
Exercises                                                          198
Suggested Writing Assignment                                       200

**20 FIRST DRAFT**
*Imaginative Leads*  201
Exercises                                                          207

**21 FORM**
*Visual Form*  210
Exercises                                                          215

**22 REWRITING AND EDITING**
*The Paragraph as a Unit of Thought*  217
Exercises                                                          222
Editorial Checklist for Part Four                                  226

**READINGS**  Back to Basics: Good or Bad?  *Debbie Zwick (student essay)*    227
New Myth on Campus  *Roger Rapoport*    230
Hey Kid, Wanna Buy a Used Term Paper?  *Phyllis Zagano*    234

# PART FIVE  Writing About Ideas, Issues, and Values  237

**23 PERCEPTION**
*Expository Patterns of Perception*  239
Exercises                                                          248
Suggested Writing Assignment                                       250

**24** **AUDIENCE AND FORM**
*Shaping the Formal Essay*  253

The Workaholic in You, Warren Boroson   260
Exercises                                 266

**25** **REWRITING**
*The Art of Coherence*  268

Exercises                                 274

**26** **REWRITING**
*The Challenge of Simplicity*  277

Exercises                                 280

**27** **EDITING**
*Proofreading and Mechanics*  282

Editorial Checklist for Part Five         298
**READINGS** The Option of Marriage or Cohabitation
     *Pamela J. Drake (student essay)*    299
Disability Isn't Beautiful   *Nancy Weinberg*  301
Understanding Rape   *Susan Brownmiller*  303


**PART SIX    Formal Analysis    307**

**28** **PERCEPTION**
*Developing an Awareness of Critical
    Thinking*  309

Exercises                                 317

**29** **PERCEPTION**
*Critical Reading*  321

We Have No "Right to Happiness," C. S. Lewis   325
Exercises                                 334
Suggested Writing Assignment              336

**30** **FORM**
*The Structure of Formal Analysis*  337

Exercises                                 343
*A Critical Analysis of "A Letter to Landers,"*
    Jan Kuntz (student essay)             343

*A Little Distortion Never Hurt Anyone—Much,*
John Restrepo (student essay)                               346
Editorial Checklist for Part Six                           349

**READINGS**   The Abortion Culture   *Nick Thimmesch*      350
Should Seat Belts Be Mandated by Law?
*Bud Shuster*                              353


## PART SEVEN   Critiquing the Arts   357

### 31 PERCEPTION
#### *Developing an Awareness of the Arts  359*

*Traveling Through the Dark,* William Stafford             364
Exercises                                                  367
*The River-Merchant's Wife: A Letter,* Ezra Pound          367
*The Taxi,* Susan Fromberg Schaeffer                       370


### 32 PERCEPTION
#### *Reading for Literary Significance  373*

*The Book of the Grotesque,* Sherwood Anderson             376
Exercises                                                  384
*Piano,* D. H. Lawrence                                    385
*A Blessing,* James Wright                                 386
*in Just-* E. E. Cummings                                  387
*The Parable of the Good Samaritan*                        388


### 33 FORM
#### *The Formal Critique  389*

Exercises                                                  395
*Truth in the Grotesque,* Diane Key (student essay)        395
Suggested Writing Assignment                               398
Editorial Checklist for Part Seven                         399

**READINGS**   During Wind and Rain   *Thomas Hardy*       400
from A Street in Bronzeville, The Mother
*Gwendolyn Brooks*                              401
What Were They Like? (Questions and Answers)
*Denise Levertov*                              402
The Pennycandystore Beyond the El   *Lawrence Ferlinghetti*                          403

Sonnet LXXIII   *William Shakespeare*            *403*
Lullaby   *Leslie Silko*                          *404*
A Conversation with My Father   *Grace Paley*     *411*

**PART EIGHT   Scholarly
Research   417**

**34   PERCEPTION AND AUDIENCE**
*Preliminary Steps in Research   419*
Suggested Writing Assignment                      *428*

**35   PERCEPTION**
*Thoughtful Note-Taking   430*
Exercises                                         *437*

**36   FORM**
*Organizing Complex Material   442*

**37   FIRST DRAFT AND REWRITING**
*Drafting and Documenting   448*

**38   REWRITING AND EDITING**
*Self-Criticism   456*
Exercises                                         *460*

**39   EDITING**
*The Whole of It   462*
Exercise                                          *468*
*Disorder? Or Just Different?* Donna Pastor
   (student research paper)                        *473*

*Index   491*

# From Sight to Insight

# The Writing Process

Poet Marvin Bell tells a story about the beauty of Korean teapots. Sometime during the past century Japanese potters became frustrated with their own efforts. They knew that Korean masters turned out the most beautiful teapots in the world. No one knew how. The Japanese elected a committee of distinguished artisans to study and analyze Korean pots. After years of labor the committee announced they had discovered ten irreducible elements of beauty. Japanese potters, they said, must reproduce those ten elements if they wished to achieve superior works of art. Try as they might, the Japanese turned out stiff and awkward pots, mere copies, lacking all grace and virtue. Korean pots remained mysteriously more beautiful. Only later did the answer become clear: the committee of experts had studied form, symmetry, color, even quality and density of clay. The Japanese potters bravely attempted to imitate each of the findings, but the findings were based on conscious analysis of finished products. The committee had not investigated the largely unconscious process used by the Korean masters in their daily work, in the actual making of the pots. It was the process, not the product, that held the secret.

Effective writing also seems like a mysterious accomplishment to many people. You may be one of those for whom writing has always seemed impossible. You may even hate to write. A lot of people do. One reason may be that so many teachers and students have always sought out the nature of good writing in the finished work, in essays and poems of famous authors. They've analyzed well-written arguments by George Orwell or profound moral essays by Bertrand Russell, and they have indeed found basic elements of good writing; they've categorized how great authors organized, shaped, selected, and envisioned their material. We even have names for the most successful and traditional models: narration, argumentation, exposition, and so on. But when we try to use such models for our own work, most of us feel frustrated and helpless. I always have. What I have to say never seems to fit into such honored rhetorical patterns. Over the years, I've found most of my students feeling the same frustration. By comparison to the masterpieces of English prose, our awkward essays read like failures, lacking all grace and virtue. Unfortunately, without intending to do so, teachers sometimes reinforce the negative feelings by focusing on student errors—on the number of ways their students failed to match up to the standard. But maybe, like Japanese potters, we've been looking too long at the product instead of the process. The best analysis of a well-written novel (or memo or report or research paper) cannot reveal the false starts, the thrown-away words and paragraphs, or the agony the author felt each morning staring at the blank page. Nor does it reveal how an author finally discovered what it was he or she wanted to say.

This book then is about a process instead of a product. I confess I'll sometimes analyze or explain a rhetorical model, and there will be many discussions of craft, but I hope it will be seen only in a context of finding a method, a *way* of getting ideas onto the page, not as a standard by which to judge one's own worth. And there *are* ways of working that seem to help writers. Because we are individuals, the process is not always identical for each of us. It can't be, just as there can't be ten irreducible elements of beauty or sixteen rules for playing the piano. But by investigating the methods successful writers go through, we find that certain phases seem to recur, enough so that we can identify six general steps most writers seem to follow.

## Step One: Perception of the Subject

All writers need to know about their subject; they also need to learn how to know about it, how to look, how to investigate, how to see relationships. In many ways this first step in the writing process is the single most important element in achieving meaningful, intelligent prose.

Perception begins as a sensory act. You must see your subject (and sometimes hear it, taste it, touch it, smell it). Ideas do not float in midair. You discover them in the process of looking at specific details, searching out patterns, bringing together seemingly unrelated parts. A business executive makes a special trip to Texas, where she personally observes the market for her product; she listens to opinions from local officials; she surveys needs of the community; she takes notes on facts found in a government report; she studies statistics provided by a university analysis.

Only then does she write her report to the company president. A social worker needs funds to develop housing projects for the aged. He searches for supporting evidence in local welfare records; he interviews supporters of the project; he selects two good examples from over fifty case studies; he makes a visual survey of the neighborhood to gather concrete impressions. Only then does he begin to write his grant proposal. No matter what your goal in writing, the first step is to see the subject clearly.

Yet the mind can be overwhelmed by too many details. Part of the perception process involves learning how to focus intensely on a manageable part of the whole subject and then how to select only the most significant details from that smaller part. Learning how to focus and select requires practice. Most writing assignments, whether in your school or in your career, will already have some degree of focus: write a ten-page analysis of economic relations between Cuba and Haiti; write an essay on character growth in *Huckleberry Finn*. But even these subjects will usually prove too broad. The writer always has the responsibility for narrowing a subject. Otherwise, a jumble of impressions leads to a confused and unfocused paper, like a home movie that jumps from "Our Vacation in the Rockies" to "Esther's Third Birthday." Focusing and selecting must become automatic steps for every writer.

Perception is ultimately the source of your ideas. In working through facts, details, statistics; in listening to others' opinions; in personal observation, you begin to combine and compare, to differentiate, to see relationships and patterns. For many, the understanding of a subject, the ideas and insights, will occur even before a word has been written; for others, like myself, the act of writing may be the only way of forcing the mind to shape and order the material. Obviously, I am using the term *perception* in a general sense to include a great many acts that go on in the mind, but the original meaning of the term includes the notion of "seeing all the way through a subject," of reaching "understanding." I think then that if we accept the concept in its broadest sense, we can fairly say that a well-written paper is the result of an intense perceptive process that may take as much training and development as the actual writing of sentences and paragraphs.

## Step Two: Recognition of the Audience

We're all aware that writing is an act of communication. Few beginning writers realize how significant a determining factor the audience is in terms of both the way we perceive the subject and the way we write about it.

The audience may well influence the way you go about looking at a subject. If a lawyer writes a brief for a judge, it had better be logical and concise; it must be documented with facts and precedents. But in turn, that means the lawyer must *see* the subject in the same way. His client may have wrecked a car one warm summer night when waves pounded against the beach and the scent of orange blossoms hung in the air. Those are all good sensory details derived from perception. But they won't influence the judge. A different selection of details is called for: the lawyer had better find facts on road conditions: a broken safety barrier and the number of other accidents that have recently occurred on that same curve. The details a writer searches for depend not only on the subject but also on the audience—and on the way the writer hopes to affect that audience.

Writing is almost always a private act. But the product (the essay, report, critical analysis) is a public performance. As in all social actions, convention and custom influence the parties involved. The shaping of your ideas, the voice you speak in, the level of your vocabulary, the formality of your sentences, even your grammar and punctuation may be influenced by the type of audience you're trying to reach. You would probably agree that safety instructions to plant employees should be written in short, declarative statements that allow for no ambiguity. Regardless of the shop supervisor's poetic spirit or need to express his inner self, that supervisor cannot be allowed to write safety instructions in free verse. Yet an essay written for a Shakespearean scholar assumes a different audience with a different set of expectations. We can speculate that the Shakespearean scholar might quickly become bored with a paper written in short, declarative sentences. Why, she asks the student, can't you let a little more of yourself come through? Where is your own voice, the flow and rhythm of some kind of personal style? Successful writers anticipate the needs of the reader. They recognize that conventions exist, not as unbreakable rules, but as traditional patterns that have proved successful in easing communication.

Recognition of the audience and its needs must occur almost simultaneously with *perception of the subject*. Honest writers will not change their ideas to please a particular audience, but they must often be willing to change many other elements—selection of evidence, organization of details, tone and level of vocabulary—all for one reason: to communicate their ideas as effectively as possible.

## Step Three: Discovery of Form

In spite of Wordsworth's famous assertion that poetry is a "spontaneous overflow of emotion," no writing, not even poetry, is ever totally spontaneous. No doubt, the best writing often sounds spontaneous, but some sort of organization or form always disciplines content. In prose, most forms, such as the essay or narrative, are open-structured, allowing enormous freedom for exploring and developing a subject. Other than a few obvious requirements like beginnings, middles, and ends, no inflexible patterns exist. You may be suspicious of the whole notion. Organizing, shaping, forming have always been the great stumbling blocks to professional writers as well as students. The reason is easy to identify: finding form in a subject is a process of ordering chaos. In other words, it's hard work. You may have focused your subject, selected your details, and clearly identified your audience; but if you're like me, you'll still have a head jumbled with subpoints, half-formed ideas, images, and hunches. No outburst of spontaneous writing will magically shape that material into a coherent message. Exhilarating moments of inspiration do occur from time to time, but most attempts to organize require sustained effort.

Placing *discovery of form* as the third step in the process, however, is merely arbitrary. The shape or organization of a paper may be determined by the writer's special perception of the subject or by the limitations and biases of a particular audience. Form may be consciously organized with a Roman numeral outline, or it may evolve gradually from the writing itself. Knowledge and practice of techniques developed by professional writers can often ease your way. For example, professional writers have developed something called the "lead." A lead quickly defines and limits your subject, establishes tone, and suggests a pattern of organization, all in a sentence or two. Other successful writers make line-by-line drawings to "design" their work with boxes, circles, and pyramids. Still others depend upon traditional forms, arguing that they can give more attention to internal subject matter if they allow convention to establish external outlines. Each of these different methods will be discussed later to provide you with a number of options for any one writing situation.

## Step Four: Writing a First Draft

Ray Bradbury once said that "writing must be as immediate as life, or there are no juices, no chance to involve yourself or others in your vitality." I've known many students who approached the act of writing with such dread that the product they produced expressed little of their lives and nothing of their vitality. So many student papers read as if they were written by a first-generation computer with faulty wiring: awkward sentences, distorted vocabulary, too many words and not enough substance, a stumbling lack of logic. Where are the juices? Where are the human beings that never seem to emerge from these shapings of their native language? And yet other students write with remarkable fluency, with a zest that reveals their own voice and spirit. Some even feel free to let ideas grow out of accidents, to play with words. Surprisingly, the difference does not seem to lie in natural ability as much as in the initial attitude a writer brings to the blank page. Perhaps one of the most serious misunderstandings about the writing process is a failure to envision the first draft, not just as a separate stage, but as a stage requiring a separate mental attitude.

In writing about creativity, psychologist Abraham H. Maslow said we must distinguish between a primary phase and a secondary phase. During the primary phase, writers lose their pasts and their futures. They live only in the moment, "immersed, fascinated and absorbed in the present, in the current situation, in the here-now, with the matter-in-hand." While writing the first draft, you must become willing to suspend—at least temporarily—a critical attitude. You must teach yourself to "let it flow," to write fast, talking to the page about what you know; you must allow digressions to occur. The first draft is the point where you get down your perceptions, follow your hunches, *see* the subject intensely in your mind as you write, often ignoring your notes and your outline. The first draft is the stage where you allow yourself to make mistakes, where you don't worry about any of the rules, the right word or the conclusion. You just write. There will be time later to judge what you've written, to rewrite, to correct. But unless you've captured the subject in your own voice, you'll have nothing to improve upon. Vitality in writing usually has its origin in the first draft stage.

## Step Five: Rewriting

I once knew a friend who rewrote her material with the same attitude she had when she wrote a first draft. She simply began again, almost without reference to what she had just written. Each draft was composed in the light of what she had learned about her subject in the previous draft. She pushed ahead, trusting her mind to develop ideas further, to clarify logic and order. Each draft was a rediscovery of her subject with renewed excitement and more depth.

I always envied her, but I could never work that way. Once I've completed a first draft, I spread out with red pencil, black pen, scissors, and tape. My attitude is more self-critical than during the first draft. I cross out sentences, draw arrows, write new ideas in the margin. I juggle the order by cutting out paragraphs and taping them into new arrangements. From time to time I stop and retype whole sections. The retyping reveals new flaws. Sometimes I read aloud and let my ear catch the imprecise word, the tangled sentence. My friend and I approach rewriting in almost opposite ways. Other writers follow other patterns. But all of us rewrite until the shape of a subject begins to find its wholeness. Some students believe that novels like *War and Peace* simply burst forth from the mind of an author, each perfect sentence following the next. The experienced writer knows better. Painters, architects, sculptors—and writers—all work from rough sketches that only gradually take on shape and substance.

I heard recently about a business executive who ordered a new advertising campaign. When a team of writers submitted the proposed material, he let it lie untouched on his desk for three days, then called the authors to his office. "Is this the best you can do?" he asked. No, they admitted sheepishly. There had been time pressure, other interruptions. They could do better. A week later they submitted the advertising campaign again, and again the executive let it lie unread on his desk. When he called them three days later he asked, "Is this the best you can do?" No, they admitted—but with more reluctance and a sense of frustration. No, they could do better. The process was repeated; the material, resubmitted. On the third day the executive asked, "Is this the best you can do?" This time the team of writers insisted it was. Yes. This was the best. "Good," the executive replied. "Now I'll read it."

Obviously, it would be a mistake to think that good writing is demanded only in college or that rewriting is not one of the essential steps in the process.

## Step Six: Editing

After drafting and rewriting, much remains to be done. Editing requires a cool, slow, line-by-line examination. For some, this step may partially overlap the rewriting phase. For others, it seems most successful as a final and separate act. Often the work is laid aside, the intense involvement in the subject, allowed to cool. Later, the writer returns to the paper with a critical eye, acting as his or her own editor.

As an editor you bring to your manuscript the attitude of an old craftsman. You want every word to be precise; you feel that every unnecessary word should be eliminated and every verb should be strong. Sentence structures must be grammatically acceptable. You want each sentence to move the idea, the feeling, the rhythm of your voice easily toward the next sentence. Paragraphs must reveal a coherency, a central focus, and a sense of unity. Each paragraph must relate to the preceding and following paragraphs. As an editor you won't hestitate to relocate a paragraph or strike it entirely if it does not contribute. Finally, the order and logic of the whole must seem apparent. The title must be considered as carefully as the conclusion. No detail is forgotten, not even (alas!) punctuation and spelling.

Learning how to edit means learning when to edit. If you begin too soon in the writing process, you may edit out your own personality in favor of safe, anonymous-sounding prose; you may even prevent your ideas from reaching their most developed form. That's why an understanding of the process can be so valuable to your writing. Editing must constitute the final phase (or at least occur no sooner than the rewriting phase). Editing must come at the point when what you have to say is important enough that every detail about how you say it seems worth perfecting.

Final editing of your manuscript is your responsibility. Someday you'll need to write a lab report for your team manager or a regional analysis for your county supervisor or a critical evaluation of court procedures for your law firm. No English instructor will be standing by to correct your paper in red ink. And it seems unlikely that your secretary will be better educated than you are. Better to set high standards now and teach yourself how to reach them. Editing will not in itself make for good writing, but good writing is simply not possible without careful editing.

## The Final Synthesis

The *writing process* is not mechanical formula. At best it should suggest a pattern, not a rigid prescription. As you work on assignments, you'll find that some steps in the process merge or overlap. I've already noted that recognition of the audience affects the voice you choose to write in. To divide subject, audience, and voice into individual steps is an act of analysis. To draw them all together, as eventually you must, requires an act of synthesis. Just as you learn tennis by studying the forehand, backhand, and serve separately, consciously, you must eventually begin to play the game intuitively. We do not know how intuition works. We cannot teach it in the classroom. Yet this inner thing, this inner sensing for which we have no satisfactory explanation, is as much a part of successful writing as the process outlined here.

Gradually, with hard work and self-discipline, practice in the writing process sets in motion an inner growth. Those Korean teapots were not beautiful merely because of correctly learned skills and techniques; they were beautiful because in the process of creation the artisan discovered something about himself and the clay. The teapot became an expression of some part of him. By working through the writing process, you work through the very process necessary to begin an understanding of yourself; you work with the way the mind perceives, selects, shapes, and envisions the world. Good writing is always an exploration and articulation of our intelligence, of the uniqueness of individual human natures. That is why writing is, or should be, a humanistic act. It extends our imaginations and makes us receptive to our intuitions. Writing increases our sensitivity to emotion, clarifies thought, and makes judgment more rigorous. The writing process is the beginning of movement from sight to insight.

# PART

## Writing from Experience

# ONE

*Creativity is the encounter of the intensively conscious human being with his world.*

—Rollo May

Writing about the self or about personal experience is not necessarily easier than writing an objective report. In some ways it may be more difficult because it requires a courage and self-scrutiny that, say, writing a research paper on sixteenth-century art does not. Yet "personal writing" is the most natural place to begin a course in writing. In seeking to find out how to write effectively, we discover that effective writing is (or should be) a natural extension of an inner voice. Writing about personal experience allows us the opportunity to discover and explore that voice before a sympathetic and willing audience.

# 1 *Exploring the Senses*

All human experience begins with sensory perception. We may know some things intuitively, and like most other animals we probably possess innate drives—to defend a plot of land, to reproduce sexually. But even our awareness of such primal elements in human nature comes from our ability to see and hear. Anthropologists know something about human social development because they have *observed* it in varying cultures. Psychologists know something about the workings of the mind because they have *listened* to thousands of patients. As a child you learned about the world only through your sensory perceptions of it. You learned that rocks taste slick and cold when you suck on them, that dandelions smell pungent, that the touch of your mother's hand feels warm. Our emotions are especially affected by sensory experience. You do not fall in love with an abstraction. You love a specific young man or woman with red or blond hair, with blue or black eyes, with soft voice and a dimple in the chin— and a name: Lynn, Bob, Garvin, Maria. Most of us even feel differently when we see a sunny sky than when we wake up and see dark rain streaking our window. All intellectual and emotional experience begins in the senses, in seeing, hearing, smelling, touching, and tasting.

Because effective writing usually begins with a subject before it begins with words, your perception of the subject is the natural starting place for every essay, every research paper, every report, every business letter. Good writing is essentially good thinking. And good thinking derives from the ability to perceive critically, to discriminate between important details and unimportant details, to be sensitive to subtleties, to recognize relationships. Each of these concepts involves an act of perception. Beginning now to exercise and extend your perceptive ability through the senses—as well as imaginatively and critically—leads to the process of self-education that is the ultimate goal of a university experience.

Professional writers have always known the value of the senses: they know that because we learn about the world through sight and sound, they must use language that communicates as directly as possible to the eye and ear. The more sensory details, the more the reader is likely to get involved, not just intellectually, but emotionally and even physically with what he or she is reading. Advertisers know they can sell dishwashing detergent if they say it smells like lemons; they can sell mouthwash by asserting that because it tastes like medicine, it must be good for us; they can sell automobiles by calling attention to the heavy thunk when the door slams. The appeal to sensory experience actually makes us willing to spend hard-earned money even when we may not need the product.

In 1932, James Agee visited the home of a tenant farmer in Georgia. Agee felt deeply moved by the experience, by the poverty, the shattered lives. He wrote about his first overnight stay with the family. Had he not known the value of sense perception, this is what he might have told us:

> The bedroom was as shabby as the rest of the cabin and very uncomfortable. I lay down on the bed but found it difficult to sleep. It was miserable and the mattress made noises. After a while I discovered bugs. Just lying there was more than I could stand, so I tried to kill as many as I could find.

But Agee knew that if he wanted us to share his experience, he had to provide sensory details. He had to stimulate our sight and touch the way his had been stimulated. Here is what he actually wrote in *Let Us Now Praise Famous Men:*

> [I saw] how the shutters filled their squares of window and were held shut with strings and nails: crevices in the walls, stuffed with hemp, rags, newsprint, and raw cotton: large damp spots and rivulets on the floor, and on the walls, streams and crooked wetness; and a shivering, how chilly and wet the air is in this room. . . .
>
> I sat on the edge of the bed, turned out the lamp, and lay back along the outside of the covers. After a couple of minutes I got up, stripped, and slid in between the sheets. The bedding was saturated and full of chill as the air was, its lightness upon me nervous like a belt too loosely buckled. The sheets were at the same time coarse and almost slimily or stickily soft: much the same ma-

terial floursacks are made of. There was a ridgy seam down the middle. I could feel the thinness and lumpiness of the mattress and the weakness of the springs. The mattress was rustling noisy if I turned or contracted my body. The pillow was hard, thin, and noisy, and smelled as of acid and new blood; the pillowcase seemed to crawl at my cheek. I thouched it with my lips: it felt a little as if it would thaw like spun candy. There was an odor something like that of old moist stacks of newspaper. . . . I began to feel sharp little piercings and crawlings all along the surface of my body. I was not surprised; I had heard that pine is full of them anyhow. . . . it was bugs all right. I felt places growing on me and scratched at them, and they became unmistakable bedbug bites. . . . To lie there naked feeling whole regiments of them tooling at me, knowing I must be imagining two out of three, became more unpleasant than I could stand. I struck a match and a half-dozen broke along my pillow: I caught two, killed them, and smelled their queer rankness. They were full of my blood. I struck another match and spread back the cover; they rambled off by the dozens. I got out of bed, lighted the lamp. . . . I killed maybe a dozen in all; I couldn't find the rest; but I did find fleas, and, along the seams of the pillow and mattress, small gray translucent brittle insects which I suppose were lice. . . .

Nearly half a century has passed, yet Agee still involves us directly in his experience.

| | |
|---|---|
| *sight* | shutters held together with string |
| | crevices in the wall stuffed with rags |
| | bedbugs bloated with blood running in the match light |
| *touch* | chill in the air |
| | wetness on the walls |
| | slimy sheets |
| | a ridgy seam |
| | bedbugs crawling on his body |
| *sound* | the rustling mattress |
| | the striking match |
| *smell* | the odor of old moist newspapers |
| | a pillow that smells like acid and new blood |
| | the queer rankness of the bedbugs |

In order to use sensory experience as part of your writing, you must first train yourself to perceive more clearly and fully. I know that by the time I reached college, I had become dulled to my senses. I was no longer excited as I had been as a child by the touch of a shiny doorknob or the brand-new taste of chocolate chips melting on my tongue. Nor did I even trust my experience to be important or meaningful to others. Yet writing that omits sensory details leaves out the human element of our world, and, more often than not, the human element makes writing interesting, even vital to a reader. With effort and practice all of us can reinvigorate our senses and make ourselves once more conscious of our aliveness. Only when we begin to see clearly will we begin to write clearly.

## EXERCISES

Here are some games you might try in a journal. Some may sound overly simple, but most will prove surprisingly difficult, either because we have allowed so much of our sense perception to fade away or because we so seldom articulate sense perception in detail.

### Sight

Describe as many sight details about your left hand as possible. Do not stop after two or three sentences. Fill at least a page. Report the color, texture, line, shape, size, knuckles, fingernails, rings, hair, scratches, wrinkles—everything you can see.

### Sound

Write a detailed sense report of the sounds made by a machine (a lawn mower as it moves close to you, then away from you; a pinball machine; a quarter falling through a Coke machine). Start by listening, jotting down every word that comes to mind. Don't be afraid of strange or unusual words. This is a game. Let your mind play with what you hear. Then try to write a full paragraph on the sounds of the machine, using the best words or phrases from your list.

### Smell

Trace the history of a smell. Write down every odor when someone lights up a cigarette, cigar, or pipe. Smell the match or lighter. Smell the first whiffs of smoke. Keep going. Does the smell change after several minutes? After ten minutes? After the cigarette has been crushed out in an ashtray? Several hours later?

### Touch

A very old game is to blindfold yourself and then list all the words you can think of that describe the feel of a quarter or a ring. Keep touching until you have ten or twenty sensations.

### Taste

Taste is one of the most difficult senses to capture in words because we tend to describe our reactions (good, delicious, awful) rather than the taste itself. Try to write about the taste of something you can suck on slowly like a hard candy or, better yet, a plug of chewing tobacco. Find the words or phrases that report the actual taste; avoid the generalizations commercial advertisers use for such products, such as *natural flavor* or *long-lasting enjoyment*.

## SUGGESTED WRITING ASSIGNMENTS

In writing about personal experience, the beginning writer often wants to deal immediately with profound emotion. The result is usually a melodramatic outburst ("I am lonely! Lonely!"). Rather than feeling moved by such a cry, the reader is usually embarrassed. A professional writer knows that emotions are stimulated by real things in the world. To share experience with a reader, the writer must imaginatively portray the *thing* that inspires the original feeling. Begin small. Do not try to write about large emotions until you can first handle a simple but genuine experience arising from a simple cause.

1. Write a single paragraph on the sensory quality of an ordinary, everyday fruit or vegetable. Perhaps the most difficult writing of all is the kind that asks you to write about that with which you are familiar. We grow so accustomed to eating a carrot or a prune or a pickle that we may no longer really taste (or hear or smell). Do *not* do this exercise from memory. Sit down with a banana or a grape, and make a list of all the sense experiences it provokes.

2. Write a single paragraph on an object owned and valued by you or some member of your family. For example, your mother may own a wicker basket brought from Italy by her great-grandmother in 1822. Your brother might think his collection of arrowheads is the most magical thing in his life. Your father may have a battered trumpet he played in the University of Miami marching band. Your job is to look at the object, perceive it physically (sight, smell, touch, taste, sound), and write a paragraph that conveys it fully to the reader. You may, of course, want to identify its history or the emotion it brings to the person who owns it, but 90 percent of the paragraph should focus on the object itself. Here is Frank Conroy in *Stop-Time* describing a Yo-Yo he prized as a young boy. Note how much detail can be found in a simple object.

The common yo-yo is crudely made, with a thick shank between two widely spaced wooden disks. The string is knotted or stapled to the shank ... but looped over it in such a way as to allow the wooden part to spin freely on its own axis. The gyroscopic effect thus created kept the yo-yo stable in all attitudes. ...

The string was tied to my middle finger, just behind the nail. As I threw ... a short bit of string would tighten across the sensitive pad of flesh at the tip of my finger. That was the critical area. After a number of weeks I could interpret the condition of the string, the presence of any imperfections on the shank, but most importantly the exact amount of spin or inertial energy left in the yo-yo at any given moment—all from that bit of string on my fingertip. As the throwing motion became more natural I found I could make the yo-yo "sleep" for an astonishing length of time—fourteen or fifteen seconds—and still have enough spin left to bring it back to my hand. Gradually the basic moves became reflexes. Sleeping, twirling, swinging, and precise aim. Without thinking, without even looking, I could run through trick after trick involving various combinations of the elemental skills, switching from one to the other in a smooth continuous flow. On particularly good days, I would hum a tune under my breath and do it all in time to the music.

3. Most of you have known a special place at one time in your lives. It may have been the attic in your grandmother's house or perhaps a clubhouse you built in the woods or even a dark crawl space behind the furnace in an old apartment building—some place you felt was yours. Write a paragraph about it. Help the reader see, smell, and touch. Select the details that will help the reader to appreciate your feelings about it.

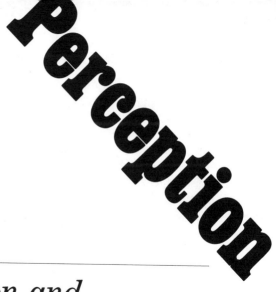

# 2 Perception and Language

Along with Shakespeare, Tolstoy, Mark Twain, and other writers who have endured, James Agee knew a simple truth about words: concrete, specific, and particular words stimulate sensory pictures in the mind. They help a reader share your experiences more fully. Concretions are words that suggest or name something we can see, hear, touch, smell, and taste, such as *trout, french bread, daffodils,* and *silk.* By contrast, general, abstract terms identify classes, qualities, or ideas, for example, *fish, nutrition, vegetation,* and *clothing.* The ability to abstract is one of the distinctions that separates our brains from the brains of other animals. Truly to think, we must abstract from sensory experience and reach an understanding of it. Indeed, without higher abstractions like *justice, democracy, hope,* and *human nature,* our thoughts would be severely limited. But such terms tend to be vague and, when overused, meaningless. More to the point, in writing about personal experience, if you allow yourself the comfort of the easy generalization, you'll find yourself failing to stretch your senses, failing to *look* for the real and immediate level of experience, and, of course, failing to share anything significant with your reader.

Here, for example, is a student's description of his three-year-old cousin.

Willa has beautiful hair. It smells nice and feels wonderful.

The writer obviously wants us to know how lovely his cousin is. He tries to bring in sight, smell, and touch. But in each case, the choice of words fails to help the reader experience anything. The description is so vague that no one could ever select Willa out of a crowd. *Beautiful, nice,* and *wonderful* are words that express the author's opinion of his subject. They tell us what he thought about his perception, but they don't *share* his perception in a sensory or specific way. The same is true of this effort by student Carol Eisley.

> There was no chance of working well at home. First I dropped my pencil and it made an interesting sound as it struck the floor. I was trying to decide how to describe it when my little brother came in making lots of ugly noises.

The reader has little idea what interesting *sound* the pencil made and cannot even guess at which of the thousands of *ugly noises* the writer's little brother happened to be making. Both *sound* and *noise* are too general; we can think such words, but we can't hear anything specific in them.

Here is the same scene after Carol went back in her memory and attempted to share the actual experience.

> There was no chance of working well at home. First I dropped my pencil. It skittered across the tile floor. I was down on my knees looking for it under the refrigerator when my six-year-old brother skipped in whistling a two-note song he had invented. He watched me, first on one foot, then on the other. He began sucking through the gap in his front teeth. It sounded like garbage water sucked down an open drain. I had my arm under the refrigerator as far as I could reach. All I could find was a broken potato chip sticky with green mold, so old and mossy it seemed to have eyes. The mold smelled like curdled yogurt. My little brother began making a wet plopping sound by sticking his thumb inside one cheek and popping it out.

Concrete, specific words name things or describe sensory details, objects, emotions, and facts in such a way that the reader can actually experience in the imagination the named quality. When a pencil *skitters* across a tile floor or when a little brother *sucks* through his front teeth or makes a *wet pop* by pulling his thumb out of his cheek, readers can hear it in their imagination, just as they can see and smell a *green, moldy potato chip.* Specific names or details call up whole pictures that affect both mind and emotion. By knowing in advance that you must describe details in your experience, you discipline your senses to work more actively. To be specific, you must first look and listen for the specific. Knowing a vocabulary of the senses thus works in two ways: it stimulates you as a writer to search deeply into your experience, and it stimulates the imagination of the reader, helping him or her to share your experience.

Concrete, specific words are not limited to personal writing. Even philosophers have known that the more abstract an idea is, the more difficult it is to communicate. Plato, for example, in writing his famous allegory of the cave, attempts to show that most of us live in darkness and that we are reluctant to face higher truths. Plato describes—in sensory images, not in abstractions—the problem of several prisoners who live their lives in a cave with their backs to the entrance. On the back wall of the cave, the men watch shadows pass back and forth. They insist that shadows are real life. But one prisoner is forced to walk to the cave entrance where he is dazzled by the light. He would almost prefer the shadowy illusions on the wall to the pain of exposure. Yet, Plato argues, after finally accustoming himself to the sun and lake and trees, the prisoner would rather die than return to the misery of the cave. Plato's dialogue deals with the nature of truth and the manner in which people both find and resist it. He constructs his argument on a simple, sensory-based story. The senses provide us with a tangible point from which Plato hopes we can reason to higher levels.

In your writing you will need both kinds of words, general and abstract terms as well as concrete, specific terms. You should make yourself aware of the differences and attempt to become rich in both vocabularies. Knowing a language of the senses can increase your powers of perception, just as knowing the words that express ideas helps you to think about ideas.

---

### CLIMBING THE ABSTRACTION LADDER

In S.I. Hayakawa's famous *Language in Thought and Action*, Hayakawa presents a diagram of the various levels of abstraction and concretion. Depending on your intention and the message you wish to share, the ladder illustrates that you have a choice of words ranging from the almost totally general and abstract to highly specific and concrete.

organism
|
animal
|
quadruped
|
bovine
|
cow
|
Bessie

Adapted from *Language in Thought and Action,* 3d Ed., by S. I. Hayakawa, copyright © 1972 by Harcourt Brace Jovanovich, Inc. Reprinted by permission of the publisher.

1. Can you find a higher generalization than *organism?* Or a more specific term than *Bessie?*

2. At what levels would you insert words like *livestock, Hereford, farm asset, red and white spots with a star on the forehead?*

3. With some of your classmates, build your own ladder of abstractions, using the following: property, Ford, rusty, mode of transportation, jalopy, vehicle.

4. Is it possible to find the point on the ladder at which you begin to communicate an *idea* instead of naming a *thing?*

## Creating Images

The use of concrete, specific words, especially sensory words, creates *images.* An image is a sensory picture in the mind. If I write that *several people came into my shop,* you receive the communication in the abstract. You understand what I mean. I have used proper grammar and good syntax. But you have no particular image in you mind; you don't know whether six Chinese diplomats came into my shop or twenty-two Nebraska farmers. But if I write, *the Hell's Angels Gang stomped into my shop,* you'll probably have a fairly instant recognition. *Hell's Angels* suggests motorcycle jackets, chains, greased back hair, black boots, and perhaps an undercurrent of tension or fear.

The word *imagination* is built from the word *image.* Our imaginations are created by sensory experience. A person without an imagination is a person who neither sees nor helps the reader to see. We might say then that one of the first principles of good writing is to *show* instead of *tell,* for showing affects the imagination. Show the reader through some kind of concrete, sensory related words, if possible, instead of merely telling the reader in abstract concepts. General, abstract words inform the rational side of our minds; specific, concrete words stimulate the imagination.

Telling Is Vague
I hurt my finger

Showing Is Specific
I poked a needle through my finger.

Telling Communicates an Idea or Concept
Downtown traffic was heavy.

Showing Demonstrates an Idea or Concept
City buses coughed black smoke; taxies honked at a stalled delivery truck. Even a policeman on a motorcycle couldn't squeeze through the rumble of cars.

Many young writers believe that abstract language sounds more intellectual. Some writers use abstract generalities in the hope of impressing the reader with their intelligence. The impression quickly wears thin. Most of us are soon bored with a continuous dose of abstraction, and often it sounds pretentious. George Orwell once demonstrated this principle by calling attention to how simply and specifically the following passage from Ecclesiastes is written.

> I returned, and saw under the sun, that the race is not to the swift, nor the battle to the strong, neither yet bread to the wise, nor yet riches to men of understanding, nor yet favor to men of skin; but time and chance happeneth to them all.

Orwell then rewrote the passage entirely in abstractions.

> Objective consideration of contemporary phenomena compels the conclusion that success or failure in competitive activities exhibits no tendency to be commensurate with innate capacity, but that a considerable element of the unpredictable must inevitably be taken into account.

The passages say approximately the same thing, but the second version speaks only to the mind, whereas the first speaks to our mind, our imagination, and our emotions.

### EXERCISES

1. Consider the type of words each writer below is using. Look closely: circle the general, abstract terms; underline the concrete, specific terms.

> The rain fell periodically on my window. Soundless. Each blurred streak looked grey and warped. I could hear my dog Harper sleeping in the kitchen. He snores when he sleeps and bubbles ooze between his lips. The rain had begun to melt the old rusted snow in the gutters.
>
> —Student journal

> The influence of custom is indeed such that to conquer it will require the utmost efforts of fortitude and virtue, nor can I think any man more worthy of veneration and renown, than those who have burst the shackles of habitual vice.
>
> —Samuel Johnson

> At sunset I sometimes make bread or roast a chicken in a camp oven on the little islet with twenty eager helpers shrieking, exclaiming, running to throw rotten eggs in the sea or to fetch firewood for a dying fire.
>
> —Margaret Mead

> When a grasshopper landed on my study window last summer, I looked at it for a long time. Its hard wing covers were short; its body was a dead waxen yellow, with black-green indecipherable

marks. Like all large insects, it gave me pause, plenty pause, with its hideous horizontal, multijointed mouthparts and intricate, mechanical-looking feet, all cups and spikes. I looked at its tapered, chitin-covered abdomen, plated and barred as a tank tread, and was about to turn away when I saw it breathe, puff puff, and I grew sympathetic. Yeah, I said, puff puff, isn't it. It jerked away with a buzz like a rasping file, audible through the pane, and continued to puff in the grass.

—Annie Dillard

My father is a great guy. The whole family looks up to him and admires him. Ever since I was old enough to walk, I think I wanted to be just like him and I still find myself imitating him all the time.

—Student essay

2. Rewrite each abstract ''telling'' given below. Make it concrete.
   a. I ate a good dinner.
   b. May is a pleasant month of the year.
   c. She dresses funny.
   d. I just love nature and the woods and all that.
   e. Roberto looked terrible after the fight.

## SUGGESTED WRITING ASSIGNMENTS

1. Take a notebook with you to a Laundromat, a basketball game, the lobby of your dormitory, or to a comfortable location on campus under the shade of an old elm tree. Spend at least thirty minutes recording what you see, smell, hear, and feel. Look for the specific, concrete elements of your experience that would help a reader share that experience with you. Then rewrite in a full paragraph the most important sensory details. Use no abstractions or generalizations.

2. Recall a particularly good experience in your life caused by a simple event (perhaps the day you picked apples in the sun for eight hours and earned thirteen dollars or the day you and three friends drove to the beach or the Christmas Eve you and your father made popcorn balls). Write a page or more focusing on sensory details from that experience. Begin or end your short essay with a generalization that summarizes the total quality of the experience, but use no general or abstract terms in the body of the essay.

3. Read the following from Robert Pirsig's *Zen and the Art of Motorcycle Maintenance*. Pirsig describes a personal experience he once had when traveling with his eight-year-old son on a motorcycle trip to Canada. How many of the senses does Pirsig use to help his reader share in the experience? A few generalizations are used at the beginning and end of

the excerpt. Why? What is the proportion of general to specific? Does Pirsig create images in your imagination?

> We were on a little six-and-one-half horsepower cycle, way over-loaded with luggage and way underloaded with common sense. The machine could do only about forty-five miles per hour wide open against a moderate head wind. It was no touring bike. We reached a large lake in the North Woods the first night and tented amid rainstorms that lasted all night long. I forgot to dig a trench around the tent and at about two in the morning a stream of water came and soaked both sleeping bags. The next morning . . . I thought that if we just got riding the rain would let up after a while. No such luck. By ten o'clock the sky was so dark all the cars had their headlights on. And then it really came down.
>
> We were wearing the ponchos which had served as a tent the night before. Now they spread out like sails and slowed our speed to thirty miles an hour wide open. The water on the road became two inches deep. Lightning bolts came crashing down all around us. I remember a woman's face looking astonished at us from the window of a passing car, wondering what in earth we were doing on a motorcycle in this weather. I'm sure I couldn't have told her.
>
> The cycle slowed down to twenty-five, then twenty. Then it started missing, coughing and popping and sputtering until, barely moving at five or six miles an hour, we found an old run-down filling station by some cutover timberland and pulled in.
>
> At the time, like John, I hadn't bothered to learn much about motorcycle maintenance. I remember holding my poncho over my head to keep the rain from the tank and rocking the cycle between my legs. Gas seemed to be sloshing around inside. I looked at the plugs, and looked at the points, and looked at the carburetor, and pumped the kick starter until I was exhausted.

Write a 500-word essay about an experience you may have had on a trip, even if it was only crosstown on the subway. (Focus on a single incident, not the whole trip.) Do not "make it up"; do not try to write a fictional story. Report in simple images what you experienced so that the reader can share it with you.

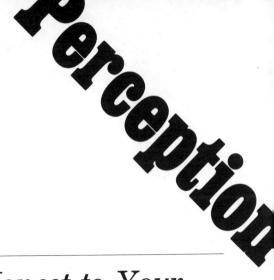

# 3 *Being Honest to Your Experience*

Nothing should be easier than writing down what you see and hear in simple, concrete terms. Yet not only do your emotions, hopes, and fantasies get in the way, so also do the biases of the world you grow up in—especially when you are writing about personal experience. Ernest Hemingway spoke for most of us when he said that one of the great difficulties for a writer was to discover what "you really felt rather than what you were supposed to feel. . . ." Honesty of perception seems to be an ideal we constantly slip away from, tempted as we are to produce the familiar response or the trite phrase. We have a seemingly instinctive desire to please by writing down what we think others want to hear instead of what we truly see or think for ourselves.

Here, for example, is what Greg Eaton wrote in a freshman class when assigned to write about the sunrise:

> In that hushed moment before dawn broke and the sky was like black velvet, there was a hovering solitude as all creatures waited for Midnight to disrobe her garments. Suddenly, golden light radiated forth from the trembling clouds. The branches of the trees began to do deep knee bends to get the circulation going again and all the awaiting animals began a symphony of noise: birdlings warbled in chorus, puppies yapped in counterpoint, insects buzzed in

harmony—while the concert master, the breeze himself, tickled the undersides of the leaves in the trees.

Greg wrote down what he thought an English instructor would approve of. He tried to imitate the gleanings of some vaguely remembered poetry, but he did not look or smell or listen for himself, probably because he did not yet have the courage to trust his own perceptions. If, as he thought, writers from earlier centuries had written about the "hovering solitude" before the dawn, then why shouldn't he? Who was he to say that branches don't do deep knee bends or that the breeze is not a concert master running around tickling leaves on their bottoms. The essay does not express his own perceptions because it seemed both safer and easier to describe the dawn in acceptable "literary" terms. This kind of faking does not necessarily imply a conscious attempt to deceive. Usually, such dishonesty is unintentional. We simply don't know we are not yet seeing for ourselves. We assume that the way we think something has always been done is the way it should be done. We may actually know of no other words to express something because it has always been expressed in the same words. We tend to grow familiar and comfortable with conventional ways of looking at the world. Trying to challenge the norm either leaves us with a dark hole into which our imagination refuses to leap or we get a headache thinking about it.

But here is what Greg wrote when urged to report the scene again as he honestly perceived it with his own senses:

I shivered in the dark. My nose started to run. On the other side of Hennly's pasture, about a quarter of a mile away, diesel trucks rumbled along the highway with their lights on. I sat on a mean rock in the dark listening to the trucks.

The last truck by thundered away down the highway. The sound faded away to a mute grumble. For several minutes there was a silent red glow in the distance, and I couldn't hear anything at all because my ears were still filled with the engines and whirring tires. Then the glow faded and my ears went empty. I heard the weeds brushing against my feet. I felt a soft wind come up. Sometimes I could hear water lapping in the creek that wound through the pasture. After a few moments I heard another truck coming, just a whisper at first, mumbling real low like it was pushing the sound ahead of it kind of angry, then louder and louder until it was booming right in front of me, the tires zinging over the pavement, then past me with the engine growing dull and retarded and passing another truck coming from the other direction in a flash of mixed up lights, with the new sound grumbling back toward me.

And somehow it was light. I don't know when or how. I just realized I could see mist hovering over the creek like faint smoke.

A few cars appeared on the highway, some without lights, zizzing along like dark beetles.

Just light. Gray at first. On the other side of the highway the woods took shape, black and smoky and wet. While the mist in the pasture faded gradually and the rim of the mountain in the east looked silver.

Little of Greg's second essay deals with the sun coming up at all. In the process of trusting his own experience to tell him what was genuine and real, he discovered a sensory world he had previously ignored. Instead of birdlings singing in chorus, Greg had diesel trucks thundering, grumbling, mumbling, whirring, their tires zinging on the pavement. Instead of branches doing deep knee bends, he saw a black and smoky woods. The light itself appeared so gradually it was almost unnoticed—all this while sitting on a "mean rock" with his nose running. This second attempt convinces the reader. Greg is no longer faking. As an almost inevitable consequence, the writing is more powerful, more memorable. Greg has begun to see honestly, and the reader shares the uniqueness of his experience. The reader begins to trust the writer and the telling.

## The Villainous Cliché

Part of Greg's problem in his first essay was his dependence on clichés to do his thinking for him. A cliché is a phrase that has been repeated so often it no longer communicates anything fresh. A cliché may be false or true, but it is so familiar to our ear that we simply don't think about it. Clichés fool us into thinking we are saying something meaningful. More than one student writer has found that he or she could pad a whole essay with clichés, although seldom with the wit Peter Carlson uses in this excerpt from *Newsweek:*

As every school child knows, the cliché has a long and glorious history here in the land of the free. Clichés were here long before I was born and they'll be here long after I'm dead and buried. Clichés traveled from the Old World to the New to follow their manifest destiny. They crossed the Great Plains, forded the rushing rivers and traversed the burning sands of the steaming deserts of this teeming continent until they stretched from sea to shining sea. . . .

And these clichés did not crawl out of the woodwork. Many of our founding Fathers added their 2 cents to the nation's great storehouse of clichés. Jefferson, Lincoln, and Roosevelt created enough clichés to choke a horse, and Franklin coined more phrases than Carter has pills. Since then, these immortal words of wisdom have become landmarks on the American scene. . . .

Let's face facts: You can fool some of the people some of the time, but you can't change human nature. This is a free country and a man has a right to say what he pleases—even if it's a hackneyed cliché. In this increasingly complex society, where the only constant is change, clichés still occupy a warm spot in our hearts. They are quicker, easier, and more economical than other forms of talk. They also require less energy than thoughtful, carefully constructed sentences. And in this day and age, that's nothing to sneeze at.

Carlson makes appropriate fun of the cliché, but unfortunately there is a serious side to all of this. Because clichés are used so often, they deaden our perceptive powers; they stifle our ability to think for ourselves. Clichés substitute for a genuine attempt to express the uniqueness of our experience.

Here's what one student wrote when asked to describe someone she cared about deeply:

The first time I met Hodges he came up to the desk in the library with determination written all over his face. I could tell he was buried deep in thought, perhaps about an assignment that had been given in class that morning. I'm sure he didn't know I was in the same class with him so I just asked him how I could help, but inside I had butterflies in my stomach.

Although the reader gets a certain feel for the situation here, the author makes it difficult for us to trust her perceptions. Did Hodges really have "determination written all over his face"? There must have been some actual physical quality, but neither the author nor the reader has seen it. And what about being "buried deep in thought"? What exactly did Hodges do or say that made the author think so? Is it even possible to be buried in thought and show a face with determination written on it at the same time? The clichés begin to sound like easy substitutions for what really happened in the author's experience. The final statement about "butterflies in my stomach" confirms such a judgment. This is lazy writing in which the author has made no honest effort.

Yet it is not enough to say that a writer must avoid clichés. We must also say how to avoid them. The answer does not lie in turning to a thesaurus for an alternative word or phrase. The fault lies not in language, but in the substitute of old language for new perception. *Only by seeing what is actually there instead of what you think you are supposed to see will your writing become meaningful.* The honesty of the writer demands an honesty to his or her experience—and perhaps the only way to begin is with a series of questions: Is my experience here real, or am I feeling this way because my parents or teacher expect me to? Am I hearing or seeing something in a certain way because the cliché tells me I am supposed to hear and see in that way? Just because something has always been said this way before, are the words true to my experience? Here is a revision of the Hodges paper:

> I was working from nine to midnight behind the checkout desk when Hodges came in. He marched straight up to the desk and let a book drop on it. I remember how I watched his jaw thrust out and pull back. At the time I was so fascinated by him I thought the thrusting jaw meant that he was a determined young man who demanded his own way, but later I came to realize that he did it whenever he was nervous. He kept his eyes on the lighted computer board behind the desk while his slender fingers twisted the corner of the book. The other girls only giggled and pretended to be busy. I had to cross ten feet of open space to get to the counter. It felt like I had forgotten how to walk. I felt my arms and legs were sponging about in all kinds of directions. When I reached the counter I took hold, hung on, and asked if I could help, all without ever looking at his eyes.

This time, in using her five senses and then in attempting to be exact in describing them, the writer has eliminated clichés. Her experience now seems genuine to us. It may be impossible to eliminate all clichés from your writing. Yet only when you begin to challenge yourself to see and feel what is really there in front of you can you be sure you are at least making an honest effort. Honesty may sometimes be painful, yet it is essential if you are to begin the process of finding truth in your experience of the world about you.

### EXERCISES

1. Make a list of all the clichés you can think of. (Your class might split into small groups to do this project so that you and your classmates can contribute to the list.) Using the clichés you've gathered, write a brief description of a handsome person, a flower, a sunset, or whatever. Or write a poem, using as many clichés as you can:

> They lingered under a silvery moon.
> He told her he worshiped her rose red cheeks
> And pearly white teeth.
> He told her he adored her raven black hair
> And button nose.
> He told her he would love her till the seas ran dry.
> She told him he was a turkey.

2. Go back to exercises or assignments you may have written earlier in the course. Circle any cliché you find. Be tough on yourself. Did you use a cliché because it was easy, because it was too hard to find a differ-

ent phrase or too demanding to use your own sense perceptions? Can the cliché be eliminated by revising—that is, by "reseeing"?

### SUGGESTED WRITING ASSIGNMENTS
1. Write a paragraph on an experience you had with someone who is important to you. Look deeply into your memory for the actual details, and do not depend upon clichés to express what you saw and felt. Here is how James Agee described a small boy confronting his grandmother in the novel *A Death in the Family*.

> He walked over to her as quietly as if she were asleep, feeling strange to be by himself, and stood on tiptoe beside her and looked down into her sunbonnet towards her ear. Her temple was deeply sunken as if a hammer had struck it and frail as a fledgling's belly. Her skin was crosshatched with the razor-fine slashes of innumerable square wrinkles and yet every slash was like smooth stone; her ear was just a fallen intricate flap with a small gold ring in it; her smell was faint yet very powerful, and she smelled like new mushrooms and old spices and sweat. . . .
>
> "Now kiss her," his father said, and he drew out of the shadow of her bonnet and leaned far over and again entered the shadow and kissed her paper mouth, and the mouth opened, and the cold sweet breath of rotting and of spice broke from her with the dry croaking, and he felt the hands take him by the shoulders like knives and forks of ice through his clothes. She drew him closer and looked at him almost glaring, she was so filled with grave intensity. She seemed to be sucking on her lower lip and her eyes filled with light, and then, as abruptly as if the two different faces had been joined without transition in a strip of moving-picture film, she was not serious any more but smiling so hard that her chin and her nose almost touched and her deep little eyes giggled for joy. And again the croaking gurgle came, making shapes which were surely words but incomprehensible words, and she held him even more tightly by the shoulders, and looked at him even more keenly and incredulously with her giggling, all but hidden eyes, and smiled and smiled, and cocked her head to one side, and with sudden love he kissed her again.

2. Write a 1,000-word paper (about four typed pages, double-spaced) in which you recount a significant event in your life, one about which you have strong feelings or one that you think had an important influence on shaping your personality. You'll probably want to avoid events that fall too easily into clichés, like graduations or birthdays. Instead,

choose an occasion involving a direct confrontation with a family member or an experience that was particularly painful but revealing. A student essay is included at the end of this unit to provide you with an example. Before you actually begin to write, you might want to read Chapter 4 on the importance of voice and audience and Chapter 5 on how to get started on the first draft.

# 4

# *Discovering Audience and Voice*

As you've looked at the world about you and sharpened your senses, you've also been redefining yourself. Consciously or unconsciously, you've been exploring concrete relationships between yourself and your immediate environment. In that sense, writing from personal experience may sometimes seem to be a private act. But almost all writing, even the most personal, has an audience. Although writing often serves to help us formulate a better understanding of ourselves, it never ceases to function as an act of communication. One of the earliest steps in the writing process, then, perhaps an almost simultaneous step with the *perception of subject* stage, is the identification of your audience. Who are your readers? Why are they reading? What do they expect from you?

## The Ever-Changing Audience

If you were writing an objective research paper for a history professor you might begin like this:

> Our knowledge of Queen Elizabeth's era is limited by the scarcity of unbiased historical data. According to C. P. Sharksey, Professor of History at Oxbridge, historical information from the sixteenth century is drawn almost entirely from men directly involved in making the history and, therefore, must be seen as containing an inherent favoritism toward one party or the other.

But you would not write a letter home in the same manner. Instead, you would probably relax and compose sentences exactly as they came from the top of your head.

> Hi Mom,
> Working on a historical paper for old Donaldson this week. He's crotchety. Wants footnotes. The whole works. I've been up to 3 A.M. every night. Got kicked out of the library Thursday night for eating chocolate cake in the rare book room.

Professor Donaldson would never accept the informality of your letter; your mother would never accept the rather stiff voice you used for Donaldson. You make such adjustments because you know each reader expects something different from you. All successful writers know they must make repeated shifts in word choice, sentence length, voice, and tone if they are to convince whatever reader they are addressing at the moment. When, for example, an advertising copywriter turns out a TV script for Crispy Pop Cereal, she writes with a vocabulary and voice that she hopes will sway an audience of children; when a bank president writes his annual report, he writes to inform the bank's stockholders; and when a student writes a paper on Freud's Oedipal theory, he or she usually writes to convince a single professor that he or she has understood the subject. Yet writing *for* an audience does not mean that you abandon your own ideas or standards; it does not mean "selling out." Rather, it means using common sense. It means learning to be flexible enough to meet your readers where they are, even when the ultimate goal may be to lead those readers somewhere else. And that requires you to know something about the audience *before* you begin to write.

What then should you know about the audience for personal writing? By its very nature, writing found in personal letters, journals, and essays is usually addressed to a more intimate group of friends or at least to a sympathetic reader. Such an audience is presumed to be interested in sharing insights drawn from your observations and experiences. Your aim may be nothing more than to entertain, or it may be to inform and persuade a reader about values and personally held truths. Either way, one common element holds all personal writing together: the natural voice. The reader will expect it and may even be offended by overformality.

## The Natural Voice

Listen for a moment with your inner ear to the voice of Virginia Woolf. The year is 1929, the location, a women's college in England.

> Here was my soup. Dinner was being served in the great dining-hall. Far from being spring it was in fact an evening in October. Everybody was assembled in the big dining-room. Dinner was

ready. Here was the soup. It was a plain gravy soup. There was nothing to stir the fancy in that. One could have seen through the transparent liquid any pattern that there might have been on the plate itself. But there was no pattern. . . . Next came beef with its attendant greens and potatoes. . . . Prunes and custard followed. . . . Biscuits and cheese came next, and here the water-jug was liberally passed round, for it is the nature of biscuits to be dry, and these were biscuits to the core. That was all. The meal was over. Everybody scraped their chairs back; the swing doors swung violently to and fro; soon the hall was emptied. . . . conversation for a moment flagged. . . . a good dinner is of great importance to good talk. One cannot think well, love well, sleep well, if one has not dined well. [But] the lamp in the spine does not light on beef and prunes.

Virginia Woolf sees clearly. She senses, names, shares the experience in concrete images. But she also talks to us in a human voice, a warm and familiar voice—almost conversational but a little more rhythmical and controlled as prose must always be. Look closely and you find simple sentences (*Here was my soup),* simple words (*biscuits, beef,* and *prunes),* mixed only occasionally with a longer, more complex thought. Among other qualities, it is this intimate voice of a real person speaking to our inner ear that makes *A Room of One's Own* such a forceful essay. Yet one misfortune of our educational system is the tendency for all of us to write in the same voice: an objective, impersonal monotone.

Listen to Irwin Parker, in his first term at college, trying to write about a personal experience in high school:

The most interesting course that was taken by me in high school was taught by Mr. Frank. It was a course in chemistry. Mr. Frank developed student minds by involving them in experiments which were a daily part of the content of the experience that Mr. Frank wanted them to have. One liked the course because of the excitement. One never knew what exciting type of experiment Mr. Frank would come up with next.

After Irwin Parker had read this paper to the class (this is only the first paragraph), he admitted he did not talk that stiffly in real life. It sounded nothing like his own voice. In fact, the class decided the essay was rather boring.

One problem was tone. *Tone* is the attitude or feeling the writer takes toward both subject and audience. Parker's tone is distant and rather cold.

*The most interesting course that was taken by me. . . . One liked
the course. . . . One never knew what exciting . . .*

Any reader would find it difficult to feel "excitement" when the prose is so
stiff. The use of the third-person *one* instead of the first-person *I* removes
the human element. Other forms of writing—a critical analysis, a laboratory report—demand that the writer take an objective tone toward his or
her subject. But the personal essay ought to sound personal.

Irwin tried to rewrite using a more natural voice. "Begin again," the
class told him. "Keep it simple, and try talking to the page."

> I liked Mr. Frank because he was a good chemistry teacher in my
> high school. He made us think. We were always doing experiments
> in class, and sometimes we would get so involved that no one
> would hear the bell. Once, Mrs. Shaw, the principal, had to come
> in and drive us out because we were all late for our next class.

"Better," the class told Parker after he read the second version. Much
more human and more readable. This would probably be an acceptable
voice for a personal essay. But it was still not the voice Irwin Parker used
outside the classroom walls. Could he tell it to the page as if the page were
his friend? Could he tell the page concretely what he saw in his memory
and pretend his audience was not an English teacher but a group of his
own peers?

> Mr. Frank was a super dude. He wore bow ties so big they held up
> his chin. A little guy, all squeezed up in an old suit spotted with
> chemicals and this giant butterfly of a bow tie. We would start ex-
> perimenting with iron sulfide and hydrochloric acid, and pretty
> soon the whole room would smell like a rotten egg, and then
> everybody would be wiping his or her eyes and gasping and laugh-
> ing, and old Mr. Frank would be dancing around the room saying,
> "Wow, it worked. You see what happened? You see what happens
> when you make hydrogen sulfide?" And that's when old Mrs.
> Shaw would stumble in gasping and holding a pink handkerchief
> over her nose. "You've all god to ho to quass." She would turn red
> and Mr. Frank would act shocked, like how did he know what time
> it was, and we would all just be laughing so hard you couldn't
> breathe.

"Good!" said the class. "Now we can hear the genuine voice of Irwin
Parker. "And notice what has happened in the process of working toward
that voice. The first essay is almost totally abstract.

*One liked the course because of the excitement.*

But in the final paper Parker involves the reader by using concrete, sensory details.

*. . . pretty soon the whole room would smell like rotten eggs, and then everybody would be wiping his or her eyes and gasping. . . .*

By finding his natural voice, Parker has been able to let his imagination flow more freely. The tone has become informal, even colloquial; and the reader feels the emotion and excitement of the class.

*. . . like how did he know what time it was, and we would all just be laughing so hard you couldn't breathe.*

In listening once again to all three versions, the class decided that the first voice probably revealed Parker's nervousness about writing anything. He wrote stiffly, perhaps on the assumption that his audience would expect "dignified," formal writing at college. In the second version, he wrote more directly to a particular English instructor who told him that he could relax and be natural. But in the third version, he wrote for his fellow students, using the same voice he would actually talk in.

The point is clearly that beginning writers should become aware that they have a choice of voices, just as they have a choice of vocabulary, and that the audience as well as the subject helps determine which voice is appropriate for the purpose. Writers who find themselves locked into the same voice in every paper, no matter what the audience or intention, find themselves locked into repetitive dullness. Even the most formal research paper can be made more lively and interesting by a carry-over of a genuine voice. What we are talking about here is a matter of degree. The beginning writer must recognize that dull writing lacks any voice at all. It sounds anonymous, as if written by committee. Effective writing, even formal and scientific prose, can still have a voice to it, a liveliness or felicity or uniqueness that makes the reader say, "This could only come from Irwin Parker or Salinda Rorequez or Hiawatha Golden."

## Exploring Your Own Voice

Finding a natural voice may open doors to your imagination that a wrong voice will permanently block. The right voice relaxes you, frees you to speak your mind. The wrong voice makes you uncomfortable and distracts your attention from the subject to the writing itself.

Listen to Jim Brown, a star football player of the late fifties and early sixties.

I get a little weary of hearing broken homes blamed for 96.3 percent of American youth's difficulties. . . . My guess is that thanks to all the yakking about broken homes, a lot of kids have found a good excuse to get into trouble. The broken home is their crutch in Juvenile Court. I am not dogmatic about this. Looking back on my own boyhood, there were many times when I came perilously close to becoming a no-account.

Compare Brown's voice to that of E. B. White, a novelist and an essayist.

One summer, along about 1904, my father rented a camp on a lake in Maine and took us all there for the month of August. We all got ringworm from some kittens and had to rub Pond's Extract on our arms and legs night and morning, and my father rolled over in a canoe with all his clothes on; but outside of that the vacation was a success and from then on none of us ever thought there was any place in the world like that lake in Maine.

Both voices sound natural, informal, relaxed. Both put the reader at ease. Yet they are not the same voice. Brown uses more colloquial words. The term *colloquial* derives from the Latin for conversation, and hence colloquial words reflect the vocabulary we use in our most casual speech, for example, Brown's *I get a little weary ... My guess is ... all the yakking about ... a lot of kids ... becoming a no-account.* Of course, no written language is identical to the spoken voice. But good writing almost invariably has the sound of the spoken voice. Brown achieves that sound, the impression that he is speaking to us from the page.

E. B. White achieves the same effect, but his word choice is *informal,* not colloquial. Excluding the more casual or slang vocabulary found in colloquial writing, the informal voice simply uses everyday words and phrases: *We all got ringworm ... but outside of that ... and from then on ... there was any place in the world like.*

The following chart contrasts informal and colloquial language to a more formal vocabulary.

| Colloquial | Informal | Formal |
|---|---|---|
| yakking | talking | discussing |
| kids | children | youth |
| a no-account | a problem child (or delinquent) | a delinquent (or social offender) |
| my guess is | I would guess | I would estimate |

Such a chart is arbitrary. Words considered informal by one generation may be considered appropriate formal terms by the next. (For example, contractions like *isn't* and *haven't* were once strongly rejected in a formal paper. Today even conservative periodicals print essays using contractions.) Still, the contrast reveals that a significant choice is available to a

From "Once More to the Lake"—August 1941—in *One Man's Meat* by E. B. White. Copyright 1941, 1969 by E. B. White. By permission of Harper & Row, Publishers, Inc.

writer—and also confirms that material written in one voice may be changed or translated into another voice.

Jim Brown, for example, must have felt comfortable writing in a colloquial style. His ideas presumably came to him most readily in the voice closest to his own speaking voice. But if his audience had been a convention of psychologists instead of the casual reader, Brown might have returned to his material and translated it into formal prose:

> I am disturbed at hearing broken homes blamed for 96.3 percent of American youth's difficulties. . . . I estimate that because of excessive discussion about broken homes many young people have found a good excuse to become social offenders.

The point is clearly that by writing in your own natural voice you allow your imagination to flow; your attention can be focused where it should be—on the subject. But later you can (and should) return to your first draft and double-check the *appropriateness* of the voice you have written in. Once your ideas and experiences are on the page, the voice can be adjusted to match the expectations and needs of your audience.

## The Appropriate Voice

Every voice has its limitations. A *colloquial* voice may be highly successful for entertaining a sympathetic, casual audience. It is appropriate for humor or light entertainment. But such a voice usually prevents you from discussing more serious material—that is, if you want to be taken seriously. An *informal* voice, however, may be considered a solid bridge between colloquial and formal. It may be both entertaining or serious. E. B. White often shifts easily from pleasant memories into thoughtful reflections on human values. The informal voice is the most flexible of all styles: friendly, relaxed, conversational, yet at the same time more polished and edited than the colloquial. The informal voice is especially appropriate for essays. Unless you are highly skilled, however, the audience for a research paper, critical analysis, or report will probably expect a more *formal* voice. The need for objective data, factual information, and logical analysis requires a tone of high seriousness to convince the reader.

Know your audience, then; know what it expects and needs. But also know yourself. If you write more freely and comfortably in one voice, use it to its best advantage, especially on the first draft. Write fast, keeping your subject vividly and imaginatively before your mind's eye. Use the most natural voice. Then be willing to return later and make whatever adjustments are necessary for your ideas and experiences to be communicated effectively to your audience.

### EXERCISES

1. Here are a series of paragraphs, each by a different author, each with a distinctive voice. Consider the audience for each voice, and suggest the

type of character behind the voice. Discuss the limitations of each voice—that is, would it be effective for a convention of physicists or for an informal audience reading for pleasure? Are there any voices here you find annoying to your ear? Any you feel you might like to emulate in your own writing?

> Among the most comprehensive of the existing synthetic models that do not use human-capital approach is that by Stiglitz, who integrates the distribution of income into its major sources, *viz.*, wages and profits. Stiglitz examines the distribution impact of nonlinear saving functions, heterogeneity of labor skills, material-capital inheritance policies, variable reproduction rates of different income classes, tax policies, and the nature of the stochastic elements in the accumulation process.
>
> —Gian Singh Sahota, "Theories of Personal Income Distribution:
> A Survey," *Journal of Economic Literature*

> Just to paint is great fun. The colours are lovely to look at and delicious to squeeze out. Matching them, however crudely, with what you see is fascinating and absolutely absorbing. Try it if you have not done so—before you die. . . . One begins to see, for instance, that painting a picture is like fighting a battle; and trying to paint a picture is, I suppose like trying to fight a battle.
>
> —Winston Churchill,
> *Painting as a Pastime*

> Wednesday, Mr. and Mrs. Johnnie Gann went to Kansas City. Sure was a hot day but enjoyed our trip. Couldn't hardly sleep that night. They were gone but they came after we were there for some time. We took the lawn chairs, went out in the back yard to keep cool until James came. He took us over to Bobbys to get something to eat. We just got a hot dog when we got to the Bus Station. Bobby works late, comes home after dark. When Jame's wife came home they came to get us. Went over there for supper.
>
> We saw several sight-seeing different places. Was close to an airplane. Went under several overhead bridges. The Bus Station sure is a nice large building, has nice seats, two lunch counters.
>
> We saw the Kaw river going down it was full. Steamboats were sailing.
>
> —Mrs. Johnnie Gann,
> Lily Grove News,
> *Tri-County Weekly*, July 1, 1970

There are, of course, other ways to account for the songs of whales, They might be simple, down-to-earth statements about navigation, or sources of krill, or limits of territory. But the proof is not in, and until it is shown that these long, convoluted, insistent melodies, repeated by different singers with ornamentations of their own, are the means of sending through several hundred miles of undersea such ordinary information as "whale here," I shall believe otherwise. Now and again, in the intervals between songs, the whales have been seen to breach, leaping clear out of the sea and landing on their backs, awash in the turbulance of their beating flippers. Perhaps they are pleased by the way the piece went, or perhaps it is celebration at hearing one's own song returning after circumnavigation; whatever, it has the look of jubilation.

—Lewis Thomas, *Lives of a Cell*

a. To what extent does sentence length affect the voice in each piece?

b. Does the use of *I, we,* or *you* change the feeling in the voice?

c. Many writers have observed that the use of Anglo-Saxon words (simple three- and four-letter terms like *pig, man, live, hand*) creates a different reaction in the reader than the use of words with Latin origin (*heterogeneous, preterition, lactiferous*). Do you find these writers using one or the other with any consistency? Does it affect their voice?

2. Here is a student writing about a personal experience. Has he chosen the right voice? What *specific* problems, if any, do you detect?

My most embarrassing moment was having the zipper of my pants split apart during church. Since church services traditionally demand one's attire to be elaborate, to see a person with his fly open must be quite striking to the observer and embarrassing to the observed. The abashment that followed the accident was humorous at the initial thought of the situation. Uncontrollably following was a nervous and very desperate search for the most logical path to use for an exit. The path hopefully would serve the purposes of a stealthy departure from the congregation and to allow unnoticed repairs to take place. Once repairs had taken place to fix the obvious defect, the feeling of complete isolation flooded my brain in order to contribute in dismissing all possibilities of the situation reoccurring. The end of the service was reached to find my body outside the church in the parking lot hastily waiting the departure home in the most inconspicuous manner possible. Consequently, when the time to dress for church services arrives in the future, a special precaution related to the strength and durability of zippers in pants will be unforgettably performed.

# 5 Facing the Blank Page

The time arrives. You've explored your subject with all your senses. You've considered who your audience is and what it expects from you. Now you have to write.

You spread out paper, pens, typewriter, erasers, dictionaries. You adjust the desk lamp. Perhaps you smoke a cigarette or drink a coke. You doodle little circles inside big circles. You stack old records on the stereo and listen for a while to your favorite group.

But the blank paper remains—white and glaring. There is no escape. At some point you must face the single most difficult part of the writing process: beginning to write.

## How the Process Works

One of the great misunderstandings about writing involves the concept of *failure*. We need to get it out of the way at the beginning. For the successful writer, failure is normal to the process. To say such a thing may sound like a paradox, but actually, without failure, most of us would never be able to say what we wanted to at all. In fact, most of us probably would not know what we truly think and feel without first saying what we did *not* think and feel. In the first draft of this very paragraph I have written a dozen sentences that did not express what I wanted to say. Why did I do that? Because until I saw the words in front of me, I could not be sure. I "knew" (like an unvoiced urge) that I should say something about failure.

But I had never articulated the ideas before. The first two sentences of the paragraph appear here exactly as I wrote them. Success. But the third sentence did not come until I had first *failed* at several false starts. I had to work through some awkward, inaccurate, and actually misleading sentences until I came to the next one that seemed right to me. I wish I could say that it wasn't necessary. I wish I could say that with practice each sentence will flow out upon the page. But, in reality, even the best writers know they must work *through* the failures to arrive at success.

In 1926, William Butler Yeats wrote "Sailing to Byzantium," a thirty-one-line poem. The manuscript reveals that Yeats wrote nineteen pages of material in pencil, ink, and typescript, each page averaging about fourteen crossed out, reworked, and abandoned lines. No line now in the final poem appears in the manuscript before the tenth page. In other words, Yeats wrote approximately 140 lines before he found even the first few rough images that satisfied him; and he still had another 126 lines to struggle through: a total of some 266 lines to achieve thirty-one lines of poetry.

Theodore Geisel is author of the famous Dr. Seuss books for children. Simple lines, simple rhymes. Nothing like the complex moral vision of William Butler Yeats.

> The sun did not shine
> It was too wet to play
> So we sat in the house
> All that cold, cold, wet day.

Yet Geisel admits that *The Cat in the Hat,* a book of sixty-one pages (only 223 words), took ten months to write.

No one, of course, will expect you to spend ten months writing a college theme, but the more words you're willing to explore on any one writing project, the more likely you'll eventually discover what it is you want to say and how you want to say it. What you need to know is what the professional knows: that the first draft will be only a sketch of the writer's ideas, of the facts and details of perception, and that much of it will be almost inevitably badly written. If you, too, can know in advance that you are never going to show that first awkward draft to any audience, if you can know that the first draft is *your* copy and that its sole purpose is to provide you with a work sheet, a place to sketch out in as much detail as possible your ideas in rough form, and that it is absolutely *normal* for your first draft to seem like a failure, you will probably find yourself less threatened, less fearful of the blank page. What you are about to do is to explore, and every explorer must chop through a lot of tangled underbrush to reach the crest of a hill. You must be willing to take wrong turnings, be willing to make mistakes. You cannot know the path in advance, nor can anyone else. So take a chance and start with the first word.

## The Habits of Writing

Certain types of preparation and mental attitudes can make your approach to the first draft, if not easier, at least more productive.

**1. Make Writing a Habit**   As long as writing is an occasional thing, it will seem strange, even threatening. If you practice the piano or the trumpet or guitar a little every day, it becomes a familiar instrument; you feel comfortable with it. Familiarity in any situation helps you relax. Better to write an hour a day, every day, than to postpone an assignment until the night before and attempt a twelve-hour marathon. Work for an hour or two a day on a private journal, on a lab report, on two pages of a fifteen-page research paper—it really does not matter as long as you're writing every day.

**2. Find a Regular Time and Place**   Try to write at approximately the same time each day. We are creatures of regularity. Football coaches know how important it is for a team to practice at the same hour, five days a week. The body—and the mind—has its rhythm. Whether you write best in the early morning or at midnight makes little difference so long as you find the tide of your personal rhythm and flow with it every day.

Most successful writers have also discovered they need a special place in which to work. Some prefer absolute silence; others write well immersed in noise. Find what works for you and stick to it. Create your own nest. Surround yourself with books or paintings or bare walls—whatever makes you comfortable. The German writer Schiller claimed to work well only when he could smell rotten apples. Most of us aren't that eccentric, but having your own special place helps to establish a pattern for writing that almost all of us need.

**3. Do Warm-up Writing When Necessary**   When Kurt Vonnegut was still employed by General Electric Company and not yet famous for his novels of fantasy and science fiction, a story was told about how he would arrive for work each morning, immediately sit down to his typewriter, and pound on it for about ten minutes describing nothing more than the eggs he ate for breakfast, the rumbling of the subway that morning, and the feel of snow in the air. He called it his warm-up. To use the analogy of an athlete or musician again, trying to perform cold, without preparation, may be possible; but the performance will usually be halting and error-prone until the mind or senses are fully tuned in. The best preparation for beginning the first draft may be to begin on something else for ten minutes. A warm-up can never substitute for honest effort on the main writing project. But don't hesitate to play a little at first. Write about anything that comes into your head. If nothing comes, write: Mary had a little lamb; then find a new rhyme to go with it, then another. Play. Exercise. But start writing fast. Time yourself and do not stop writing for at least ten minutes.

**4. Write Fast**   Once you begin work on your real subject, write with as much intensity and speed as possible. Because the mind usually moves faster than the hand, it may prove valuable to train yourself to write a first draft on the typewriter or in some sort of shorthand. You might even want to try dictating your ideas into a tape recorder. But work fast.

Most successful writers have found that the more slowly you write the first draft, the more slowly ideas tend to come. The more words you get on the page, the more the words themselves seem to activate the imagination. Words call up words. Images call up images. Slow writing may allow time for you to become overly critical. You may begin consciously to challenge the sentence you've just completed (Is it the best way to phrase what you want to say? Did you spell that word correctly? Should you be varying your sentence structures more?). Once this sort of self-criticism begins, you're no longer writing. You're editing. Writing and editing are different steps in the writing process. During the first draft, fast, intensive writing focuses your mind on the subject. Ideas will grow only out of an encounter with the subject, not out of concern for grammar or spelling. After you've finished the first draft, there will be time (and need) to rewrite, to edit, and to polish.

# Form and the Personal Essay

Form refers to the shape or pattern of your experience, to the way you organize your material. In personal writing, form is usually subjective. It tends to develop from the natural sequence of events you are writing about (this happened and then this happened) or from subconscious "associations" (one word calls up a second; one image leads to another). I can't tell you not to outline or plan before you write. Many writers find it helpful. But because part of the aim of writing about personal experience is to explore yourself and your own voice freely, for the time being you'll probably find that conscious concern for form should follow the first draft, not precede it. Yet two traditional elements of form tend to be associated with most personal essays. Knowing them in advance may help you focus even your rough draft more clearly.

First, although the whole range of human experience is open to you, you cannot successfully write about ten years of life, or even twenty-four hours, in only four or five pages. The personal essay may be organized around a single, unique experience, one that you develop in great detail, helping the reader to see, hear, smell, and touch. Or the personal essay may be organized around two or three smaller experiences that reveal some kind of pattern—a series of ordinary daily situations that are typical or that lead to general insight. Either way, you will need to *select* only the one major incident or the two or three typical incidents and to exclude all the millions of others that compose your life.

Second, the elements of experience you select to write about should show the reader how they led you to some type of growth, insight, or understanding, even if it is a humorous one. You do not necessarily need to explain the meaning of the experience in abstract, general terms (although you can do so), but the meaning must be evident or implied by the end of the essay. After all, why write about it if it had no meaning to you?

### EXERCISES

As the blank page is often the most difficult step to overcome in writing, warm-up games are played by even professional writers. The warm-up game must be unthreatening and without consequences—something you do only for yourself to get the words flowing. It should also be fun and fast. Here are some suggestions.

1. Write for ten minutes about your earliest memory. Share every element of the memory—sound, smell, sight. Write fast. Do not look at the words on the page; look into your memory at this moment. See it now in detail in your imagination. Do not remove your pen from the page for ten minutes. If you get stuck, find another detail in your memory and keep going. Allow one association to call up another.

2. Write about a total sensuous experience like eating breakfast. *See* the breakfast in front of you as you write. Do not look at the words you are writing. Look at the breakfast. Begin your first sentence with, *I can see it now. . . .* Do not stop writing for ten minutes.

3. Write on any associations you have had with the word *petadactril* (or *Garvis, scissors, glass casket, stone*—a word you may have heard during the day or dreamed about last night). No one but you will ever read what you have written. Let the word call up images (pictures) in your imagination. Write fast. Share it with the page. Be concrete. See it as you write it. Let the images and your associations lead you. Do not stop writing for ten minutes.

# 6 Rewriting for Precision and Feeling

*Interviewer*  How much rewriting do you do?
*Hemingway:* It depends. I rewrote the ending of *Farewell to Arms* thirty-nine times before I was satisfied.
*Interviewer:* Was there some technical problem there? What was it that had stumped you?
*Hemingway:* Getting the words right.

—*Paris Review*

The real work of writing begins when you determine to make your prose say exactly what you want it to say. You may find it effective to create a wholly new second draft, a complete reworking with the same speed and intensity as in your initial effort. Or you may find that for you rewriting is a somewhat slower, more calculated study in which some inner feeling suggests that the words you've used do not yet express what you hoped they would; in which you rephrase, cross out, and begin again, testing each new sentence against the old. In either case, your focus remains primarily on the subject—on ideas and feelings—but you find that your attention edges toward a conscious effort at finding the right word, the most meaningful sequence of ideas or images, and toward achieving an overall unity of effect.

# Searching for the Right Meaning

If you're like most of us, you take language for granted. In terms of influencing our lives, we tend to place words somewhere between sunshine and potato chips. But language has a remarkable, almost awesome power over us. Words spoken by someone you love on an autumn afternoon unite the two of you forever. Words written on a letter of application get you accepted to law school. Words spoken on television by a local disk jockey campaigning for mayor make you slam a book on the table in anger. The power of language is such that almost two-thirds of the world's governments forbid newspapers to publish freely. Priests in many early cults and religions were often feared because they knew magic words that summoned up the gods. Telling stories, fables, and fantasies around the campfire led to complex mythologies that eventually became the cultural fabric of civilization. Indeed, without words, we would have no civilization at all. Language is inseparable from being human. As a beginning writer, you need at least a rudimentary understanding of some of the ways words affect you and your reader.

Here's how one freshman (who had not yet developed a feeling about words) began an early draft of an essay on his grandfather:

> Royster R. Matting lived an immemorial life. He began as a surveyor in Montana, made and lost a fortune as a miner, once owned a railroad in Virginia, became a judge in Maryland, and raised thirteen children who honored his loins.

Well, maybe, we say with hesitation, but the writer seems to have encountered two kinds of language problems, both related to accuracy. One is a matter of denotation; the other, a matter of perception.

*Denotation* is the explicit (or dictionary) meaning of a word. Obviously, using a word with the correct denotation is essential to clear communication. *Immemorial,* for example, means reaching beyond the limits of memory, beyond even recorded history. As admirable a life as Royster R. Matting may have had, it surely wasn't beyond memory's scope. The student has clearly wanted to express the breadth and energy found in his grandfather's life, but the word *memorable* (something worth remembering) probably comes closer and expresses his feelings more exactly. Mark Twain's famous remark still applies: "The difference between the right word and the wrong word is the difference between lightning and a lightning bug." Words are symbols. Unless we use them with generally agreed upon meanings, confusion and disorder result. In this case, the student has simply chosen the wrong word. Thirty seconds with any dictionary would have revealed the problem.

But dictionaries are not always the solution to achieving accuracy. Accuracy begins in clarity of perception. If you are not seeing your subject clearly, you obviously won't find clear and precise words to communicate it. The freshman who wrote about his grandfather admitted that he felt uncomfortable with the phrase "thirteen children who honored his loins," but it had a Biblical ring to it and he hoped it would work. The student accepted the first phrase that sounded good to his ear (something that's fine to do on a first draft), but that uncomfortable feeling should have signaled a need for challenging the phrase in the second draft. Surely, these thirteen children honored more than their father's prodigious sexual abilities. The problem here is not that the student has chosen a wrong word, but that he has not truly identified what it was about his grandfather the children honored. Was it his remarkable career? His achievements? His human compassion? We don't know and neither does the student. At this point a dictionary won't help.

Rewriting the first draft often means reseeing the subject—a matter of *revision* (from the Latin for "looking again"). This student should have asked himself a series of questions: if I haven't found the precise word, is it because I haven't found the right insight? If I haven't found the right insight, is it because I haven't looked honestly, haven't struggled to find the small details that make up the total? What is it about my subject that I'm not yet seeing?

The answer in this case was not difficult:

> Royster R. Matting lived a memorable life. He began as a surveyor in Montana, made and lost a fortune as a miner, once owned a railroad in Virginia, became a judge in Maryland, and raised thirteen children who always honored the model of courage and discipline he established.

Before submitting a final typed version of his essay, the student reread it and again refined the accuracy by penciling in the term *self-* before discipline. Now the reader can be convinced. Self-discipline and courage indeed can make for a memorable life. Precise words strike home more forcefully than a page of words that only circle the subject. The "almost right" word is never the right word.

## Searching for the Right Feeling

If you were hired to write menus for Top of the Town Restaurant, you might find that correct denotation was only half the problem. Here are two versions of the same menu, each conveying a similar denotative meaning.

> Succulent roast beef served in its own juice with tiny young peas and mashed potatoes . . . $12.50

> Bloody cow's flesh with tiny young *pisum sativum* seed and squashed tubers . . . 75¢

No doubt most of your customers would prefer to pay $12.50 for the first dish, even though the seventy-five-cent meal is identical. Words do more than communicate messages. The *connotation* of a word is the feeling it suggests to us.

*Nursing* merely names a medical occupation, but the word has about it an aura of feelings: tenderness, care, perhaps even sacrifice. The nature and intensity of feeling associated with a word may be peculiar to your individual relationship with it. If you were raised in Alabama, where some people call themselves *red-neck* with pride, the word might have a different feeling than if you were raised in Boston, where *red-neck* is a contemptuous term. Other words, however, seem to share a general *connotation* throughout a given culture—snake, for example.

Sometimes the feelings we have about words become so strong that they actually replace the original denotative meanings. In the Middle Ages the word *mistress* meant a woman who had control of the house. Possession of numerous keys to pantries, cupboards, and wine cellars symbolized her control. The word was equivalent to the male appellation *master* and projected a similar positive connotation. During Shakespeare's time, *mistress* began to be used metaphorically as in "mistress of my heart," suggesting the woman who possessed keys to, or control of, her lover's emotions. Apparently the metaphor seemed so right that a *mistress* began to be associated more with love than home. By the seventeenth century, the denotation had actually changed to "an illicit lover" and the connotation had become negative.

---

Compare your emotional responses to each of the following words with similar denotations. The positive or negative feeling you experience is the connotation. Words that evoke no feeling are said to be connotatively neutral.

| | | |
|---|---|---|
| Negro | black | nigger |
| excrement | defecation | shit |
| amour | love affair | making it |
| Mexican | chicano | wetback |
| cancer | malignancy | tumor |
| female activist | feminist | women's libber |
| rest room | powder room | john |

---

Words evoke feelings, but communicating the *exact* feeling is not easy. Several years ago a student of mine, Kiki Nikoni, wanted to write about a painful moment from childhood. Kiki stumbled into what is probably the most common danger among beginning writers—overwriting, telling too much, using words that are too emotional or that suggest an inappropriate connotation. In listening to her first draft, the class argued that her essay sounded melodramatic. Kiki rewrote it several times to make it more genuine, but at the same time she wanted it to be forceful because the real experience had been important to her. Read the original version through before you read the revision.

Original

1 Where I used to live there was
2 a train. I would hear it but I
3 never really listened until
4 after my father died. Once I was
5 alone at night by the window.
6 Frankenstein-shadows seemed as
7 deathly cold as I felt inside.
8 Then I heard the whistle like a
9 moaning screaming animal some-
10 where far outside. The silence
11 roared about me! Then the
12 whistle blew again, this time
13 closer but still painful and
14 really lonely. I remember
15 thinking for a moment that it was
16 like I was out there and my heart
17 was broken and torn out of me
18 and lost, like a father's ghost
19 crying out! It hurt my ears,
20 it hurt my heart until the tears
21 ran down my cheeks.

Revision

In Japan I used to live near a train. Each night I would hear its whistle but I never really listened until the night after my

father's funeral. I was alone at the window and the shadows seemed thin and cold. Then I heard the whistle, high and far away, like a child's toy in the dark. The

silence afterward seemed unsteady, as if something whole had been sliced. The whistle blew again, this time closer but still hollow and lonely. For a moment I felt some part of me was out there, like my father's

ghost. Then the whistle again, but

further away, faint and fading. After a while I couldn't hear it. There was just moonlight on empty fields.

Both versions reveal problems with connotations, but the first presents serious difficulties. The class objected especially to lines 13 through 21. Kiki's listeners felt she was crying out in abstractions (*painful, lonely, lost, hurt*) and that she was perilously close to clichéd melodrama (*a broken heart, a ghost, tears running down her cheeks*). Kiki had tried to select words and images she thought would convey an honest feeling of pain. The opposite effect resulted. The class doubted the sincerity of her description.

In the second version Kiki tried to resee the scene in her memory. She removed most of the abstractions and substituted concrete images, using words that might *suggest* the feelings of pain and loss (*a hollow whistle, a faint and fading whistle, moonlight on open fields*). She removed the references to her broken heart, replacing it with the generalization: *some part of me.* The class agreed that this was a time when the generalization worked more successfully because it seemed less melodramatic. In the context (and connotation is always affected by context) *some part of me* by its very abstractness suggested emptiness and helped promote the appropriate feeling.

Kiki made a number of other changes you might want to consider:

1. Why did she add *Japan* to line 1? How does a specific place suggest feeling? Would the connotation have been different had she lived in Little Rock at the time?

2. Why did she change *after my father died* in line 4 to *after my father's funeral?*

3. Why shadows *seemed thin and cold* instead of *Frankenstein-shadows* in line 6?

4. What was gained or lost in changing *moaning screaming animal* in line 9 to *high and far away, like a child's toy in the dark?* How do the connotations of either one relate to the loss of a father, and which seems most appropriate for the mood Kiki wants to convey?

5. What kind of feelings does *moonlight on empty fields* in line 19 connote for you? Why did Kiki think that it could substitute for the original *tears ran down my cheeks?*

As a young writer you need to develop the confidence that words can be played with. Just because you've written a word on the page, you should not think it's sacred. Indeed, you may not know exactly what you want to say until you've tried to say it in several different ways. By understanding something about how language affects all of us, you learn how to discover and express your own ideas with more force.

### EXERCISES

William Faulkner said there are three things a writer needs: paper, tobacco, and whiskey. To that list we need to add a good, large dictionary. It may not do for you what tobacco and whiskey will, but it is an essential tool of any educated person, not just the professional writer.

1. *The Oxford English Dictionary* (usually called the *OED*) traces word histories, providing you with a thorough sense of a word's past and, by implication, its denotative and connotative developments.

Investigate the history of the following terms. In your own words write up the history as you understand it, giving some of the examples listed in the *OED*.

| | |
|---|---|
| science | gay |
| woman | humanities |
| sophisticated | text |

2. Look up the following terms in a dictionary of synonyms. Find three synonyms for each and in your own words suggest the differences in connotation. For example, *Roget's Thesaurus* lists *dowager* and *relict* among the synonyms for *widowhood*. For me, widowhood suggests loneliness, dark dresses, and silence, whereas *dowager* suggests strength in a woman's old age, a widow with power and authority, and something vaguely Elizabethan. Frankly, I'm surprised to find *relict* there at all. If relict is a synonym for widowhood, then it suggests a decrepit woman, the leavings of a man's life, a woman without value. (I wonder what the feminist movement would think of that one!)

| | |
|---|---|
| submission | regret |
| money | marriage |
| cool | truth |
| trust | student |

3. Rewrite each of the following sentences, first with positive connotations, then with negative connotations, but always retaining essentially the same meaning.

| Neutral | Positive | Negative |
|---|---|---|
| Jill is overweight. | Jill has the fullness and ripeness of a Renoir model. | Jill's a hog. |
| The Vietnam village was taken by an American tank force. | The Vietnam village was liberated from Communist captors by Capt. "Smiley" Bonner and his 33rd Motorized Division. | The Vietnam village was savagely overrun by invading forces using blazing tanks against peasants with pitchforks. |

   a. Stephanie was a good employee.
   b. Juan is a Mexican-American.
   c. Lawrence's first novel was widely read.
   d. She's a cautious driver.
   e. Grandma has a houseful of art objects.
   f. She prefers conversation to dancing.
   g. I could smell her father's cigar in the living room.
   h. Georgette payed a very low price for her new car.
   i. Tim and Michele have seen a lot of each other lately.
   j. "... whenever any form of Government becomes destructive of these ends Life, Liberty and the pursuit of Happiness, it is the Right of the People to alter or abolish it. ..."

4. Select any one of your previous exercises, and evaluate every sentence in the light of what you now know about connotations and

denotations. Does every word contribute to the precise meaning and feeling that you want it to? Are there some words or phrases that seem inappropriate? Rewrite your exercise to make it more effective. (If you submit a rewritten version to your instructor, be sure to include a copy of the original.)

# 7 *Editing Sentences for Unnecessary Words*

The distinction between editing and rewriting is somewhat arbitrary. For more experienced writers, editing techniques blend naturally with the process of exploring the subject in second and third drafts. The goal of both steps in the writing process is to improve the effectiveness of writing so that you find means of conveying your subject clearly and convincingly. But many necessary aspects of writing involve the mechanics of effective expression: sentence structure, sentence variety, paragraphing, logical order, accurate documentation. When such qualities are emphasized too early in the learning process, a beginning writer tends to be overwhelmed by what he or she perceives as rules and restrictions. The results can often create stillborn prose and the "I hate to write" attitude. It might be best (even if somewhat oversimplified) to think of rewriting as a phase in which your primary focus remains on developing the subject, and of editing as a phase in which your attention shifts to achieving the most polished and effective form of expression.

## The Editor's Job

Editing involves selecting, arranging, and correcting a manuscript. Your papers may not be intended for publication, but as most audiences are accustomed to thinking of "good writing" as that which they see published, your writing will usually be judged by similarly high standards. You must become your own editor. You must learn some essential skills of editing. Almost without exception, you'll find their application to every essay report or research paper will make the difference between average work and good work.

Editing requires an attitude almost opposite to the one you were urged to adopt in writing the first draft. Instead of spontaneous, fast writing, instead of suspension of all concern for sentence structure and correctness, editing requires a cool, slow, self-critical act. Most writers find that they need to turn away from their writing for a while, distance themselves from it, and later return with a coldly skeptical attitude: every word, every sentence must prove its worth. As a student you may not have the ideal amount of time to pause between rewriting and editing, but you can still train yourself to approach your material with an editor's eye.

© 1972 United Feature Syndicate, Inc.

Because the sentence is the shortest complete unit of thought, it seems the best place to begin the practice of editing. The first step in forming a solid, readable sentence is to make it say only what it needs to say and nothing more: that means eliminating unnecessary words. Unfortunately, many students have been taught that short simple sentences should be avoided. Long, complex-compound sentences seem to get all the praise. Some students go out of their way to use as many words as possible in every paper. Editing down to simple, irreducible elements may seem in conflict with everything you've been taught. But a major misconception is at work here. Long sentences in themselves are neither better nor worse than short sentences, but extra words are deathly to all forms of writing. The first goal of sentence editing is to clear away clutter that distracts from meaning. *Every word or phrase that can be cut should be cut.*

Here's a typical early-draft sentence:

Having just finished college myself, I can testify that mental discipline is the greatest asset a college student can have while he's in school.

Fair enough. But not good enough. The simplest editorial act strikes out excess.

> *Cut:* Having just finished college [~~myself~~], I can testify that men-
> tal discipline is the greatest asset a [~~college~~] student can have
> [~~while he's in school~~].

By eliminating six redundant words or phrases, we have a cleaner sentence that conveys its message directly.

Here's another example from a freshman theme:

> At an early stage in his career, Johnny Bench met a coach who
> kept urging him to go and analyze his motions while he was up at
> the plate.

No two editors would necessarily find the same weaknesses in this sentence. Right and wrong answers are seldom clear-cut in editing. But most
editors would probably agree that almost half could be eliminated without losing the meaning of the sentence.

> *Cut:* [~~At an~~] early [~~stage~~] in his career . . .
> ("Early in his career" says the same thing.)

> *Cut:* . . . Johnny Bench met a coach who [~~kept~~] urg [~~ing~~] him to go
> and analyze . . .
> (*Kept urging* adds little to the concept of *urge,* and *to go and* sim-
> ply distracts from the stronger word, *analyze.*)

> *Cut:* . . . his motions [~~while he was up~~] at the plate.
> (As we seldom think of someone being *down* at the plate, *while he
> was up* contributes nothing to meaning.)

A final edited version might now read like this:

> Early in his career, Johnny Bench met a coach who urged him to
> analyze his motions at the plate.

We have eliminated ten words, made the sentence simpler, and, in the
process, allowed the meaning to come through more clearly.

Sometimes prepositions are special offenders to wordiness.

> The federal government has sponsored several programs *to* assist
> *in* providing *for* funds *for* the college student.

Prepositions are essential to English grammar, but if you find them pop-
ping up like dandelions, do some weeding.

> The federal government has sponsored several programs to assist
> college students.

## The Backward Sentence

In early drafts we often tend to write about what something is not rather
than what it is. Again, the process seems normal. In trying to figure out
what we want to say, we may need to circle and come in from behind.

Editing can be the time where we reconsider and consciously reshape the sentence to strengthen the meaning.

> There is no doubt that Ellen looked as though she were not feeling well.
>
> *Cut:* [~~There is no doubt that~~] Ellen looked as though she were not feeling well.
>
> (Introductory phrases that use the word *that* can almost always be eliminated.)
>
> as if she were sick
> *Tighten:* Ellen looked [~~as though she were not feeling well~~] .
>
> (It is almost always more effective to say what something is instead of what it isn't. "He was not a weak man" suggests weakness by the very presence of the word; "he was a strong man" suggests the strength that is actually there.)
>
> sick
> *Tighten again:* Ellen looked [~~as if she were sick~~] .
>
> (Sometimes a short, blunt sentence is the most forceful of all.)

Here's the sentence before editing:

> There is no doubt that Ellen looked as though she were not feeling well.

And after editing:

> Ellen looked sick.

The editing process eliminated eleven unnecessary words and reversed the thrust of the sentence from what Ellen was not to what she was. The result is a simple, strong statement that leaves "no doubt"—the point the writer began with.

The word *not* should be a clue. When it shows up in a sentence, challenge the sentence. Obviously, there will be many times when *not* works well; but if you're a good editor, you'll probably find an equal number of times when the direction of the sentence needs reversing or when a single word will substitute for a phrase.

| | |
|---|---|
| I did *not* remember. | I forgot. |
| I did *not* believe his statistics. | I distrusted his statistics. |
| It did *not* seem important. | It seemed unimportant. |

## Who, Which, and That

Like the word *not*, the words *who, which,* and *that* should be seen as clues. Every time they occur, challenge their necessity. About half the time they serve no function.

> *Cut:* I lived in a room [~~that was~~] over the garage.
>
> ("I lived in a room over the garage" says the same thing.)

*Cut:* How could I know that her mother, [who was] short and dumpy, would oppose our marriage?
(Make it sound more like the spoken voice: "How could I know that her short, dumpy mother would oppose our marriage?")

*Cut:* [I think that] we owe first responsibility to our own moral conscience.
("We owe first responsibility to our own moral conscience" is stronger and more direct.)

# Adjectives

Adjectives modify nouns: a *red* house; a *grouchy* professor. They can be helpful at times. But the beginning writer often overuses them, sometimes attaching a string of adjectives to a single noun or even an adjective to every noun in a mistaken belief that "adjectives are colorful" or that in some way they will make up for weak writing. Successful writers have learned from experience that a strong noun in itself is more colorful than a weak noun propped up with one to six adjectives. Nouns, not adjectives, are the foundation blocks of every sentence. Use of an adjective should cause you to question the noun to which it's attached. Can the adjective be eliminated, either because it's unnecessary or because a stronger noun will supplant it?

*Challenge:* I ate a [red apple] .

*Winesap* might be a better noun ("I ate a Winesap") because a Winesap is both red and an apple. A concrete noun simplifies the sentence (one less word) while making it more sensuous. *Winesap* does more than suggest red; it suggests a shade of red (wine-colored) and a taste (wine plus sap).

*Challenge:* I studied a [small brown] insect that I found by an [old gray] rock.

Why not name the *insect?* A cricket, for example, is both *small* and *brown* (a two-word saving). And aren't all rocks *old?* In this case, we would know more if the adjective identified some less predictable quality. Was the rock covered with lichen or moss?

I studied a cricket that I found by a mossy rock.

(If you must use an adjective, at least make sure that it tells us something we didn't already know.)

*Challenge:* A [big, red, growling, thundering, incredible, bell-clanging] fire engine came down the alley.

A string of adjectives attached to a single noun is called an adjective pileup. In this case, *fire engine* is a strong enough noun, but more than two adjectives in a row should cause the writer to think twice. Here are some steps we might go through to reconsider:

1. *Big* seems weak because of its vagueness. How big is big? In this context, *thundering* probably connotes bigness anyway.

2. *Red* is generally associated with fire engines and, therefore, adds nothing to the image.

3. *Thundering* and *growling* suggest similar sounds but with slightly different connotations. We need to choose between them. As both are stronger than the verb, one or the other might replace the verb.

4. *Incredible* might be valuable, but, as it's used here, it seems lost amid the other adjectives.

5. *Bell-clanging* adds another dimension of sound and might be an adjective we want to retain.

Here, then, are several possible revisions:

A bell-clanging fire engine thundered down the alley.

A clanging fire engine growled down the alley.

An incredible, bell-clanging fire engine thundered down the alley.

The context in which a sentence occurs, your purpose, and your own ear will have to help you decide. But, in general, two or more adjectives in a row should be seen as a caution signal. Editing is probably called for.

## Adverbs

What the adjective is to the noun, the adverb is to the verb. It helps, but often with only moderate success.

*Challenge:* I [really] felt strange and uptight.

The reader can only respond that *really* feeling is still feeling and hasn't added enough extra dimension to justify letting it live in this sentence.

*Challenge:* Both of us ran [very] fast.

We can accept *fast* as an adverb (I suppose one could run slowly), but what does *very* add? What is the difference between *very fast* and *fast?* A smidgen at best, and not worth the extra word.

Maybe we can come up with a general principle: Adverbs and adjectives should be used so sparingly that their effectiveness is increased by the rareness of their appearance.

## A Reminder

In each of my examples in this chapter I have edited a sentence out of context. Obviously, in your own papers, word choice and sentence length must be evaluated within the flow and meaning of the whole essay. (See

Chapter 17.) But remember that editing occurs at the end of the writing process. Do not worry about editing discussed here while you are still in the first draft or rewrite stages. If you begin to edit too early, you take your mind off the subject matter. Content must precede form. Get the content on the page; then shape and form it afterward.

However, do not think you can ever skip the editing phase. Content alone is never effective. The way you express yourself is as important as what you have to say. If your ideas are submerged in an ocean of unnecessary words, you'll find your reader unwilling to make the dive for fear of drowning. The best of the writers—Hemingway, Fitzgerald, Thomas Wolfe—all had editors. The rest of us must learn to become our own.

## EXERCISES

Although you must eventually learn to edit your own material, it may at first be easier to identify wordiness in someone else's sentences. Try some of the following games before you begin editing your own papers.

1. In each of the following sentences, eliminate every unnecessary word or phrase. Do not change the meaning of the sentence itself. When it is necessary, replace a cluttered phrase with a single word or with a more concrete and specific word.

   a. Owing to the fact that he was late, he missed seeing the President.

   Because
   *Cut:* [~~Owing to the fact that~~] he was late, he missed seeing the President.

   b. I ~~do not approve~~ of the methods ~~he employs~~. [*disapprove* ... *his*]

   c. His tale is ~~very~~ old and strangely ~~different~~.

   d. His brother, ~~who is~~ a member of the same firm, was indicted by the grand jury.

   e. This ~~is~~ a subject ~~that~~ has always interested me.

   f. Her sweater has a red glow ~~to it~~.

   g. ~~The question as to whether he succeeded~~ has not been decided. [*His success is undecided.*]

   h. ~~The~~ people ~~who stood~~ around ~~outside in~~ the street had a better view than those who stayed inside.

   i. Mike was different ~~from him~~. His face was ~~quite~~ round, ~~and a pale white color~~. ~~On his chin~~ he had a [*thin*] beard which was thin and scraggy in some places. He wondered where he was ~~at~~. [*pale*]

2. Here is a paragraph from E. L. Doctorow's *Ragtime,* a novel about the 1920s. The main character in this passage is "Mother's Younger Brother." He has no other name. I have rewritten the paragraph as it might have looked in a first-draft version. Edit out every word you feel is unnecessary. Then compare your editing to Doctorow's version, which follows. Don't cheat by looking ahead. Right and wrong answers are seldom available in editing. Context, purpose, and your own inner ear must

determine your answers. Test your ear against that of a professional writer.

> The air was very salty-like in your nose. Mother's Younger Brother in his white linen suit and boater had rolled his trousers up to almost his knees and taken off his shoes and was walking barefoot in the salt marshes. Sea birds were startled by his approach and flew up into the blue sky. This was the time in our history, which was before most of us were born, when Winslow Homer was doing his painting. A certain type of light was still available along the whole Eastern seaboard. Homer painted the light in his paintings. The light gave the sea a very heavy, dull menace and shone very coldly on the black rocks and rough shoals of the New England coast.

Here is Doctorow's edited version:

> The air was salt. Mother's Younger Brother in his white linen suit and boater rolled his trousers and walked barefoot in the salt marshes. Sea birds started and flew up. This was the time in our history when Winslow Homer was doing his painting. A certain light was still available along the Eastern seaboard. Homer painted the light. It gave the sea a heavy dull menace and shone coldly on the rocks and shoals of the New England coast.

3. Edit two of your previous short exercises. Eliminate every unnecessary word. Look especially for clutter words like *of, at, to,* and *the.* Try to eliminate or find single-word substitutes for unnecessary phrases like *the fact that, whether or not,* and *the question of.* Be careful of overusing *who* and *which;* they can be eliminated about half the time.

It is possible to overwork a piece of writing. Sometimes your first instinct is best. If you feel yourself becoming angry or frustrated, stop for a while. Go over it again later when you feel cooler. For many people, the process works better in the back of the mind than on paper. For others, it's always a word-by-word battle, crossing out and starting over. Never think you are alone. Everyone from Thomas Jefferson to William Faulkner has worked in exactly the same way.

4. Edit any one of your previous exercises by making it at least one-third shorter than the original version. Do not cut anything that is essential to the meaning or feeling, but be brutal; throw away everything that doesn't directly, concretely contribute to the total effect. (If you submit this work to your instructor, be sure to include your original.)

## Editorial Checklist for Part One
*Writing from Experience*

_____ Have you included sensory details?

_____Sight (especially light) _____Touch _____Smell

_____Sound _____Taste

_____ Have you used concrete, specific words and images to help your reader see?

_____ Have you observed honestly with your own powers of observation?

_____ Have you been faithful to your experience?

_____ Have you eliminated all clichés? Both in language and perception?

_____ Have you identified your audience? And considered their needs?

_____ Have you adopted the most natural voice possible for that specific audience?

_____ Have you searched for the right words instead of trying to get by with half-right words?

_____ Have you double-checked for connotations? Have you overwritten just to impress?

_____ Have you edited out every unnecessary word? Have you used ten where five would do?

_____ Have you told what is instead of what isn't?

_____ Have you eliminated unnecessary *whos, whiches,* and *thats?*

_____ Have you used strong nouns? Concrete nouns?

_____ Have you used adjectives and adverbs selectively?

_____ Have you cared enough to rewrite and edit until you feel you've achieved the best, polished prose possible at this time?

David Hinkle, a biology major, wrote the following personal essay as a freshman. Hinkle begins and ends with several appropriate generalizations, but the body of the work focuses on two specific events portrayed in concrete detail. The essay entertains, but it also leads us to a conclusion about the significance of the experience.

# The Championship Move
## David Hinkle

I always loved to play basketball. Although I was never a good ball handler, I had a high arching shot that fell in from any range when I was hot. I was proud of that shot. People called it everything, especially unorthodox and ugly, but I got many compliments on its accuracy.

I always wanted to play on an organized team because I felt I could be a good team player. I liked setting hard picks that stopped defenders; I liked running through fast plays, slinging quick passes to teammates, and rigidly freezing myself, establishing good position.

I finally got my chance when I was sixteen. Five friends and I joined a league at a city recreation center. I played in that league three years. The first two were horrible. We lost eleven of eighteen games and fought and argued with referees and opponents.

As we rode to one of those games, we tried to joke with each other. Niece, the center said, "Man I'm gonna gun tonight and get fifty points." I knew he could do it because he was six-foot-four, two-hundred-eighty—a giant compared to the opponents.

At the start of the game everyone walked out to the green circle at center court and surrounded it, waiting for the jump ball. Niece tipped the ball to Wendell, a five-foot-nine guard who zipped up court for a one-armed lay in. But as the game progressed, we became isolated androids, slowly stumbling up and down the court, missing easy shots, shooting unnecessarily, and feebly raising our weary arms attempting to play defense. With nine minutes left in the game, Niece was charged with a foul. He bulldozed to the referee with slanted eyebrows, flared nose looking like a double-barreled shotgun and voice booming. I felt glad when he did that because he intimidated the referee. Whenever he would try to say something, Niece would cut him off, yelling, proving his innocence. The referee threw up his thumb and said in a beaten voice, "You're outta the game." With our main player gone, we decided to go out in style. The guards fouled out, trying to steal every ball they could. Smacking arms, scratch-

Reprinted by permission of the author.

ing hands, poking eyes, and tripping over feet of the opponents. I was ejected when an opponent reached around me. I bent my arm in a sixty-degree angle and whacked my elbow against his ribs. He withered back, clutching his chest with a compressed look on his face. The referee glared at me. His face grew redder and redder. He looked like a pressure cooker ready to explode. He shouted at me, "Get outta here." All our players yelled at him in my defense. He flung his arms up and blasted a shrill note from his whistle. "This game is over," he screamed. We found it hard to look at each other in the locker room.

My third and final year on the team was different. We were strengthened by six new talented players. (Two played on a high school state championship team.) I knew we were going to win the city championship. We played superbly that year, beating one team seventy to fourteen and another fifty-four to twelve. Our record was seven and one. We were in second place and had to play the first place team for the championship.

I didn't expect to play much that game, but if I did, I was going to go all out. I felt good vibes when we did our warm-ups before the game. Everyone was clapping in rhythm as we shot and did lay-ups. Whenever anyone made a basket, we would compliment and cheer him. When we finished, I got the shock and thrill of my life. Our captain announced the starting lineup. He said, "Me, Niece, Pig, Effley, and Dave will go in first." The air went out of my lungs and I stared at him in disbelief. I knew he had to be wrong because I played forward and was only five-eleven. The other forwards were six feet, six-one, six-two, and six-three. I asked the captain if he really meant me. He said, "Yeah man, you know that." I felt a wide grin ready to explode over my face. I ran into the bathroom to hide my happiness. While I was in there, I smiled at myself in the big mirror on the wall. I convinced myself I deserved to start and then casually pimped back into the tension-filled gym, trying to look cool and calm.

The game got underway. Niece, as usual, tipped the ball to Wendell but was quickly stopped by two muscular defenders. We set up our offense and Pig threw a behind-the-back pass to Effley, who plowed his way towards the rim for two points. I got the ball and missed a free, fifteen-foot jumper from the side. I felt I was the worst on the team. The score was dead even for the first seven minutes; then they built a six-point lead. One of them shot a short shot; Effley and I leaped for it with out-stretched arms. It swished in. We crashed in midair and banged to the hardwood floor. Their bench cheered approvingly. We called a time-out. I felt I wasn't contributing enough, so I asked Slim, a six-two forward, if he would take my place. He looked at me eagerly and said, "Cool." For the rest of the game we easily overpowered them by hitting most of our shots. We were aggressive on offense and stingy on defense. Wendell and Pig flew up and down the court controlling the ball, and Niece and Effley muscled command of the boards. We won by eighteen points. We had risen from the bottom to the top and were the champions. I felt my move was the reason. It had hurt to take myself out of the game, but it hadn't hurt as much as when I had tried to make myself important by being ugly and mean. It hurt in a new way and I walked off the court feeling lighter than I ever had before.

---

Julius Lester is a noted songwriter and author of numerous books on the black experience in America. *To Be a Slave* was a Newbery Honor Book in 1969; in 1972 Lester was a National Book Award finalist. The following personal essay, first printed in *Ms.* Magazine, presents a humorous account of Lester's attempt to come to terms with his maleness.

# Being a Boy
## Julius Lester

As boys go, I wasn't much. I mean, I tried to be a boy and spent many childhood hours pummeling my hardly formed ego with failure at cowboys and Indians, baseball, football, lying, and sneaking out of the house. When our neighborhood gang raided a neighbor's pear tree, I was the only one who got sick from the purloined fruit. I also failed at setting fire to our garage, an art at which any five-year-old boy should be adept. I was, however, the neighborhood champion at getting beat up. "That Julius can take it, man," the boys used to say, almost in admiration, after I emerged from another battle, tears brimming in my eyes but refusing to fall.

My efforts at being a boy earned me a pair of scarred knees that are a record of a childhood spent falling from bicycles, trees, the tops of fences, and porch steps; of tripping as I ran (generally from a fight), walked, or simply tried to remain upright on windy days.

I tried to believe my parents when they told me I was a boy, but I could find no objective proof for such an assertion. Each morning during the summer, as I cuddled up in the quiet of a corner with a book, my mother would push me out the back door and into the yard. And throughout the day as my blood was let as if I were a patient of 17th-century medicine, I thought of the girls sitting in the shade of porches, playing with their dolls, toy refrigerators and stoves.

There was the life, I thought! No constant pressure to prove oneself. No necessity always to be competing. While I humiliated myself on football and baseball fields, the girls stood on the sidelines laughing at me, because they didn't have to do anything except be girls. The rising of each sun brought me to the starting line of yet another day's Olympic decathlon, with no hope of ever winning even a bronze medal.

Through no fault of my own I reached adolescence. While the pressure to prove myself on the athletic field lessened, the overall situation got worse—because now I had to prove myself with girls. Just how I was supposed to go about doing this was beyond me, especially because, at the age of 14, I was four foot nine and weighed 78 pounds. (I think there may have been one 10-year-old girl in the neighborhood smaller than I.) Nonetheless, duty called, and with my ninth-grade gym-class jockstrap flapping between my legs, off I went.

To get a girlfriend, though, a boy had to have some asset beyond the fact that he was alive. I wasn't handsome like Bill McCord, who had girls after him like a cop-killer has policemen. I wasn't ugly like Romeo Jones, but at least the girls noticed him: "That ol' ugly boy better stay 'way from me!" I was just there, like a vase your grandmother gives you at Christmas that you don't like or dislike, can't get rid of, and don't know what to do with. More than ever I wished I were a girl. Boys were the ones who had to take the initiative and all the responsibility. (I hate responsibility so much that if my heart didn't beat of itself, I would now be a dim memory.)

It was the boy who had to ask the girl for a date, a frightening enough prospect until it occurred to me that she might say no! That meant risking my ego, which was about as substantial as a toilet-paper raincoat in the African rainy season. But I had to thrust that ego forward to be judged, accepted, or rejected by some girl. It wasn't fair! Who was she to sit back like a queen with the power to create joy by her consent or destruction by her denial? It wasn't fair—but that's the way it was.

But if (God forbid!) she should say Yes, than my problem would begin in earnest, because I was the one who said where we would go (and waited in terror for her approval of my choice). I was the one who picked her up at her house where I was inspected by her parents as if I were a possible carrier of syphilis (which I didn't think one could get from masturbating, but then again, Jesus was born of a virgin, so what did I know?). Once we were on our way, it was I who had to pay the bus fare, the price of the movie tickets, and whatever she decided to stuff her stomach with afterward. (And the smallest girls are all stomach.) Finally, the girl was taken home where once again I was inspected (the father looking covertly at my fly and the mother examining the girl's hair). The evening was over and the girl had done nothing except honor me with her presence. All the work had been mine.

Imagining this procedure over and over was more than enough: I was a sophomore in college before I had my first date.

I wasn't a total failure in high school, though, for occasionally I would go to a party, determined to salvage my self-esteem. The parties usually took place in somebody's darkened basement. There was generally a surreptitious wine bottle or two being passed furtively among the boys, and a record player with an insatiable appetite for Johnny Mathis records. Boys gathered on one side of the room and girls on the other. There were always a few boys and girls who'd come to the party for the sole purpose of grinding away their sexual frustrations to Johnny Mathis's falsetto, and they would begin dancing to their own music before the record player was plugged in. It took a little longer for others to get started, but no one matched my talent for standing by the punch bowl. For hours, I would try to make my legs do what they had been doing without effort since I was nine months old, but for some reason they would show all the symptoms of paralysis on those evenings.

After several hours of wondering whether I was going to die ("Julius Lester, a sixteen-year-old, died at a party last night, a half-eaten Ritz cracker in one hand and a potato chip dipped in pimiento-cheese spread in the other. Cause of death: failure to be a boy"), I would push my way to the other side of the room where the girls sat like a hanging jury. I would pass by the girl I wanted to dance with. If I was going to be refused, let it be by someone I didn't particularly like. Unfortunately, there weren't many in that category. I had more crushes than I had pimples.

Finally, through what surely could only have been the direct intervention of the Almighty, I would find myself on the dance floor with a girl. And none of my prior agony could compare to the thought of actually dancing. But there I was and I had to dance with her. Social custom decreed that I was supposed to lead, because I was the boy. Why? I'd wonder. Let her lead. Girls were better dancers anyway. It didn't matter. She stood there waiting for me to take charge. She wouldn't have been worse off if she'd waited for me to turn white.

But, reciting "Invictus" to myself, I placed my arms around her, being careful to keep my armpits closed because, somehow, I had managed to overwhelm a half jar of deodorant and a good-size bottle of cologne. With sweaty armpits, "Invictus," and legs afflicted again with polio, I took her in my arms, careful not to hold her so far away that she would think I didn't like her, but equally careful not to hold her so close that she could feel the catastrophe which had befallen me the instant I touched her hand. My penis, totally disobeying the lecture I'd given it before we left home, was as rigid as Governor Wallace's jaw would be if I asked for his daughter's hand in marriage.

God, how I envied girls at that moment. Wherever *it* was on them, it didn't dangle between their legs like an elephant's trunk. No wonder boys talked about nothing but sex. That thing was always there. Every time we went to the john, there *it* was, twitching around like a fat little worm on a fishing hook. When we took baths, it floated in the water like a lazy fish and God forbid we should touch it! It sprang to life like lightning leaping from a cloud. I wished I could cut it off, or at least keep it tucked between my legs, as if it were a tail that had been mistakenly attached to the wrong end. But I was helpless. It was there, with a life and mind of its own, having no other function than to embarrass me.

Fortunately, the girls I danced with were discreet and pretended that they felt nothing unusual rubbing against them as we danced. But I was always convinced that the next day they were all calling up all their friends to exclaim: "Guess what, girl? Julius Lester got one! I ain't lyin'!"

Now, of course, I know that it was as difficult being a girl as it was a boy, if not more so. While I stood paralyzed at one end of a dance floor trying to find the courage to ask a girl for a dance, most of the girls waited in terror at the other, afraid that no one, not even I, would ask them. And while I resented having to ask a girl for a date, wasn't it also horrible to be the one who waited for the phone to ring? And how many of those girls who laughed at me making a fool of myself on the baseball diamond would have gladly given up their places on the sidelines for mine on the field?

No, it wasn't easy for any of us, girls and boys, as we forced our beautiful, free-flowing child-selves into those narrow, constricting cubicles labeled *female* and *male*. I tried, but I wasn't good at being a boy. Now, I'm glad, knowing that a man is nothing but the figment of a penis's imagination, and any man should want to be something more than that.

---

Carson McCullers (1917–1967) was one of America's finest novelists and writers of short fiction. Her works include *The Heart Is a Lonely Hunter* and *The Ballad of the Sad Cafe*. In the following essay, from *The Mortgaged Heart*, McCullers recalls the sensuous impressions of a childhood Christmas and the conflicting emotions that accompanied it.

---

# Home for Christmas
## Carson McCullers

Sometimes in August, weary of the vacant, broiling afternoon, my younger brother and sister and I would gather in the dense shade under the oak tree in the back yard and talk of Christmas and sing carols. Once after such a conclave, when the tunes of the carols still lingered in the heat-shimmered air, I remember climbing up into the treehouse and sitting there alone for a long time.

Brother called up: "What are you doing?"

"Thinking," I answered.

"What are you thinking about?"

"I don't know."

"Well, how can you be thinking when you don't know what you are thinking about?"

I did not want to talk with my brother. I was experiencing the first wonder about the mystery of Time. Here I was, on this August afternoon, in the tree-house, in the burnt, jaded yard, sick and tired of all our summer ways. (I had read *Little Women* for the second time, *Hans Brinker and the Silver Skates, Little Men,* and *Twenty Thousand Leagues under the Sea.* I had read movie magazines and even tried to read love stories in the *Woman's Home Companion*—I was so sick of everything.) How could it be that I was I and now was now when in four months it would be Christmas, wintertime, cold weather, twilight and the glory of the Christmas tree? I puzzled about the *now* and *later* and rubbed the inside of my elbow until there was a little roll of dirt between my forefinger and thumb. Would the *now* I of the tree-house and the August afternoon be the same *I* of winter, firelight and the Christmas tree? I wondered.

My brother repeated: "You say you are thinking but you don't know what you are thinking about. What are you really doing up there? Have you got some secret candy?"

September came, and my mother opened the cedar chest and we tried on winter coats and last year's sweaters to see if they would do again. She took the three of us downtown and bought us new shoes and school clothes.

Christmas was nearer on the September Sunday that Daddy rounded us up in the car and drove us out on dusty country roads to pick elderberry blooms. Daddy made wine from elderberry blossoms—it was a yellow-white wine, the color of weak winter sun. The wine was dry to the wry side—indeed, some years it turned to vinegar. The wine was served at Christmastime with slices of fruitcake when company came. On November Sundays we went to the woods with a big basket of fried chicken dinner, thermos jug and coffee-pot. We hunted partridge berries in the pine woods near our town. These scarlet berries grew hidden underneath the glossy brown pine needles that lay in a slick carpet beneath the tall wind-singing trees. The bright berries were a Christmas decoration, lasting in water through the whole season.

In December the windows downtown were filled with toys, and my brother and sister and I were given two dollars apiece to buy our Christmas presents. We patronized the ten-cent stores, choosing between jackstones, pencil boxes, water colors and satin handkerchief holders. We would each buy a nickel's worth of lump milk chocolate at the candy counter to mouth as we trudged from counter to counter, choice to choice. It was exacting and final—taking several afternoons—for the dime stores would not take back or exchange.

Mother made fruitcakes, and for weeks ahead the family picked out the nut meats of pecans and walnuts, careful of the bitter layer of the pecans that lined your mouth with nasty fur. At the last I was allowed to blanch the almonds, pinching the scalded nuts so that they sometimes hit the ceiling or bounced across the room. Mother cut slices of citron and crystallized pineapple, figs and dates, and candied cherries were added whole. We cut rounds of brown paper to line the pans. Usually the cakes were mixed and put into the oven when we were in school. Late in the afternoon the cakes would be finished, wrapped in white napkins on the breakfast-room table. Later they would be soaked in brandy. These fruitcakes were famous in our town, and Mother gave them often as Christmas gifts. When company came thin slices of fruitcake, wine and coffee were always served. When you held a slice of fruitcake to the window or the firelight the slice was translucent, pale citron green and yellow and red, with the glow and richness of our church windows.

Daddy was a jeweler, and his store was kept open until midnight all Christmas week. I, as the eldest child, was allowed to stay up late with Mother until Daddy came home. Mother was always nervous without a "man in the house." (On those rare occasions when Daddy had to stay overnight on business in Atlanta, the children were armed with a hammer, saw and a monkey wrench. When pressed about her anxieties Mother claimed she was afraid of "escaped convicts or crazy people." I never saw an escaped convict, but once a "crazy" person did come to see us. She was an old, old lady dressed in elegant black taffeta, my mother's second cousin once removed, and came on a tranquil Sunday morning and announced that she had always liked our house and she intended to stay with us until she died. Her sons and daughters and grandchildren gathered around to plead with her as she sat rocking in our front porch rocking chair and she left not unwillingly when they promised a car ride and ice cream.) Nothing ever happened on those evenings in Christmas week, but I felt grown, aged suddenly by trust and dignity. Mother confided in secrecy what the younger children were getting from Santa Claus. I knew where the Santa Claus things were hidden, and was appointed to see that my brother and sister did not go into the back-room closet or the wardrobe in our parents' room.

Christmas Eve was the longest day, but it was lined with the glory of tomorrow. The sitting-room smelled of floor wax and the clean, cold odor of the spruce tree. The Christmas tree stood in a corner of the front room, tall as the ceiling, majestic, undecorated. It was our family custom that the tree was not decorated until after we children were in bed on Christmas Eve night. We went to bed very early, as soon as it was winter dark. I lay in the bed beside my sister and tried to keep her awake.

"You want to guess again about your Santa Claus?"

"We've already done that so much," she said.

My sister slept. And there again was another puzzle. How could it be that when she opened her eyes it would be Christmas while I lay awake in the dark for hours and hours? The time was the same for both of us, and yet not at all the same. What was it? How? I thought of Bethlehem and cherry candy, Jesus and skyrockets. It was dark when I awoke. We were allowed to get up on Christmas at five o'clock. Later I found out that Daddy juggled the clock Christmas Eve so that five o'clock was actually six. Anyway it was always still dark when we rushed in to dress by the kitchen stove. The rule was that we dress and eat breakfast before we could go in to the Christmas tree. On Christmas morning we always had fish roe, bacon and grits for breakfast. I grudged every mouthful—for who wanted to fill up on breakfast when there in the sitting-room was candy, at least three whole boxes? After breakfast we lined up, and carols were started. Our voices rose naked and mysterious as we filed through the door to the sitting-room. The carol, unfinished, ended in raw yells of joy.

The Christmas tree glittered in the glorious, candlelit room. There were bicycles and bundles wrapped in tissue paper. Our stockings hanging from the mantlepiece bulged with oranges, nuts and smaller presents. The next hours were paradise. The blue dawn at the window brightened, and the candles were blown out. By nine o'clock we had ridden the wheel presents and dressed in the clothes gifts. We visited the neighborhood children and were visited in turn. Our cousins came and grown relatives from distant neighborhoods. All through the morning we ate chocolates. At two or three o'clock the Christmas dinner was served. The dining-room table had been let out with extra leaves and the very best linen was laid— satin damask with a rose design. Daddy asked the blessing, then stood up to carve the turkey. Dressing, rice and giblet gravy were served. There were cut-glass dishes of sparkling jellies and stateliness of festal wine. For dessert there was always sillabub or charlotte and fruitcake. The afternoon was almost over when dinner was done.

At twilight I sat on the front steps, jaded by too much pleasure, sick at the stomach and worn out. The boy next door skated down the street in his new Indian suit. A girl spun around on a crackling son-of-a-gun. My brother waved sparklers. Christmas was over. I thought of the monotony of Time ahead, unsolaced by the distant glow of paler festivals, the year that stretched before another Christmas—eternity.

# PART

## Describing People and Places

# TWO

*Accuracy of observation is the equivalent of accuracy of thinking.*

—*Wallace Stevens*

You've been describing and narrating since you were old enough to talk. Description and narration are among the oldest forms of discourse in oral tale-telling. Why then a whole unit on something we're all so familiar with? Why especially when description and narration seldom exist as forms of writing by themselves?

The answer does not lie in their formal qualities. You may never be called upon in college or your career to write straight description or straight narration. Yet both description and narration make up integral parts of almost all other forms of writing. To compose a laboratory report on a chemical experiment, you must *describe* the procedure and *narrate* the sequence of events and results. To write a business report on market conditions in the textile industry, you must *describe* consumer demands and *narrate* monthly buying patterns. To write a law brief, you must *describe* the case in detail and *narrate* events that led to your client's arrest. To apply for a federal grant, you must *describe* your need for money and *narrate* how and when it will be spent. The list is endless. Practice in writing description and narration is solid preparation for incorporating them into more complex patterns of writing at a later stage.

An even more important reason for their study derives from the mental discipline description and narration impose upon perception. In personal writing you may pick and choose among the details of your world as they affect you, but narration requires you to see an ordering in your experience, and description (because it can be so boring if not well done) requires you to train your eye to select the most significant detail for presentation to the reader. *To see an ordering, to select significant detail*—these are two primary steps that shape, discipline and impose necessary limitations on random experience.

# 8 *Focusing Perceptions*

To describe is to picture, to create a scene in the reader's imagination.

> As I walk along the stony shore of the pond in my shirt sleeves . . .
> it is cool as well as cloudy and windy, and I see nothing special to
> attract me. . . . The bullfrogs trump to usher in the night, and the
> note of the whippoorwill is borne on the rippling wind from over
> the water. Sympathy with the fluttering alder and poplar leaves al-
> most takes away my breath; yet, like the lake, my serenity is rip-
> pled but not ruffled. These waves raised by the evening wind are
> as remote from storm as the smooth reflecting surface. Though it
> is now dark, the wind still blows and roars in the wood, the waves
> still dash, and some creatures lull the rest with their notes.

That is how Thoreau described Walden Pond in a memorable chapter on solitude, and that is how many of us first think of description—as
something associated with nature.

But this is also description:

> A distractingly pretty girl with dark brown eyes sat at the edge of
> our group and ignored both the joint making its rounds and the
> record player belching away just behind her. Between the thumb

and middle finger of her left hand she held a pill that was blue on one side and yellow on the other; steadily, with the double-edged razor blade she held in her right hand, she sawed on the seam between the two halves of the pill. Every once in a while she rotated it a few degrees with her left index finger. Her skin was smooth, and the light from the fireplace played tricks with it, all of them charming. The right hand sawed on.

This paragraph, by Bruce Jackson, is taken from a magazine article on drug abuse. The article has nothing to do with rippling wind and whippoorwills, yet the same attention to specific details engages our imagination.

Here, too, is description:

Squirrel monkeys with "gothic" facial markings have a kind of ritual or display which they perform when greeting one another. The males bare their teeth, rattle the bars of their cage, utter a high-pitched squeak, which is possibly terrifying to squirrel monkeys, and lift their legs to exhibit an erect penis. While such behavior would border on impoliteness at many contemporary human social gatherings, it is a fairly elaborate act and serves to maintain dominance hierarchies in squirrel-monkey communities.

Scientist Carl Sagan, writing about the evolution of human intelligence in *The Dragons of Eden,* is a long way from Thoreau, writing about waves on Walden Pond. But both use an identical process of focusing upon selected details. All three writers describe the ordinary world about us, yet each has sharpened his perceptions so that the reader's consciousness is heightened, magnified. The commonplace is no longer common when seen by a focused intelligence. We are made to experience the newness of our world.

How does a beginning writer learn to select the best details from all those thousands of images registering on the senses every moment? Over the years, experienced writers have discovered some general principles that may help.

## Descriptive Focus

1. If a detail isn't interesting to you, you probably won't be able to make it interesting to your reader. Don't include it just to fill up the page.

2. Sometimes you may fail to recognize the interest value of a detail because you haven't looked closely enough. If your senses have dulled or your mind has grown lazy from lack of challenge, you may never see the element in the detail that makes it significant. Look again. Focus your mind like a camera moving in for a close-up.

3. Use all of your senses: listen, taste, touch, smell, look. Make mental or written lists of more details than you can ever use. From thirty visual details, select two or three that will help your reader *see*.

    a. Look especially for light. Without light, other details remain in the dark.

    b. Choose one detail that suggests the predominant character, atmosphere, or impression of the thing observed.

    c. Select one detail that personalizes the subject or that seems to be the unique feature setting it apart from all others.

If I look about my office, for example, I see brick walls, a dull red carpet, shelves of literature books, a Chinese evergreen with yellowed leaves, an ashtray on the desk, a telephone, morning light falling through the window, stacks of unread freshman papers, and so on. What should I choose? Probably the morning light because, in addition to lighting the scene, the word *morning* gives us a type of light, an angle to the light, and a time of day—all of which open the scene to the mind's eye. Then I might select the rows of books or toppling piles of freshman papers; either would suggest the predominant atmosphere. Finally, I might focus on the milk-glass ashtray with red lettering stamped around the rim: COWBOY BAR— PINEDALE, WYO., U.S.A. The ashtray suggests something personal, something that sets me apart from other college instructors. (Do I spend my summers herding cattle in Wyoming? Could I have stolen it one wild and drunken night?)

4. Select the small detail most representative of the larger whole. Fly specks on a water glass in a restaurant may be the only detail needed to suggest an unsanitary restaurant. A comb poking from the Levis pocket of a teen-age boy may suggest his pride or vanity. A hesitant pause before answering a question may give a clue to a congressman's use of slush money.

5. Look for details that reveal contradictions, conflict, or contrast, either in the subject itself or in what you anticipate the audience expects from the subject. A white picture is heightened by contrasting it with a dark matting. A man's strength may be emphasized by the tenderness with which he holds his six-month-old daughter. The character of a sixty-year-old woman may be revealed when she jogs in the Boston Marathon.

Obviously, every subject may call for its own special treatment, yet these guidelines can suggest a starting point for observation. Here's part of an essay in which freshman Gary Svoboda described an occurrence on a beach in North Carolina—before he had trained himself to select:

> Later on that night I went out to the beach and met several people who were hauling in a fishing net. One was named Jim and there was a woman whose name I didn't catch. I asked if I could help, just for the fun of it, and I worked with them for about an

hour pulling fish and all kinds of sea life out of the net. They gave me a couple of fish for my help. We worked hard and I was tired by the end.

Gary has described, but he has failed to evaluate the effectiveness of his details. Both randomness and abstraction show that he hasn't yet disciplined his perceptions. A woman whose name he didn't catch creates no picture in our mind; neither does feeling tired after an hour's work or pulling "sea life" from a fishing net. Nothing here engages our imagination. After hearing his class react indifferently to the essay, Gary complained that in his hometown this was just an ordinary event. How could he do more than write an ordinary description? As an experiment, we asked him to name twenty details from the experience. Here are only a few that Gary listed on the blackboard.

| Gary's Details | Class Response |
| --- | --- |
| a man named Jim | The detail lacks significance. |
| fish tossed in piles | What kind of fish? |
| croakers, sand sharks | Good. The names create images. |
|  | What did they do with the sand sharks? Do croakers croak? |
| The fish got tangled in the net. | Fair. Keep going. |
| Skates made a clapping noise trying to escape. | What are skates? How do they clap? Why didn't you tell us this before? |

The interest shown by the class in certain types of details helped Gary rewrite.

Later on I went out on the beach and walked along the sand in the moonlight. There was a small crowd gathered around some fishermen hauling in a net. I watched for a while and then asked if I could help. The rope felt like a steel cable cutting into my hands. When the net came out of the waves it sounded like someone clapping, like applause. At first I thought it was the bystanders and then I realized it was the skates caught in the net and clapping their wing-like bodies, trying to desperately escape. I put on a pair of gloves borrowed from one of the fishermen and knelt in the wet sand and helped them untangle the fish from the net. There were croakers and sea trout, sand sharks, and horse shoe crabs. The fish were tossed in a heaping pile on the sand. We heaved the skates and crabs back into the surf. We let the two-foot-long sand sharks die on the beach. They were still there the next morning. They had their mouths open and I felt like their eyes were staring at me.

Although the writing here needs editing, Gary's second version contains details that involve the reader in the experience. Gary has omitted dull points (surely "a man named Jim" did not stir interest even in Gary), and he has replaced them with sensory details (moonlit beach, a cutting rope), with details that contrast to the reader's expectations (skates that clap their bodies in an effort to escape), and with small details that suggest a larger significance (their mouths gape open; eyes seem to stare at him).

A unique style, correct grammar, a large vocabulary—all are wasted unless you also develop a disciplined mind eager to encounter the realities of an ordinary world—the fabulous realities as Thoreau calls them. To describe with precision one must see with precision.

## Narrative Focus

In the process of reseeing details in his subject, Gary Svoboda also discovered a natural, chronological ordering for presenting his experience. His description moves clearly from nighttime setting to early next morning; the rope is pulled; the net, hauled onto the beach; the fish, removed—all in the sequence in which they obviously occurred.

Few students experience any difficulty with narrative. Chronological sequence seems to come naturally to us: this happened; then this happened; then this happened. But good narrative—the ordering of events—requires a mental discipline similar to that required by description: to order or arrange, you must select. Some aspects of an event must be omitted in favor of other aspects. Time must be shortened here, dwelt upon in more detail there.

Not all narrative is chronological, of course. Sometimes a writer begins with the present, moves to the past, then to the distant past and back to the present. This is the beginning of form: selection and ordering for the sake of emphasis, clarity, interest. All professional writers, writers of fiction as well as of nonfiction, know that the ordering of events affects the reader's ability to follow a story or essay logically, as well as it affects the pace or speed with which the essay seems to flow.

Here is an example of superb ordering and pacing from *Black Elk Speaks* as recorded by John G. Neihardt. Black Elk describes the butchering at Wounded Knee:

> I had no gun, and when we were charging, I just held the sacred bow out in front of me with my right hand. The bullets did not hit us at all. . . .
> The soldiers had run eastward over the hills where there

From *Black Elk Speaks* by John G. Neihardt, copyright © 1932, 1959 by John G. Neihardt, published by Simon and Schuster Pocket Books. Reprinted by permission.

were some more soldiers, and they were off their horses and lying down. . . .

We followed down along the dry gulch, and what we saw was terrible. Dead and wounded women and children and little babies were scattered all along there where they had been trying to run away. The soldiers had followed along the gulch, as they ran, and murdered them in there. Sometimes they were in heaps because they had huddled together, and some were scattered all along. Sometimes bunches of them had been killed and torn to pieces where the wagon guns hit them. I saw a little baby trying to suck its mother, but she was bloody and dead. . . .

When we drove the soldiers back, they dug themselves in, and we were not enough people to drive them out of there. In the evening they marched off up Wounded Knee Creek, and then we saw all that they had done there. . . .

Many were shot down right there. The women and children ran into the gulch and up west, dropping all the time, for the soldiers shot them as they ran. There were only about a hundred warriors and there were nearly five hundred soldiers. . . .

It was a good winter day when all this happened. The sun was shining. But after the soldiers marched away from their dirty work, a heavy snow began to fall. The wind came up in the night. There was a big blizzard, and it grew very cold. The snow drifted deep in the crooked gulch, and it was one long grave of butchered women and children and babies, who had never done any harm and were only trying to run away.

Notice how the flow of this narrative is maintained by the first sentence in each paragraph:

I had no gun, and when we were charging . . .
The soldiers ran eastward over the hills . . .
We followed . . .
When we drove the soldiers back . . .
Many were shot down right there . . .
It was a good winter day when all this happened . . .

Of course, the power of Black Elk's story depends equally upon the descriptive details. Narration almost always works hand-in-hand with description. Practice in describing and narrating is practice in perceiving and shaping experience. Teaching yourself how to *select* and *order* is the first major step in disciplining the senses and in moving eventually toward logic and critical judgment.

### EXERCISES AND SUGGESTED WRITING ASSIGNMENTS

1. In order to both discipline and focus your sense of sight, sketch in detail (with a pencil or ink) a small object like a key or a school ring as it

rests on a table. Try to capture texture, light, shadow, shape, dimension, and depth. You're not expected to be an artist, but because an artist has a trained eye, he or she sees details many of us miss. We can learn much about training our perceptions by imitating the techniques of artists. Once you've completed your sketch, write a single paragraph describing the object in detail, this time using words to capture the same texture, light, shadow, shape, dimension, and depth.

2. Description should have direction or purpose. A random listing of details has little interest even for the writer. The purpose may be nothing more than creation of mood or feeling. Here is Joan Didion's opening paragraph from a short story. By focusing her perceptions on selected details, she creates an atmosphere that suggests the quality of life along a particular stretch of highway in California. Her purpose is to make you see and feel that quality.

> Imagine Banyan Street first, because Banyan is where it hap-
> pened. The way to Banyan is to drive west from San Bernardino
> out Foothill Boulevard, Route 66: past the Santa Fe switching
> yards, the Forty Winks Motel. Past the motel that is 19 stucco
> tepees: SLEEP IN A WIGWAM—GET MORE FOR YOUR
> WAMPUM. Past Fontana Drag City and the Fontana Church of
> the Nazarene and the Pit Stop A Go-go; past Kaiser Steel through
> Cucamonga, out to the Kapu Kai Restaurant-Bar and Coffee
> Shop, at the corner of Route 66 and Carnelian Avenue. Up Carne-
> lian Avenue from Kapu Kai, which means "Forbidden Seas," the
> subdivision flags whip in the harsh winds. HALF-ACRE
> RANCHES! SNACK BARS! TRAVERTINE ENTRIES! $95
> DOWN. It is the trail of an intention gone haywire, the flotsam of
> the new California. But after a while the signs thin out on Carne-
> lian Avenue, and the houses are no longer the bright pastels of the
> Springtime Home owners but the faded bungalows of the people
> who grow a few grapes and keep a few chickens out here, and then
> the hill gets steeper and the road climbs and even the bungalows
> are few, and here—desolate, roughly surfaced, lined with euca-
> lyptus and lemon groves—is Banyan Street.

Write a paragraph describing a street that leads to your home or school. Focus your perceptions in such a way that you select only details that suggest what it would be like to live there. Do not "tell" the reader through abstractions; "show" in carefully selected concrete images.

3. Describe and narrate one minute of a college wrestling match or other sporting event. Be careful to avoid clichés both in language and perception. Use selected concrete words and images.

4. Describe and narrate in no more than two or three paragraphs the most important two or three scenes (one per paragraph) of your high school graduation. Select carefully both descriptive details and the *chronological ordering* of events. Try to help the reader see and feel the flow of your experience.

Now rewrite the whole experience with a different narrative ordering. Begin at the end, flash back to an earlier stage, and narrate up to the same point you described in your first sentence.

Which version do you find more effective?

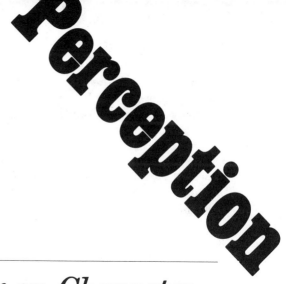

# 9 Focusing on Character

At one time I lived in a small village on the side of a mountain in South America. The village priest, Padre Bolanos, was also the mayor. A thin, almost gaunt man who wore a faded black cassock and drove a jeep, the padre seemed to be everywhere, organizing a festival, laying a water pipe from a spring to the village, building an electrical generator to light the church, petitioning for government funds to construct a small bridge, initiating a soccer game in the rain in which he ran wildly through the mud, his black cassock flaying the wind, his boots kicking the splattered ball high into the air. Everyone loved Padre Bolanos.

As I was one of the few outsiders ever to stay in the village, the padre invited me to live in his home behind the church. I had hardly settled in when I discovered that a young woman and her small son also lived with the Padre. The very mention of the young woman to others in the village caused raised eyebrows and knowing smiles. "The Padre is only human," one man told me. I quickly found a room with another family. For six months I felt contempt for the priest. That the villagers loved him made him only more hypocritical in my eyes. I avoided him, spoke coolly to him. And then once, in an emergency of sorts, I found I had to ask him to drive me to the nearest large town where I could find a doctor. Padre Bolanos acted without hesitation. Within minutes he had the jeep bouncing down the mountainside. On the way, he told me a story.

He told how a priest had once visited the capital city of his country and walked late at night through the poorest *barrio*. As he walked among the broken streets, the priest heard muffled cries from an alley and found there a young girl who had just given birth among the rags and ashes. The girl was fourteen. She had been a prostitute since she was eleven. The priest had taken the girl home with him where for several years now she served as housekeeper. He knew many people felt horrified that a priest should have an ex-prostitute for a housekeeper; others, more cynical perhaps, felt certain the priest kept the girl as mistress. In a few weeks she would be eighteen and leaving for the capital city again. She did not like living in a rural village. The priest would continue to raise the little boy, at least for a while, until the girl found a job. The priest's only regret was that the girl was still not a Christian. She did not believe in God.

I sat quietly, ashamed. How could I have misjudged him so badly? As we pulled up to the doctor's office, Padre Bolanos turned to me. "You know," he said, "for a long time I thought you were a sullen young man, perhaps even a little arrogant. But I apologize to you for my mistake. I see now that you are only shy." I had climbed out of the jeep. "Character," he said, "is a difficult thing. Too often I don't know what to look for, or I judge too quickly." He smiled at me and added in English, "I must learn to look most closely."

After two years in South America I returned home. I wanted to write about the economic consequences of a village market on sociological development—big words, big ideas. Most college writing deals with ideas and issues. But I found I could not separate my ideas from the people I had known. Ideas and issues do not exist in a vacuum. People with complex characters create ideas, cause events, stir up issues, invent machines, change the course of history, and indulge in little acts of human kindness. Describing people requires that we learn to look "most closely" and is perhaps the best training we can have for the development of writing skills. Good writing begins with perception of the subject. Teaching yourself to perceive people in all their complexities is a major step in teaching yourself to perceive the complexity of the world people have created—and perhaps in making us all a little more human.

## Perception of Character

What exactly is "character"? What do we mean when we say (in the abstract) that "Gomez is a real character"? Or "Loretta has a super personality"? Even though you may not plan to write novels, novelists are one of the better sources to learn from, for a major tradition in the novel for 150 years has been the creation of character.

Here is David Copperfield describing (concretely) his stepfather's sister, whom he has never met and who has just arrived by stagecoach.

> It was Miss Murdstone who was arrived, and a gloomy-looking lady she was; dark, like her brother, whom she greatly resembled

in face and voice; and with very heavy eyebrows, nearly meeting over her large nose, as if, being disabled by the wrongs of her sex from wearing whiskers, she had carried them to that account. She brought with her two uncompromising hard black boxes, with her initials on the lids in hard brass nails. When she paid the coachman she took her money out of a hard steel purse, and she kept the purse in a very jail of a bag which hung upon her arm by a heavy chain, and shut up like a bite. I had never, at that time, seen such a metallic lady altogether as Miss Murdstone was.

. . . Then she looked at me, and said:

"Is that your boy, sister-in-law?"

My mother acknowledged me.

"Generally speaking," said Miss Murdstone, "I don't like boys."

Charles Dickens is famous for his ability to create a sense of character within a short space, sometimes by exaggeration, but more often by seeing with an accurate eye the precise details that contribute to making a person unique. If we look closely at this description of Miss Murdstone, we find—either through direct concrete description or by implication—almost all of the major qualities that create in our minds an image of character.

# Physical Description

As always, we begin with *seeing*. The way people look, the way they dress, the physical qualities of their person—these suggest something about character. Miss Murdstone is dark with heavy eyebrows that almost meet over her large nose (suggesting a perpetual scowl); she carries a hard steel purse in a jail of a bag with a heavy chain. Now although it might be possible that Miss Murdstone is actually delicate, kind, happy, and charming, her physical appearance suggests the opposite. And although we have always heard we should not judge a book by its cover, the fact is we do. We tend to judge people, rightly or wrongly, by their physical appearance.

We can begin to make a distinction between fact and inference. A *fact* is a direct observation of the senses that can be verified by someone else making the same observation. "John has a black eye." An *inference* is a conclusion about something that you cannot observe directly but that the facts suggest to you. "John has probably been in a fight."

The facts of physical appearance lead us to inferences about character. If we see a thirty-five-year-old man wearing shoulder length hair, slopping around in sandals, and dangling a 1968 Peace symbol about his neck, the facts that all can verify lead to inferences about his character—inferences that may or may not be correct. Physical appearance, then, is our first contact with character. But we need more details of another nature to confirm our impressions.

## Actions

Actions can overcome the impressions made by outward physical appearance, or they can confirm our impressions. In the paragraph by Dickens, Miss Murdstone is seen performing only two significant actions: paying the coachman for her ride and speaking to David Copperfield's mother. We see her in more action later in the novel; but even at this stage, in our introduction to her, we begin to sense a quality of her personality by the way she takes her money from a steel purse (that shuts with a bite) and by the bluntness—could one say rudeness?—of her speech. Dickens tells us nothing in the abstract. He never says, "Miss Murdstone was greedy and cruel." But the *fact* of her actions causes us to *infer* that she is.

Look at the actions of people around you. Perhaps you have a grandfather who locks himself in a fruit cellar when your grandmother gets angry. Perhaps you have a college roommate who sticks wads of used chewing gum on the bottom of a desk. You've probably encountered the college instructor who is never in his or her office during posted office hours. About all those people you make inferences as to their character. Neither physical appearance nor actions by themselves give a complete picture of character, but together, they build impressions.

*level of educ inferred from diction*
*Repetition of revealing phrases*
*punctuation*

## Speech

What we say and how we say it reveal an almost infinite number of qualities. Miss Murdstone's blunt dislike of children could not be made more stunning than by her single line, "Generally speaking, I don't like boys." Physical details and physical actions can suggest inner qualities, but speech has the potential of directly revealing values, ideas, rigor of intellect, attitudes, beliefs—even educational and cultural background. There is a striking difference between the character who says, "I ain't gonna put up with no more crap!" and another who says, "Your suppositions about me are highly distressing and I refuse to tolerate further insinuations."

Yet speech, too, must be weighed against other perceptions, for it is one thing to hear a man say, "Your President is not a crook," and another thing to accept the *fact* of the statement at face value.

## Self-created Environment

The type of environment we surround ourself with, the physical nature of the room we live in, the condition of our home, the car we drive—all contribute to perception of character. For example, Miss Murdstone apparently surrounds herself with metallic hardness. She carries her belongings in *hard* black boxes on which she has her initials pounded in *hard* brass nails. She even carries her money in a *hard* steel purse hung on her arm by a metal chain. Dickens would have created a different character in our minds had he described her as carrying a silk umbrella, a purse made of see-through wicker with wild straw flowers on top, and a trunk painted with fragile blue forget-me-nots. *can tell manners, sets mood, beliefs*

## Background

Background may or may not be important in creating a sense of character. We know nothing about Miss Murdstone's background when we first meet her, and we probably don't need to. At other times, background can be the single most vital quality in explaining why someone acts as he or she does—for example, an actress may have had a "stage mother" who drove her relentlessly to become famous, or the president of a giant corporation may have learned his dedication as a boy by getting up at 4 A.M. to milk cows on his father's Missouri farm. But writers must be cautious about background details. If you tell us, "Mr. Harper was born on July 9, 1932. He lived in a small town until he was six; then he moved to a large city where he attended elementary school, . . ." you will bore all of us to death. Background details must be striking and essential to understanding current qualities of character, or they must be avoided altogether. Dickens, like other successful writers, uses background material with careful selectivity.

## Others' Reactions

Finally, the way other people react to character helps to establish the validity of a writer's observations. Any writer may be biased in judgment. As we've already seen, it's possible to select only details with negative connotations or only those with positive connotations to sway the reader's impression. A second and third opinion can help us as readers to believe that the writer is reporting fairly and honestly. In the scene of Miss Murdstone's arrival, we have no reactions from other characters, but later we find that people tiptoe around Miss Murdstone, no one dares speak loudly to her, and others obey shamefacedly when she commands. Their reactions to her confirm our original impression of her character.

Although one could probably name several more aspects of life that shape our attitudes toward character, these six attributes—balanced off against each other—seem to be the most frequently observed and used by successful writers:

> Physical appearance
> Actions

Speech
Self-created environment
Background
Others' reactions

As Dickens shows, a writer need not present all six qualities to evoke a sense of character. Some writers have achieved solid, believable characters by using only dialogue or by using only action and speech but without physical description. You must train yourself to look for the most interesting and important qualities in your subject, the unique elements of human nature that separate the person you're writing about from all others.

## How Describing Character Relates to Other Forms of Writing

Of course, you're not going to write novels or short stories—at least not most of you. So why learn how to describe character?

First, any training in how to select factual details that lead to logical inferences is simply good training for every paper or report you'll ever write in college or in your career. But the suggestions for selecting those details that I've listed in this chapter are also crucial: it is one thing to say, "Learn how to select good factual details"; it is another to question, "How?" The strategy of looking for *physical details, actions, speech, environment, background,* and *others' reactions* provides you with a focus for selection that goes beyond "character." For example, with only slight modification, you might use the same criteria of selection for a history paper on the battle of Marathon:

1. What physical details were significant? What type of armament, protective shields, and supplies affected the outcome?

2. What actions were significant? Why did the Athenians form a battle line that was thin in the middle and heavy on the flanks?

3. What speech was significant? Who convinced the Greeks to meet the Persians on the plain of Marathon instead of awaiting battle at Athens?

4. What elements in the environment were significant? How did the shape of the hills and the narrow passes affect the outcome?

5. What elements of background are important? Why were the Plataeans willing to aid the Athenians; where did the Athenian generals learn their tactics?

6. How have other historians reacted to the battle? To what good fortune does Herodotus attribute the victory?

In other words, the six attributes a novelist looks for in "character" can be used as six strategies any writer can look for in developing almost any subject. In later chapters, I'll develop this approach more fully.

But it must also be said that perception of character—and the ability to share that perception in writing—goes beyond a mere set of techniques. The need to extend our awareness, to sense and feel the qualities of another man's life, is one of the great steps out of self-centered adolescence and into adulthood. Only by training ourselves to sympathize (and ultimately to empathize) with other people in their fears, their ideals, their frustrations, their convictions—only in developing the ability to project ourselves into others—can we begin to know and better evaluate our own lives by contrast. As Padre Bolanos said, we "must learn to look most closely."

## SUGGESTED WRITING ASSIGNMENTS

1. Write a paragraph describing the physical details and actions of someone you *don't* know. Look for, select, and organize the details in such a way that they imply something about the person's character as you perceive it.

Be careful. If you tell us that a gentleman on the bus wore a brown suit and white tie and brown shoes and carried a raincoat over his arm, we will only yawn. Search out unique features that make the person special, that make him come alive as an *image* in the reader's mind. Perhaps the gentleman on the bus has a yellow wart in the corner of his eye; perhaps he draws circles in the steam on the bus window when he thinks no one is looking; perhaps he takes a comb from his pocket and strokes his moustache with loving care. One or two sentences of carefully selected concrete details will be more effective than a page of common description.

2. Reveal character through action. You may do this exercise from memory or from watching someone closely. Actions may be as small as gestures made by the hands or as large as decisions made in the face of great crises or danger. Here is how Ray Bradbury characterized a grandmother in *Dandelion Wine*. Notice how each sentence reveals an action that, in turn, reveals an element of the grandmother's character.

> She was a woman with a broom or a dustpan or a washrag or a mixing spoon in her hand. You saw her cutting piecrust in the morning, humming to it, or you saw her setting out the baked pies at noon or taking them in, cool, at dusk. She rang porcelain cups like a Swiss bell ringer, to their place. She glided through the halls as steadily as a vacuum machine, seeking, finding, and setting to rights. She made mirrors of every window, to catch the sun. She strolled but twice through any garden, trowel in hand, and the flowers raised their quivering fires upon the warm air in her wake. She slept quietly and turned no more than three times in a night,

as relaxed as a white glove to which, at dawn, a brisk hand will return. Waking, she touched people like pictures, to set their frames straight.

Here is how a college freshman handled actions (along with other "characterizing" details):

I was walking down Main Street near dusk when I noticed him staggering toward me. He was an old man. The skin on his face was wrinkled and parched. His glasses kept sliding down his nose with each step and he would periodically stop to push them up. His baggy trousers and shirt were shabby and frayed at the cuffs. The olive-green sweater buttoned crooked, making the right side longer than the left. A battered brown hat sat lop-sided upon his head. As he walked, his untied shoe-strings flapped back and forth. He clutched a small paper bag in his right hand. The smell of liquor nauseated my senses as he passed me. He turned his head slowly to the left then to the right, but he never looked back. Satisfied that no one was watching, he raised the wrinkled bag to his lips and swallowed quickly. Then he looked around again to see if anyone had seen him. He cradled the bag to his chest with both arms as he continued to sway down the walk.

3. Interview your roommate or a friend. Find out everything you can about his or her *background*. As you listen, consider whether each detail being revealed would interest your audience. Look for a small detail from the past that suggests or explains a larger meaning today. Look for contradictions or conflict. Do not be satisfied with birthdays and names of elementary schools. Probe for the unique story, the summer your roommate painted fire hydrants in Fairbanks, Alaska, or the loneliness he or she felt at growing up an only child. Select *only* the most significant details, and write up a single paragraph of background material that reveals something about your roommate's character. *Focus* the paragraph on the most significant one or two details. Be concrete.

Sandra Brooks, a sophomore nursing major, handled the exercise like this:

When you see Elizabeth, the first thing that comes to mind is the image of the perfect woman athlete. Her legs and arms are muscular and her voice booms like that of a football coach. She lives her life according to a schedule. Everything she does is timed and carried out in step-by-step method. I asked Elizabeth why she was so orderly. She glanced anxiously at her watch before she answered. Today is Monday and she has worked from nine to five. She has to get home, eat dinner, and change for her exercise class at seven. By ten o'clock she will be in bed. Elizabeth replied, "When I was fifteen my father died. Before his death he taught me how to do everything a son was supposed to do. My father wanted a son, but after my mother had me she couldn't have any more children. A couple years after I was born, she became an invalid. There was nothing really wrong with her; she just seemed to lose interest in life. After my father died, I had to take care of the house. That's when I started doing things by a schedule. It was the only way I could get everything done. As I grew older I found that it had become a part of me. Keeping busy made me forget what I was missing in life." The entire time that Elizabeth was talking to me she constantly twisted her watch around and around her wrist. "It makes me feel secure to know that I have a schedule to keep. It keeps me from wondering what I'll be doing at a certain time each day. I don't have a family to take care of anymore, and I have to fill the time some way." Elizabeth tried to glance at her watch without my noticing. I saw that she wanted to leave, so I thanked her for her time. As she hurried to her car, I thought how sad it was to live each day by a list or according to a schedule.

4. Write a 1,000-word paper (about four typed pages, double-spaced) in which you describe the character of someone who has had a special influence on your life. Avoid writing about your latest girlfriend or boyfriend; choose instead a relative, a teacher, a neighbor, or a lifelong friend. Focus upon no more than one to three events in which you show your reader the special qualities of the character. Narrate events according to a determined sequence; focus your description on *selected* details of action, physical qualities, speech, background, a self-created environment, and others' reactions. A student essay is included at the end of this unit to provide you with an example. Before you begin to write, read Chapter 10 on how to create a scene—it should help you organize your material more effectively.

# 10 Creating a Scene

That night Demirgian lay in his combat clothes—his steel helmet, the damp fabric of his shirt and trousers, his canvas boots—and Demirgian had a wet black rifle on the soil beside him as with intricate fingers he made himself a glass of grape juice. Slower than a caterpillar chews on a maple leaf his fingers tore a small paper packet of Kool-Aid and quieter than a dandelion loses its fluff his hand shook the light purple powder into his Army canteen. The cold stars above, the cool earth below him kept their complete silence as Demirgian tilted his rubber canteen to its left—right—left—right with the slow periodicity of a pendulum. One long minute of this and Demirgian took a quiet sip. And ah! Demirgian had come alive! He's in the grape-juice generation! He buried the torn paper packet quietly in six inches of Vietnam's soil.

This paragraph is not taken from a short story or a novel, although it seems to have all the qualities we expect in fiction. Actually, it was written by John Sack, a professional writer describing in an article for *Esquire* a true character involved in the Vietnam War. Sack writes nonfiction, but like many successful writers, he incorporates the techniques of fiction into his work to make it more interesting. In almost any type of personal writing and in many other kinds of writing, the various elements of perception, language, and form that have been covered in the first nine chapters of this book (especially in description and narration) can be drawn together into a fiction technique labeled the *scene*. Understanding the components of scene can give you both an effective device for beginning an essay, as well as structural unit for shaping your first draft.

# Elements of Scene

A highly respected teacher of writing, Wilson R. Thornley, has identified seven major elements in the prose scene:

> *Light.* The stage in a theater cannot be seen without light, nor can your reader see a prose scene in his imagination without some mention or implication of light.
>
> *Time.* Light often suggests time: a "November dawn" for example gives time of year, time of day, and type of light. We do not need time as given in detective novels (it was 6:42 P.M. when the murder occurred) but we do need a general range of time like morning, evening, noon or whatever.
>
> *Place.* We all live in a real world, in a real setting, and we cannot imagine people functioning in a vacuum. A sentence or two can suggest the gates of a castle, a Victorian living room, the path in a dark forest.
>
> *Character.* Common sense tells us that character is the focal point of any scene. Light, time and place are all background to the character who walks, talks, acts and reveals for us the vital qualities of his or her life.
>
> *Position.* The character in a scene, whether it is you or someone else, holds a position in relation to the other characters and to the setting or place itself. The vice-president of a company sitting firmly behind his oak desk suggests a different quality of character to the reader than a vice-president meeting you at the door of his office, showing you a chair, and sitting beside you by a round coffee table. This positional relationship is surprisingly important in suggesting a feeling about the character's relationship to the world he lives in.
>
> *Purpose.* Nothing can be more dull than a scene that doesn't go anywhere. No scene in a play or in your own writing should exist without some clear intention. Purpose can lie in demonstrating some aspect of character, or in setting the mood for what is to follow, or in presenting a problem or conflict that will need to be solved.
>
> *Five senses.* The theater can successfully suggest only sight and

sound to the audience. Prose can involve as many of the five senses as possible or necessary to absorb the reader physically and emotionally in the scene.

If we go back for a moment to John Sack's opening paragraph about a soldier in Vietnam, we find all of these qualities: the first sentence sets up time (night, stars out); we know immediately that a character (obviously a soldier wearing combat clothes and a steel helmet) is lying on the ground, a detail that provides both his position and our first indication of place—which turns out to be Vietnam soil; the larger setting of the article will follow. In addition to sight, sensory details include touch (a wet rifle, cold earth) and sound ("quieter than dandelion fluff"). Sack's purpose here is not as immediately clear. We do gain some insight into the soldier's personal, human qualities as we see him mixing Kool-Aid grape juice in his canteen. Actually, it is not until the next paragraph (which I have not quoted) that the author makes his point: while a soldier is on ambush patrol, nothing ever happens. The scene becomes clear. The soldier is doing what soldiers have always done—lie in the mud, wait, and find some way to pass the time.

Scene is a literary device, but it is so only because we all live every day in a scene, as you are doing at this moment. Knowing the elements of scene gives you a method for observing and recording. Description and narration should not consist of random details. Selection should be made from those qualities most likely to convey to the reader's imagination the actual and most vivid elements of life itself. Thus scene: *light, time, place, character, position, purpose,* and *sensory experience.* Scene provides you with the first major step in creating form; a scene *is* form.

# Organizing Within the Scene

The elements of scene can be organized into whatever pattern is most effective. There are no rules, but there are some conventional organizations that you should be familiar with and that might help you in your own writing.

## General to Specific

Because a reader needs orientation, it can often be helpful to begin with the larger frame and focus in step-by-step toward the more significant detail. Here is how one student, Olivia Bertagnolli, began an essay on her seventeenth summer:

> On Saturday morning I crossed the hollow to Leo Auffman's house and sat on the back porch where the sunlight pooled and dropped into the narrow slats between the wooden steps. I watched the round speckled sparrows with purple ridged beaks squatting along the chicken wire fence that stretched behind Leo's woodshed. The

sparrows chattered and scratched the sides of their beaks back and forth against the wire.

I whistled just to be whistling. I didn't feel seventeen years old sitting there in a white blouse and Levis the color of blueberry stains on cheesecloth. I didn't even feel eight, or ten, or twelve, but just as old as the ripening blueberries that grow blue-misted in summer.

July brought yellow days, warm wind, and blueberries. Blueberries as big as the end of your thumb; blueberries so bloated with thick, purple juice that the tight skins burst when the sun touched them; and the ebony meat slipped from the tarnished sacks leaving the wrinkled skins to hang from the stems like bits of purple rag. The blueberries didn't ripen all at once, but just a few at a time, some still clinging to the stems as hard as green peas. The plumper berries pushed a few of the smaller ones away from the sun, squeezing the blueness from their skins. They turned yellow and shriveled against the stem leaving the others waiting to be picked.

Olivia begins with the larger frame. She leads us across a "hollow" to Leo Auffman's house, then to his back porch. We scan the general area, observing a few sparrows, a chicken-wire fence, a woodshed (although within that general frame Olivia still points out specific selected details such as the purple-ridged beaks of the sparrows). The second paragraph again begins with the general—this time a general feeling, an emotion caused apparently by being young and alive and free in summer sun. But in that general emotion, a single image occurs ("blueberry stains on cheesecloth"). The image seems to trigger a focusing of memory, and the third paragraph moves quickly from July to yellow days and warm wind (the general) to blueberries and all their particulars (the specific). The third paragraph focuses on a single ordinary element of life with such accuracy and precision of observation that every element of our imagination is stimulated.

This pattern of movement is often used at the beginning of essays. The same pattern, usually called the *panoramic scene,* can be seen in a number of TV shows and movies: we begin with the overview, a large city with tall buildings. The camera zooms in toward a single building, then focuses on a single window in the building; we move inside, where we find Mary Tyler Moore dancing on a desk. Movement from the general to the specific orients the audience, leading its attention toward the detailed point the writer wants to make.

The panoramic technique can be especially helpful for the writer during the first draft because the mind, too, needs orienting, needs to follow a process of focusing. By allowing yourself to begin with the general, you help the words flow. It is usually easier to write about large elements than about small (easier to begin with "It was a July morning" or "All over Brooklyn the rain was falling") and then to lead your own mind into the finer details.

## Specific to General

The alternative is obvious. John Sack's scene about Demirgian begins with the soldier lying in the mud. Not until the end do we find out he is in Vietnam. We clearly move from the focused detail to the larger frame. Here is Billy Whitmore, a sophomore, following such a technique in an essay on his coach:

> His hand reached out and slapped my helmet. An explosion like a dull boom thundered inside my head. His shoulder clipped my shoulder and the pads made a vicious smack! I felt myself spinning for a moment off balance, the sun flashing past my eyes, blue sky, then the cold plastic grass coming up at my nose. I was reaching out to catch myself when something hit me from behind like three heavy mattresses falling on me at once, smashing me down. Then someone's knee drove itself into my kidneys and the pain arched across my back. My ribs poked into my lungs. For a moment everything was just still, only the sounds of several people panting. Huffing. Then the weight lifted off me and I heard the coach yelling, "Jesus H. Christ, Whitmore, where's your head? You were out of position? Get yourself up before I kick your ass all the way to Rolf Hall!"
>
> It was the third day of practice. Coach Harley was standing over me and between his legs I could see the afternoon sun dripping down over the empty bleachers. The dull thundering in my ears had not gone away. His voice sounded as if he were shouting at me through a cloud. I got to my knees and in spite of the pain burning in my back I pulled myself up. The other guys trying out for the team had drifted back over to scrimage line and were looking away from me, pretending not to notice. It was the third major mistake I had made that day and something in Coach Harley's face told me it would be my last.

Although the reader can quickly tell that the author is writing about football (the helmet and the shoulder pads appear in the first two sentences), we know nothing of the larger situation until the second paragraph. Only gradually do we perceive the more general setting (a sinking sun, empty bleachers, other football players, the coach). And not until the final sentence of the second paragraph do we get a suggestion of purpose or direction.

Beginning with selected details has the value of thrusting the reader immediately into your writing. The audience is caught up in an event or a description without knowing exactly why and must keep reading to find out. Therein lies the risk. The reader will stay with you only so long—perhaps a few paragraphs or a page before you must provide some general orientation. But either organizing technique—general to specific or specific to general—provides you with a relatively easy and sequential pattern to follow in getting the first few paragraphs of an essay flowing.

## Scene and the First Draft

As the first draft often presents the most difficult obstacle to overcome in writing, an understanding of scene and its components can provide you with an immediate place to begin writing: create a scene in which you show us your subject; write a series of scenes showing different aspects of your subject. In the first draft the scenes need not even be logically connected. You can always return later and fill in the relationships, add commentary or personal reflection, and draw conclusions. A scene or a series of scenes can be the organizing unit of a complete essay: it can serve as a sensory and dramatic introduction to an essay or it can provide an effective and often moving conclusion. The readings collected at the end of this unit provide several examples.

The function of a scene is not to tell but to dramatize. A scene helps you select and order your details by focusing your attention on light, time, place, character, and purpose. It provides a manageable shape for organizing details, either from specific to general or general to specific. Ford Madox Ford, an early twentieth-century writer, said you must always write as if your subject were acting out its life before you on a stage. If you see nothing in your mind's eye, you can be sure your reader won't see anything either. Especially in writing about character or in writing any form of description and narration, keeping the elements of scene in the back of your mind while keeping a picture of the thing you're describing in the front of your mind, can help make words flow onto the page.

### EXERCISES

Analyze the following scene by John Knowles from his novel *A Separate Peace*. Identify each of the elements of scene. Has he left any out?

No one else happened to be in the pool. Around us gleamed white tile and glass brick; the green, artificial-looking water rocked gently in its shining basin, releasing vague chemical smells and a sense of many pipes and filters; even Finny's voice, trapped in this closed, high-ceilinged room, lost its special resonance and blurred into a general well of noise gathered up toward the ceiling. He said blurringly, "I have a feeling I can swim faster than A. Hopkins Parker."

We found a stop watch in the office. He mounted a starting box, leaned forward from the waist as he had seen racing swimmers do but never had occasion to do himself—I noticed a preparatory looseness coming into his shoulders and arms, a controlled ease about his stance which was unexpected in anyone trying to break a record. I said, "On your mark—Go!" There was a complex moment when his body uncoiled and shot forward with sudden metallic tension. He planed up the pool, his shoulders dominating the water while his legs and feet rode so low that I couldn't distinguish them; a wake rippled hurriedly by him and then at the end of the pool his position broke, he relaxed, dived, an instant's confusion and then his suddenly and metallically tense body shot back toward the other end of the pool. Another turn and up the pool again—I noticed no particular slackening of his pace—another turn, down the pool again, his hand touched the end, and he looked up at me with a composed, interested expression. "Well, how did I do?" I looked at the watch; he had broken A. Hopkins Parker's record by .7 second.

| | |
|---|---|
| ____light | ____sight |
| ____time | ____touch |
| ____place | ____sound |
| ____character | ____taste |
| ____purpose | ____touch |
| ____position | ____smell |

### SUGGESTED WRITING ASSIGNMENTS

1. Observe a scene in real life. Make a list of all the elements of scene—try to find several items for each element. For example, you might observe a teen-age girl buying a frozen yogurt cone at a dairy bar. How many different elements of light are present? Bright afternoon sunlight falling through the dirty window? Greenish fluorescent lights over the counter? A whirling light from a neon sign atop the frozen-yogurt machine? Draw up a list for each of the required elements of scene; then select the best and write a short paragraph describing the scene.

2. Practice writing a "panoramic scene." Look out of your window. Describe the general location; record the light (try to imply "time" through the light); then focus in, step-by-step, on a simple but important or characteristic detail selected from the whole. Here is how freshman Mark Bostic attempted it:

*general overview*   It was another gloomy Monday and the light was beginning to fade for the day. The clouds in the sky grew darker and darker. Then the rain began, lightly at first, barely touching the leaves of the trees outside my *focusing in*   house. I saw my neighbor in his driveway with his car

*smaller focus*    hood up. Then the rain began to fall harder. I saw it bouncing furiously against the top of his car. He slammed down the hood with a disgusted look on his
*specific focus*    face. As he ran around the side of his car he tripped over his tool box. "Damn," he yelled, "Who in the hell set this here?" He raced into the house to get out of the rain.

3. Write a scene involving two characters. Do not fictionalize. Observe and listen to two secretaries as they go about their work or two janitors leaning on their brooms in the hall or two professors having a cup of coffee. Catch the actual dialogue, the gestures. Look especially for opposition. Select details about each character that must reveal their personalities. Focus on actions and speech. Include all other elements of scene necessary to orient the reader: light, time, purpose, place, position, five senses. Writing about two characters is at least twice as difficult as writing about one. Ease the way by organizing either from the general to the specific or the reverse. Do not merely list details at random.

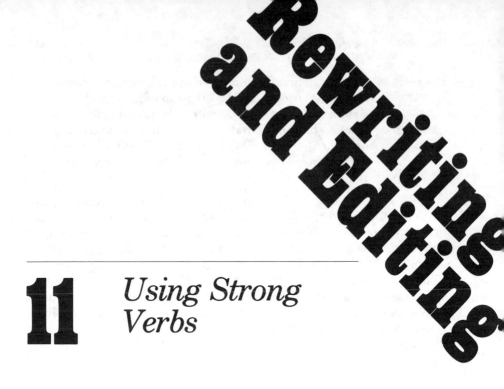

# 11  Using Strong Verbs

I remember as a student that style always seemed one of those vague things others "had" and I was supposed to "get." But no one could tell me how. For a long time I thought that style meant being flowery or dramatic or writing like William Faulkner. Only gradually did I come to discover that it meant, among other things, using your own most natural voice. Indeed, some professional writers insist that style *is* voice, the revelation of your spirit, your biases, your vitality as it speaks to us from the page. In an earlier chapter I emphasized that you could probably discover your natural voice while writing spontaneously during the first draft. Another surprising way of finding that voice, of developing strength and vigor in your style, is through the conscious search for strong verbs during the rewriting or editing phase of the writing process.

## Weak and Strong Verbs

You may think of verbs (if you think of them at all) as grammatical elements in a sentence, as words that connect subjects to objects. Verbs do much more. Verbs move. Verbs laugh. Verbs dash, cry, dance, and shout. Successful writers have found that verbs are the most important element in creating lively prose.

We can divide verbs into two general categories:

1. *Weak verbs* use some form of the construction "to be" (*is, was, were, am, are, has been,* and so on), or they use what is generally

called a "passive voice" (*The line was hit by the fullback,* instead of *The fullback hit the line.*). Sometimes weak verbs are merely those vague little words like *get, do, make, come,* and *go* that fail to give statements a forceful impact because they are so innocuous.

2. *Strong verbs* by contrast, create a sense of direct, specific action, and because they are often concrete words, they tend to create an image in the reader's mind (*slump, crackle, shove, roar,* and so on).

An overdependency on weak verbs leads to dreary, styleless prose. One reason may be that there are only a dozen "to be" forms in the language. Their repetition in sentence after sentence grows dull to the ear. They've already been overworked by thousands of other writers. Contrast, by example, the almost infinite number of strong verbs available for the single sentence: A snake *is* under the porch.

> A snake *coiled* under the porch.
> A snake *slithered* under the porch.
> A snake *rattled* under the porch.
> A snake *hissed* under the porch.
> A snake *died* under the porch.

The list might go on for pages. Strong verbs offer you an almost unlimited number of choices. And strong verbs make writing more precise, more sensory. *A snake* is *under the porch* locates the snake but nothing more. It doesn't show us anything for the imagination to grab hold of. *Coiled, slithered, slid, rattled, hiss,* and *died* convey exact concrete details about the snake. The specific choice you make gives your writing a voice that distinguishes it from the choice someone else makes, even for the same sentence on the same subject.

Weak passive verbs also create problems with wordiness, often requiring an extra preposition to support the verb.

> It *was brought* to my attention *by* Dr. Lewis that I had failed to define my terms.

Strong verbs eliminate unneeded prepositions and purge your style of clutter.

> Dr. Lewis *told* me that I had failed to define my terms.

Professional writers, like journalists, must be especially conscious of verbs. Stories have to move; action must keep the reader interested. Few reporters could get away with a story that relied on weak verbs. Notice how the writer of this *Newsweek* article used strong verbs to make the event more concrete, more specific, more active, and more interesting:

> She *strolled* into a New Orleans Motel, calmly *demanded* money in the cash register and *warned* the clerk: "I'm going to spill your

guts." When the disbelieving clerk *resisted,* the teenage holdup girl *stepped* behind the reservations counter and *slashed* the clerk in the belly with a 3-inch knife.

While he *lay* bleeding on the floor, several motel guests *walked* in. The girl *made* change for one of them from the stolen money, *handed* a room key to the second and *checked* out the third.

Even the newspaper-headline writer knows that verbs sell a story by capturing the reader's interest:

PRESIDENT WRESTLES WITH INFLATION
STRANGLER STRIKES AGAIN
PROFITS SOAR ON WALL STREET
YANKEES CRUSH REDSOX

The value to your writing of the strong verbs cannot be overemphasized. More active verbs make sentences more concrete and sensory, they eliminate extra words, they emphasize the most important facts in the sentence, they make details more precise, they make all forms of writing sound vigorous, and they offer you the opportunity to express your own voice, to make your writing stand out from the crowd.

How does a professional writer pull all of that together? In this selection from "A Christmas Memory," Truman Capote describes making fruitcakes. The strong verbs have been italicized.

The black stove, *stoked* with coal and firewood, *glows* like a lighted pumpkin. Eggbeaters *whirl,* spoons *spin* round in bowls of butter and sugar, vanilla *sweetens* the air, ginger *spices* it; melting nose-tingling odors *saturate* the kitchen, *suffuse* the house, *drift* out to the world on puffs of chimney smoke. In four days our work is done. Thirty-one cakes, *dampened* with whiskey, *bask* on the window sills and shelves.

## Editing for Strong Verbs

For the beginning writer, finding strong verbs is usually an editorial act. After several years of practice, such verbs may come to you as early as the first-draft stage: the weak passive voice may seem almost unnatural. But too much conscious effort at the first-draft stage may cause inhibitions as much as excessive concentration on proper punctuation. Unless you already write in active verbs, it would be better to work with them during the rewriting or editing phase of the process.

As in other forms of editing, there are few clear rights and wrongs. Some sentences may work successfully with a passive verb, and every effort to change to an active verb will only distort or strain the flow. *Never force a strong verb into the sentence merely for its own sake,* but do test every sentence you write.

1. In many cases, the strong verb is already in the sentence. Find the word that seems to carry any action at all and rebuild the sentence around it.

*Original*
The truck was overloaded by the workmen with watermelons.
*Find the action*
overloaded
*Rebuild the sentence around the action.*
Workmen overloaded the truck with watermelons.

*Original*
His work shirt had dark rings where it had been stained with sweat.
*Find the action*
stained
*Rebuild the sentence around the action.*
Dark rings of sweat stained his work shirt.

Note that, in both of these examples, editing for the strong verb also eliminated several unnecessary words. In each case, the active sentence reads more smoothly, simply, and effectively.

2. Avoid especially the "to be" verb form at the beginning of sentences. Such constructions as *There are, There is, It is,* and *It was* can often be eliminated.

*Original*
There are two basic types of verbs you may have studied in high school.
(a sentence taken from my own first draft of this chapter)
*Find the action.*
studied
*Rebuild the sentence around the action.*
You may have studied two basic types of verbs in high school.

*Original*
It was her decision to become a banker.
*Find the action.*
decision
*Rebuild the sentence around the action.*
She decided to become a banker.

Changing verbs, of course, may also change the meaning. "It was her decision" may suggest that a question existed regarding *who* made the decision. "She decided" loses such an implication. You must make editorial changes within the context of your whole essay. If the passive construction is actually more accurate, then use it. But if a strong verb can be substituted without distorting the accuracy or if it actually increases the accuracy, then by all means make the change.

*Original*
> The elderly are thought by some people to be a burden on society because wages are not earned by most of them.

*Find the action.*
> thought . . . earned

*Rebuild the sentence around the action.*
> Some people think the elderly burden society because they earn no wages.

3. Finally, certain active verbs in themselves remain dull and empty because they lack concrete imagery. *Got, have, come, go,* and *made* serve better than a passive form, but not much better. Usually, a more precise action can improve the sentence.

*Original*
> I got in late at night.

*Revision* (that is, reseeing in more precise or sensory terms)
> I tiptoed in late at night.
> I slipped in late at night.
> I stomped in late at night.
> I thundered in late at night.
> I crept in late at night.

Most readers consider Shakespeare the finest writer in English because of the combined breadth and depth of his perception into human nature, but also because of the superiority of his craftsmanship. Critics long ago identified his use of strong verbs as a major element in that craftsmanship. One scholar estimates that Shakespeare uses approximately four active verbs for every passive verb. In the following passage from *King Lear,* Shakespeare uses no passives at all.

> Lear: *Blow,* winds, and *crack* your cheeks! *rage! blow!*
> You cataracts and hurricanes, *spout*
> Till you have *drench'd* our steeples, *drown'd* the cocks!
> You sulphurous and thought-executing fires,
> Vaunt couriers to oak-cleaving thunderbolts,
> *Singe* my white head! And thou, all-shaking thunder,
> *Smite* flat the thick rotundity o' the world!
> *Crack* nature's moulds, all germens *spill* at once,
> That make ingrateful man!

It would be misleading to state that style or voice is nothing more than the use of strong verbs. Style is ultimately the reflection in language of your total personality. But the conscious search for vigorous, forceful verbs can be a major step in learning to control language so that it speaks for you and through you. The verb may be the key element in making your writing sound fresh as well as energetic and exact.

### EXERCISES

1. In the following paragraph by John Steinbeck, almost all verbs have been left out. Fill in every blank with a strong, vigorous verb. (Some of the blanks require present participles—verb forms ending in *ing*.)

Don't try to guess what verbs Steinbeck might have used; try to come up with your own. Then compare your choice to the choice of others in your class. If you're like most people, you'll find that you overlap with someone else on no more than five or six out of the twenty-two blanks. Selection of the strong verb almost automatically helps you find your own voice.

The sun _settled_ on the grass and warmed it, and in the shade under the grass the insects _stir_ .... And over the grass at the roadside a land turtle _crawled_ , turning for nothing, _carried_ his high-domed shell over the grass. His hard legs and yellow-nailed feet _trudged_ slowly through the grass, not really walking but _tugging_ and _dragging_ his shell along. The barley beards _bounced_ off his shell, and the clover burrs _landed_ on him and _rolled_ to the ground. His horney beak _sported_ partly open, and his fierce, humorous eyes, under brows like fingernails, _peered_ straight ahead. He _trudged_ over the grass leaving a beaten trail behind him and the hill, which was the highway embankment, _loomed_ up ahead of him. For a moment he stopped, his head held high. He _sniffed_ and _searched_ up and down. At last he started to climb the embankment. Front clawed feet _stretched_ forward but did not touch. The hind feet _pushed_ his shell along, and it _scraped_ on the grass, and on the gravel. As the embankment _grew_ steeper and steeper the more frantic were the efforts of the land turtle. Pushing hind legs _struggled_ and _pumped_ , boosting the shell along, and the horney head _reached_ as far as the neck could stretch.

2. Although not all of the following sentences use passive verbs, all contain at least one weak verb. Rewrite each sentence to make it as strong and vigorous as possible. In the process, eliminate other unnecessary words.

a. Several important statistics were found in the document by the search committee.

b. The torn drapery was repaired by the stage crew.

c. For many years the country was under the totalitarian rule of a dictator. The dictator was self-appointed.

d. The Dimley brothers were thought by many of us to have grown up on a farm.

e. It is very important for speakers to have the gift of being able to give their speeches emotional force.

f. Mrs. Roosevelt's feelings for him are shown by her staying with him when he was ill with polio.

g. A satisfactory decision was made by the students regarding the use of the campus union.

h. All men possess certain doctrines of natural rights that have been instituted by God.

3. Read two of your earlier assignments. Circle every weak verb. Rewrite both exercises, substituting strong verbs in every possible case (but don't make the sentence sound unnatural to your ear). Do try to eliminate each case in which two or more passives appear in a single sentence or in which two or more sentences in a row use weak verbs. If Shakespeare used an average of four active verbs for every passive, set yourself a goal of using at least one active for every passive. If you fall below the fifty-fifty ratio, you're probably not seeing the potential for vigor and action in your own material. Be sure to submit to your instructor both the original version and your edited version.

## Editorial Checklist for Part Two
### *Describing People and Places*

————————— Have you included concrete images? Avoided unnecessary abstractions?

————————— Have you observed honestly with your own senses?

————————— Have you used a natural voice?

————————— Have you double-checked for connotations?

————————— Have you organized descriptive passages from specific to general or from general to specific?

————————— Have you organized narrative passages in an effective sequence?

————————— Have you included major elements of characterization?

————physical description ———— actions ———— speech ———— self-created environment ———— background ———— others' reactions

————————— Have you organized your essay around the basic elements of scene?

————light ———— time ———— place ———— character ———— position ———— purpose ———— five senses

————————— Have you edited out every unnecessary word?

————————— Have you eliminated unnecessary *whos, whiches, theres,* and *thats?*

————————— Have you used strong nouns? Concrete nouns?

————————— Have you used adjectives and adverbs selectively?

————————— Have you used strong verbs in 50 percent of your sentences?

Sandie Ell, a music major, wrote the following character sketch as a freshman. The body of her essay is composed of narration and description, providing us with a series of typical events that develop her grandfather's basic qualities. To give the essay unity, Sandra opens and closes with two scenes that also help us realize the fullness of her experience.

# Grandpa and Me
## Sandie Ell

Grandpa sat in his old squeaky rocking chair, a bottle of beer in one hand. His eyes were closed and his head hung forward resting comfortably against his chest. Only a few gray hairs combed back over his ears and over the peak of his forehead remained. The shiny bald spot on the back of his head looked red as usual; his small black-rimmed glasses rested on the tip of his nose. Grandpa was in his seventies, but seemed older. The dust danced in the sunrays through the window as the fan buzzed, turning back and forth. His loud rhythmic snore accompanied the squeak in the rocker. Suddenly, as if awakened by a dream or an unfamiliar noise, Grandpa looked up. He glanced around the room and then at the clock on top the television.

"Four o'clock? Didn't know I slept that long. Seems time goes by faster every day." He sipped the warm beer. "Come over here and sit on Grandpa's lap, child." I ran over to him and jumped on his lap. Mom had to remind me to be careful. I always felt like a queen when I sat in Grandpa's rocker. None of us were allowed to sit in his chair unless they were given permission, but since I was the youngest, Grandpa always let me sit with him.

On Sundays the whole family would meet at Grandpa and Grandma's for dinner. I loved eating there. When everyone else ate baked rabbit or pheasant, Grandma always made my favorite bacon and cracker sandwiches.

After dinner we would go into the living room and the grownups would talk. Grandpa entertained the children by telling old stories about times he was young or in the war. Half the stories we had heard before but it didn't matter.

Sometimes we would talk him into playing his harmonica, usually with a little help from my brother Gary pleading with him. He would play "She'll be comin' 'Round the Mountain," and we'd get up and start singing and dancing as loud as we could. Grandpa would grin. He never

Reprinted by permission of the author.

showed his teeth when he smiled, just kind of turned up the corners of his mouth, but you always knew when he was happy.

Two huge apple trees stood in the backyard and when the apples got ripe enough to pick, Grandpa would get two bushel baskets from the garage and we'd help him pick them. Once I pulled a green apple and my brother Richie told me Grandpa would make me eat it—worm and all. I started to cry but Grandpa came over and hugged me and told Richie if he wasn't careful he'd be eating the worm.

Every summer each one of the grandchildren would get to spend a week with Grandpa and Grandma. Grandpa always slept upstairs in the attic in an old brass bed. I slept with Grandma downstairs. We used to hear Grandpa snoring louder than a thunderstorm. We knew he was doing it on purpose and we'd both begin to laugh. Grandma always kept the scraps from dinner and in the mornings we'd get up and go in the backyard and feed the birds. Grandpa said we had the best-fed birds in the country.

Grandpa and Grandma had very little money, but what they did have seemed to be spent on us kids. Holidays were great. Enormous packages scattered around the popcorn-trimmed Christmas tree filled half the living room. Easter was even better. Huge solid milk chocolate Easter bunnies that took us through summer to finish, and Easter baskets filled with jellybeans and Grandma's homemade chocolate chip cookies.

Of all the memories I have of my grandfather, the one that I remember most is the time he showed me a picture of himself and Grandma. I had been bothering him for quite a long time to show me some pictures. One afternoon I persuaded him to take me to the attic where the light fell in shafts through the small window. He pulled out an old snapshot from the top dresser drawer of the vanity. He handed it to me. The picture was taken on the farm where my father grew up. Grandma and Grandpa stood in front of the old white house, arm in arm. They didn't look any younger, but it had been taken twenty years ago. I looked up at Grandpa and he looked sad.

"Grandpa, why are you so sad?" I asked. He turned and looked at me and grinned. He took me into his arms and hugged me.

"I'm not sad, child; in fact I'm happy."

"But Grandpa, if you're not sad, then how come your face looks it?"

He smiled and for the first time in my life I remember him opening his lips to smile. He hugged me even closer. I still didn't understand why someone could possibly look so sad and really be happy, but Grandpa told me someday I would, and he was right.

My grandfather is dead now. He's been dead for almost ten years. I still remember his grin and his harmonica, and the stories he told. He cared so much. Of all the people I've known in my life, my grandpa was one of the kindest and most generous friends I've ever known, and for the sole reason that he gave what so many of us are afraid to give.

Loren Eiseley was both scientist and humanist. As an anthropologist, he published numerous books and technical articles, but he also wrote poetry and essays that related his scientific studies to questions of human value. The following is excerpted from one of his best-known works, *The Immense Journey*.

# from The Bird and the Machine

## Loren Eiseley

The cabin had not been occupied for years. We intended to clean it out and live in it, but there were holes in the roof and the birds had come in and were roosting in the rafters. You could depend on it in a place like this where everything blew away, and even a bird needed some place out of the weather and away from coyotes. A cabin going back to nature in a wild place draws them till they come in, listening at the eaves, I imagine, pecking softly among the shingles till they find a hole and then suddenly the place is theirs and man is forgotten. . . . I got the door open softly and I had the spotlight all ready to turn on and blind whatever birds there were so they couldn't see to get out through the roof. I had a short piece of ladder to put against the far wall where there was a shelf on which I expected to make the biggest haul. I had all the information I needed just like any skilled assassin. I pushed the door open, the hinges squeaking only a little. A bird or two stirred—I could hear them—but nothing flew and there was a faint starlight through the holes in the roof.

I padded across the floor, got the ladder up and the light ready, and slithered up the ladder till my head and arms were over the shelf. Everything was dark as pitch except for the starlight at the little place back of the shelf near the eaves. With the light to blind them, they'd never make it. I had them. I reached my arm carefully over in order to be ready to seize whatever was there and I put the flash on the edge of the shelf where it would stand by itself when I turned it on. That way I'd be able to use both hands.

Everything worked perfectly except for one detail—I didn't know what kind of birds were there. I never thought about it at all, and it wouldn't have mattered if I had. . . . I snapped on the flash and sure enough there was a great beating and feathers flying, but instead of my having them, they, or rather he, had me. He had my hand, that is, and for a small hawk not much bigger than my fist he was doing all right. I heard him give one short metallic cry when the light went on and my hand descended on the bird beside him; after that he was busy with his claws and his beak was sunk in my thumb. In the struggle I knocked the lamp over on the shelf, and his mate got her sight back and whisked neatly through the hole in the roof and off among the stars outside. It all happened in fifteen seconds and you might think I would have fallen down the ladder, but no, I had a professional assassin's reputation to keep up, and the bird, of course, made the mistake of thinking the hand was the enemy and not the eyes behind it. He chewed my thumb up pretty effectively and lacerated my hand with his claws, but in the end I got him, having two hands to work with.

He was a sparrow hawk and a fine young male in the prime of life. I was sorry not to catch the pair of them, but as I dripped blood and folded his wings carefully, holding him by the back so that he couldn't strike again, I had to admit the two of them might have been more than I could have handled under the circumstances. The little fellow had saved his mate by diverting me, and that was that. He was born to it, and made no outcry now, resting in my hand hopelessly, but peering toward me in the shadows behind the lamp with a fierce, almost indifferent glance. He neither gave nor expected mercy and something out of the high air passed from him to me, stirring a faint embarrassment.

I quit looking into that eye and managed to get my huge carcass with its fist full of prey back down the ladder. I put the bird in a box too small to allow him to injure himself by struggle and walked out to welcome the arriving trucks. It had been a long day, and camp still to make in the darkness. In the morning that bird would be just another episode . . . I sucked my aching thumb and spat out some blood. An assassin has to get used to these things. I had a professional reputation to keep up.

In the morning, with the change that comes on suddenly in that high country, the mist that had hovered below us in the valley was gone. The sky was a deep blue, and one could see for miles over the high outcroppings of stone. I was up early and brought the box in which the little hawk was imprisoned out onto the grass where I was building a cage. A wind as cool as a mountain spring ran over the grass and stirred my hair. It was a fine day to be alive. I looked up and all around and at the hole in the cabin roof out of which the other little hawk had fled. There was no sign of her anywhere that I could see.

"Probably in the next county by now," I thought cynically, but before beginning work I decided I'd have a look at my last night's capture.

Secretively, I looked again all around the camp and up and down and opened the box. I got him right out in my hand with his wings folded properly and I was careful not to startle him. He lay limp in my grasp and I could feel his heart pound under the feathers but he only looked beyond me and up.

I saw him look that last look away beyond me into a sky so full of light that I could not follow his gaze. The little breeze flowed over me again, and nearby a mountain aspen shook all its tiny leaves. I suppose I must have had an idea then of what I was going to do, but I never let it come up into consciousness. I just reached over and laid the hawk on the grass.

He lay there a long minute without hope, unmoving, his eyes still fixed on that blue vault above him. It must have been that he was already so far away in heart that he never felt the release from my hand. He never even stood. He just lay with his breast against the grass.

In the next second after that long minute he was gone. Like a flicker of light, he had vanished with my eyes full on him, but without actually seeing even a premonitory wing beat. He was gone straight into that towering emptiness of light and crystal that my eyes could scarcely bear to penetrate. For another long moment there was silence. I could not see him. The light was too intense. Then from far up somewhere a cry came ringing down.

I was young then and had seen little of the world, but when I heard that cry my heart turned over. It was not the cry of the hawk I had captured; for, by shifting my position against the sun, I was now seeing further up. Straight out of the sun's eye, where she must have been soaring restlessly above us for untold hours, hurtled his mate. And from far up, ringing from peak to peak of the summits over us, came a cry of such unutterable and ecstatic joy that it sounds down across the years and tingles among the cups on my quiet breakfast table.

I saw them both now. He was rising fast to meet her. They met in a great soaring gyre that turned to a whirling circle and a dance of wings. Once more, just once, their two voices, joined in a harsh wild medley of question and response, struck and echoed against the pinnacles of the valley. Then they were gone forever somewhere into those upper regions beyond the eyes of men.

Poet Donald Hall is a Harvard graduate and Rhodes Scholar who has authored and edited more than twenty books since 1955. In *Remembering Poets* (1978), Hall recounts his early experience at meeting Robert Frost, T. S. Eliot, Ezra Pound, and Dylan Thomas. In the following excerpt, Hall tells of accompanying Thomas to a reading at Oxford. At the time, Thomas was already a major British poet with a reputation for heavy drinking and outlandish behavior.

# Remembering Dylan Thomas
## Donald Hall

We started for Oxford at nine-thirty, which was a good thing, because the reading was at half past eight that night. We stopped in Laugharne while Dylan, ever the good son, said goodbye to his mother and father. We stopped for petrol once, and people at the pumps were making noises I could not decipher; Dylan confirmed that it was Welsh, and that he couldn't understand a word. In the first hour we drove steadily, but at ten-thirty the pubs opened, and in the next four hours I suppose we spent about forty-five minutes driving. At one pub Dylan challenged me to a game of darts; he let me *almost* win, then swept me off the board with his delicate, practiced wrist. In another pub we played shove ha'penny; same thing. The publicans greeted Dylan fondly, at least for the first hour or two; reminiscence flowed. At noon Dylan led us to a glittering pub in a city we drove through—I can't remember the city—and we ate sausages and Scotch eggs and potato salad with half-raw potatoes.

At two-thirty we were able to drive again. Most of the afternoon in the car we improvised on the American game which awards points for hitting pedestrians, high scores for degree of difficulty—like zapping a pole vaulter carrying his pole—or for degrees of cruelty. Dylan had never encountered this scheme. He loved to *develop* jokes, carrying them on for hours and hours. His ultimate invention he scored for twenty points, and I remember it well: "a crippled nine-year-old blind orphan nun, leading a three-legged kitten on a string." Then he added, "It's worth three more points if she's pregnant."

It was a near thing, getting to Oxford. At about four-thirty, Dylan led us out of our way to park beside a closed pub where he knew the landlord *well*, and was *certain* that the landlord would open up for us. It never occurred to me to argue with Dylan, or to disobey him; he gave no orders, but his charm was so engaging, his bosom friendship so overwhelming, that you did what he asked. We knocked and knocked. Fortunately, the landlord never opened up.

We arrived in Oxford at six-fifteen and drove directly to New College, where the sherry party began at six. When Dylan heard where we were taking him, he told us that he hated sherry, and hated sherry *parties* worse than sherry. Was there a pub we could go to? There was a tiny local near New College called The Turf, which you could find only by assiduous search. We drank beer again in the minuscule public bar, a coal fire burning in October. Meanwhile, back at the sherry party, forty-seven leading Oxford poets were convinced that we would never arrive. The three of us showed up precisely at seven, time to go to Oxford's Café de Paris for supper.

After a superb reading, we took Dylan back to our flat on Banbury Road, and brought with us half a dozen Oxford poets. I had laid in a supply of beer, and Dylan sat in a corner chair drinking and talking quietly. He took a fancy to one young woman, but he did not give her the *Advocate* treatment; she was flattered more than she was embarrassed, and his fancy though passing was true enough. When people made motions as if to leave, Dylan felt called upon to provide a curtain. From his chair in the corner he improvised a story. It was clear that he made it up as he went along. He spoke slowly, mimicking, telling about a keeper in the London Zoo who fell in love with a warthog. I'm not sure that Dylan knew what a warthog looked like, but he knew warts and he knew hogs, and warthog was good enough for him. The keeper Dylan invented—he knew him from a pub, he said, when he lived near the zoo—had a wife, but preferred the warthog, and grumbled in bed at night at his bad luck in sleeping companions. Then the warthog took sick, and Dylan made stories out of the keeper's anxiety, his increasing resentment of his healthy wife, and his devices for curing the ailing beast. At the end of the story the keeper bought a large fish, and artfully rotted it in his warm kitchen at home, until it reached a level of putrefaction which revived and restored the exhilarated warthog of the London Zoo.

Oxford poets took off on their bicycles, and Dylan and I drank the last bottle of Tolly. I was complaining about some Sunday paper critic who used phrases like "death-wish." Out of brutal innocence I added, "What a dumb idea anyway. Who wants to die?"

Dylan looked up at me. "Oh, I do," he said.

"Why?" I said. I thought of what I had heard in Laugharne the night before.

"Just for the change," he said.

In the morning he looked rested, bright-cheeked, with an orange-red shirt and a blue bow tie with white polka dots. He wore gloves as usual, with a jacket but no top coat, and we set off after breakfast for the depot, and arrived early and drank horrid British Railways coffee. Then he touched me for two pounds and went off to London—to the BBC and the Mandrake and somebody's bed, Caitlin's rescue, and a five-day hangover, and death in a year's time.

# PART

## *Objective Reporting*

# THREE

*Someone once said, "There is no such thing as a true general-*
*ization, including this one," but we can come pretty close to a*
*true generalization when we say that every writer must first be a*
*reporter.*

—John DeWitt McKee

Reporting is the process of collecting, evaluating, and conveying facts. It incorporates the techniques of sensory observation, description, and narration that you practiced in the first two units; but it requires you to take a new attitude toward the world about you—it requires you to look for *objective* facts instead of *subjective* impressions. Most professional writers consider reporting an essential skill upon which all other types of writing can be based. Many of our major American authors— Mark Twain, Stephen Crane, Sherwood Anderson, Theodore Dreiser, Ernest Hemingway, Tom Wolfe—first learned their craft as reporters. Reporting techniques form the underlying structure of many essays in our best magazines and journals, from *The New Yorker* to *Atlantic*. And the ability to write a formal report may be a requirement for your future career: a medical researcher who has invented a new device to measure cardiac output and heart rate must report on it in a medical journal; a city manager who has decided to promote a new process for converting garbage to electrical energy must present a report to the city council; a government economist detecting a downturn in employment must write a report to the undersecretary of labor. Simply put, reporting is the way we convey factual information. But reporting involves more than learning how to craft certain types of sentences; it involves learning how to seek out and evaluate the facts about a subject <u>imaginatively</u> so that, for both you and the reader, <u>new insight</u> is acquired.

# 12 Perception and Objectivity

For thousands of years, no one understood how typhus was spread. Some thought by touch; others, by air; still others speculated that typhus dropped from moon rays. Not until Charles Nicolle saw the relationship of several previously ignored facts did he discover the true carrier. Nicolle was a medical doctor in Tunis when a typhoid epidemic struck in 1909. Nicolle noticed that patients already inside his hospital did not catch the disease from newly arrived victims. Nor did the nurses and doctors catch it. One day, in the act of stepping over a typhus victim who had collapsed on the hospital steps, Nicolle realized that something must be actually stopping the spread of typhus at the hospital doors. He traced procedures back to the admission process and found that new typhus victims were bathed and their clothing burned. The carrier obviously had to be something the patient carried on the outside of his body. Nicolle determined that it could be nothing but a flea.

> The fact that I had ignored this point, that all those who had been observing typhus from the beginnings of history . . . had failed to notice the incontrovertible and immediately fruitful solution of the method of transmission, had suddenly been revealed to me. I feel somewhat embarrassed about putting myself into the picture. If I do so, nevertheless, it is because I believe what happened to me is

**117**

a very edifying and clear example. . . . I developed my observations with less timidity.

*He developed his observations with less timidity.* Perception of specific factual details that others had never bothered to investigate literally led to insight.

Heraclitus told us more than twenty-five hundred years ago:

Men who wish to know about the world must learn it in its particular details.

Only by observing the details of a subject—and then only after observing them with imaginative concentration—does sight lead to fresh understanding or, more importantly, to discovery of new and previously unseen relationships. But there are many different ways of "observing." Charles Nicolle suspended his emotional reactions, ignored all previous opinions, and tried to see the facts—and their relationships—with an objective eye. The key word is *objective.*

In the first two units of this book I have urged you to pursue sensory details in order to intensify awareness of yourself in relation to the world around you. The pursuit of objective detail requires the same type of concentrated effort and uses the same sense receptors: sight, hearing, taste, touch, and smell. But a search for factual detail requires a shift from emotional experience to reasoned experience, from an extension of emotional awareness to an extension of intellectual awareness.

## Objectivity Versus Emotion

*Objectivity* requires the observation of phenomena uninfluenced by feelings. For most of us, subjective feeling comes first. We have to train ourselves, consciously, to suspend feeling and to see only the fact itself.

| Subjective Observation | Objective Observation |
|---|---|
| That's a beautiful sunset. | The sunset has streaks of yellow and lavender in it. |
| This fried chicken tastes terrible. | This fried chicken has a burned metallic taste. |
| Burt Reynolds is in this movie, so it must be good. | Burt Reynolds is in this movie. |

If all life were this simple, the distinction between objective and subjective observation would also be simple. Unfortunately, emotion may be subtle and may influence observation without our knowledge.

Abortion is murder.

(Here an implied judgment based on some deep inner belief—on some inner feeling about what is good and what is evil—may cause the observation to *seem* like an objective fact to the observer, but the term *murder* has such negative connotations that we should be immediately alert to a subjective intrusion.)

Abortion is the removal of a live fetus from a mother's womb.

(Here a simple description retains objectivity because no judgment about good or evil and no hidden emotion apparently influence the observation. The connotations are neutral.)

Industry has poisoned our air and water.

(This observer may believe he or she has stated an objective fact, but again the connotations suggest a negative emotion underlying the observation.)

Industry has disposed of its waste material and by-products through the air and water.

(Without the word *poisoned,* the observation seems more readily acceptable as objective fact—no negative feelings intrude.)

The various emotional influences in our lives and how they affect observation and judgment can be a complex subject. The problem will be explored more fully in a later chapter about critical thinking in Part Six. In the meantime, two common forms of *subjective* influences need to be understood now.

## Inference

While walking across campus this morning, I noticed a student who wore shoes but no socks. Such a sight might have disgusted me, and I might have inferred that the student was lazy or dirty, or I might have felt sorry for him and inferred that he was poor, or I might have laughed and inferred that he was following the latest fad. A *fact* is a quality that can be verified by a second observer. A second person could easily have verified that the student I saw wore no socks. But an *inference* is a conclusion drawn from the fact. Inferences may be logical and true. Or, as my examples here show, an inference may be influenced by emotion: my disgust, my pity, my laughter could each lead me to interpret the objective fact differently. *An inference is not a fact.* A second observer cannot verify which, if any, of my conclusions might be true. The first step in removing emotional elements from my observations is to suspend judgment, to withhold inference, until I am in possession of more facts.

As a beginning writer, you may observe facts accurately; but because of this confusion between fact and inference, you may report the inference (the judgment) as if it were the fact. Here is what one student wrote when sent out to interview a local official:

> The warden was unhappy when the noon whistle drowned out his conversation.

The student insisted this was a fact. But the term *unhappy* is an inference drawn from concrete details that the student observed with his senses but that he has not reported to the reader. Perhaps the warden stopped talking in mid-sentence and held his breath until his face turned red, or perhaps he chewed on his lower lip and pounded the table with his pistol butt until the whistle stopped blowing. Any or all of these concrete details may have led the student to infer that the warden was "unhappy." The student's judgment may have been accurate. But the facts, the concrete details, should have been presented to us so that in our role as readers, we could also function as the second observer.

Here is another student, reporting on birth control methods at her college:

> I surveyed twenty-six women in my dormitory. Nineteen of them indicated they had used some form of birth control at some point or another. The other seven were evidently less promiscuous. . . .

The first sentence can be accepted as a factual statement. A survey has been taken, and a specific number of answers has been collected. A second observer could verify the information. But to infer that the first group of women were more or less promiscuous than the second cannot be verified because no information on the frequency or casualness of sexual contact is provided. To infer that women who use birth control are promiscuous is to allow personal feelings to obscure the original topic.

## Opinion

Although somewhat different from an inference, an *opinion* raises a similar problem. In an older legal sense, an opinion represents a judgment based on available data and logical argument, as in "The judge delivered the court's opinion on the Harris case." But more current and popular use of the term reduces opinion to personal taste. "Henrique loves jazz." "Ann Marie thinks wooden clogs are ugly." Such opinions cannot be substantiated by another observer because they deal not so much with the thing observed as with personal feelings. In the most extreme use of the term, an opinion may not be drawn from any objective evidence at all, as in "I feel sure life exists in many galaxies besides our own" or "Man is by nature loving and good." Although such opinions may be held with confidence, they're based on speculation or intuition, not on verifiable, objective facts. Yet because opinions, like inferences, are expressed as conclusions—as judgments—they often sound more forceful and convincing than facts.

> People who want gun control are un-American.
> The energy crisis is a hoax created by the oil companies.

Such bold, declarative statements are simplistic and easy to grasp. An opinion stated or held with conviction uses language itself to obscure our perceptions, to make us think no more seeking of fact is necessary because we supposedly already possess the truth.

If you are to train yourself in objectifying perception, you must be aware of the difference between a fact observed, an inference drawn from it, and an opinion expressed about it.

| Objective Fact | Inference or Opinion |
|---|---|
| Toadstools are growing in the forest today. | It must have rained last night. I think toadstools are pretty. The soil there is probably rich in humus. |
| Rembrandt once painted a picture only three inches by five inches. | Small paintings sell for much less. He was too poor to afford a large canvas. Rembrandt was the world's greatest painter. |
| The stock market fell fourteen points in April. | The stock market is for gambling fools. Investors are afraid of inflation. Now's the time to buy stock. |

# Objectivity and Abstraction

Finally, I've found that some students confuse being objective with being abstract. These qualities are not related. Objectivity is an attitude of the mind. It is a way of approaching a subject. The subject itself may be concrete (a scientist looks objectively at a very tangible frog; a medical doctor looks objectively at the specific colorations and flesh tone of his or her patient), or the subject may be general and abstract (a philosopher attempts to study the question of justice by withholding all personal bias; a sociologist studies the relationship between poverty and behavior by quantifying the data). To be objective does not require you to be abstract *or* concrete. It requires you to perceive the subject—whatever it is—with as little intrusion of your emotion as possible.

Obviously, as human beings, we can never be totally objective, nor would we want to be. But training ourselves to observe and report with an objective attitude provides excellent mental schooling: it sharpens powers of observation; it clarifies the separation between self and nonself, strengthening the ability to think and argue with finer distinctions; and it improves linguistic awareness, helping us to recognize how language itself may influence observation and judgment. A sound objective attitude continues to require all our sensory and perceptive powers.

**EXERCISES**

1. In the following conversation, identify which observations are influenced by emotion and which might be considered factual—that is, which could be verified by a second observer.

| | |
|---|---|
| Bob: | That drunk almost hit me. |
| Mary: | What drunk? |
| Bob: | The one in that weaving car. He drove right up over the curb and I had to leap out of the way. |
| Mary: | What did he look like? |
| Bob: | A big ugly guy. He was aiming at me. You could see in his eyes he wanted to kill someone. |
| Mary: | The car had a license from Montana. |
| Bob: | It was some cowboy who's never been in the city before. |
| Mary: | Are you all right now? Your face looks pale. |
| Bob: | I'm OK. I just don't like drunken cowboys. |
| Mary: | I read in the paper that there are still fifteen thousand people who make their living as cowboys. |
| Bob: | Boy! Are you gullible! Not everything in the paper is fact, you know. |

2. Here is a statement containing both opinions and inferences. Rewrite it so that the same information is conveyed as objectively as possible.

Grade-point averages are higher today than ten years ago, but the fact is that kids aren't smarter; teachers are just easier. Ten years ago, a $C$ was considered a good grade in college. The average grade was 2.2 on a 4-point scale. Today anybody who goes to class can get a $B$. The average grade across the country is 3.2. Over 85 percent of the Harvard class of 1977 were graduated with honors, which proves how low the standards have fallen. One report from the U.S. Office of Education stated that teachers blamed grade inflation on the Vietnam War. A lot of cowards who didn't want to fight for their country hid out in college and as long as they got good grades, they were draft-deferred. But once the teachers started giving grades for reasons other than performance, there was no more objective standard to judge by, so everyone had to get $A$'s.

3. The following statement is factual. How many different kinds of inferences can be drawn from it?

Since 1901 five vice-presidents have moved up to the presidency owing to the death, assassination, or forced retirement of the president. Since Eisenhower no president has even served two complete terms in office: Kennedy was shot; Johnson, pressured not to run for reelection; Nixon, forced to resign or face impeachment; Ford, defeated for reelection after less than two years.

Write a brief paragraph in which you begin with a statement that could be considered a reasonable inference drawn from the preceding facts. Now organize and expand upon the facts provided so that they will support your inference.

4. Study the engraving by William Hogarth below. Based on the specific details portrayed in the engraving, draw a reasonable inference about what is happening. Now write a brief paragraph that begins with your inference and is then supported by a description of the engraving that can be verified by a second observer. Compare your paragraph to those written by others in your class. Were your inferences the same? Can more than one inference be supported by the same data?

*William Hogarth,* Hudibras Catechized, *engraving.*

## SUGGESTED WRITING ASSIGNMENTS

1. Write a brief objective report of a classroom lecture or a student meeting. Include no opinions or inferences of your own. Avoid emotional influences of any kind, but try to select the facts that are most interesting or most important.

2. Write an objective report on something you have deep personal feelings about. For example, report the objective facts about your first date or about the loss of a best friend. Give no opinions; avoid all emotionally influenced words. Present only facts that could be verified by a second observer. Be as specific and concrete as possible.

**13** *Finding and Selecting Facts*

Until a few years ago I thought my job complete once I had advised students to pursue facts objectively, once I'd established the proper "attitude." What more could I do? That the writer also needed to select only the most important facts about a subject was self-evident. How the writer was to separate the significant from insignificant seemed more mysterious—something I could explain only by the words *intuition* or *experience*. Then I had the opportunity of spending several days with a reporter for a large city newspaper. I hurried after him through the corridors of a state-government office as he pursued a story on alleged payoffs to several low-ranking bureaucrats. I stood to one side while he researched dusty files and ledgers. I watched in amazement as he flirted with secretaries, all the while drawing out fragments of information. I waited outside closed doors while he interviewed officials. As it turned out, no evidence for payoffs could be found. For my friend the story was a dead end, but for me it had been a revelation.

## The 4 C's of Observation
A reporter knows a great deal that could benefit any writer in any career about how to seek and find facts. Reporters know, for example, that whatever story they write has to be interesting because it has to sell papers,

and to make it interesting they need to search out facts that affect the largest number of readers. They know that details with the most impact tend to be found by training the mind to look for certain aspects of a subject that I've grouped under four headings: *change, contrast, consequence,* and *characterization.* Although my friend would wince to hear his methods so labeled, I've come to call them the 4 *C*'s of observation. They are guidelines only. Any subject may suggest its own unique approach, and audience requirements may place restrictions on any writer. But the 4 *C*'s provide an effective *starting point* for developing an eye for factual observation.

## Change

Events, ideas, values, social customs can all be studied according to how they are changing (or sometimes failing to change). Here is how sophomore Larry Kinde approached the subject of childbirth:

> At the center of the delivery room was a soft, padded chair, something like a dentist's chair, only angled more, so that a woman in it would have been half-reclining, half-standing. Toward the bottom of the chair were stirrup-like contraptions for the woman's legs to rest in. The room was painted a soft blue and there was even a speaker on the wall for music. Where was the white sterility of the old-fashioned delivery room? Where was the flat table with leather straps that held the woman down? Where the bright overhead lights?

We could study childbirth delivery rooms for many qualities other than change. But in this case change was the key element for entry into the subject. It provided the focus for selecting important facts about new developments, and even though Kinde's report is objective, there is nothing dull about it. The focus on change stimulates interest in the subject.

## Contrast

People clash and so do ideas. Republicans battle Democrats; psychotherapists disagree with behaviorists; environmentalists fight industrialists. Forces in opposition provide a natural focal point around which a writer can approach a subject.

> ... a basic contention developed from the whole philosophy behind prisons. Those who guard and manage the prison tend to believe that its function is to punish the prisoners. Those who counsel and serve as probation officers tend to believe that a prison should reform the prisoners. Both sides were able to provide me with statistics and facts supporting their position.

This student writer has stepped into the middle of controversy. Almost every issue or event stimulates an opposing view. Contrast, conflict, contradiction, and opposition are not only eternally interesting to readers, but they also provide natural ways of selecting, shaping, and organizing factual information. Looking for contrast in every subject should become habitual as you develop a reporter's eye.

## Consequences

Interesting facts are useful. Significant facts are vital. To find the significance in a subject, a writer must look for facts that have the most impact, the most consequence, on people directly involved. Here is how a student reporter for a college newspaper zeroed in on the consequences of an action:

> The faculty voted Wednesday to change from a "course system" meeting four days a week for an hour per day, to a "credit-hour system," meeting on Monday, Wednesday, and Friday for an hour a day. The majority of the faculty argued that the credit-hour system was used by most colleges and that we were out of step.
>
> However, it could also be considered that while Faculty members would teach a lighter load under the credit-hour system students would need to take five courses per semester instead of four in order to graduate in the same number of years.

On the surface, a change in the organization of credits and class hours is being carried out to increase conformity with other colleges. Those are the facts. But the significance is revealed only by questioning the consequences of those facts: students will need to carry more courses per semester; instructors will teach fewer hours. Actions, ideas, events— all produce consequences. To describe the action, idea, or event objectively is important. By asking whom the consequences affect, the writer begins to focus his or her attention on what is most significant.

## Characterization

In an earlier chapter I described a number of ways for selecting details that would characterize a person. Because ideas, values, and issues seldom exist or have interest for us apart from the human being whose lives are affected by them, knowing how to bring people—character— into almost any essay or report can increase the impact it has on the audience. But "characterization" has a larger potential: the same techniques that bring people alive on the page of a novel can be applied as guidelines for selecting details from other types of subjects. If you wanted to report on a business operation in the Bahamas, for example, or on current developments in nuclear reactors, you could look for the same categories you sought out in characterizing your grandfather: *physical details, actions, background, speech, environment, and others' reactions.* To characterize is to give a full, rounded view of a subject. Here is how Kathleen Mills characterized the physical education facilities at her high school:

| | |
|---|---|
| *Physical details* | The gymnasium was drafty and cold. The old wooden floor had splinters in it and the windows at either end were broken out and boarded over. Lockers had no locks; the showers had only cold water. The basketball team from North High refused to dress in our locker rooms. They dressed on their bus and their coach was |
| *Others' reactions Speech Actions A self-created environment Actions* | quoted as saying, "It was nothing personal." The students at Jefferson were part of the problem. They had torn out the toilets two years before after losing a game. They ripped locker doors off the hinges. Three times during the four years I attended, the local PTA tried to raise funds for restoring and painting but the neighborhood had deteriorated since the 1950's. Some apart- |
| *Background* | ments were empty and boarded up. A large percentage of the population was on welfare. The tax base no longer supported the school, we were told, and the remaining residents would not support the PTA. Finally, |
| *Action* | in my senior year, ten seniors took to the school board a petition signed by over 200 students. They demanded |
| *Lack of action* | better facilities. The school board promised to look into the situation but nothing was ever done. |

Using the 4 *C*'s of observation offers no guarantee you'll find the most important factual details in every subject, but if you encounter a subject you don't know how to write about or a report you don't know where to begin on, ask yourself:

1. Is there an element of *change?* Is it the most interesting or important point in the subject?

2. Does any element of the subject involve *contrast, conflict, contradiction,* or *opposition?* Could the best details be organized around one of those categories?

3. What quality about the subject has led to significant *consequences?* To whom or to what aspect of the subject are these consequences important? Whose lives are affected?

4. How could this subject be *characterized?* Which of the elements of characterization seem most consequential? (Physical description? Action? Background? Speech?) Is a full, rounded view of the subject what the reader needs or expects?

# Obtaining Facts from Others

Relying solely upon personal experience, however, suggests its own obvious inadequacies: we cannot be in all places at once; we cannot always separate our emotions from the facts observed; we cannot be experts in all subjects. Others' views are necessary to formulating an objective and balanced understanding of a subject. In careers outside the academic world, writing often depends upon interviewing as a major source of information. Historians talk to those who were there; biographers talk to those who remember; technical writers talk to engineers; medical writers talk to researchers. Even within the university, a student of political science, social work, anthropology, psychology, or sociology will recognize that significant amounts of data, almost all in many cases, are derived from surveys or interviews. An interview often provides information unobtainable from any other source, and it offers the writer a natural way to introduce human interest into an otherwise objective report.

## Questioning

The value of the information acquired in an interview is determined in part by the type of question you ask. Avoid the question that requires only a yes-or-no answer.

> Do you believe we ought to have a better campus police force?

Such questions might be valid for a survey, but you want more depth from a personal interview. Always formulate a number of questions in advance based on what you already know and on what you need to know.

> Thirteen rapes were reported on the State University campus last year. Do we face that kind of problem here?

> Recently a number of letters to the editor in the campus paper have complained about theft in the dormitories. Do you think the problem is "out of control" as one letter writer suggested?

The phrasing of each question is vital. If you reveal bias or seem to be attacking the person you're interviewing, you'll probably create a situation that brings the interview to an abrupt end.

> Campus security is obviously inadequate. What are you going to do about it?

The shape of such a question, the emotional tone, inhibits a free exchange of information. Take time in advance to compose wording that makes each question seem open-minded, fair, and objective.

> Do you feel campus security is inadequate?

> Are measures being taken to improve campus security or do you feel current procedures are working effectively?

Follow up answers by asking for supporting facts or concrete examples.

> Can you provide me with statistics on that?

Exactly how many cases of theft were reported to your office last year?

Are records available to show whether crime on campus has increased or decreased?

## Listening

Most professionals insist that learning how to listen is the most vital element in an interview. A good interview must flow like a good conversation. If you merely read off that prepared list of questions or if you fail to follow up on answers, you might as well conduct the interview by mail. Here is the wrong way to go about it:

*Question:* Do you feel America has an evenhanded policy in the Middle East?

*Answer:* We've had one of the most biased and misguided policies that could have been devised.

*Question:* How important is Saudi Arabian oil?

The person interviewed can only rightly assume you haven't listened to the answer or that you're not genuinely interested. Future answers will become more perfunctory. You'll probably find it more helpful to repeat the central point of an answer (this helps you remember it while making clear to the person interviewed that you're listening) and then to ask for further clarification or explanation.

*Follow-up question:* You say "biased and misguided." Could we look at each of these points separately? In what way has American policy been biased? In whose favor? And why?

Now you've engaged in a dialogue. Perceiving that you're alert and interested, the person interviewed will freely expand upon his or her ideas.

A dialogue, however, does not mean you should take sides. Even if you personally disagree or find flaw in what you're hearing, avoid a direct argument:

But you're contradicting yourself now. You don't have a single fact to prove your point.

Instead, phrase your follow-up in such a way that you press hard for the answer but seem to be attributing your aggressiveness or disagreement to what others might say when they read your report:

I wonder if others would see this as a contradiction to a point you made earlier?

Could you give me some statistics to support that point?

Listen intently. Follow up. Train your ear to select important facts from

others' observations in the same way you train your eye to observe minute details from personal experience.

## Evaluating

Just as you cannot always separate your own emotions from external
facts, neither can others. You must assume that many answers you hear
will reflect some degree of self-interest or bias. It will always be your job,
both during and after an interview, to distinguish facts from opinions or
inferences. You must ask yourself, Does this answer show a hidden emotional element? What are the consequences of such an answer? Am I
hearing an opinion or a verifiable fact?

Opinions may form a part of any objective report so long as they are
attributed to your source ("Dr. Harrison believes ..." "Captain Miller
thinks ...") and do not derive from your own bias. For some subjects,
opinions may be as important as the facts themselves. But any interview
that tends to be opinionated should be balanced with an interview providing that other side of the issue. You have no control over others' opinions, but you must demonstrate your own objectivity by presenting a
balanced and fair report that includes equal representation of every point
of view.

Learning how to obtain information from others extends your range
of observation. Combined with the 4-*C* approach, it provides you with a
tool for moving outside the limitations of personal feelings and personal
experience—as you must if you are to begin to explore and write about
the world you live in. Learning how to find facts and how to select significant facts are both essential steps in developing writing and thinking
skills.

### EXERCISES

1. Discuss how *change, contrast, consequences,* or *characterization* might be a way of finding the best factual details about the following.
Which of the 4-*C* methods or which combination might be useful in investigating each topic?

> dormitory rules
> the grading system at your college
> motorcycle-helmet law in your state
> drinking on campus
> the newest fad in clothing
> student sexual behavior
> off-campus housing
> censorship policy for the student newspaper
> parking regulations
> athletic scholarships

> bookstore policies
> your state's law on marijuana use
> campus grounds and environment
> class attendance regulations
> grade inflation
> co-ed dormitories
> campus security
> cafeteria food

2. Make a list of people you might seek information from for three or four of the above topics.

### SUGGESTED WRITING ASSIGNMENTS

1. Write a short, objective report based on one of the above topics or a topic assigned by your instructor. Organize your report into three paragraphs. (a) In your own words introduce the subject by *characterizing* the main elements as specifically and factually as possible. (b) Interview someone directly involved or affected by the subject. Seek out that person's opinions and any facts he or she can provide. Summarize the information from the interview in the second paragraph of your report (be sure to identify your source). (c) Finally, write a concluding paragraph in which you draw a reasonable inference based on your total findings.

2. Write a 1,000-word report on an event or issue at your college or place of employment. (For example, report on the losing football season or the resignation of the dean or the latest change in course requirements.) Gather as much factual information as possible from observation and interviews. If you obtain more than one interview, devote a separate paragraph to each and clearly identify your sources. Most information from interviews should be summarized in your own words; use quotations for only the most significant statements. Maintain an objective attitude throughout your report, avoiding any intrusion of your own opinions and biases. (Begin your investigation now, but before you begin to write, read Chapter 14 on purpose and voice and Chapter 15 on basic forms.)

# 14 Context, Purpose, and Voice

Unlike personal writing, for which you could expect a sympathetic audience, perhaps even a friendly audience that wants to share your feelings and experience, no such simple generalization can be made for informative writing. Too many variables exist. In certain situations, the audience for informative writing may want straightforward, no-nonsense facts. In other situations, your audience may appreciate a more informal voice, even a personal voice, while still reading for objective information. Everything depends upon four interacting elements: the subject, the audience's needs, the context (or situation), and your own purpose.

Most of the time these four factors are defined for you in advance. In college your instructor assigns an essay on the French Revolution (*subject*); your paper will be evaluated to determine how well you know the subject and it will count as part of your final grade (*context*); your instructor alone will read it (*audience*); and in the process of investigating the subject, you determine which particular aspect you wish to explore and what you want to say about it (*purpose*). In the career world, a similar situation will usually influence your writing projects. Your supervisor will assign you to write a report on whether your company is meeting environmental regulations (*subject*); the report will be used by company officials to prepare for an upcoming federal inspection (*context*); your supervisor, the company vice-president, and several government agents

**133**

will read it (*audience*); and although the report must be accurate, it must also present the company's efforts in a positive light (*purpose*).

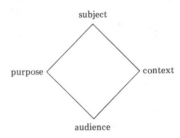

Once you make the leap from personal writing into more objective forms of writing, the demands upon you increase rapidly. Yet this relationship of subject-audience-context-purpose does not necessarily make the act of writing as difficult as it may sound. In many cases, knowing the four points of influence actually simplifies your job by clearly defining what you need to write about and how you must approach it. All four points in combination also determine the voice and tone you will use. Because that voice can be significantly different from the voice you use in personal writing, we need to look at some of the options open to you.

## Objective Reporting with a Formal Voice

The most objective writing is usually found in scientific work where the voice must be formal and the tone objective. No element of your personality or inner feelings should be apparent. In scientific reporting, your audience will desire facts alone. Here is a report on Martian landing sites from *Scientific Results of the Viking Project*:

> Both sites are dominated by a variety of rocks among fine-grained material, and both have the brownish to orange color of the surface and the sky. Beyond this superficial similarity the sites are quite different in their appearance. The Chryse site topography is undulating and has a great range of rock size and type from rocks a few centimeters across to one nearby large rock almost 2 m across and others in the distance much larger. . . . No evidence of life has been found in the pictures at either site.

The tone here is factual and unemotional. The avoidance of either positive or negative connotations modulates the voice and creates a neutral effect. Even the last sentence shows no trace of personal emotion (although it may have stirred a feeling of regret in the scientists). Instead, we receive only a straightforward statement of observable fact—in this case, concrete sensory details observed in a photograph.

The use of the pronoun *one* in place of *I* or *we* is sometimes associated with formal writing. The *one* creates a distance between writer and reader and may sometimes be necessary. But note that the NASA scientists who reported on the Viking Project avoided its use altogether. The use of *one* too often creates awkward sentences where the pronoun tends to pile up in clusters that sound contrived. Here is how a university scholar misuses it in a book on poetry.

> When one begins writing poetry one tends to use language that convinces one that it is truly poetry that is being written. One uses a special voice . . .

Try reading such sentences aloud, and you find that the excessive repetition of *one* begins to feel like marbles in the mouth.

The use of *one* can be necessary at times, but it works best when it does not call attention to itself. Here is an objective report on Alaskan snow in which the *one* blends easily and unobtrusively.

> There are different kinds of snow. New-fallen snow yields almost silently underfoot. Midwinter snow is dry, and squeaks and crunches as one walks through it, while spring snow is tired and crackles as the crust resists, then breaks. Wind-driven snow is riffled like lace or like the whitecaps of the sea, and it sparkles with flashes of blue, yellow, orange, and green.

Tom Walker, writing in a book titled *We Live in the Alaskan Bush,* has so skillfully blended the objective *one* into this passage that a reader might miss it entirely—which is what should happen.

## Objective Reporting with the Informal Voice

In many situations, when context and audience are appropriate, the informal voice may be quite successfully used with objective writing. Naturally, the author must still avoid intrusion of personal feelings or emotions, but the notion that all objective writing must be dull is mistaken. Here is a report on the Sloth bear from the *Audubon Society Book of Wild Animals:*

> *Termites are a staple of the sloth bear (Melurus ursinus) of the* Indian subcontinent and Sri Lanka, and to get at the insects this

dim-sighted creature has evolved a snout that approximates a vacuum cleaner. The lips of the sloth bear are hairless and flexible and can be protruded like a tube a considerable distance from the mouth. The bear can close its nostrils whenever it wishes. After digging open a termite mound, the bear literally huffs and puffs to uncover and ingest its prey. Puckering its lips into a tube, with its nostrils shut to keep out dust, it blows away the loose dirt to expose the termites, then sucks them in, a process facilitated by a gap in its teeth resulting from the absence of two upper incisors.

Although the reporting here is objective—each fact can be verified by a second observer—the tone is lighter and more casual. The active verbs (more than ten in five sentences) and the humorous imagery (a snout like a vacuum cleaner, huffing and puffing, sucking termites between a gap in the teeth) make the writing lively and interesting. Yet neither personal emotion, nor opinion, nor bias appears. The Audubon Society has produced a book for informative reading but one meant to entertain at the same time. Context and purpose justify the informal voice.

## Objective Reporting in the First Person

Writers for more popular magazines often use the first-person while still reporting objective information. The admission that a human being is behind the observation tends, naturally, to create a more personal and informal tone. At one time, such reporting was avoided. Writers went to great length to objectify or disguise their presence, sometimes using such awkward phrases as "This reporter saw . . ." or "The writer has noticed that . . ." Today the trend is toward an honest admission that *I,* the writer, exists as a person but that he or she also has the ability to report objectively. After all, the use of *one* or the neutral, objective tone in the scientific voice is only a subterfuge. A writer still exists. He or she is a human being and from the very fact that the writer has consciously selected some details to present while omitting others, we know that the writer's personal imagination is actively involved. Total objectivity is impossible.

Here, then, is how Jane Winslow Eliot reports for *The Atlantic* on winemaking in Spain in the 1930s:

By the light of one small candle I saw three men inside the vat. Their coats were off, their trousers rolled above the knees. They hung onto knotted ropes which were looped over the rafters, and, barefoot, they rhythmically stomped the slippery grapes. Sweating, faces distorted by candlelight, they shouted back and forth as friends came to watch. Fumes began to rise, and their footing became less sure, their laughter louder. A new basket of grapes was tipped into the vat. Twirling around and around, one man lost his grip. With a splash he fell into the richly reeking mash.

The concrete details make the scene rich and sensuous, perhaps even evoking emotion in the reader. Yet the writer herself injects no undue inferences or opinions. Eliot presents a verifiable report, but she uses a personal voice that candidly admits, "I was there, and I'm reporting what I saw." In a different context, of course, and for a different purpose and audience, this voice might be highly inappropriate. You must determine the subject-audience-context-purpose *before* you begin to write; otherwise, you will find yourself working in a vacuum and merely guessing or hoping that the way you treat your material might be successful.

### EXERCISES

1. Read each of the following selections. (a) Identify the level of formality or informality. (b) Describe a *context, purpose,* and *audience* for which each passage might be appropriate. (c) Describe a *context, purpose,* and *audience* for which the voice and tone would be highly inappropriate or less effective.

(a) Some hermit crabs have developed a relationship with a group of anemones that benefits both creatures. Relations like these are called symbiotic relations. Once it has found a shell, the hermit crabs find a special kind of anemone that has tentacles which sting and irritate fish and other potential enemies. In some cases the anemone climbs on the hermit crab's shell and plants itself there. In other cases there seems to be some complex communication based on touch between the hermit crab and the anemone. They tap and touch each other, and the anemone then releases its grip on the rock it clings to and plants itself on the hermit crab's shell.
—Judith and Herbert Kohl, *The View from the Oak*

(b) The top of a maple leaf is dark green with green-yellow lines running through it. These lines are fairly straight and seem to branch off into smaller and smaller lines, which give the surface of the leaf a scale-like appearance. The leaf is thin, about the thickness of two sheets of paper. It is about four inches wide, measuring from tip to tip, and about four inches long. At the bottom of the leaf there is a thin, pliable tube which seems to connect with the largest of the green-yellow lines.

—Student Report

(c) The eel is a fish which believes in long journeys. It is spawned in the Sargasso Sea in the western Atlantic, and from there will travel back to its fresh water haunts in this country or in Europe to feed and grow up in the rivers and streams frequented by its parents. The young eel or elver is still only 2 or 3 inches longer after its immense journey, and is transparent and yellowish. . . . As with cats, there is more than one way to skin a fresh eel. We prefer the following. Slip a noose around the eel's head and hang the other end of the cord on a hook, high on the wall. Cut the eel skin about 3 inches below the head all around, so as not to penetrate the gall bladder which lies close to the head. Peel the skin back, pulling down hard—if necessary with a pair of pliers—until the whole skin comes off like a glove.

—Rombauer and Becker, *The Joy of Cooking*

(iv) Committing the mind to one approach for a long period of time with no evident prospect of success is a mistake. Of course, the length of time one should devote to any one approach cannot be stated in advance. It depends on the difficulty of the problem. But if one does not seem to be making any progress the thing to do is to try to break from that pattern of thought, though it is very hard to give up once one starts to think along that line. What one should do is probably forget the whole thing and come back to it sometime later when that mental groove has disappeared.

—Morris Kline, *The Creative Experience*

2. Rewrite the passage on the sloth bear (page 135). Make the voice sound more formal and the tone less entertaining.

3. Rewrite the following passage to make it more informal. Use the personal *I* instead of *one*. Try to find strong verbs to replace weak ones.

A decline in energy is observed as the team continues its workout. The gymnasts who are on the rings show fatigue early. One notices that the faces begin to turn red and the veins bulge in the throat. If one looks closely, one also sees a slight quivering in the biceps as the exercises continue. Even after the rings have been released and the student is back on the mat, the shoulder and back muscles often can be observed to twitch involuntarily.

# 15 Basic Forms in Factual Reporting

For most writers, not just beginning writers but all of us, finding the right order for the right content becomes a major stumbling block to success. To avoid the struggle and to save time, news reporters sometimes use a formula for organizing factual information. By knowing the formula, they have an automatic form in which to shape their material. You should know it as well because it is the simplest and easiest of all forms to learn and because it provides a natural starting point for objective reporting. It teaches you how to discipline facts, and it can be used for many other types of informative writing.

## The 5 W Lead

As you develop your writing skills and become involved in complex interpretation and analysis of a subject, you will need to practice the art of creating an effective *thesis statement* (Chapter 24), but straight reporting of objective facts requires a simpler, although equally effective type of introduction. Professional writers call it the *5 W Lead*. A lead informs the reader of the five most important facts about the subject: *who, what, where, when* and *why*. The facts may be organized in any sequence, according to which elements are most important.

The 5 *W* lead began as a journalistic device, and an experienced reporter can usually handle all five elements in the first sentence alone:

        *who*                    *where*
Sen. Howard M. Metzenbaum, D–Ohio, said in Washington
    *when*              *what*
Saturday he will introduce a major piece of legislation
                    *why*
next week, designed to upgrade parks, playgrounds, and

other recreational areas in American cities.

   *where*      *when*        *who*         *what*
In Baltimore last week Peter L. McCrystal, 15, broke the
                    *why*
world's gumchewing record just to win a ten-cent bet.

The 5 *W* lead groups and organizes information that might otherwise have appeared randomly throughout a news story. By shaping the material in this way, the reader receives all major facts immediately. Everything that follows the lead will support or elaborate on the major facts. But just as you probably don't plan to become a novelist who writes about character, you probably don't plan to become a journalist. How, then, does the 5 *W* lead apply to the type of writing you may be doing?

Here is how one student began a report for a sociology class:

    *who*                     *where*     *what*
A white, Anglo-Saxon Protestant in America is socially
                 *why*
mobile because achievement rather than background is the
                 *who*
determining factor. For blacks and Jews, social mobility
     *what*                *why*
is restricted regardless of achievement since color and

religion are influencing factors.

By selecting all the important facts and organizing them according to the 5 *W*'s, the student has pulled together a surprisingly clear statement about her subject. The reader knows immediately what to expect in succeeding paragraphs—development or elaboration of details that support the statement and perhaps, depending on the type of report, an explanation of why such different patterns of social mobility exist.

Here is another example of the 5 *W* lead used for a business report in a class on macroeconomic theory:

    *when*
During the second half of 1977 and the early months of
    *who*                *what*
1978, the administration's price guidelines apparently

were 6 percent. Price increases of up to 6 percent
*why*
were tolerated since they corresponded to what was thought
*who*
to be the basic rate of inflation. But the Office of
*what*
Budget and Management ignored all evident signs that the basic

inflation rate was actually closer to 12 percent.

This student has obviously begun a factual narrative by shaping his opening sentences around the most important facts in an inflationary period. The reader is now prepared for succeeding paragraphs to provide evidence that supports the 5 *W* claim.

Even students of the humanities have found the 5 *W* lead effective. Here is how one sophomore began a report for a literature class:

*where*        *when*        *who*
In *The Bell Jar,* first published in 1963, Sylvia Plath
     *what*
recounts the events of a young girl's twentieth year,

her attempted suicide, and her struggle to avoid madness.

The 5 *W* lead is an all-around serviceable introduction for almost any kind of informative writing. It communicates the facts clearly and concisely. And as starting a first draft is often the point at which writers have the most difficulty, the 5 *W* lead provides a simple strategy for organizing information and getting the first sentence or first paragraph on the page.

Equally important, the lead can immediately suggest an organization for the rest of your report.

# The Inverted Pyramid

Let's return one more time to how all this was developed by journalists. Because of the constriction of space in a newspaper and because hurried readers often do not read to the end of a news story, the 5 *W* lead became a technique for presenting vital information as quickly as possible. But the nature of journalism also imposed another constriction on the reporter and predetermined the organization of remaining material. Until the final moments before a newspaper goes to press, neither the reporter nor the editor may know how much space is available for any one story. The writer must be prepared, then, for the editor literally to take scissors to a report so that it will fill the appropriate column. This means that all important supporting details must be presented early, followed by interesting details and finally mere details. The editor can easily clip off the "mere" details without any great loss. The editor can even cut the story in half and remove the "interesting" details, still without damaging the important supporting information that follows the lead. The reporter has thus learned to envision the organization of his or her story in the form of an upside-down pyramid:

The technique is also used in laboratory and engineering reports as well as in formal business reports. A busy executive, for example, does not necessarily have time to read through twenty pages of details. The executive wants and needs to know important information immediately, at the beginning of the report. He or she does not want to be kept in suspense as to what it all means. But the inverted pyramid design also creates a problem because, by its nature, it fails to come to a conclusion. Other than in the field of journalism, few situations exist in which you will ever be allowed to drift off with "mere" details. On the assumption that you have engaged your intelligence with the subject at all, you will want to do more—and your reader will expect more. If nothing else, you must at least summarize your findings. Better, you must draw a reasonable inference from the facts you have gathered and come to a concluding generalization. Even the business executive will expect a final paragraph that at least restates or reinforces the 5 *W* lead. Here, then, is how we might modify the inverted pyramid so that it can serve you as a visual pattern for organizing objective essays in college and in other career situations:

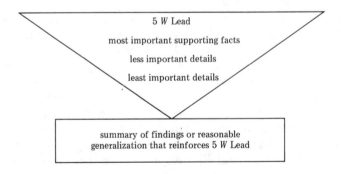

Freshmen Michelle Newburg and Ted Larkin used such a form to organize a report assigned as part of a group project on pornography for a class in religion and contemporary values. Here are excerpts from that report that illustrate the pattern:

| | |
|---|---|
| *5 W Lead* | According to Ralph Hendleman, the manager of the World Cinema, customers for his *x*-rated movies are generally upper-class businessmen from the exclusive suburb of Marlborough Heights, where the theater is located. . . . |
| *Most important supporting facts* | We spent a total of six hours observing the type of customer entering and leaving the theater on two separate afternoons. During that time we counted sixty-one men and four women entering the theater, all well dressed, some carrying briefcases. Only seven seemed to be younger than twenty-five. The majority seemed to be in their forties and fifties. Forty-seven arrived alone in automobiles that were parked to the side of the theater. Of the forty-seven cars, nine were Cadillacs; nine were Buicks, Oldsmobiles, or Toronados; seven were foreign sports cars, including one red Porsche driven by a woman. . . . |
| *Interesting details (background)* | Until 1971 the theater showed traditional Hollywood films but lost money, according to Hendleman. Since the introduction of *x*-rated films, the theater has shown a profit each year. . . . |
| *Least important details* | The theater is located next door to a shoe store and an exclusive jewelry shop. . . . |
| *Concluding generalization* | Since we did not interview any of the customers, we cannot speculate on the psychology that motivates attendance at this particular *x*-rated theater. But from our observations we believe that the customers seemed to be financially well off, primarily male, and probably of the upper managerial level. Other theaters might attract a different type of customer. We believe, however, that it is reasonable to conclude that the World Cinema shows pornographic films because there is a willing-to-pay audience among the supposedly better educated and socially higher classes in our society. |

This most-important-to-least-important method of organizing is not the only pattern that can evolve from using the 5 *W* lead. Any one element or combination of elements from the lead may form the focus of your organization. The lead for the student's paper on social mobility (page 140), for example, might suggest that the *why* is the key question a reader would be interested in. The writer could provide supporting factual evidence to defend the lead, then move quickly into an interview with a sociologist on why such a social pattern exists. The lead might equally suggest that the report will be organized around the contrast between the two groups being discussed (in several later chapters I will develop the contrast design more fully). In turn, the lead for the student business report (page 140) implies that the *what* and *who* will be pursued: what went wrong and who was responsible for soaring inflation? In other words, the value of the 5 *W* lead lies in its potential for serving you and the reader with a concise, clear statement of your findings in the first sentence or paragraph and then in *suggesting* a possible organization to follow. The very act of looking for the 5 *W* lead in your material actually forces you to begin a process of discovering your purpose, selecting the most important facts, and organizing them concisely.

A word of caution, however. Formulas like the 5 *W*'s and the inverted pyramid quickly grow dull if repeated in everything you write. Use such formulas selectively. When the subject-context-audience-purpose calls for a simple but factual presentation, they will serve you well. But do not trap yourself into using them for everything you write, for other contexts and audiences may be responsive only to fresher and more creative designs. Eugene O'Neill once said that "a man's work is in danger of deteriorating when he thinks he has found the one best formula for doing it." The 5 *W* lead and the inverted pyramid design should be learned and used wisely, but different leads and organizations will be discussed in further units throughout this text so that by the end you will have a wide variety of organizational patterns to choose from.

**EXERCISES**

1. Identify the 5 W's in the following leads.

> A spokesman for the firemen's union said Wednesday that negotiations with city hall have been broken off until the mayor is willing to be more flexible.

> Marketing conditions have remained unstable during the last six months because of inflationary pressures. The Federal Reserve Bank in Washington has increased prime interest rates three times. Investment conditions could not be worse.

> The English Advisory Board believes that current requirements in the English Department are arbitrary and inflexible. A review of requirements at other colleges shows that students elsewhere have more opportunity to make selections from clusters of related-area courses.

> Professor Mike Kepple, chairperson of the Chemistry Department, at Milligan College, has been elected chairperson of the

National Honors Colloquium, to be held on the University of Southern California campus next fall.

2. Write three different 5 *W* leads based on the same set of facts:
   a. John Smith is director of public relations at Simkon Foundry.
   b. The foundry has decided to donate $5,000,000 to the United Appeal.
   c. United Appeal will divide the money among the Boy Scouts, the Children's Hospital, and Mothers for Peace.
   d. Bentley V. Cunningham is chairman of the board that made the decision.
   e. The stockholders voted last April on the issue.
   f. The vote passed by only 52 percent.
   g. Smith made the announcement public on Tuesday, August 7.
   h. Cunningham hopes the gift will create good will for the foundry.
   i. Simkon Foundry has been located in the city for twenty years.
   j. Claire Wilson, representative of a minority group of stockholders, spoke out against what she called a "giveaway" of stockholder profits.
   k. Cunningham personally delivered the check into the hands of Bennett Goodman, president of the United Appeal.

3. As an exercise, write a one-page objective report on health or counseling services available at your college. Begin with a 5 *W* lead. Use the inverted pyramid for the overall design, organizing material from the most important facts to the least important. Conclude with a reasonable inference based on the evidence you present in the report. Share your report with others in your class, and discuss the strengths and weaknesses of such an organization.

## 16 Reshaping, Rearranging, Integrating

*I can't understand how anyone can write without rewriting everything over and over again.*

—Leo Tolstoy

The most serious error the beginning writer can commit is to write only a single draft and assume the writing process is complete. You might at first believe that objective reporting would require less rewriting than a personal essay. After all, you're dealing with facts, not struggling to express inner feelings. But although the problems seem different, the demands upon you are similar: to find precise words, to discover the best arrangement of parts, to blend or join each part so that the whole of it reads clearly. If we consider the various needs for informative reporting, the complexities become more apparent:

1. Objective observation of factual detail.
2. A focus on elements of change or contrast (if significant).
3. A focus on major consequences.
4. Characterization of the subject as a whole (including actions, physical description, background, and so on).

5. Understanding of the subject-audience-context-purpose.

6. A lead that clearly presents all major facts in a sentence or two.

7. An organization that flows naturally out of the lead and serves the subject-audience-context purpose.

To do all of this well in a first draft would be impossible for most of us. Even when we feel we have a subject well in hand, some elements of a paper always seem to get muddled. Here are four paragraphs of a rough draft by freshman Melvin Chase. In the first paragraph the 5 *W* lead shows he has found his purpose and made a clear statement that ought to lead him into an easy-flowing organization. With only minor editing the second paragraph can probably stand as it is, for it does provide specific support for the lead. But the next two paragraphs present serious problems.

*5 W Lead*

A new organization in Cleveland, The Committee Against Cancer, is working to ban all cigarette advertising. The CAC claims that dangerous products should be forbidden public promotion. A pamphlet distributed last Wednesday on the Western Reserve campus claimed that an average reader of newspapers and magazines is exposed to 3,000 advertisements for cigarettes each year. But not only is the CAC claim suspect; the organization's efforts may be unconstitutional.

*Specific,
factual details*

First, to test their claim, I surveyed newspapers and magazines subscribed to by my own family. In the October issue of *McCall's,* I counted five cigarette advertisements. There were nine in the same month's issue of *Playboy* and three in the Wednesday, October 3rd, edition of the *Cleveland Plain Dealer.* The Sunday, October 7th, edition of the paper contained one full-page color advertisement for True and four other half- or quarter-page ads for other brands. If my family is typi-

*Evaluates facts*

cal, it might read as many as 100 advertisements for cigarettes each month in such publications—a total of approximately 1,200 per year and far below the CAC claim.

*Source not
identified
fully—who is
Brooks?*

When I interviewed Benjamin Brooks, he said, "The evidence is tenuous. Our own research is ongoing and not yet conclusive either, but we've found that moderate smoking does no more damage to your health than moderate drinking of wine at mealtimes or moderate

*Connection to
first
paragraph is
unclear
Doesn't speak
directly to the
issue*

eating of candy or almost anything else taken in moderation. I'm just not convinced that because rats get cancer when forced to smoke a hundred cigarettes a day that people who are smoking only maybe twenty a day

*Quotation becomes too long, rambling*

are going to get cancer. There are dozens, hundreds of kinds of cancer, you know. Well, I can't understand why people want to ban advertising tobacco as if it caused all those kinds. No one wants to ban alcohol or beer or candy advertisements and they could cause cancer too for all we know. It's our legal and constitutional right to

*Finally relates to advertising*

advertise like any other product. Even if you ban all cigarette advertising it won't stop people from smoking. After they banned it on TV our sales actually went up."

*Good, but his authority should come earlier*

I asked him about his qualifications to speak on the subject and he told me that he had worked as District Representative for the R. J. Reynolds Tobacco

*Characterization details are adequate but seem tacked on*

Company for ten years. He is a large, robust man with blond hair that is going bald. He smoked a cigarette while I interviewed him in his office. He spoke very forcefully.

Chase was aware of the problems encountered in his report as it moved along, but he felt unsure about how to solve them. For him, as for most of us—especially when working with facts and opinions collected from others—rewriting is often a process of selecting only the best statements for quotation, summarizing other parts, and integrating the two. We must sharpen the focus of our own essay while being careful not to distort the meaning of the information provided by the source.

## Summarization

To summarize is to restate concisely in your own words the essence of a larger work or idea. A person you interview or material you read may provide more information than you need or material not directly relevant to your paper. The long quotation in Melvin Chase's report is an example. Much of it could be selectively omitted; most of it can be summarized in a sentence or two.

Professional writers know that good quotations make writing seem lively. But lengthy quotations or too many quotations can become as tedious as none at all. The reader expects a balance between summary and direct quotation. In general, approximately 80 percent of material taken from other sources (through interviews or reading) should be summarized in your own words. You should summarize only the information or ideas that directly relate to your subject, while being careful not to distort, oversimplify, or in any other way change the meaning of the original. Only the most important element should actually be quoted.

Here is how Melvin Chase summarized a portion of Brooks's statement. Note that although unrelated details have been omitted, the essence of Brooks's ideas has not been changed, only condensed.

| Original | Summary |
|---|---|
| The evidence is tenuous. Our own research is ongoing and not yet conclusive either way, but we've found that moderate cigarette smoking does no more damage to your health than moderate drinking of wine at mealtimes or moderate eating of sweets or almost anything else taken in moderation. | Cancer research by the cigarette companies is inconclusive. The companies believe that moderate smoking is no more harmful than moderate drinking. |
| I'm just not convinced that because rats get cancer when forced to smoke a hundred cigarettes a day that people who are smoking only maybe twenty a day are going to get cancer. There are dozens, hundreds of kinds of cancer. Well, I can't understand why people want to ban advertising tobacco as if it caused all those kinds. No one wants to ban alcohol or beer or candy advertisements and they could cause cancer too for all we know. | The result of laboratory experiments on rats may not apply to people. Brooks doesn't understand why tobacco should be selected for an advertising ban when products like beer and candy are not. |

The summary has shortened the original by half. By restating only the main points, the reader's attention is focused more clearly on ideas that contribute directly to the subject.

## Quotation

To quote another person means to use the *exact* words you've heard or read. Although you have a great deal of flexibility in how you integrate those words into your text, you will seldom be forgiven an inaccuracy of even the smallest nature. A word omitted or a phrase inverted can change the total meaning of an idea. If you cannot be sure of the exact words, place the idea in your own terms and give credit to your source, but do not use quotation marks unless you can be precise.

The most important element of Benjamin Brooks's statement came at the end. Melvin Chase decided that here Brooks's exact words should be retained.

It is our legal and constitutional right to advertise like any other product. Even if you ban all cigarette advertising it wouldn't stop people from smoking. After they banned it on TV our sales actually went up.

Only three of Brooks's nine sentences will now be used as direct quotation.

## Integration

Finally comes the task of blending all the parts.

As the purpose of Chase's report deals with cigarette advertisements, the beginning of the third paragraph needs to show a related emphasis. Brooks's statement on advertising originally appeared at the end of the interview and seemed lost in all the discussion about cancer, candy, and alcohol. Moving it to the beginning of the third paragraph will more clearly focus the report on the main subject. Many students aren't aware that they have the right to alter a sequence of information from the way it appeared in an original source. *So long as no change in meaning or emphasis is created,* however, you have every obligation to your reader to reorganize and shape your material so that it seems clear and unified. (More techniques for achieving unity will be discussed in Chapter 25.)

Here is how Chase drew related concepts together:

Original end of second paragraph
>... If my family is typical, it might read as many as 100 *advertisements* for cigarettes each month in such publications—a total of approximately 1,200 per year, and far below the CAC claim.

New third paragraph
>To hear the cigarette companies' side of the issue, I interviewed Benjamin Brooks, who said, "It is our legal and constitutional right to *advertise* like any other product."

Now the reader moves smoothly between paragraphs, and the connection between related ideas is clearer.

The next step is to identify Brooks's authority to speak on the subject. In general, a speaker needs to be described or identified *before* his or her ideas are given. Chase rewrote the opening of the third paragraph one more time.

Authority inserted
>To hear the cigarette companies' side of the issue, I interviewed Benjamin Brooks, district representative for R. J. Reynolds Tobacco Company. Mr. Brooks said, "It is our legal and constitutional right to advertise like any other product."

Depending upon the audience, context and purpose, details describing character may have no place in a formal report. But for a more informal report, or one in which you want to add an element of human interest, such details should be integrated as if you were creating a scene. We need to *see* actions and description at the same time that we *hear* Brooks speak. Here then is how Melvin Chase pulled everything together in the third and fourth paragraphs, omitting unnecessary elements, summarizing related points, and integrating character details and authority into the quoted passages.

> To hear the cigarette companies' side of the issue, I interveiwed Benjamin Brooks, district representative for the R. J. Reynolds Tobacco Company. Mr. Brooks, a robust, balding man spoke forcefully about the "legal and constitutional right to advertise like any other product." He leaned forward in his chair to emphasize his point. "Even if you ban all cigarette advertising," he said, "it won't stop people from smoking. After they banned it on TV our sales actually went up."
>
> Mr. Brooks stressed that cancer research by cigarette companies is inconclusive. The companies believe that moderate smoking is no more harmful than moderate drinking. Brooks himself feels that tobacco products are unfairly selected for an advertising ban when advertisements for other potentially dangerous products such as alcohol and candy are ignored.

The function of first draft is to explore ideas, to get facts on the page. The function of rewriting is to reshape, rearrange, integrate, and develop the facts and ideas. The normal process for almost all of us is to move from awkward, stumbling prose toward a gradually emerging clarity.

### EXERCISES

1. Summarize the following passage in no more than two sentences. A summary should be written in your own words and should constitute the essence of the original without distorting the central idea.

> The mentally healthy freshman comes with a basic sense of industry. Industry is the positive identification with those who know things and know how to do things, with workmanship and task mastery; it is the capacity to learn how to be, with skill, what one is in the process of becoming; it is the sure knowledge of personal competence. . . . This sense of industry is severely tested. Not necessarily because the academic tasks are too difficult or onerous, but because of the unimaginable number of distractions, temptations, annoyances, and interruptions that ensnare and drag one down to exhaustion. The student is surrounded by seducers, exploiters, entrepreneurs, manipulators, many hedonists, and a few nihilists.

—Hal Crowley, *Forum for Honors*

2. Assume that you are writing a report on the community relations—or lack of relations—between your college and the surrounding neighborhoods. You obtain an interview with the local mayor or borough representative. From the following exchange, select the most important statement for a quotation, decide which material is irrelevant to your study, and summarize the remainder in no more than a couple of sentences.

*Interviewer:* Do you feel Learning University has achieved satisfactory community relations?

*Mayor:* We're very proud to have Learning University as a part of our great community.

*Interviewer:* Some people have suggested that the university locks itself away in an ivory tower and ignores the concerns of the surrounding neighborhoods.

*Mayor:* Well, you know, I am an alumnus of old Learning U. and it was a fine school. Class of 1955. We had a winning football season for the first time in a decade. Do you play a sport?

*Interviewer:* No, sir. But I wonder if you might elaborate on how the community looks at the university. Are there specific problems that ten thousand students create? How do the merchants feel? Or the police force?

*Mayor:* Well, there are always problems, you know. I suppose that we are concerned about the off-campus parking. A lot of residents complain about cars blocking their driveways, that type of thing.

*Interviewer:* What about the tax base? The university pays no taxes as I understand.

*Mayor:* That's a particularly sore point with me. Everybody's taxes in this community are higher because of the university. There are four streets, fifteen light poles, a dozen sidewalks that all cut through the university, but the city has to maintain them. That means some little old lady on social security has to pay property taxes to repave streets for freshmen to ride their bicycles on. And then there's the cost of fire and police protection. Yet the university doesn't pay one cent for all the services we provide!

3. It is sometimes easier to identify faults in others' papers than to see them in your own. Here is a portion of a first draft. Rewrite it by rearranging whatever is necessary, omitting irrelevant detail, summarizing, and integrating related parts. The focus of the paper should be on the lack of social life at this student's college.

I did a survey of Milligan Hall and found that only 40 percent of the students remained on campus last weekend. One student, who shall remain nameless because he doesn't want to be identified, told me: "I just hate it around here. For kicks I go down and do my laundry or maybe watch the squirrels bury nuts in the south quadrangle. I mean, I think the school ought to bring in more movies or speakers. We were supposed to have a dance in February but only fifteen people showed up. Thirteen were girls." As I talked to this student, he told me that he came from a small farm in Iowa and that his father owned over one hundred milk cows. He is a freshman planning to major in economics.

Another comment I got came from a junior. She told me, "I think everyone complains because they don't have enough imagination to think of something on their own. I've never been bored a minute here. The school has a choral group, a theater club, a dance ensemble, a chess tournament, you name it, but everyone wants to be entertained instead of getting involved in something and entertaining themselves. Do you see what I mean?" Her name is Barbara Walker, and she is a chemistry major from Detroit. She also plays flute in the university symphony and paints for a hobby. The day I interviewed her, she wore patched Levis and an old paint-spotted sweat shirt.

# 17   *Editing Sentences for Rhythm, Variety, and Emphasis*

Have you ever "listened" to your writing? Here's a paragraph from a student who hasn't:

> Professor Shirley Baxton is in the English Department. The interview was held in her office. She told me that she believed writing should be required in the whole university. She didn't believe it should be just required for English. She has a reputation for having high standards. She says writing is an expression of the inner self. She says it should be part of the experience we have in every class.

These are perfectly correct sentences, but not the sentences of real life. This student has not listened with his inner ear and the result is Dick-and-Jane monotony. People don't talk this way. And even though good writing is not identical to speech, it should sound like speech. Good writing should reflect all the variety and points of emphasis found in the best conversation; it should express the rhythms of the human voice.

# Rhythm

Rhythm means flow. Effective writing has a flow to it that suggests the sound patterns of living speech. And yet rhythm involves more than sound; it is inseparable from clarity, coherence, unity, order, and all the other elements of style as they work together within a specific context. Prose with little meaning is almost always accompanied by weak rhythms, and, in turn, weak and awkward rhythms signal that meaning may not yet be clearly expressed. Many of our best writers insist that one must develop an ear for the silent rhythm of the printed page. The best method for doing so—and the one least likely to be attempted by most students—is to listen to good prose as it's read aloud. The ear is more sensitive to rhythm than the eye.

Read aloud the following passage from Abraham Lincoln's First Inaugural Address. Listen to the voice you hear.

> I am loath to close. We are not enemies, but friends. We must not be enemies. Though passion may have strained it must not break our bonds of affection. The mystic chords of memory, stretching from every battlefield and patriot grave, to every heart and hearthstone, all over this broad land, will yet swell the chorus of the Union, when again touched, as surely they will be, by the better angels of our nature.

Lincoln begins with a short sentence, followed by another short sentence lengthened only slightly by a second clause. He returns to the short pattern and then moves on to what might be considered a sentence of medium length. The final sentence begins a long sweeping role where clause after clause delays the most important words, like a symphony building toward a final musical statement. Read it aloud and the passage sings. But did you? I've taken surveys of my own students and found that when I give this exercise, two-thirds continue to read silently. Yet rhythm, which is so essential to effective prose, cannot be learned in silence. If you would learn to play the drum, you must bang on it and listen to the sounds; if you would learn to write well, you must read aloud both good prose by professional writers and your own prose. And you must listen to the rhythms. If, out of laziness or shyness or whatever, you choose not to read aloud, you ignore one of the primary techniques our best authors have found successful. Quite simply, the student who reads aloud will have an advantage over the one who doesn't.

Let's return to the Lincoln passage and see what can be learned. Perhaps, most important, we discover that rhythm is not a part of any one sentence. Rhythm is always found in context. That is why neither I nor anyone else can establish a "correct" or "model" sentence for you to imitate. There are none. A sentence is not a static or rigid absolute. A perfectly good sentence in one context will fail miserably in another. The *subject-audience-context-purpose* and your own voice must all be considered—consciously at this stage, where you may feel unsure of yourself, intuitively at a later stage, when practice and experience can be supported by the ear of your imagination. Lincoln's prose reflects his own personality, his own voice. We know that to be true because, in this particular instance, we have not only the four drafts that Lincoln worked on, but we also have a first draft written by William H. Seward, who was to become Lincoln's secretary of state. Here are Seward's words:

> I close. We are not, we must not be, aliens or enemies, but fellow countrymen and brethren. Although passion has strained our bonds of affection too hardly, they must not, I am sure they will not, be broken. The mystic chords which proceeding from so many battlefields and so many patriot graves, pass through all the hearts and hearths in this broad continent of ours, will yet again harmonize in their ancient music when breathed upon by the guardian angel of the nation.

Seward's proposal has its own rhythm, but Lincoln improved upon it. Compare Seward's blunt and unsatisfactory first sentence to Lincoln's still brief but more melodious version. In turn, compare the simplicity of Lincoln's second sentence to the choppy (and somewhat clichéd) second sentence of Seward. Read both versions aloud. What other changes in the next three sentences improve the flow? Can you determine how changes in rhythm have paralleled clarification (and simplification) of meaning?

If we represent Lincoln's sentences with graph lines, we might diagram the paragraph so:

Sentence 1: _____ .
Sentence 2: _____ , _____ .
Sentence 3: _____ .
Sentence 4: _____ .
Sentence 5: _____ , _____ , _____ , _____
_____ , _____ , _____ ,
_____ , _____ , _____ .

Obviously, variety of sentence structure and length are key elements. Look again at the student example that begins this chapter. You'll find that a major problem arises from the dull sameness of each sentence. In art, music, dance, and language, rhythm is always achieved by theme and variation, by establishing a pattern and then varying the pattern.

## Editing for Variety in Sentence Patterns

Sentences can be simple, compound, complex, or even compound-complex. If you're unsure of the differences, you might want to look into a handbook on grammar. Yet knowing definitions for sentence structure is not as important as knowing that every sentence ought to organize a thought into a clear, coherent pattern that flows well within the larger context of your essay. Two editing steps discussed in earlier chapters (omitting needless words and using strong verbs) should help you begin. Return to the student example on page 154. If we graph-lined that paragraph, it would look something like this:

Sentence 1: _____ .
Sentence 2: _____ .
Sentence 3: _____ .
Sentence 4: _____ .
Sentence 5: _____ .
Sentence 6: _____ .
Sentence 7: _____ .

The variation here is slight at best. Each sentence makes a simple statement with a subject-verb-object sequence; each is approximately the same length as its neighbor. The monotony is deadening. But through careful editing, we can combine some of those Dick-and-Jane construc)tions into sentences of varying lengths and rhythms.

*Circle unnecessary or repetitive words. Find the action and re-build around it:*

Professor Shirley Baxton(is)(in)(the)English Department.(The)
    *action*
interview(was)held in her office.

*Result:*
I interviewed English Professor Shirley Baxton in her office.

Two sentences reduced to one brings about a savings of six words.

*Again, circle unnecessary or repetitive words. Find the action and rebuild around it:*

                      *action*
She (told)(me)(that)(she)believed writing should be required in the whole university. (She)(didn't)(believe)(it)should be just for English.

*Result:*
She believes writing should be required throughout the university curriculum, not just in English classes.

Even though I've added new words for clarity, we still save eight words and improve the flow.

*Circle unnecessary or repetitive words. Find the action and re-build around it:*

                                *action*
(She)(has)(a)reputation for having high standards. (She)says

writing is an expression of the inner self. (She) (says) (it) should be a part of the experience we have in every class.

*Result:*
Baxton, who has a reputation for high standards, says writing is an expression of the inner self and should therefore be a part of every classroom experience.

In the process of performing this type of editorial act, we not only clarify meaning, but also enhance it by creating a more natural rhythm. Yet when I read these new sentences aloud as a complete paragraph, the second sentence still jars my ear. It seems out of place. As I'm at a loss on how to change the sentence itself further, my "ear" suggests that the second sentence might exchange places with the third. A fortunate discovery. When this is done, the logic itself proves more convincing.

> I interviewed English Professor, Shirley Baxton, in her office. Baxton, who has a reputation for high standards, says writing is an expression of the inner self and should therefore be a part of every classroom experience. She believes writing should be required throughout the university curriculum, not just in English classes.

Now I think we have a more precise statement supported by a rhythm that, without calling attention to itself, suggests a natural, if somewhat formal, speech pattern. *The first step in editing for variety in sentences, then, is not deliberately to make sentences longer or shorter, but to make them better.* Almost inevitably, the rhythms will begin to flow.

Here is the process:

1. Circle unnecessary and repetitive words.
2. Locate the action.
3. Combine or rebuild around the verb.

# The Parallel Sentence

Effective writing needs more than just a mixture of long and short sentences, however. Rhythm does not exist for its own sake but to heighten clarity and emphasize important or related elements. For that reason, you must develop a familiarity with the concept of *parallelism*—a method of shaping sentences so that a series of related ideas is expressed in a related grammatical structure. What that grammatical structure might be does not matter—a series of similar verb forms, a series of similar prepositional phrases, a series of nouns—so long as each follows a parallel pattern on the page.

Let's begin with a single idea:

Roger's dad promised to buy him a new bicycle.

But what if Roger's dad made two promises, and the two promises were related?

> Roger's dad promised to buy him a new bicycle *and* that he would let him ride it before Christmas.

Now we have two related ideas, but the sentence structure does not show that relationship. The promised idea before the *and* is expressed differently from the promised idea after the *and*. Here's how we could make each clause show the relationship:

> Roger's dad promised to buy him a new bicycle and
>
> to let him ride it before Christmas.

In this case, infinitives have been made parallel (*to buy, to let*). The result forms a closer psychological relationship in the mind of the reader. The ideas seem to cohere more clearly.

We can create the same parallelism with other grammatical structures:

> The company wants a new taxi driver who knows the city and
>
> who has a good safety record.
>
> (adjective clauses are parallel)
>
> Chinita believes in God, motherhood, and country.
>
> (nouns are parallel)

Parallelism is not merely a grammatical device made fetish by English teachers. Parallel structure is one of the oldest techniques in our language, existing long before English grammar itself was ever set down in rule books. We can trace its importance in English to the influence of the Bible, where parallelism was a basic element of Hebrew poetry:

> Blessed are the meek for they shall inherit the earth;
> Blessed are those who thirst for righteousness for they shall be satisfied.

The effectiveness of parallel structure can be most clearly emphasized if we take such a well-known passage and rewrite it out-of-parallel:

> Blessed are the meek for they shall inherit the earth;
> And we should also bless those who thirst for righteousness so satisfaction can be obtained by them as well.

What we discover is that a failure to provide parallel structure not only makes relationships between ideas less clear, but it also weakens the forcefulness of writing in general.

Poets and statesmen have long used parallel structure for the sense of dignity and strength it creates in the ear of the reader:

Let the word go forth from this time and place, to friend and foe alike, that the torch has been passed to a new generation of Americans, born in this century, tempered by war, disciplined by a hard and bitter peace, proud of our ancient heritage, and unwilling to witness or permit the slow undoing of those human rights to which this nation has always been committed, and to which we are committed today at home and around the world.

Let every nation know, whether it wishes us well or ill, that we shall pay any price, bear any burden, meet any hardship, support any friend, oppose any foe to assure the survival and the success of liberty.

—John F. Kennedy, Inaugural Address

In every case, the rhythm emphasizes and clarifies a relationship. The result is a coherence that can seldom be more effectively achieved.

## The Balanced Sentence

A *balanced sentence* is related to parallelism, but the emphasis is achieved through the equal "weight" of each clause, not necessarily through grammatical structure.

I come to bury Caesar, not to praise him.
/\          —Shakespeare

We have won our battle against necessity, but we don't know what to do with victory.          /\

—Sam Keen

The difference between tragedy and comedy is the difference between experience and intuition.          /\

—Christopher Fry

Both parallel and balanced structures tend to be found more in formal prose than in informal writing, but even the most casual essay may reach a point where the relationship of ideas needs to be stressed clearly, and an otherwise informal style can often increase its impact on the reader by use of carefully selected balanced sentences. Such symmetry is not only appealing to the ear, but it also suggests an almost irrefutable logic and can be especially effective in clarifying contrasts or in ending an essay with dramatic finality.

Do writers create balanced sentences or parallel structure on a first draft? No doubt, some do. After becoming familiar with the technique, you might do so as well. But the place to teach yourself such forms is in the rewriting or editing phase. Any series of related ideas can be expressed in similar grammatical form, whereas contrasting ideas can be expressed in a balanced style. Do not be afraid to rearrange the parts of a sentence or to combine several sentences to achieve the desired emphasis.

# The Periodic Sentence

Emphasis can be achieved in other ways. The most amateurish way is to add an exclamation mark! Or <u>worse</u>, to underline <u>important</u> words just to make <u>sure</u> your reader gets the point!!!! Both exclamation marks and underlining have a place, but they quickly grow tiring, and in the long run they are merely external punctuation. A truly good sentence should achieve its emphasis from within. By arranging word order to fall at exactly the right point in a sentence, you can control the reader's reaction. When a sentence delays the most important words for last through the use of several interior clauses, we call it a *periodic sentence*. The trick is to postpone the important words, as Lincoln did in the final sentence of his First Inaugural Address, to delay and create suspense, to build the reader's anticipation, and then to fulfill it with a bang.

> *Simple sentence:* Beverly decided to run for president.
> *Periodic sentence:* Beverly, who had so often thought of herself only as a housewife, a servant of others, and a woman of no special talents, decided to run for president.

The order should follow the natural intensity of the details. Build from the least important to the most important, and the rhythms as well as the suspense will create a sense of controlled effectiveness.

> The dictator exploited his country's resources, stole from the common people, executed those who opposed him, and trampled over their corpses.

Sentences have movable parts and you should feel free to experiment with their arrangement. Move the parts about. Combine and recombine. Read each of your experiments aloud and test it with your ear.

> We have a responsibility to look further into how we were drawn into the war. A nation like ours has a high moral tradition. Perhaps what we find will teach us a lesson about the future.

*Try an experiment. Combine and rearrange the parts:*

> To learn what lessons it will teach us about the future, we have a responsibility, as a nation with high moral traditions, to know how we became drawn into the war.

*Experiment again. Recombine the parts:*

> A nation like ours, with its high moral tradition, has a responsibility to discover how we were drawn into the war and to learn what lessons it will teach us about the future.

By attempting several versions and by reading each aloud, you will quickly detect the difference in emphasis and rhythm. Of course, if you turned every sentence into a periodic sentence or a balanced sentence, you would not have theme and variation. Lincoln used three relatively short, simple sentences and one medium-length sentence before building to a crescendo in a final periodic sentence. The short rhythms made the long rhythms more effective. A blunt sentence can often be its own best way to emphasis, especially at the beginning or end of an essay. Short sentences have force. They make a point. Use them. But use them with recognition that they must be rhythmically varied with other types of sentences for the total effect to seem natural to our human patterns of speech.

## Emphasis Through Word Order

The components of even a simple sentence may be arranged to affect emphasis. Your purpose determines what is placed at the beginning of each sentence:

*Purpose: to emphasize Eisenhower's leadership*
Dwight D. Eisenhower directed the Normandy invasion from a small base in England.

*Purpose: to describe the invasion*
The Normandy invasion was directed by Dwight D. Eisenhower from a small base in England.

*Purpose: to recount England's role in the invasion*
It was from a small base in England that Dwight D. Eisenhower directed the Normandy invasion.

But the traditional point for emphasis in the sentence (as well as in the paragraph) is at the end.

*Weak emphasis:*
The concept of "giving until it hurts" derives from an irrational guilt, in my opinion.

*Strong emphasis:*
In my opinion, the concept of "giving until it hurts" derives from irrational guilt.

By arranging your words so that they build toward the most forceful term or phrase, you lead the reader toward the most important idea. Your purpose is more effectively achieved.

| Weak Emphasis | Strong Emphasis |
|---|---|
| Our neighborhoods are still unsafe and dirty, Councilman Moody told me. | Councilman Moody told me our neighborhoods are still dirty and unsafe. |

| My father remained a widower for twenty years. The women he met always lost out, and Dad lost out, too, because he compared them to my mother. | For twenty years my father remained a widower. By comparing the women he met to my mother, the women always lost, but Dad lost, too. |

In some ways, all of this is only common sense. The order of words affects the meaning. Writers and speakers knew that long before text books were dreamed of. And, no doubt, you already knew it and make use of it in your everyday speech, especially when trying to be forceful or "make a point." Rhythm, variation, and emphasis are natural to speech. You must make them equally natural to your prose. During the editing phase, read aloud, *listen* to what you have written, and be willing to combine, rearrange, or rewrite until each sentence sounds strong and natural, as if spoken in your own voice.

### EXERCISES

1. Identify the method by which each of these sentences achieves its effectiveness.

Balanced

    a. There is an appointed time for everything, and
        a time for every affair under the heavens.
     A time to be born, and a time to die;
        a time to plant, and a time to uproot the plant.
                              —Ecclesiastes

Balanced

    b. In proportion as men delight in battles, bullfighting, and combats of gladiators, will they punish by hanging, burning, and the rack.
                              —Herbert Spencer

    c. The best writing, both prose and poetry, as Shakespeare preeminently shows, makes use, with condensation and selection, of playful, impassioned, imaginative talk.
                              —Sidney Cox

    d. Consider what had happened to me: I had thought myself lost, had touched the very bottom of despair; and then, when the spirit of renunciation had filled me, I had known peace.
                        —Antoine de Saint-Exupéry

2. Rewrite the following passages to achieve a more natural rhythm. First, circle unnecessary and repetitive words. Second, find the action. Third, combine sentences or rebuild sentences around the verb.

    a. The *College Chimes* is the campus newspaper. I interviewed Tony Rosenblatt, who is the editor of the *Chimes*.

The inteview was conducted in the *Chimes* office located in the basement of the Student Union. Tony Rosenblatt is a senior majoring in English. Tony was dressed in faded jeans and a wrinkled shirt that said, "Country Time Lemonade" on the front.

b. Brown's family was not a particularly religious one at all. His grandmother made him attend a religious revival that was taught by a man with particularly narrow views about the Bible and religious areas. He was a traveling evangelist. The man's name was LeRoy Jedson. His sermon was filled with hellfire and brimstone and threats of what would happen to sinners.

3. Make each of the following sentences parallel. First identify each idea that needs to be related. Then choose a pattern of expression and rewrite each idea to fit the pattern.

a. The ballerina is light, very agile, and moves with grace.

| | |
|---|---|
| *Identify the related ideas.* | light<br>very agile<br>moves with grace |
| *Choose one pattern.* | light ← *possible choice*<br>very agile<br>moves with grace |
| *Express each idea in the same pattern.* | light<br>agile<br>graceful |

*Rewrite the sentence in parallel form.*
The ballerina is light, agile and graceful.

b. Henry advised him to forget time and forge ahead for victory.
c. All work and not playing makes life dull.
d. Julio promised to bring a copy of the play and that he would not be late.
e. A few generations ago children learned early in life to obey their parents without question, to consider all adults their superiors until told differently, and they had much better table manners.
f. It was a time not for words but action.
g. The French, Italians, the Spanish, and Portuguese all speak a form of language that derives from the Romans.

h. A perfect croissant is tender, flaky, and, of course, delicious.
i. My objections are, first, the injustice of the measure; second, that it is unconstitutional; and third, an inhumaneness.
j. Each room in the dorm is complete with little closet space, no air conditioning, bedroom and living room combined in one room, no appliances, and the sharing of bathroom facilities with forty other students.
k. We shall not always expect to find them supporting our view; but their own freedom is something they have to put their support behind.

4. Edit your last writing assignment for rhythm, variation, and emphasis. Do not make changes merely to make changes. Read each passage aloud. Rewrite only those sentences that need to be improved so that the whole of it sounds natural to your ear.

## Editorial Checklist for Part Three
*Objective Reporting*

_____ Have you investigated your subject for

_____ change? _____ contrast? _____ consequences? _____

characterization?

_____ If you have characterized an aspect of your subject, have

you included

_____ actions? _____ physical description? _____

background?

_____ others' reactions? _____ speech? _____ environment?

_____ Have you looked for objective facts as distinct from opin-

ions or inferences?

_____ If you have interviewed others, have you considered

whether the information provided to you was fact, infer-

ence, or opinion?

_____ Have you opened your report with a 5 *W* lead that includes

*who, what, where, when,* and *why?*

_____ Have you attempted to organize from most important to

least important?

_____ Have you written a conclusion that summarizes or general-

izes upon your findings?

_____ Have you integrated quotations with summaries?

_____ Have you read aloud and listened to the rhythms of your

sentences?

_____ Have you consciously worked to achieve the best word

order and emphasis?

_____ Have you eliminated unnecessary words? Found the action

in every sentence and, if necessary, rebuilt the sentence

around the verb?

Karl Ott, a freshman music major, wrote the following report on a new curricular development in his field of study. Karl interviewed several faculty members and students and then rewrote his essay four times before it reached a final form.

# Jazz Studies
## Karl Ott

According to Ray Eubanks, director of Jazz Studies at the Capital Conservatory of Music, the new jazz curriculum provides an excellent opportunity for students to direct their studies toward performance. Eubanks began the program two years ago when he saw a need to "diversify the conservatory." At that time, 80 percent of the students majored in music education.

Mr. Eubanks estimates that half the entering freshmen will drop out of the jazz program because "they realize that they simply don't have the ability." But he claims that he doesn't play God and does not tell students they lack talent. "Generally, they can figure it out for themselves if they're seniors playing sixth trumpet in the second band." Yet the high standards established by Eubanks have not discouraged students from enrolling. The program now has thirteen freshmen, five sophomores, and twelve juniors.

These thirty-three students study in a curriculum similar to the "legit music" curriculum, although courses include improvisation and jazz arranging instead of the more traditional classes in counterpoint and nineteenth-century orchestration. In addition, the jazz major is required to take all traditional university requirements such as freshman English, ethnic studies, and religion. As Barney Rooker puts it, "Some of the courses that jazz majors think are a waste may turn out to be the ones most helpful to them in later life." Barney Rooker is sax instructor at the conservatory. A soft-spoken man, he has long brown hair and black-rimmed glasses that give him the appearance of a philosopher. "I know a lot of guys get caught up in this mysticism of being a jazz musician," he told me, "all the drugs, being late, dressing and acting weird." But as intriguing as it may seem to some, Rooker insists that students have to recognize they are attending college, not doing a gig in some dark New Orleans bar. "The point is, by the time they get out of here, we want them to be well-rounded, educated individuals. Not just musicians."

Rooker's philosophy is supported by the other staff members, eight altogether, who were chosen for their "understanding of music and their ability to teach it." All eight members of the faculty are active, performing jazz musicians in and around the city. To augment the regular faculty,

Eubanks has also been able to attract to the school top-name jazz artists. Last year, Clark Terry, Ladd McIntosh, Will Watrous, Tom Scott, the Brecker Brothers, Phil Woods, and others performed with the Jazz Arts Group and taught classes at Capital.

The jazz department currently sponsors five performance groups: two big bands, two octets, and the Fusion Music Orchestra. The Fusion Band, so-called because it plays a wide variety of music, is the most advanced group, a prize of sorts for the better talents. It has played at the Glasboro Jazz Festival and the Ohio State University Jazz Festival, as well as performing on a fairly regular basis at the Dell, a local night spot.

But as one student asked me, what can one do with a jazz performance degree after college? I talked to Ray Eubanks at length on this topic. Eubanks is in his thirties and almost boyish in his appearance and enthusiasm for jazz. "No degree guarantees a job anymore," he admitted. "Even an education degree doesn't guarantee a job. And I know countless people who hold jobs that have nothing to do with their majors." On the other hand, a performance degree can help a student enter graduate school. And as many other colleges are now developing jazz programs, teaching positions should be available. What about performance with professional groups? The degree means nothing, Eubanks confessed. But four years of training, practice, and discipline mean a lot. "If a student has the personality and drive, and even a little talent, we can cultivate that talent and give him a healthy start on a career."

Jazz studies, then, cannot be seen as a program designed to turn out hot players, although a few might eventually succeed as artists. Instead, the program offers a student with a love of music the opportunity to develop his or her abilities to the maximum. And as part of a regular college curriculum, it offers the opportunity to pursue that love in a university atmosphere dedicated to developing well-rounded, educated human beings.

The following article is printed in its entirety from *Women's Work,* a magazine devoted to revealing the career possibilities open to women. Author Elizabeth Breed Clark has used the 5 *W* lead and the inverted pyramid organization. You might want to note as well how she has integrated quotations and summary and how clearly she has identified each source of information.

# Policewomen
## Elizabeth Breed Clark

The 1970's have brought major changes in the role of women in police forces throughout the country. Long confined to the so-called "Women's Bureau" or to the Youth Division, their assignments focusing on work with juveniles, female suspects or victims of sex offenses, police women usually have drawn salaries lower than their male counterparts—despite the fact that greater educational credentials have been frequently required of women. With promotions coming from uniformed patrol officers—and women traditionally barred from uniform patrol—chances to rise in the hierarchy of the police department have been extremely limited for females. In 1971, *fewer than a dozen policewomen were on patrol in the United States;* by 1974, they numbered close to 1,000. While 1971 saw a handful of women in police supervisory positions, in 1974, there were several hundred women sergeants, lieutenants and captains supervising male and female patrol officers and detectives. Spurred by the women's rights movement, civil rights legislation and research findings, experiments in Denver, St. Louis, Washington, D.C., and New York have demonstrated successfully the use of women in patrol work. Now, more and more women are being given the chance to go out on uniformed patrol, with opportunities and responsibilities equal to their male counterparts.

The average female officer still has to be a little better to be accepted on an equal basis, says Katherine Kurtz, the first female training technician for the Los Angeles Police Department. "But," she adds, "men are slowly conceding the fact that women can do the job as well—and sometimes better."

Studies in both Washington, D.C., and St. Louis Co., Mo., show that women can perform police patrol duties equally as well as men. While women exhibit a less aggressive patrol style and make fewer arrests than males, they are still just as effective in managing distraught and angry people. Also, according to the results, citizens rate policewomen high in sensitivity.

Opening up patrol duties to women has helped dispel the old myths about women being too weak and emotional to cope with the dangers and pressures of active police work. The Vera Institute of Justice, a private research agency based in New York, has reported that opponents of policewomen argue that, "when faced with danger, female officers would tend to panic, that they would be more likely to use a gun when threatened and that they could lack the stamina and strength necessary to chase a suspect or to carry an injured person." After comparing the performances of male and female officers in New York, the Institute found that "the women's style of patrolling was almost indistinguishable from the men's."

Capt. Joyce Leland, the first female sergeant to work in uniform for the Washington, D.C., police department and now the highest ranking woman officer in the country, believes that patrol gives a woman "the chance to use all your abilities and give service to the community. It constantly challenges you." "Police work is several careers in one," says Inspector Gertrude Schimmel, the highest ranking woman in the New York police department. "No other field offers so much variety of experience."

Areas open to women in police departments around the country include patrolling in uniform, which may lead to a supervisory position on the force, and investigating evidence for homicide, sex, burglary or fraud. Hiring specifications differ from one locality to another, but all applicants must be U.S. citizens and have at least a high school education. Some jobs require a college degree. Patrolwomen usually must be over 21, possess a driver's license and be in good physical condition. Generally, a written competitive Civil Service examination must be passed. Police officers also must undergo physical and psychological tests.

A six-month training period at the police academy in basic law, first aid, community relations, "pursuit driving" and the operation of firearms usually comes next. Incidentally, while height, weight and physical agility requirements have been abolished by most departments, one may be expected to pass a fitness test after initial training at the academy.

Street work, cruising, investigating and detective work in homicide, sex squad, fraud or vice; undercover narcotics work; park policing and work in youth divisions are among the fields now open to patrolwomen.

Salaries for patrol officers start around $12,000, with openings determined by the city's budget and needs.

Rachel Carson (1907–1964) was an award-winning science writer, conservationist, and marine biologist. Because of the effective reporting of Carson and others like her, concern for ecology became a national issue and pesticides like DDT were eventually banned. The following essay is excerpted from her most famous work, *Silent Spring* (1962). Although some of the information the book contains is now out of date, Carson's ability to find and select objective facts—and to present them in an interesting way—still illustrates the value of the reporter's eye.

# The Poison in Clear Lake
## Rachel Carson

Water must also be thought of in terms of the chains of life it supports—from the small-as-dust green cells of the drifting plant plankton, through the minute water fleas to the fishes that strain plankton from the water and are in turn eaten by other fishes or by birds, mink, raccoons—in an endless cyclic transfer of materials from life to life. We know that the necessary minerals in the water are so passed from link to link of the food chains. Can we suppose that poisons we introduce into water will not also enter into these cycles of nature?

The answer is to be found in the amazing history of Clear Lake, California. Clear Lake lies in mountainous country some 90 miles north of San Francisco and has long been popular with anglers. The name is inappropriate, for actually it is a rather turbid lake because of the soft black ooze that covers its shallow bottom. Unfortunately for the fishermen and the resort dwellers on its shores, its waters have provided an ideal habitat for a small gnat, *Chaoborus astictopus*. Although closely related to mosquitoes, the gnat is not a bloodsucker and probably does not feed at all as an adult. However, human beings who shared its habitat found it annoying because of its sheer numbers. Efforts were made to control it but they were largely fruitless until, in the late 1940's, the chlorinated hydrocarbon insecticides offered new weapons. The chemical chosen for a fresh attack was DDD, a close relative of DDT but apparently offering fewer threats to fish life.

The new control measures undertaken in 1949 were carefully planned and few people would have supposed any harm could result. The lake was surveyed, its volume determined, and the insecticide applied in such great dilution that for every part of chemical there would be 70 million parts of water. Control of the gnats was at first good, but by 1954 the treatment had to be repeated, this time at the rate of 1 part of insecticide in 50 million parts of water. The destruction of the gnats was thought to be virtually complete.

The following winter months brought the first intimation that other life was affected: the western grebes on the lake began to die, and soon more than a hundred of them were reported dead. At Clear Lake the western grebe is a breeding bird and also a winter visitant, attracted by the abundant fish of the lake. It is a bird of spectacular appearance and beguiling habits, building its floating nests in shallow lakes of western United States and Canada. It is called the "swan grebe" with reason, for it glides with scarcely a ripple across the lake surface, the body riding low, white neck and shining black head held high. The newly hatched chick is clothed in soft gray down; in only a few hours it takes to the water and rides on the back of the father or mother, nestled under the parental wing coverts.

Following a third assault on the ever-resilient gnat population, in 1957, more grebes died. As had been true in 1954, no evidence of infectious disease could be discovered on examination of the dead birds. But when someone thought to analyze the fatty tissues of the grebes, they were found to be loaded with DDD in the extraordinary concentration of 1600 parts per million.

The maximum concentration applied to the water was 1/50 part per million. How could the chemical have built up to such prodigious levels in the grebes? These birds, of course, are fish eaters. When the fish of Clear Lake also were analyzed the picture began to take form—the poison being picked up by the smallest organisms, concentrated and passed on to the larger predators. Plankton organisms were found to contain about 5 parts per million of the insecticide (about 25 times the maximum concentration ever reached in the water itself); plant-eating fishes had built up accumulations ranging from 40 to 300 parts per million; carnivorous species had stored the most of all. One, a brown bullhead, had the astounding concentration of 2500 parts per million. It was a house-that-Jack-built sequence, in which the large carnivores had eaten the smaller carnivores, that had eaten the herbivores, that had eaten the plankton, that had absorbed the poison from the water.

Even more extraordinary discoveries were made later. No trace of DDD could be found in the water shortly after the last application of the chemical. But the poison had not really left the lake; it had merely gone into the fabric of the life the lake supports. Twenty-three months after the chemical treatment had ceased, the plankton still contained as much as 5.3 parts per million. In that interval of nearly two years, successive crops of plankton had flowered and faded away, but the poison, although no longer present in the water, had somehow passed from generation to generation. And it lived on in the animal life of the lake as well. All fish, birds, and frogs examined a year after the chemical applications had ceased still contained DDD. The amount found in the flesh always exceeded by many times the original concentration in the water. Among these living carriers were fish that had hatched nine months after the last DDD application, grebes, and California gulls that had built up concentrations of more than 2000 parts per million. Meanwhile, the nesting colonies of the grebes dwindled—from more than 1000 pairs before the first insecticide treatment to about 30 pairs in 1960. And even the thirty seem to have nested in vain, for no young grebes have been observed on the lake since the last DDD application.

This whole chain of poisoning, then, seems to rest on a base of minute plants which must have been the original concentrators. But what of the opposite end of the food chain—the human being who, in probable ignorance of all this sequence of events, has rigged his fishing tackle, caught a string of fish from the waters of Clear Lake, and taken them home to fry for his supper? What could a heavy dose of DDD, or perhaps repeated doses, do to him?

Although the California Department of Public Health professed to see no hazard, nevertheless in 1959 it required that the use of DDD in the lake be stopped. In view of the scientific evidence of the vast biological potency of this chemical, the action seems a minimum safety measure. The physiological effect of DDD is probably unique among insecticides, for it destroys part of the adrenal gland—the cells of the outer layer known as the adrenal cortex, which secretes the hormone cortin. This destructive effect, known since 1948, was at first believed to be confined to dogs, because it was not revealed in such experimental animals as monkeys, rats, or rabbits. It seemed suggestive, however, that DDD produced in dogs a condition very similar to that occurring in man in the presence of Addison's disease. Recent medical research has revealed that DDD does strongly suppress the function of the human adrenal cortex. Its cell-destroying capacity is now clinically utilized in the treatment of a rare type of cancer which develops in the adrenal gland.

The Clear Lake situation brings up a question that the public needs to face: Is it wise or desirable to use substances with such strong effect on physiological processes for the control of insects, especially when the control measures involve introducing the chemical directly into a body of water? The fact that the insecticide was applied in very low concentrations is meaningless, as its explosive progress through the natural food chain in the lake demonstrates. Yet Clear Lake is typical of a large and growing number of situations where solution of an obvious and often trivial problem creates a far more serious but conveniently less tangible one. Here the problem was resolved in favor of those annoyed by gnats, and at the expense of an unstated, and probably not even clearly understood, risk to all who took food or water from the lake.

It is an extraordinary fact that the deliberate introduction of poisons into a reservoir is becoming a fairly common practice. The purpose is usually to promote recreational uses, even though the water must then be treated at some expense to make it fit for its intended use as drinking water. When sportsmen of an area want to "improve" fishing in a reservoir, they prevail on authorities to dump quantities of poison into it to kill the undesired fish, which are then replaced with hatchery fish more suited to the sportsmen's taste. The procedure has a strange, Alice-in-Wonderland quality. The reservoir was created as a public water supply, yet the community, probably unconsulted about the sportsmen's project, is forced either to drink water containing poisonous residues or to pay out tax money for treatment of the water to remove the poisons—treatments that are by no means foolproof.

# PART

---

## *Factual Investigation*

---

# FOUR

*We assume all too readily that observation comes by nature, that we are born "naturally observant." But the truth is that most of us are born lazy, and observation beyond the necessities of life has been too great for voluntary exertion. The result is that we live in a world of which we know little more than a dog or a cat; we are familiar with a few things from long association; we have a nodding acquaintance with a number of other things; but as far as our scientific observation of them goes, we can scarcely be said to be even curious.*

—A. E. Orage

An investigation or inquiry goes beyond reporting. It requires a more active curiosity, a healthy skepticism, and a determination to discover the truth. The following unit builds upon the experience of observing and reporting, asking you to extend your imagination and to explore the relationships among the facts you discover. You will be required to research new types of sources in your pursuit of information, and you will be faced with evaluating and interpreting what you find. This unit begins to draw together all the separate activities of the writing process you've been practicing. It moves toward helping you achieve one of the major goals of any college education: a self-disciplined intelligence that knows how to investigate a problem and reason a solution.

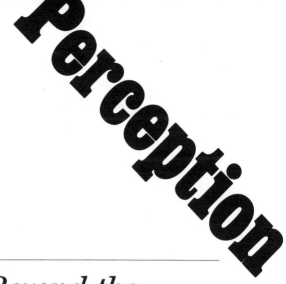
*Perception*

# 18 *Seeing Beyond the Surface*

> Imagination is more important than knowledge. For knowledge
> is limited, whereas imagination embraces the entire world.
> —Albert Einstein

In June, 1972, two local Washington, D.C., reporters were assigned to investigate a burglary of Democratic Headquarters in the Watergate apartments. Bob Woodward and Carl Bernstein, both in their twenties, had never investigated anything more serious than an unsanitary restaurant. For the next two years the two men worked on almost nothing else. They quickly discovered that one of the burglars formerly worked for the CIA and was currently employed by President Richard M. Nixon's Committee to Reelect the President. Address books belonging to two other burglars contained the name of E. Howard Hunt, an employee of one of the highest-level assistants to the president. Although the White House denied any connection, calling the affair a "third-rate burglary attempt," Woodward and Bernstein had in front of them a number of inexplicable, seemingly incredible facts.

After the denial by the White House and, later, after a grand jury indicted only the men directly involved in the break-in, other reporters and news organizations drifted away from the story. Although many suspected a cover-up, further investigation seemed fruitless. Almost no one felt that top aids to the president of the United States might be involved. Not even Woodward and Bernstein suspected the complicity of Richard M. Nixon.

During the next eighteen months the two young reporters pursued thousands of separate clues: telephone records, library cards, mysterious checks from Mexico, reports of cash handed out in brown envelopes, tips from interviews (each reporter interviewed or telephoned as many as a hundred people a week). Eventually, their notes filled four filing cabinets. No information was ever printed unless it could be verified by two sources in addition to the original source. Woodward wrote the first drafts of each story; Bernstein rewrote and polished. At several points the investigation seemed to die. Other newspapers ignored their reports; national newscasters felt no more significant facts would be uncovered. Most of the evidence was circumstantial; concrete proof seemed lacking. But the pile of inexplicable, seemingly incredible facts kept growing.

Truth is difficult to define, difficult to prove. At best we can usually work toward probable truth. We can have the curiosity, the skepticism, the open mind—all needed to pursue the facts beyond a mere surface accounting—but, ultimately, success seems to rely on our ability to evaluate and interpret the facts, on our persistent desire to find an order, a pattern, a meaning that the facts reveal. Woodward and Bernstein were not solely responsible for the exposure of Richard Nixon. But their tenacity in the face of such odds and their ability to sense the relationship of seemingly unrelated facts eventually led to the prosecution and conviction of a former attorney general, a former secretary of commerce, and ten presidential assistants and aids. The president of the United States resigned after being faced with the first impeachment proceedings in over one hundred years.

A serious inquiry into a subject goes beyond mere reporting, beyond observing the facts or listening to facts or gathering facts. *To investigate means to pursue detail in such a way that you begin to perceive a pattern or association that suggests a reasonable meaning—a probable truth.* Although there are as many ways of organizing an inquiry as there are subjects to investigate, three general phases can be identified in the inquiry process: narrowing your focus to a single, manageable portion of the subject; pursuing and selecting facts or informed opinion that seem most significant; and interpreting results.

## Narrowing the Focus

Your eye functions as the lens of your imagination. You have the ability to see the whole of something or to focus on minute detail. Successful writers have found that the most effective and significant work usually has a narrow focus on one or two specific areas of a larger subject. Woodward and Bernstein did not investigate "American Politics." They focused on an attempted burglary and a cover-up. They tirelessly traced each small connection, each relationship. Although results of their work eventually produced enough information to fill a book, *All the President's Men,* the focus never shifted.

Many, if not all, topics you'll be assigned in college will be too large to handle successfully. Train yourself to break the topic down into its own various components, then to focus on only one or two specific segments. Here's an example of how you might begin.

### Assignment
*Investigate dormitories at Slippery Sands State College*
As a topic, "dormitories" is too broad. It covers hundreds of categories composed of various components and specific details. If you try to write on dormitories, you'll end up producing either vague generalization or a very large book.

First, break down the subject into its major categories.

dormitories
- physical buildings
- student facilities
- residents
- social life
- traditions
- rules
- living conditions
- administration
- cost
- maintenance
- student counselors

Next, select one category and break it down into its various components.

social life
- movies
- organized floor activities
- charity drives
- entertainment council
- beer blasts
- dances
- fall picnic
- regulations
- participation
- pool tables
- expenses

Now you've got enough material for only a small handbook. If you want to write an essay or report, better break it down one more time.

Focus on *one* specific area. Begin asking questions, specific questions that can produce facts from which you can reasonably expect to draw conclusions.

Here's a more complex example.

### Assignment

*Investigate an ethnic custom*

First, break down the subject into its major categories.

ethnic custom
{
types of food
funeral ceremonies
initiation rites
hand gestures
marriage ceremonies
dress
greetings
sibling relationships
}

Next, select one category and break it down into its various components.

marriage ceremony
{
dress
bride's family
traditional music
invitations
groom's family
religious ritual
food
blessings
traditional gifts
announcements
}

Finally, focus on one or two areas and investigate the specific facts.

bride's family
groom's family
{
What is expected of the bride's parents?
What is expected of the groom's parents?
Why? Where do the expectations come from?
Why does the bride's father "give away" his daughter?
Why doesn't the groom's father "give away" his son?
Are the families expected to meet? To exchange symbolic gifts?
Who offers the first toast at the reception? Why?
}

> Are the families aware of the reason behind the customs? If not, why do they follow the customs?
> What is the function of custom and ceremony in this situation?

The answer to these questions will require much research. You'll probably need to investigate written sources, perhaps a history book or a work on anthropology or sociology. For some questions you may find no concrete facts at all. You may need to rely on inference and informed opinion. But with enough persistence and enough determination, a probable truth can still be found.

---

Here is a general topic for you to practice on. Narrow the focus by breaking it down, first into its general categories, then into major components, then into one specific area of concern around which you can formulate some initial questions for inquiry.

                                        categories
topic: funeral customs          _____
                                _____
                                _____
                                _____
                                _____

                                major components:
                                _____
choose one category             _____
_____        _____
                                _____
                                _____

                                specific questions:
choose one component            _____
_____        _____
                                _____
                                _____
                                _____

---

# Pursuing and Selecting Details

Almost half of the previous chapters in this text have dealt with the pursuit or selection of specific detail. Each method and technique discussed earlier may apply at some point during an investigation of any subject. It would probably be best to keep them all in the back of your mind, selecting from them as the subject itself seems to call them forth.

**Look for the 5 W's**   Think of the 5 *W*'s as more than a technique used in writing a lead. *Who, What, Where, When,* and *Why* are the questions that apply to every subject as a whole.

**Look for Change**   Change may be the key element. Why is change occurring or not occurring? Whom does the change affect? When will it occur? How will it be brought about?

**Look for Contrast**   Contrast, conflict, contradiction, or opposition may lead to the center of an issue. Why is there a conflict? What does it grow out of? Who is involved? Where and when did it begin?

**Look for Consequences**   How does one fact influence another? What facts have the most serious impact? Who is affected? When will the impact take place? What will be the result?

**Look for Characterization**   Major actions, speech or written documents, background, others' reactions or opinions, and the physical description or environment (when appropriate) all contribute to the total pattern of almost any issue or event.

**Look for the Elements of Scene**   The concrete sensory elements of a scene are the elements of life. Subjects for investigation exist in a real world, in a place and setting, in a time frame, and with people who have purpose or motivation. An objective search for truth does not mean we abandon the concrete world for the sake of abstractions. See your subject in its real setting, in its world context, both for yourself and for your reader's fullest understanding.

**Look for the People Behind the Subject**   Whether through observation, interviews, or library research, keep your own eyes open to the human element both to make your writing more interesting and to retain a human perspective on the issue.

# The Role of Feeling

To all these previous techniques, we need to add a few points about mental and emotional attitudes during an inquiry. We've already seen that to reach even a probable truth, we need an objective approach. It seems self-evident that personal bias or an emotional attitude will only lead a person to prove what he or she already believes. Yet we face a paradox here. The best writing and probably the most important discoveries derive from intense involvement, from deep personal feelings about a subject. I began this book with two units on personal writing because my experience with students has led me to believe that the human voice speaking out of honest personal observation rings truest in the ear of the reader. Unless we are able to *feel* a subject as well as perceive it objectively, we have not truly explored it in all its fullness.

You must approach a subject with an open mind, but also with a sense of caring. That is what it means to be sensitive. Pierre Curie, a French scientist and husband of Madame Marie Curie, entered into a ten-year investigation of piezoelectric crystals because of their beauty. Beauty involves aesthetic appreciation. In other words, it was an emotion that motivated and sustained objective research. In Curie's case, the emotion and the objective facts complemented each other and enriched the inquiry process. On other occasions, you'll find that objective facts oppose inner feelings. You can never ignore the facts or slight them or distort them because of that. The facts must always be fairly and accurately presented, no matter how painful it may be. Surely, the nation felt a deep sense of regret about the Watergate affair. There can be no question that the objective facts needed to be revealed and the truth discerned by reasonable men. Yet the agony—the emotion—suffered by a whole nation became part of the truth. The meaning of the facts is increased by that recognition. Emotion and objectivity may oppose or complement each other. Either way, your research and your writing will be enhanced by an intense commitment that effectively balances the two qualities.

## The Role of the Imagination

I also feel I should say something about imagination because no successful inquiry functions without it. A scientist, for example, trained in analysis and logical procedure, may suddenly follow an illogical hunch, a leap of the imagination toward an unexpected breakthrough. The years of objective empirical study may at first seem unrelated, yet it is exactly this previous preparation that helps him or her to use intuition productively. You have been training your eyes and ears to perceive specific details and facts, and it may have begun to seem like an end in itself. But it has only been preparation for a more important goal. Possession of the facts is never a substitute for understanding their meanings.

Here is what one student wrote when asked to investigate the campus cafeteria. He began with description:

> Students enter through the south door. They stand in line and have their identification cards checked. They gather up knives, forks, spoons, napkins, and trays from a stand. Then they push their trays along an aluminum rack in front of steaming kinds of food. Each student can select one item from meat, two items from the vegetables, one salad, one dessert, bread, butter, and a choice of five or six drinks. Students then separate and choose tables, usually with their friends, where . . .

No need to go on. This is objective reporting with a vengeance. Everything the writer says is verifiable by a second observer. He has successfully prevented emotional influences from affecting his observations. But nothing he says has been seen as significant. He reports objective facts without concern for their value or meaning. The real problem is that the author has made no commitment to the subject. He has not engaged his imagination. It is easy to misunderstand the nature of objectivity and to believe that your mind must act like a machine, like a camera that records but does not evaluate.

Yet here is what Tina Hawthorne wrote for the same assignment. She, too, began with description:

> The young woman sat down at the lunch table with two books under her arm. Her tray contained only a small salad of cottage cheese on wilted lettuce, and a slightly brown orange. She placed one book flat to the side of her tray. She opened the other—a nursing text on cancer—propping it against the first so that it was raised slightly. The edge of the tray held open the pages. She pushed her heavy rimmed glasses against her nose with her thumb, glanced around the line of students still shuffling past the milk machines, and then began to peel her orange and read at the same time.
>
> She used her fingernails to dig at the orange while her eyes studied the chapter on "Multiple Primary Tumors." As she read, the juice ran between her fingers and she slurped each finger slowly, never taking her eyes from the text. Again she thumbed her glasses up her nose, then began to break the orange into segments, popping each one open with small white teeth. A fine spray of juice squirted out over her tray. She leaned into the tray pushing out her chin so the juice wouldn't dribble into her lap. Eyes fixed on the book, she fed each orange slice automatically into her mouth.
>
> She reached out and turned the page with the tips of her wet thumb and forefinger. The subheading read "Malignant Melanoma." She licked her lips and fingers skimming fast. Feeling about with one blind hand, she found her fork and speared the cottage cheese.

Like the first author, Tina Hawthorne observes facts. Yet Tina's work is not only more interesting, it also strikes me as more meaningful. Tina does not merely report objective details, but she also begins to write toward an idea. We begin to sense something about the nature of education, about the excitement of learning when involvement becomes intense and absorbing. The incongruities of the scene heighten our awareness. Tina looked at selected facts (the rest of the cafeteria is ignored), and through her eye we begin to explore the world. John Ciardi, a poet and essayist, once wrote: "The fact is that anything significantly looked at is significant. And that is significant which teaches us something about our own life-capabilities. The function of detail when ordered by a human imagination is to illustrate the universe." I know of no finer way to make the point. The eye of the scientist and the eye of the poet are not that different. Both perceive the world with imaginative discipline; both select details and weigh them for their value and significance; both reject those that are mere gloss while retaining those that illuminate larger wholes. Facts are lifeless and boring only when perceived by an unengaged mind that does not imaginatively relate them to the world we live in.

# Evaluating and Interpreting

To *evaluate* is to judge the worth of something. Each fact you obtain during an investigation must be evaluated for its worth. So must the source of each fact, for the source may affect the value of the fact in several different ways. To *interpret,* on the other hand, means to clarify or to explain the significance of something. When you evaluate, you ask whether a fact is any good. When you interpret, you ask what the fact means or what it suggests about the subject as a whole.

## Evaluating Sources

Before you can evaluate the worth of a fact, you need to consider its source. During the Watergate investigation, Woodward and Bernstein received thousands of tips from random telephone calls to their newspaper, *The Washington Post*—calls from housewives, bakers, mechanics, and department-store clerks who claimed knowledge of "inside information." As a source, such people were unlikely to have verifiable facts that only someone working within the administration might have possessed. The best facts can usually be obtained from someone considered an expert or authority on a subject. However, an authority does not need a fancy title. A housewife may be an authority on the need for women's liberation; a baker may be an authority on the nutrients in bread, and so on. Authority may derive from experience or from scholarly study. Each source must be tested against the subject. One of the key sources for the Watergate investigation turned out to be a low level accountant at the Committee to Reelect the President. The accountant had access to financial transactions that revealed the nature, size, and control of a secret fund totaling almost one million dollars. The accountant did not hold a major position in the Committee to Reelect the President; she could provide only a single element of the whole picture, but her authority on that element was considerable.

On the other hand, access to information, the title of "expert," or even a national reputation does not necessarily give a source inherent value. Motivation behind the release of information may make it suspect. Someone with a grudge or someone acting out of self-interest may provide biased or incomplete information. You must weigh each of your sources with as much care as you weigh your own personal observation. Be skeptical. Human nature is always involved. Withhold judgment until more facts or evidence can be obtained. No matter who or what your source, attempt to verify all data from a second source.

## Evaluating Evidence

Once the evidence has been gathered, it must be evaluated on its own terms. Is it fact, inference, or opinion? If the evidence seems factual, can it be verified? How or by whom? If the evidence is an inference, can you trust the source that made the inference? Is the inference confirmed by more than one source? Do other facts support the inference so that one could reasonably consider it a *probable* truth? Finally, if your information derives from opinion, is it informed opinion—that is, does it come from someone likely to be informed on a subject, or does it come from a random man on the street?

You must evaluate whether each fact is typical of the whole or special to a particular situation or context. Either may be valuable, but exceptions can always exist and may prove little more than that exceptions exist. You need information that forms an association, that seems consistent or typical, for what is typical may suggest a pattern. In the Watergate burglary, five of the original burglars were Cuban exiles. A number of people suspected that various Cuban exile groups were behind the whole plot. Because the ringleader was a former CIA employee, others suspected the CIA of direct involvement. Yet when pieced together with other evidence, these facts turned out to be exceptions. As other data accumulated, the *pattern* of the evidence suggested the burglary was directed by someone inside the White House. The nationality of the people committing the actual break-in seemed to play no significant role in that pattern. Obviously, in some cases an exception to the whole may become the focal point of your research, but you'll usually find the pattern or relationship of facts, rather than the exception, leads to the most reasonable conclusion.

## Interpreting the Results

One of the most human qualities is the desire to know, the desire for certainty. As a result, we sometimes begin to interpret or judge before we have finished an investigation. In our impatience to find the truth, we may jump to hasty conclusions before all data are available. We then find ourselves forced to distort the remaining evidence to support interpretation, or else we must back up and endure the tedious process of reevaluating and interpreting anew. But writers, artists, scientists—everyone engaged in trying to make sense of the world—report that chaos is a natural phase in the creative process and that we must move through chaos before we can discover order. In other words, we must learn to accept temporary uncertainty and confusion as normal. Few investigations move in logical, step-by-step fashion. Facts, data, quotations, opinions pile up without seeming relationship or significance. The mind seems boggled. Hours or days of struggling with the material may follow. But the intuitive or subconscious elements in our mind eventually become our ally. Psychological studies have shown that alternating periods of intense work with relaxation encourages a breakthrough. A pattern forms. A relationship is discovered.

The original meaning of the Greek and Hebrew words meaning "to know" included the concept of sexual relations: to know was to join together, to unite opposites. If we wish to know the significance of something, we must join the parts together; we must discover how seemingly opposite or disparate facts relate. Interpretation, then, is a process of reasonable inference applied to an accumulation of data. A hasty inference may cause a distorted or false interpretation. A carefully considered inference, based on all possible evidence, usually leads to a verifiable interpretation.

The human mind finds its truths in qualities that shape themselves into patterns or associations that have order and form. It is your job as a writer to discover the pattern and show it to the reader.

### EXERCISES

1. The ability to discern relationships is a major element of evaluation and interpretation. Study the three advertisements that follow. What common features do you find? Are there qualities that suggest a pattern? Make a list of the typical qualities. What reasonable inferences might you make about the nature of advertising? How could you verify your inferences?

COURVOISIER VSOP. THE BRANDY OF NAPOLEON

Reprinted by permission of W. A. Taylor & Company.

# The spirit of the Czar lives on.

It was the Golden Age of Russia. Yet in this time when legends lived, the Czar stood like a giant among men.

He could bend an iron bar on his bare knee. Crush a silver ruble with his fist. And had a thirst for life like no other man alive.

And his drink was Genuine Vodka. Wolfschmidt Vodka. Made by special appointment to his Majesty the Czar. And the Royal Romanov Court.

It's been 120 years since then. And while life has changed since the days of the Czar, his Vodka remains the same.

Wolfschmidt Genuine Vodka. The spirit of the Czar lives on.

schmidt Vodka · Distilled from grain · 80 and 100 proof · Wolfschmidt, Relay, Md.

WOLFSCHMIDT
GENUINE
VODKA
SINCE 1847
WOLFSCHMIDT

**Wolfschmidt
Genuine Vodka**

*Reprinted by permission of the House of Seagram.*

*Reprinted by permission of the House of Seagram.*

2. Here are three sources providing information on a student's application to join a college honors program. Evaluate each of the sources. Evaluate the information provided by each source. Look for patterns or relationships. Interpret the evidence by drawing a reasonable inference about the student's qualifications for honors work.

### Excerpts from Student Application Form

a. Describe the most important book you've read this year.

The best book I've read this year was *I Am Third* by Gale Sayers. Usually, I just read fiction.

b. What are your goals and ambitions?

I plan to open my own successful law office and go into politics. I'd like to be a congressman or senator some day.

c. Describe an accomplishment of which you are particularly proud.

Last spring my father was struck by a bull on our dairy farm. He received a bruised heart and a collapsed lung. My brother and I carried on the entire dairy operation for two months by ourselves while also completing high school.

d. Why do you want to participate in an honors program?

I am applying for honors because it would be a personal accomplishment. It also might help me get into law school.

### Excerpts from Letters of Reference

I have known Randolph for several years. I once treated him for hyperactivity when he was younger. Throughout the years he has matured and turned out to be a fine young man. I understand from his mother that he has applied for your honors program and I feel he would be a welcome addition.

John L. Morando, M.D.

It is a pleasure for me to recommend Randolph as a candidate for your honors program. As his guidance counselor I have known him for three years. I also taught him in a class on interpretative dance, for which he received an *A* plus. He is an excellent student whose chief areas of interest are history, psychology, and political science. We would be very proud here at Easter High School for Randolph to be selected for such a fine program.

Kathleen Spangler, Counselor

### Excerpts from High School Transcript

National Test Scores:   SAT Verbal 601/SAT Math 545

Grades in Senior Year:   English . . . A

Algebra II . . . C

History . . . A

> Physical Education . . . B
> Psychology . . . A
> Social Studies . . . A
> French II . . . A

Activities: Debating Club, Future Farmers of America, Chess Club President, Senior Class Historian, Honors Society, Senior Play.

Awards: Future Farmers of America Award for Achievement in Dairy Farming; Third Place, Wisconsin High School Chess Tournament; State Fair, Third Prize Guernsey Calf Competition; Honorable Mention, "I Speak for Democracy" Competition; Delegate to the Midwest United Nations Conference.

3. Here are several broad topics. Choose one and narrow it to a single component. Design a series of questions that would help you find specific facts and informed opinions about it.

> public school attendance
> church attendance
> local art galleries
> grading practices
> SAT exams
> cheerleading
> law schools
> core requirements

# **19** *Primary and Secondary Sources*

As John Dewitt McKee once wrote, "No writer who is any good writes solely from the contemplation of his navel. He must *know,* either through personal experience or through research." We're now ready to put together the full process by which a writer sets out to explore a subject and, one hopes, to learn something about it. We might describe a full investigation as a triangular process involving, first, your own personal observation; second, the extension of observation by using others' eyes and experience as reported directly to you in an interview or as recorded in an original document; and third, the research of secondary sources, the use of knowledge and insight accumulated throughout history by other authors.

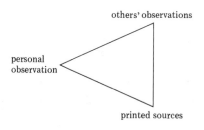

others' observations

personal
observation

printed sources

# Primary Material

A primary source provides information to you in some direct way—through a personal interview, telephone conversation, letter, diary, journal, ledger, memo, manuscript, or book that presents a firsthand account. Even your own personal experience might be considered a primary source if it directly involves your subject of investigation. If, for example, you were reporting on racial prejudice in the public schools and you had personally experienced or been involved in a racial incident, your own observations would constitute a primary source. So would interviews with others directly involved or with those who might be informed on the subject: a school superintendent, a psychologist or sociologist at a nearby university, a police report written about the incident, or an extract from a diary kept by a teacher.

# Secondary Material

A secondary source provides secondhand information or analysis and interpretation of original documents. Secondary sources may constitute the largest body of material available to you on many subjects. Your personal ability to observe is limited, as is the number of interviews or primary sources you usually have access to; but the number of books, newspapers, magazines, films, records, government reports, pamphlets, and so on is almost unlimited. A racial incident in your city's public schools may be investigated almost exclusively through primary sources, but for a fuller understanding of racism and of how the incident in your school forms part of a larger pattern, you would need to turn to secondary sources.

Students often feel that investigation of secondary material is somehow taxing, more duty than pleasure—all those hours in the library, all that note-taking. But every subject is interesting when pursued imaginatively, critically, and skeptically. If you bring a dull mind to the work, it will indeed seem dull. If you involve yourself with some sort of personal commitment, even the evolution of the aardvark can become fascinating. What is always necessary is a focused question—the question that grows out of the narrowing of your subject: does this fact relate to others? Does it conflict with others? How is it significant? Whom does it affect? Does it constitute part of a larger pattern? Is it true? Can the truth be known?

# In-text Documentation of Sources

Because the source of any information you obtain affects the value of the information, a writer must always provide complete and accurate documentation (identification) of sources. In formal papers you will want to provide footnotes and bibliographies. A report or a critical paper, however, usually requires only that you clearly identify your source *within* the text itself.

Both primary and secondary sources need to be documented. Some instructors may provide you with a preferred method; some businesses and institutions may provide a "style sheet" that lists a prescribed form. Without such guidance, you can rely on any number of methods for integrating the documentation into your material so long as it provides, in general, *who, what, where,* and sometimes *when.*

## Primary Sources

*who*      The first time information from a source is used, give the full name of the source. In addition, give the source's full title or a description of his or her authority to speak on the subject.

*what*      If a manuscript, original document, or book is involved, give the full title (or a description if it doesn't have a title).

*where*      If the source is an individual, give his or her location should the reader wish to verify the information. (If the source is a published book, you would not, of course, want to say that it is located in the library. Instead, provide the same in-text documentation described below under *Secondary Sources.*)

    *what*      *who*          *where*
A letter from Roger T. Jerome, California State Assemblyman and
        *authority*
a self-professed expert on aardvarks, claims that aardvarks have become an uncontrolled problem near the campus area.

    *who*         *where*
Bud Walker, University of Missouri freshman, claims he
had never heard of aardvarks until he became mixed up
                *authority*
with a bad crowd. Today, however, Walker raises aardvarks
in his basement.

## Secondary Sources

For secondary sources (or published primary sources), the same general information is necessary, although *when* the information was published must be added. (Some instructors may also wish page numbers to be included in the text.)

         *who*
Ex-President Richard Nixon declared, "There were no aardvarks
         *where, when*
in my administration" (*Time,* Sept. 2, 1974).

   *who*        *authority*        *where*
Dr. Harold Bley, professor of zoology, Arizona State

*when*
University, asserts in his classic 1931 study on aardvarks,
*what*
*Cognitive Configurations of Snout Development,* that aardvarks
will inherit the earth (p. 231).

Direct quotations, paraphrases, and summaries all need to be attributed to a fully documented source.

Statistics, facts, ideas, inferences, and opinions should all be attributed to a fully documented source.

The reader needs to know specifically *who* your source is, *what* information you obtained from that source, *what* authority the source had
to speak on the subject, *where* the source can now be found (if primary
material) or *where* and *when* the information was printed.

You should recognize that this demand for accurate documentation
exists not only so that material can be verified by a second observer but
because the stronger the source of information, the stronger the facts will
seem to your reader, and the more thorough your investigation will
appear.

## The Full Investigation

Many college students spend almost all their research time in a library.
The professional writer recognizes that the variety of primary and secondary sources—and their location—is so extensive that actual library
research is only one small area of the imaginative investigation. Depending upon the subject, here's a partial list of sources that might be considered for an inquiry.

> memos
> court proceedings
> accountant's ledger
> journals
> surveys
> medical libraries
> state or city historical societies
> private libraries
> newspaper files
> hotel registers
> letters
> college catalogs
> business firms' libraries
> U.S. Government libraries or depositories
> office files
> museum and art-gallery libraries
> diaries

police reports and logs
magazines
record-album covers

Not all of these sources would be available to a college student, of course, but the writer who makes the extra effort—to interview, to write a congressman, to check a telephone log, to dig through some dusty archives—that is, the writer who is alive to the richness of his or her subject, knows that all ideas are related to the world we live in.

Here is how sophomore Mary Jo Loufman investigated the profits earned by a student-run book exchange. Mary Jo interviewed two student employees, an accountant, and the finance officer at the university. She studied the regulations published by the student senate several years earlier, the quarterly statement provided by the accountant (with permission of the president of Student Government), and the minutes of the student committee that supervised the exchange at the time. Her final report was six pages long. Here are the first three paragraphs.

| | |
|---|---|
| *5 W lead* | During the last three years the Student Book Exchange has accumulated more than 1,200 dollars in excess profits because the SBX Committee has lacked authority to |
| *Inference* | deal with the money. Apparently when the Student Book Exchange was founded in 1968, no one considered |
| *Verifiable fact* | that a profit might be earned. Today, the $1,200 sits in a savings account of the First National Bank drawing 5.5 percent interest. |
| *Primary source* | Carl Green, an outside accountant hired by the SBX Committee three years ago when he was a student |
| *Authority* | working on his Master's in Business Administration, states that there was no real bookkeeping procedure when he began. |
| *Quotation* | "Even though there had always been a 10 percent handling charge on every exchange, no one seemed to have any permanent records on how that money was |
| *Summary* | handled." Green claims to have found a shoe box of receipts for various expenses, but no ledgers or accounts. |
| *More authority* | Green now runs his own accounting business but has continued to work once or twice a month at the SBX office—an enlarged closet in the basement of the Student Union. It was Green's introduction of accounting practices that revealed that SBX could and did earn a profit. That was three years ago. But the *Student Book Exchange, Governing Rules and Procedures,* a four-page dittoed pamphlet written and signed by members of the 1967–68 student government committee that formed SBX, contains only one line dealing with how that 10 |

*Sources compared*

percent handling charge is to be spent: "Money accrued from the handling charge will be used to pay for all overhead expenses and student salaries." Green claims that is exactly what is now done. But SBX still has approximately $400 a year left over.

*Secondary source*

The student government committee that oversees the SBX is aware of the problem. The published minutes for September 9, 1976, and for October 23, 1976, both reveal that concern was expressed. On both occasions a motion was considered to bring the issue to the full senate for a recommendation. No action was taken.

*Summary of findings*

*Lack of action*

However, the same concern was shown in minutes from March 3, 1975, and September 13, 1974. No action was taken at those times either.

Mary Jo Loufman eventually drew together enough facts to demonstrate that a pattern of inaction and lack of leadership had allowed the profit to accumulate. Nor did she miss the result in human terms. The two part-time student employees of the SBX might have earned an extra two hundred dollars had the money been paid in salaries. Mary Jo sifted through pages of unrelated material to discover the evidence she needed. She read three years' worth of published committee minutes, and she studied financial accounts even though she knew little of accounting. When she combined the findings with other sources, she discovered a pattern—a lack of action, and a feeling by each person involved that it was someone else's concern.

An inquiry into probable truth requires responsibility, initiative, and determination. By combining personal observation, primary sources and secondary sources, you have all the tools you need to investigate almost any subject.

### EXERCISES

1. Once you've narrowed the focus of your investigation, you need to consider the types of sources you might seek out. Here's an example of how you could begin.

TOPIC: Grade Inflation at St. Mary's College

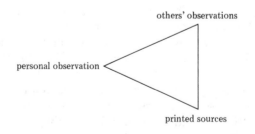

| **Personal Observation** | **Others' Observations** | **Printed Sources** |
|---|---|---|
| classroom experience | several instructors | computer printouts of grades |
| attitude of those you interview | dean of colleges | current grade averages |
| | registrar | from Dean |
| | alumni | statistics from |
| | several students | registrar |
| | | *Time, Newsweek, Chronicle of Higher Education* (for comparison to national patterns) |

Not every source will be available to you. Some sources won't provide you with information. You probably need a list twice as long as you actually plan to use just to allow for those sources that won't work out.

2. Discuss the following topics. Make a list of the various types of sources you might consider for a full investigation: back to basics movement in high schools; opportunities for women or minorities in college teaching; minority coaches in athletics; influence of federal financing or grants to college.

3. Here are four documented sources taken from student papers. Consider which are complete and informative, which have omitted essential elements needed for verification.

   a. Samuel B. Goldman, commission chairman, indicated in a speech to the accounting class on Friday that Minneapolis business conditions were unstable.

   b. As part of my study, I wrote to Georgia's Democratic congressman, Julian Bond. In a letter from his Washington office, dated January 3, 1973, he claimed to support the college-tuition tax credit for the following reasons . . .

   c. Bilingual programs were begun nationwide in all cities with more than 5 percent Chicano population, according to a *Time Magazine* interview with Dr. Kenneth Kriester, Title VII Coordinator for the U.S. Department of Health, Education and Welfare (*Time*, September 23, 1975).

   d. CBS News reported that the divorce rate had risen again in 1977 but so had the marriage rate.

4. In a sentence or two, provide all necessary documentation and the major facts for each of the following notes:

   a. "I believe the Charismatic Christian movement is just reaching its peak," *Religion Today*, Reverend Charles Mathaies, Jr., page 21, June, 1977, Church of the Good Pastor, Baltimore.

  b. Telephone conversation with Marilyn Chase, indicates that unemployment in the inner city areas is now 13 percent, mayoral candidate, councilwoman from 6th district, October 28th.

  c. P. 369, *The Origins of Evolutionary Theory,* P. Samuel Wyndcotyl, "Darwin was not the first to propose the concept of evolution," professor of biology, chairperson of the Biology Department at the University of Toronto, has published six books on evolution since 1955, copyright, 1972.

  d. "We are approaching an ecological disaster," Boston, Mass., John Pittston, Staley Lecture series, Thursday, March 5, 1975, Boston University, editor of the *Ecological Drift,* a collection of essays, spokesman for the Sierra Club.

## SUGGESTED WRITING ASSIGNMENT

Write a 1,000-to-1,500-word paper in which you investigate a narrowed subject. Choose a topic that offers the opportunity for personal observation, interviews (if possible), and access to primary and secondary sources. For example, you might want to investigate an institution (an institution involves buildings, customs, regulations, people, goals, activities, and much, much more). Your college, the local government, a nearby hospital, a library, or your place of employment might provide you with access if you have focused your inquiry on a specific concern: the latest increase in tuition or dormitory costs, the effectiveness of an urban jobs program, the entrance procedures at a hospital emergency room, the increasing theft of books and magazines from the open stacks.

Follow the steps you've read about in Chapters 18 and 19:

1. Narrow the focus from a general topic to major categories to one category and its specific components.

2. Design a series of questions using the various strategies for inquiry listed on page 182.

3. Investigate your sources. Use your own powers of observations; talk to people involved; search out primary and secondary sources.

4. As you investigate, evaluate your sources, evaluate the evidence, and interpret your findings (but avoid hasty conclusions that support your own bias).

Begin your inquiry now. Before you actually begin to write, however, read Chapter 20, "Imaginative Leads," and Chapter 21, "Visual Form."

# 20 *Imaginative Leads*

It was a pleasant summer day—warm with just a hint that it would grow hot and humid later on. Doctors moved quietly among a score of patients at the Jewish Chronic Disease Hospital in Brooklyn, giving them injections under the skin of one thigh. It was just a test of their immunity, the patients had been told. There was no real danger, though they "might feel a little discomfort and perhaps see a lump for a while." But there was one thing the patients weren't told: that the injections contained live cancer cells.

William Barry Furlong wrote the above paragraph as an introduction to an article in *Good Housekeeping*. Furlong might have written, "The subject of my report is about doctors who are experimenting with cancer on live human beings." He might have, but he didn't. Few professional writers begin an informative article or essay or even a business report with such a dull statement of purpose. As a writer you do want to tell your reader the subject of your paper. But there are boring ways and there are interesting ways.

You've already studied the 5 *W* lead in Chapter 15. Knowing other types of more imaginative leads can provide you with a surprising range of alternatives for effective introductions. Imaginative leads may be anything from a sentence to a page or more (depending on the length of the total writing project). Their intent is to involve the reader directly in some concrete element of the subject while also directly or indirectly presenting the underlying idea. The imaginative lead attempts to catch the reader's interest through the use of quotation, a question, a dramatized conflict, suspense, humor or shock—and then to lead clearly and logically into the subject itself. The lead should set the tone, provide the underlying idea of your paper, and even suggest to the reader the organization of the essay that follows. A lot for a few sentences to accomplish, but perhaps it explains why professional writers put so much emphasis on the value of the lead. Donald M. Murray, essayest, novelist, journalist, Pulitzer Prize winner, and teacher says that many writers spend 85 percent of their effort on the lead—not just to catch the reader's attention, but because of its focusing and organizing potential (Chapter 21 will go into more depth on how the lead suggests an organization).

## The Dramatic Lead

A bold, dramatic statement may be the easiest way to grab your reader's attention.

> The women's liberation movement has been a spectacular failure. Instead of freeing women to find the best qualities in themselves, it has condemned them to adopt the very worst qualities found in men.

Here a student writer has used a strong, declarative first sentence. It is actually a conclusion based on his investigation. The author does not present the facts, only the meaning he has interpreted from them. The result, standing by itself as the first sentence, can seem striking, challenging, even opinionated. But the reader is captured into reading on to see if indeed the author can support such boldness with concrete factual evidence or logical argument.

A dramatic or surprising lead may come from the situation itself rather than from a judgment about the situation as above. Here's the best example and probably the most famous lead of all time:

> In the beginning God created Heaven and earth.

Hard to stop reading at this point. The audience is almost trapped into continuing to see how He did it.

## The Contrast or Conflict Lead

Aldous Huxley was a master of the contrast lead:

> The most distressing thing that can happen to a prophet is to be proved wrong; the next most distressing thing is to be proved

right. In the twenty-five years that have elapsed since *Brave New World* was written, I have undergone both these experiences. Events have proved me distressingly wrong; and events have proved me distressingly right.

The paradox of this lead is so intriguing that the reader's interest is immediately captured. At the same time, Huxley clearly implies the focus of his topic (events confirmed or denied since the writing of his novel) as well as the probable design of the essay (half on events that proved to be right, half on events that proved wrong).

For some reason human beings have an eternal interest in conflict: cops and robbers, cowboys and Indians, girl and boy. Find a conflict or a clearly defined contrast, especially an unexpected one, and you'll probably have a natural lead paragraph.

The process of cloning may be one of the most beneficial discoveries ever made by mankind.

But cloning may also lead to loss of individual rights and freedom, political distatorship, and a more frightening world than even George Orwell imagined in *1984*.

This student writer has emphasized conflicting opinions by using two one-sentence paragraphs. Many teachers dislike the one-sentence paragraph and rightly so when it is used to make a random statement without further development, evidence, or support. In general, one-sentence paragraphs should be avoided except when a strong emphasis is desired—and that makes the lead an almost perfect place because a strong emphasis may be just what you need to catch the reader's attention.

## The Question Lead

The question lead can fail miserably if it seems to be a substitute for a more thoughtful or imaginative introduction. Try to avoid the rhetorical or dead-end question: *Can human beings live without love? What is the meaning of life? Should disease be wiped out?* A truly thoughtful question, however, can stimulate interest if it raises the reader's curiosity or seems to suggest an impact on the reader's own values, beliefs, or whatever. Here is a student lead that raises legitimate issues:

In 1974 the American Psychiatric Association voted to remove homosexuality from its category of mental illness. The ruling came after extensive gay lobbying. The new official definition uses the term "sexual orientation disturbances." But the action of the APA raises serious questions about psychiatry as a so-called science. Can the difference between illness and social deviation be determined by a vote instead of by empirically gathered evidence? If medical doctors decided to vote that a ruptured appendix is not an illness, would we accept the decision? And if psychiatrists have no more sound method for determining mental illness than by voting on it, how can we accept their testimony in, say, a trial for murder in which the accused has pleaded innocent by reason of insanity? Can psychiatry really be called a science if we know that, through lobbying and organized pressure, psychologists can so easily redefine the nature of abnormality?

In an age dominated by psychology, such questions have direct impact on us all. The question lead also sets up a natural organization for your paper: you have to answer your own question.

## Cumulative-Interest Lead

Seven dead of wounds. A twenty-one-year-old woman paralyzed from the neck down. Four widows. Twelve children left without fathers. Over $158,000 in medical and funeral expenses. Two hundred and six robberies. These were the statistics for one city—Los Angeles—during a single month without gun control legislation.

The cumulative-interest lead attempts to overwhelm the reader with a "pileup" of facts, sometimes without attaching the facts to any specific subject until several sentences into the essay. Dramatic lists or statistics seem to stimulate interest automatically.

The above lead comes from a student report. Even though it does not directly state the subject of the report, the tone and focus—even the conclusion—are implied. The author has presented a series of objective facts, yet each fact has been carefully selected for its impact. And the final sentence suggests the remainder of the paper will deal in more detail with gun control legislation. If, for some reason, the paper actually focused on robberies committed with guns, then the lead would be a failure because the last sentence implies a larger issue.

Here is a cumulative-interest lead from one of the most famous personality profiles ever printed in *Esquire:* "What Makes Sammy Run?" by Thomas B. Morgan.

In a typical ten-day period recently, Sammy Davis, Jr., had this schedule: the final week of an eighteen-day engagement at the Copacabana (sixteen performances interspersed with general frolicking, a record date, television and radio interviews, and two visits with Cye Martin, his tailor); a one-night stand in Kansas City to receive an Americanism award from the American Legion; one night at home in Hollywood and the opening night of a two-week

From "What Makes Sammy Run?" by Thomas B. Morgan. Originally appeared in *Esquire,* October 1959, and later in *Esquire: The Best of 40 Years,* 1973. Excerpted by courtesy of the author.

date in Las Vegas at the Sands Hotel. . . . The day after closing in Vegas, Davis was due for three weeks in Hollywood at the Moulin Rouge, another nightclub with which he has a five-year million dollar deal, followed by two weeks in Australia, followed by an Eastern tour. Photographer Burt Glinn and I, however, arbitrarily pursued Davis through that ten-day period . . . we wanted to find out what we could, naturally, about what makes Sammy, Jr., run.

Like all leads, this one begins to limit the subject, suggests a focus, and points to the overall organization of the essay.

## The Descriptive Lead

The descriptive lead might also be called the literary lead because it takes as its model the concept of the scene (see Chapter 10). Human beings have a natural interest in hearing stories. A scene, in effect, presents a story in miniature and is, therefore, one of the most popular and most effective means of concretely involving the reader.

> For more than half an hour thirty-eight respectable, law-abiding citizens in Queens watched a killer stalk and stab a woman in three separate attacks in Kew Gardens. Twice the sound of their voices and the sudden glow of their bedroom lights interrupted him and frightened him off. Each time he returned, sought her out, and stabbed again. Not one person telephoned the police during the assault; one witness called after the woman was dead.

The horror of this news story is intensified by *The New York Times* writer who takes us step-by-step through the event. We hear the voices, we see lights in bedroom windows, and perhaps imaginatively we see the killer's shadow stalking the young woman. Not until the final word of the paragraph do we learn the result. The emphasis we placed on sense perception in earlier chapters can be used with dramatic effectiveness in a descriptive lead. Here is student Laura Stone's opening paragraph for a sociology report on aging. She began by visiting a nursing home.

> The old woman sat with her hunched back to me. Her wheelchair faced the window that looked out on a Sunoco gas station. Greasy barrels and stacks of used rubber tires and cardboard boxes of worn-out auto parts lined the back of the station. The light coming through the window seemed greasy and faded. The old woman's hair was curled in ringlets and the light shone through giving her a halo effect. From the next room a TV voice announced that The World Turns. I made a halfhearted attempt at saying hello but the old woman did not move an inch. Over her bed hung a crucifix with a plastic rose taped to it. On a nightstand there were several bottles of green pills, pink false teeth soaking in a glass of water,

and several worn copies of *Reader's Digest.* I tried again. "Hello!" This time louder. "Hello!" Still the woman sat unmoving. The tile floors were polished, the white walls were newly painted. The bed was made. It was not a bad place. But the hunched old woman sat staring out through the window at the rear of a gas station, at the worn-out tires and generators and dead batteries.

Actually, the various types of leads are limited only by your own imagination. Furlong's lead, used at the beginning of this chapter, describing doctors injecting cancer cells into live patients, is a combination of the literary lead and the surprising statement. You could easily combine a question lead with a contrast lead or a literary lead with conflict, and so on.

It should be emphasized that a lead is not necessary. You can write an adequate informative investigation or essay without one or by using a factual, 5 *W* lead. Most students and beginning writers never use leads. Yet a lead establishes a feeling of professionalism from the first sentence; it catches our imagination and makes us think, "Now here's a writer who seems to have something to say." Leads can do for you what almost no other writing technique can: capture the audience, set mood or tone, suggest the focus and organization of your essay, and psychologically prepare the reader to be more receptive to your ideas—all at the same time.

## Finding the Lead

Few professional writers wait until they have gathered all details on a subject before writing the lead. They train themselves to search out leads *at the same time* they are investigating the subject. Leads, therefore, directly relate to the perception phase as well as to form and the first draft. If you come across a good quotation, an element of conflict, a dramatic change, a sensuous scene, or some startling fact, test it immediately in your mind: would this make a good lead? If you can come up with a lead *before* you ever sit down to write, you will have solved one of those inhibitions to writing: facing the blank page. There won't be a blank page. Instead, you'll have a sentence or a paragraph already in mind. Leads thus play a vital role for the writer as well as the reader. Knowing in advance that you've got the first sentence or first paragraph helps to release tension, helps to release the flow of ideas so that writing gets off to a good start.

Never trust yourself, however, to take the first lead that comes along. Keep looking. A better one may turn up as you explore your subject further. Always try to write out several leads before you settle on the best. Try them on friends. Read several leads aloud to a roommate. Find out which one the listener would be most responsive to, which would make him or her want to hear more. Some professional writers admit that they spend as much time on the lead as on all the rest of their essay.

On the other hand, if you haven't been able to identify a good lead during the investigation of the subject, go ahead and begin your first draft. You may find that in writing the paper a lead will appear in the middle of it or even in the last sentence. Many a writer has discovered that his or her conclusion made a better lead than it did a final paragraph. Don't be afraid to move sentences and paragraphs around. Remember that the first draft is only a process of discovery, and what you may discover is that a scene or fact or detail you hadn't recognized as striking makes a natural introduction around which the rest of your ideas logically group themselves. In other words, let the lead work for you. Try to find it while studying the subject, but if you can't, don't panic. Let it find you during the writing process itself.

### EXERCISES

1. Read each of the following leads. Discuss the technique the writer seems to be using. What type of tone or mood, if any, is established? From the brief sentence or paragraph provided, what probable design or organization of the material would you expect to follow? What specific quality about each lead makes it interesting or would make you want to read on?

All happy families resemble one another, but each unhappy family is unhappy in its own way.

—Tolstoy, *Anna Karenina*

*Ben-Hur,* as everyone knows, cost $15,000,000 to make, runs for almost four hours, has a cast variously estimated at 50,000 (by Metro-Goldwyn-Mayer) and at 10,400 (by *Time*), was directed by William Wyler, and has had the biggest advance sale ($500,000) in film history. But what no one knows who hasn't seen it is that it is lousy.

—Dwight MacDonald, *Esquire*

Politics is war without bloodshed. War is politics with bloodshed. Politics has its particular characteristics which differentiate it from war. When the peaceful means of politics are exhausted and the people do not get what they want, politics are continued. Usually it ends up in physical conflict which is called war, which is also political.

—Huey P. Newton, *The Black Panther*

They lined up four abreast, blue-clad laborers in plastic hard hats, soldiers in khaki uniforms, Tibetans and Yunanese mountain tribesmen in gaudy native costumes. Their vigil in the sprawling Gate of Heavenly Peace Square had begun at dawn. Some wept, some bowed their heads, some stared into space. Precisely at 10

A.M., the massive glass doors of the Great Hall of the People swung open, and the first of the mourners filed in to pay their final, wondering respects to Chairman Mao-Tse-tung. Throughout the day, the specially selected representatives of the Chinese masses, shuffled slowly and silently past Mao's bier, and with each passing hour, trucks and busses brought thousands more of them into the heart of Peking to view the body of China's fallen hero.

*—Time*

In the past few decades, man has become capable of controlling almost every aspect of life through modern equipment and increased knowledge and insight into and about the human body. But these medical and technical advances are having a dual effect. True, in many instances, they are prolonging life. But in many other cases, they are more accurately prolonging death.

—Student research paper

Once upon a time and very good time it was there was a moocow coming down along the road and this moocow that was coming down along the road met a nicens little boy named baby tuckoo. . . .

His father told him that story: his father looked at him through a glass: he had a hairy face.

He was baby tuckoo. The moocow came down the road where Betty Byrne lived: she sold lemon platt . . .

When you wet the bed first it is warm then it gets cold. His mother put on the oilsheet. That had the queer smell.

—James Joyce, *A Portrait of the Artist as a Young Man*

When in the Course of human Events, it becomes necessary for one People to dissolve the Political Bands which have connected them with another, and to assume among the Powers of the Earth, the separate and equal Station to which the Laws of Nature and of Nature's God entitled them, a decent Respect to the Opinions of Mankind requires that they should declare the causes which impel them to the Separation.

—Thomas Jefferson, *Declaration of Independence*

2. Create three different types of leads based on the following collection of material. Assume that this material represents the core of observations and research you have made on your subject. Which elements would be most interesting to begin with? Which elements might suggest a way of organizing the rest of the material?

   a. Marietta Bowker has lived in Bay's End, Maine, for her whole life, some ninety-three years.
   b. She raises strawberries, cabbage, corn, and tomatoes.
   c. She now walks with a cane.
   d. When she was sixteen, she married Harold Bowker and gave birth to thirteen children in the next fifteen years.
   e. "I drink a nip of whiskey every day, and sometimes I smoke a cigar," she says, laughing.
   f. She wears a red dress with white lilies on it.
   g. The ocean breezes blow through the open window of her house.
   h. Her six books of poetry have never sold more than fifty copies apiece.
   i. There are geraniums on her windowsill.
   j. She has outlived her husband and seven of her children, but she has thirty-two grandchildren and nine great-grandchildren.
   k. She last went to the movies in 1932.
   l. She walks five miles a day.
   m. She doesn't know why she has lived so long.
   n. "I just regret I didn't write more poetry," she says.

   3. Return to one of your earlier assignments and write at least three different leads for it. For example, if you wrote an objective report for Part Three, try to come up with three new ways of beginning the same paper. Write a descriptive lead, a contrast lead, and a bold statement.

   4. As audience and intention make a difference in how you begin anything you write, choose a previous assignment or exercise, and write new leads addressed to several different audiences. For example, if you wrote a character sketch for Part Two, use the same material to create three new leads: one for an essay to be published in a psychological journal; another for an essay to be distributed anonymously to your peers in a sociology class; a third for an essay to be included in a new anthology entitled *Interesting Americans,* intended for sale to a general audience.

# 21   *Visual Form*

Aldous Huxley has stated that the writer must have the urge "first of all, to order the facts one observes and to give meaning to life." To discover the pattern formed by a series of facts is to find order and meaning. Your audience shares that need with you. It cannot see meaning in your work without form or pattern. Random facts are like those disconnected dots on the page of a child's coloring book. Only when the dots are connected and only when they are connected in recognizable shapes is meaning communicated. Without order, without form or design or plan, we have only chaos, and chaos is not meaningful.

The most simple example proves the point. Try mixing up the sequence for a butterscotch brownies recipe:

> Bake for 20 minutes.
> Stir into the butter mixture.
> Sprinkle flour on the dates and figs.
> Cut into bars and serve.
> Sift ½ cup of flour.
> Pour the batter into a greased pan.
> Chop the dates and figs.
> Grease pan.
> Melt ½ cup of butter in a saucepan.
> Cool the ingredients.
> Preheat oven to 350°.
> Beat in one egg.

Without the proper arrangement, nothing makes sense.

And just as there is no one recipe that serves all types of cooking, you should not expect any one pattern or method of organization to serve all types of writing. In a personal essay, the arrangement of the parts usually grows organically out of the experience you've had with the subject. In objective writing, form may sometimes grow out of the complex subject-audience-context-purpose, or it may be based on an imitation of a traditional design. In the formal research paper, organization is usually constructed around a conventional thesis design. The frustrating part about "ordering the facts" is that for every set of facts there always seems to be a different order.

## How the Lead Suggests Form

In many cases the organization of a paper can be discovered in the process of searching out the best lead. We've already noted how the 5 $W$ lead suggested a natural sequence for an objective report. As the 5 $W$ structure provides all major information in the first few sentences, it follows logically that less and less important information must trail behind. The visual design illustrates the form.

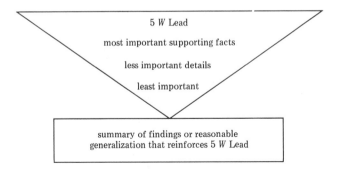

5 $W$ Lead

most important supporting facts

less important details

least important

summary of findings or reasonable
generalization that reinforces 5 $W$ Lead

Note, however, that the lead does not *create* form. Rather, in the process of searching for a lead, you find that you must sift through all the information you have gathered; you must question the value, meaning, and worth of it; and you must consider your audience, purpose, and context. Each of these factors affects your choice of a lead. But these are the same factors that influence overall organization. In the process of looking for a lead, the mind wrestles with the shape of the subject itself. Just as the 4 $C$ method of investigation gives you a strategy for finding potential meaning in a subject, so the lead gives you a strategy—a method—for finding an effective form. A lead is never something patched onto the beginning of an essay merely to make the introduction interesting. A lead is integral to the whole body of material you are working with.

As we are visually oriented creatures, professional writers have developed several specific diagrams to help themselves envision forms that often grow out of the imaginative leads discussed in the previous chapter. Once you've found a possible lead, you can test your material against the visual diagram associated with it. If the subject or some other factor suggests that this organizational pattern won't work, then you'll know that your lead doesn't truly *lead*. But if the visual pattern does correspond to your material, you're ready to write.

## The Dramatic Lead Design

Because the surprising or dramatic lead is usually a bold generalization of some sort—and usually judgmental—the nature of the lead demands that it be supported with objective evidence. Once the facts and data have been given, the strength of the lead is then reinforced by repeating it as the conclusion, usually with different wording.

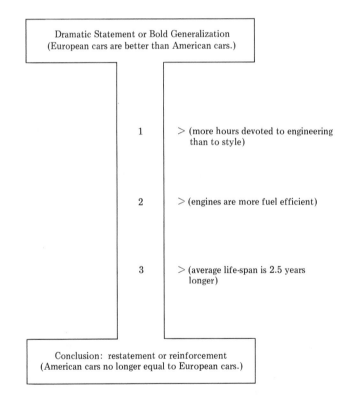

The sequence of the facts in the middle of the paper may be organized either from most important to least important or the reverse. Good arguments have been presented for both methods. By starting with your weakest facts and building to your strongest, you raise the intensity of your paper as you progress and hope to sweep the reader along with you. On the other hand, by beginning with your strongest points, you hope to demonstrate immediately the truth of your bold generalizations by providing overwhelming evidence. In the above example, I've organized from "least to most." To me, the number of hours spent on engineering is not as important as the results—better fuel efficiency and longer life. Either organization method may be effective. But do have a method: don't jump randomly from strong point to weak point. Begin forcefully, present your facts in a planned sequence, and end forcefully.

## The Contrast Design

A lead that calls attention to some type of opposition implies to the reader that you will deal equally and fairly with both sides of the conflict. For example, if you investigated the latest increase in tuition, you would find many students opposed; but you would also find explanations in support of it, perhaps from administrators. On a larger scale, an investigation of welfare costs might turn up many who would justify a large federal budget and others who would oppose it. The easiest way of organizing such information is to group all facts supporting one position into the first half of your report and all facts supporting the other position in the second half.

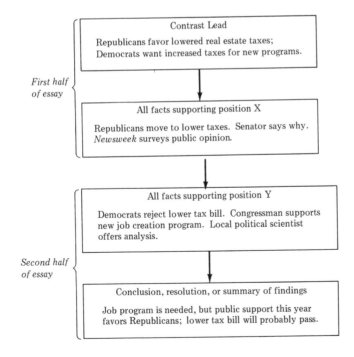

This organization has the benefit of simplicity both for you and the reader. But it is not the only organization for contrasting material. A second method reveals the conflict more directly by alternating facts supporting one position with facts supporting the other (this is usually done by giving a paragraph or a page to each in alternating sequence). Most of us like a good debate. A back-and-forth exchange creates the tension and interest of two good debaters.

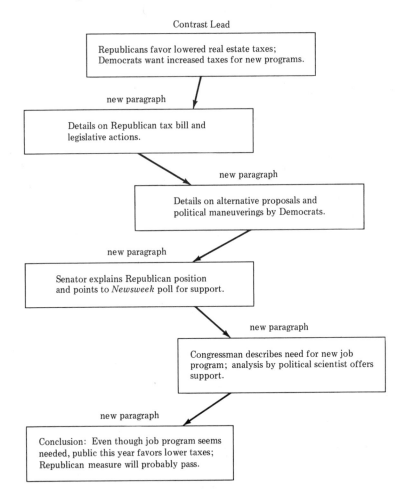

Contrast Lead

Republicans favor lowered real estate taxes;
Democrats want increased taxes for new programs.

new paragraph

Details on Republican tax bill and
legislative actions.

new paragraph

Details on alternative proposals and
political maneuverings by Democrats.

new paragraph

Senator explains Republican position
and points to *Newsweek* poll for support.

new paragraph

Congressman describes need for new job
program; analysis by political scientist offers
support.

new paragraph

Conclusion: Even though job program seems
needed, public this year favors lower taxes;
Republican measure will probably pass.

A word of caution, however. The alternating method of organization is more difficult for both reader and writer. Unless clear transitions are used at each changeover, the reader can easily become lost. Gather a good supply of transitions before you begin: *however, by contrast, in opposition to that view, but, on the other hand,* and so on. (See Chapter 25 for a further discussion of transitions.)

# The Literary Design

Both the *cumulative-interest lead* and the *descriptive lead* suggest the possibility of moving from the specific details with which each begins toward a more general or abstract understanding of the details. The conclusion, as in a work of literature, remains in suspense until the final page. This type of organization is the opposite of the inverted pyramid.

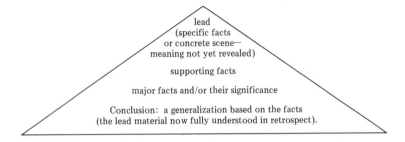

The literary-lead design has several major advantages for the objective investigation or personal essay written in a humanities or social science course. The nature of the lead captures the reader's interest immediately; the ever-increasing importance of the details maintains interest and builds step-by-step toward what you hope will be seen as an inevitable conclusion. The form suggests a logical mind at work and tends to lead the reader toward accepting the concluding generalization. As in reading a mystery novel, the reader continues to the end in order to discover the fullest realization of facts you've perceived.

If we now consider the *lead* in retrospect, we see that its role in writing can be central both for reader and writer. For the reader, a lead creates interest and captures attention. It suggests tone, mood, and direction. For the writer, it provides an excellent method of getting started on the first draft. And it suggests a design or organization for the report as a whole. Finding order in your subject need not be quite as overwhelming if, in the process of selecting the best lead, you also discover an organizational pattern for all that follows. Perhaps that's why professional writers willingly spend so much time on leads. They know that once the lead is set, the remainder of the paper will flow more easily.

Ultimately, of course, form grows out of content, not out of a predetermined diagram. Visual designs are not a substitute for engaging your mind with the subject. They offer only outlines that may help you "see" the content and discover its potential.

### EXERCISES

1. Three groupings of facts are collected below. Study the relationship within each group, and determine which of the visual designs discussed in this chapter might be best for organizing the facts. Draw the

design on a full sheet of paper, and test your proposal by filling in the appropriate spaces.

a. • Airlines and trucking should not be regulated, according to Congressman Smith.
   • Government statistics show higher costs owing to regulation.
   • Airline executives and trucking owners want regulations to continue.
   • Some costs are double because of regulations.
   • Economic analysts in Washington say that industry fears competition if regulations are removed.
   • Regulations allow small companies to survive, according to the secretary of commerce.

b. • The price of gold has gone up.
   • Oil nations want more dollars for oil.
   • Inflation is increasing.
   • The president announces, "I will support the dollar."
   • A local economist fears a recession.
   • The danger to our economy was never greater.

c. • The board of regents is concerned about a balanced budget.
   • Six men have gathered in the board-of-regents room; afternoon light filters in; coffee cups clank; discussion is heated; voices rise.
   • Board members agree to reinvest the funds in a local shoe factory.
   • Outside the windows 200 students with signs march in a circle.
   • The return on the investment is enough to pay for five faculty salaries.
   • The students are concerned about moral values.
   • Students are protesting having university funds invested in a foreign country.
   • A student leader says the funds support racism and dictatorship.
   • An investigation of the financial statement reveals that 10 percent of the funds are invested in foreign countries.

2. Study the readings included at the end of this unit. What relationship between the lead and overall design can you identify? Could you make a visual outline of the last paper you wrote for this or any other class?

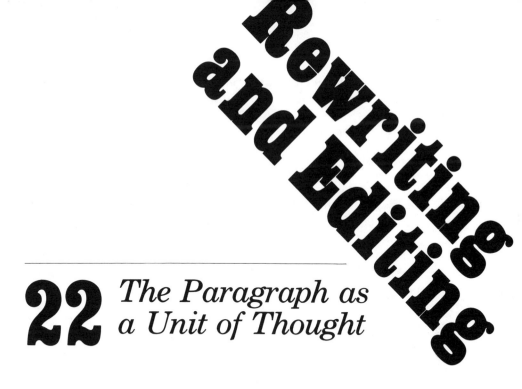

# 22 *The Paragraph as a Unit of Thought*

The more you practice writing, the clearer it becomes that order and form are integral to every phase. A sentence itself involves an ordering—using a subject, verb, and object in a sequence that communicates meaning. The next largest unit of form, the paragraph, is based on the same principle. Paragraphs must have a beginning, a middle, and an end that communicate meaning. By this point in your life, most of you have been using paragraphs as a natural device that requires little conscious thought. And that's how it should be during the first draft. During the first stages of writing your attention should be focused on the subject, not on the form. But when you reach the rewriting-and-editing phase, a more conscious attention must often be directed at the unity of each paragraph. Acting as your own editor, you must distance yourself from the material and reconsider whether sentences work in harmony to develop, illustrate or prove your point effectively. Each paragraph must be considered in its own right, as a whole, as well as part of the larger whole.

## The Ideal Paragraph

Everyone knows there can be as many different kinds of paragraphs as there are writers and subjects, but by becoming familiar with the shape and organization of the paragraph most writers and scholars think of as the standard model, you have something against which you can test your own work.

The ideal paragraph has six major components:

1. All material in the paragraph must relate to a single *unifying idea* either by providing concrete support for the idea or by logically developing or expanding a specific point or by illustrating the idea through example, anecdote, or scene.

2. The unifying idea must be developed fully, either through argument or evidence, so that the reader feels a sense of *completeness*.

3. At some point in the paragraph—usually toward the beginning, sometimes at the end—the single unifying idea must be clearly stated. Teachers often call this the *topic sentence,* that is, a sentence announcing the primary concept that holds the paragraph together.

4. Each sentence in the paragraph must lead into the next with some kind of reasonable progression so that the reader feels a sense of *coherence*.

5. The paragraph must have a *conclusion*.

6. To be effective, the paragraph should have a point of *emphasis*. The emphasis usually coincides with either the topic sentence or the conclusion.

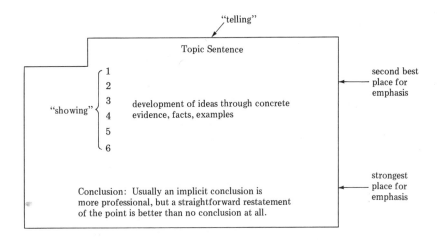

As many have long noted, this so-called ideal paragraph has the same formal requirements as an essay itself. We can even think of the best paragraphs as mini-essays, each of which is linked together to form a larger essay. Here is such a model paragraph from Henry David Thoreau, who seemed to write nothing but model paragraphs.

| | |
|---|---|
| *Transition from previous paragraph* | I left the woods for as good a reason as I went there. Perhaps it seemed to me that I had several more lives to live, and could not spare any more time for that |
| *Topic sentence announces unifying idea* | one. It is remarkable how easily and insensibly we fall into a particular route, and make a beaten track for ourselves. I had not lived there a week before my feet wore a path from my door to the pondside; and though it is five or six years since I trod it, it is still quite distinct. It |
| *Concrete details illustrate idea* | is true, I fear that others may have fallen into it, and so helped to keep it open. The surface of the earth is soft and impressible by the feet of men; and so with the paths which the mind travels. How worn and dusty, then, must be the highways of the world, how deep the |
| *Emphasis* | ruts of tradition and conformity! I did not wish to take a cabin passage, but rather to go before the mast and on the deck of the world, for there I could best see the moonlight amid the mountains. I do not wish to go |
| *Conclusion* | below now. |

Here is another model paragraph, this time from a student paper on the investigation of a local abortion clinic:

| | |
|---|---|
| *Transition from previous paragraph* *Topic sentence* | But not all the women were embarrassed. A significant number of those that I spoke with felt defiant or perhaps even angry, although they too expressed regret. One woman in her twenties, attractive and dressed in Gucci shoes, silk dress, and leather purse, told me that the demonstrators outside had attacked her. "I have a |
| *Concrete facts, quotations, opinions support main idea* | constitutional right to make my own decisions," she said. "I don't tell them what to do with their bodies; they have no right to tell me what to do with mine." Another women who was thirty-six years old and a mother of four children, was equally defiant. "My husband makes $12,000 a year. You tell me how we're supposed to feed four kids and two adults on $12,000." To have another child, she told me, would mean to con- |
| *Conclusion* | demn it to low nutrition, poor clothing, poor education. The defiant woman felt angry that the Right-to-Life crowd outside supported a principle without recognizing the consequences of the principle to both the mother |
| *Emphasis* | and child. "They want life," one woman told me, "even when it means condemning a child to a life of misery." |

# Editing the Paragraph

Three common approaches have been developed for editing paragraphs, depending upon the stage of work you have reached.

## Summarizing the Central Idea

Immediately after completing a first draft, you may find you are still searching for the idea itself. You may have facts but not yet have relationships. The first draft may be "close," but something tells you that you haven't yet said what you want. This is the point to study each paragraph and summarize *in one sentence* what you think the main idea *suggested* by the paragraph ought to be. Forcing yourself to summarize in a single sentence is excellent discipline for the mind, but don't expect to achieve a topic sentence on the first try. Try several sentences. Be patient, and let yourself discover the meaning as you work with the words on the page.

Here is a first-draft paragraph by freshman Lisa Brown that doesn't yet have a point.

> Most men probably don't believe that smoking Marlboro makes them more masculine. They didn't even have this much advertising until after World War II according to *Advertising Age*. What is it exactly that the advertiser is trying to do? The latest advertisement for the Corvair pictures three girls in bikinis playing volleyball on the beach with the car parked behind them. You have to look through the girls to see the car. Vance Packard wrote a book on *The Hidden Persuaders* in advertising that tries to make us afraid of our body odors or makes us have a false hope that our lives will be better if we buy a new model toaster. A Colonel Sanders TV commercial recently showed a working mother dancing around the table with her children when the father brings home a bucket of fried chicken, as if joy was the essence of chicken.

Lisa worked on this paragraph during an in-class editing session. Here is the first single-sentence summary she tried:

> What is it that advertising is trying to do to us?

Fair, but many of the facts in her paragraph don't seem to relate to the question as such. Here's the second effort:

> Advertising tries to persuade us that our lives will be better or at least different if we will only buy their product.

Better, but at least one more refinement is necessary:

> Advertising seems to have two goals—first to seduce us into looking at or reading the advertisements, and then to convince us that in some way our lives will be better if we will only buy something.

Most of the different points in the original paragraph are now covered by this summary. The sentence on how much advertising has developed since World War II will have to be eliminated or moved to another part of the paper. It no longer contributes to the unifying idea. The other sentences will need reorganizing.

## Rearranging Sentences

When the central idea of a paragraph is unified, the next stage is to order the supporting facts in some type of sequence. The most basic principle of organization states that like materials should be arranged together: the closer the likeness, the closer the arrangement. Lisa numbered each sentence of her paragraph, arranging the numbers in two columns according to the two points in her summary. Then, using her summary sentence as a topic sentence, she rewrote. As she did, other ideas came to her and the paragraph began to take on more details; a sense of adequacy or completeness developed.

| | |
|---|---|
| *Topic sentence* | Advertising seems to have two goals—first, to seduce us into looking at or reading the advertisement, and then to convince us that in some way our lives will |
| *Supporting facts and interpretation of first point in topic sentence* | be better if we will only buy. The latest advertisement for the Corvair pictures three girls in bikinis playing volleyball on a beach with the Corvair parked behind them. We have to look through the girls to see the car. The function of the sexy girls seems not so much to suggest that we should think that the car is sexy as to attract our attention. The words on the page deal with gear ratios, engine horsepower, and electronic ignition. Not sex. An advertisement for Marlboro shows a cool green mountain setting with a masculine cowboy on his horse. The object is obviously not to sell real estate or horses, but to attract our attention. The words on the page talk |
| *Supporting facts and interpretation of second point in topic sentence* | about nicotine and tar. But once the advertiser has our attention, he also wants us to buy, and he seems to argue that by buying we will improve our lives. Perhaps by implication, a man will think he is more masculine if he smokes Marlboros. Colonel Sanders has a commercial on TV where a working mother and her children |
| *Transition to lead reader to next paragraph* | dance around the table when the father brings home a bucket of chicken. The obvious suggestion is that all of us will feel joyful if we'll only buy. But will we? |

Lisa Brown has grouped related ideas to support a topic sentence so that the whole of it has coherence—it hangs together. And although she has no conclusion, she does provide a final sentence that ought to lead the reader clearly into the next paragraph, where we can assume some further interpretation will be provided.

Lisa isn't finished, however. The editing of the paragraph needs one final step.

# Reading Aloud

Writing is a voice symbolized upon the page. As readers, we "hear" the voice in our imagination. As a writer, reading aloud reminds you both of the existence of an audience and of your own voice speaking to that audience. You grow more aware of how your writing "sounds" to other readers.

Lisa's final paragraph seems coherent, but the sentences are still awkward and unnatural in places. By reading her work aloud, she could put herself in the place of an audience and detect any final breakdown in fluency, logic, or continuity. This technique is centuries old. Here is Samuel Butler, a nineteenth-century novelist:

> ... the mere act of reading aloud put his work before him in a new light and, by constraining his attention to every line, made him judge it more rigorously. I always intend to read, and generally do read, what I write aloud to some one; any one almost will do.... I feel weak places at once when I read aloud where I thought, as long as I read to myself only, that the passage was all right.

The oral reading occurs during the final editing stage. It can be helpful if you have an audience—a friend or roommate—but even reading to yourself slowly will help you pull together and polish each paragraph.

I would be less than candid, however, if I did not say that emphasis on perfect paragraphing has sometimes been carried to extremes. Many paragraph breaks exist only for the pleasure of the eye. A long paragraph of gray type looks boring and inhibiting. Even the so-called topic sentence is not sacred. Many effective paragraphs deal with a single, unified idea without ever formulating it into a topic sentence. And no writer that I know of ever used such a concept actually to compose a paragraph in the first draft (in spite of what some textbooks on the subject might say). Yet by knowing what the ideal paragraph looks like, you do have a model against which to test your own prose. Don't discard the model lightly. The often confused and disjointed writing that emerges from a first and even second draft must be edited. Eventually, each paragraph must develop an idea with *unity, coherence,* and *completeness.*

### EXERCISES

1. Here is a sampler of paragraphs for you to study. Some match the ideal; others use varying methods for development. The point is not to know, surely not to memorize, the 1,231 methods for organizing a paragraph, but to recognize that all good writing *is* organized and that conscious principles of unity can be applied to make your own more effective.

*Consider the*
*movement of*

This word *opinion* makes us stop and think. It is the word a hostess uses to bring to an end a discussion *this paragraph. What is the relationship of abstract to specific?*

that threatens to become acrimonious. It suggests that all points of view are equal; it reassures us, for it gives an inoffensive appearance to ideas by reducing them to the levels of tastes. All tastes are natural; all opinions are permitted. Tastes, colors, and opinions are not open to discussion. In the name of democratic institutions, in

*What is the unifying idea? How is emphasis achieved?*

the name of freedom of opinion, the anti-Semite asserts the right to preach the anti-Jewish crusade everywhere.

—Jean-Paul Sartre, *Anti-Semite and Jew*

*How does the first sentence prepare for the final two sentences?*

The chill night air brought a restlessness to many fish scattered widely throughout the sound. They were steely gray fish with large scales and a low, four-spined fin set on the back like a spread sail. The fish were mullet who had lived throughout the summer in the sound and estuary, roving solitary among the eel grass and widgeon grass, feeding on the litter of animal and vegetable fragments of the bottom mud. But every fall the mullet left the sound and made a far sea journey, in the course of which they brought forth the next generation. And so the first chill of fall stirred in the fish the feeling of the sea's rhythm and awakened the instinct of migration.

*Is there a topic sentence? Where?*

—Rachel Carson, *Under the Sea Wind*

*Locate the topic sentence. How much of the paragraph provides concrete support? How much is interpretation? How does the final sentence relate to the first?*

Minority programs have affected academic quality. At some schools the average SAT score of the disadvantaged students is nearly 200 points lower than that of other students (the national average for minorities is 100 points lower than that for non-minority students). Faced with that disparity of achievement in the classroom, the professor, feeling pressure from the minorities and suffering from white guilt, usually gives passing grades to minority students even if they are failing. But if failing students are given *C*'s, those students who would normally have earned *D*'s and *C*'s will have to be given *B*'s and *A*'s, or else, like Professor Eikopf, the professor would simply throw up his hands and give all students *A*'s.

—Alton Chase, "Skipping through College," *The Atlantic*

*What connecting words link each sentence to the one before or after? Underline them.*

Plutarch refers to a vulgar notion to the effect that females among lower animals were able to give birth to young without the aid of a male, provided they licked salt. In other words, salt was so powerful that like the shower of gold in the myth of Danae, it was able to per-

*Locate the unifying idea.*

*How does the example support the unifying idea?*

*The last sentence implies a relationship to the idea. What is it?*

form the physical (as well as the spiritual) functions of the male sex. The connection between salt and the idea of love is clear from the fact that there are a number of savage superstitions which involve the bridling of the passions at a particular time and for a particular purpose—and in such instances frequently the abstinence is not only from the joys of love, but also from the partaking of salt. For example, there are certain Indians of Mexico who revere a species of cactus. Every year the men go on a long journey for the purpose of gathering this sacred plant. From the time when the men depart to the day of the cactus festival the Indians are very careful in their conduct. Among the restrictions which they impose on themselves is that of complete restraint where human affections are concerned. Linked with this is the complete abstinence from salt.

—Philip E. Waterman, *The Story of Superstition*

*What is the organizing principle for each sentence?*

*How is the paragraph unified?*

They went down to the camp in black, but they came back to the town in white; they went down to the camp in ropes, they came back in chains of gold; they went down to the camp with their feet in fetters, but came back with their steps enlarged under them; they went also to the camp looking for death, but they came back from thence with assurance of life; they went down to the camp with heavy hearts, but came back with pipe and tabor playing before them.

—John Bunyon, *The Life and Death of Mr. Badman*

2. Here is a long passage that could use some paragraph breaks. Indicate where you would place them and justify your choice. Compare your decisions to the choices made by others in your class.

How long should your copy be? It depends on the product. If you are advertising chewing gum, there isn't much to tell, so make your copy short. If, on the other hand, you are advertising a product which has a great many different qualities to recommend it, write long copy; the more you tell, the more you sell. There is a universal belief in lay circles that people won't read long copy. Nothing could be farther from the truth. Claude Hopkins once wrote five pages of solid text for Schlitz beer. In a few months, Schlitz moved up from fifth place to first. I once wrote a page of solid text for Good Luck Margarine, with most gratifying results.

Research shows that readership falls off rapidly up to fifty words of copy, but drops very little between fifty and 500 words. In my first Rolls-Royce advertisement I used 719 words—piling one fascinating fact on another. In the last paragraph I wrote, "People who feel diffident about driving a Rolls-Royce can buy a Bentley." Judging from the number of motorists who picked up the word "diffident" and bandied it about, I concluded that the advertisement was thoroughly read. In the next one I used 1400 words. Every advertisement should be a *complete* sale pitch for your product. It is unrealistic to assume that consumers will read a *series* of advertisements for the same product. You should shoot the works in every advertisement, on the assumption that it is the only chance you will ever have to sell your product to the reader—*now or never*. Says Dr. Charles Edwards of the Graduate School of Retailing at New York University, "The more facts you tell, the more you sell. An advertisement's chance for success invariably increases as the number of pertinent merchandise facts included in the advertisement increase." In my first advertisement for Puerto Rico's Operation Bootstrap, I used 961 words, and persuaded Beradsley Ruml to sign them. Fourteen thousand readers clipped the coupon from this advertisement, and scores of them later established factories in Puerto Rico. The greatest professional satisfaction I have yet had is to see the prosperity in Puerto Rican communities which had lived on the edge of starvation for four hundred years before I wrote my advertisement. If I had confined myself to a few vacuous generalities, nothing would have happened.

—David Ogilvy, *Confessions of an Advertising Man*

## Editorial Checklist for Part Four
### *Factual Investigation*

_____ Have you focused on a single, specific component of your subject?

_____ Have you investigated *who, what, where, when,* and *why?*

_____ Have you looked for change, contrast, or significant consequences?

_____ Have you looked for those qualities that characterize a subject?

_____ Have you looked for and used both primary and secondary sources?

_____ Have you evaluated the worth of each source and the facts or opinions provided to you?

_____ Have you tried to find a pattern or relationship to the evidence that could lead to a reasonable interpretation?

_____ Have you accepted only surface answers, or have you pressed for deeper insights?

_____ Have you provided full in-text documentation of all sources and their authority to speak on the subject?

_____ Have you used an imaginative lead?

_____ Have you organized your report around some evident design?

_____ If you've used quotations, have you integrated them into your text?

_____ Have you checked each paragraph for unity, coherence, and completeness?

_____ Have you read aloud and listened to the rhythms of your sentences?

_____ Have you omitted unnecessary words and used strong verbs?

Debbie Zwick was a freshman majoring in elementary education when she wrote the following essay. After beginning with an imaginative lead, Debbie integrates both primary and secondary sources. Notice especially how her conclusion is made more effective by tying it back to the lead.

# Back to Basics: Good or Bad?

## Debbie Zwick

Afternoon sun glints through the window at the end of the hall. Students march single file to their next class. At every corner, adults monitor their charges' actions. No talking is permitted. The students' shoes clump on the tile floor. Is this a scene from a state reform school? No. It is one of the typical promises of the back-to-basics schools characterized in the 1978 February/March issue of *Today's Education.*

The back-to-basics movement began when the public became concerned about the effectiveness of today's schools. Fred M. Hechinger, a writer for *The New York Times,* reported in the same issue of *Today's Education* that "20 million Americans are functionally illiterate...." A special article in *U.S. News and World Report* (September 11, 1978) expressed similar findings: "Thirteen percent of all seventeen-year-olds are unable to read a newspaper, fill out a job application or calculate change at the checkout counter." Several sources note that scores on the National Scholastic Aptitude Test, a test designed to measure basic skills, have been declining since 1962.

Some parents and teachers blame the progressive movement of the 1960s for the decrease in basic skills among students. Instead of drilling students in the three Rs, the progressives offered a wider curriculum. Music, art, and foreign language courses were introduced. Vocational training gained immense popularity. But as test scores in basic skills declined, the public became dissatisfied with the progressive movement. Sources report that more parents are demanding local schools to return to traditional courses in reading, writing, and arithmetic. Many school administrators and teachers strongly support the back-to-basics movement, yet they are worried that the public is "drawing the strings too much" on liberal education. "Nothing is wrong with reaffirming the fundamental importance of the three Rs in the education of every child," declared Hechinger in *Today's Education.* "What is alarming is the direction the movement is taking in too many minds and too many school systems."

*U.S. News and World Report* and *Today's Education* indicate the trend of the back-to-basics movement: many people interpret the movement as a solution to problems concerning classroom discipline, declining test scores, and increasing school costs. Discipline has become the key word. Schools promoting the three Rs advocate strict enforcement of dress and discipline codes. The silent, single file march through the halls is only one of the typical promises of the back-to-basics schools. Other schools have defined their goals to Hechinger as ones that emphasize the need for "'systematic, factual, and disciplined subject matter [and] development of mind and character and of the values of truth, justice, and virtue.'"

Hechinger and many educators question the relevancy of such programs to the basics. Dr. Robert A. Kirkland, director of the Education Department at Western Miami College, stated in an interview on March 13, 1979, that "the basics won't provide the answer to classroom management. That matter is solely dependent on the teacher." The Council for Basic Education also disagrees with many of the basics schools' programs. An excerpt from a Council bulletin printed in *Today's Education* warns that "some of their programs contain simplistic battle cries of doubtful merit such as 'bring back the paddle,' 'teach truth, justice, and patriotism,' and 'what we need is a dress code.'"

Richard Pips, associate director of the National Education Commission, followed up Hechinger's report with an article discussing minimal competency standards in the February 1979 issue of *Teachers Journal*. According to Pips, thirty-one states have established some type of minimal competency standards within their schools. Although each state's approach varies, all identify the basic skill areas as reading, writing, and mathematics. Most programs rely on testing. In order to graduate, each student must pass a specially designed test. Some of the tests consist entirely of multiple-choice questions. Others require a student to apply skills in the basics by balancing a checkbook or writing a paragraph in perfect grammatical form.

Minimal competency tests are considered highly effective but are subject to the same limitations as other tests. Unfortunately, too many schools and parents equate learning with high test scores. Sources note that many teachers feel pressured to produce "acceptable" results. Some educators fear that frantic preparation for such tests distracts from the effective teaching of the basic skills. HEW Secretary Joseph A. Califano responded in Pips's article by stating, "Basic competency testing will be acceptable and effective only if we stress, along with its benefits, the critical limitations and dangers of testing. . . . The purpose of schools is not merely to produce high scores on achievement tests; it is also to educate children. . . ."

Hechinger and Pips noted that most individuals have linked the back-to-basics movement with an unrelated educational concern. Hechinger observed that rising school costs have caused taxpayers to change back-to-basics to a demand for "cutting out the frills." Robert Kirkland of Western Miami University commented, "This is the most devasting impact of the back-to-basics movement. I've observed through reading that several school districts use the term Back to Basics, when they really mean 'cut the budget.'" Kirkland believes that when people refer to frills, they are generally speaking about the fine arts. Usually, music and art are the first items that get taken off the curriculum. Then social studies and school newspapers go. "Personally," Kirkland stated, "I was glad to see a shift back to the basics, but it seems like this nation swings wide on many issues. Right now, education is swinging too far toward the basics and forgetting all the lessons we've learned about education in the past."

According to Hechinger, the present tendency to strip education to the three Rs may serve ironically to make the basic skills appear less useful to children. Past experience has demonstrated that children learn better in stimulating environments, yet the no-frills programs eliminate diversity. Knowledge in the basics can't be applied because the no-frills curriculums eliminate activities such as newspapers that require basic skills. Hechinger asks, "What is motivation if not getting the learner to connect the effort of acquiring skills with their application to something that is interesting and fun?" He also points out that many successful reading programs in the ghettos emphasize that reading can be fun. A typical factor of the antifrills supporters is to pack every classroom and have one teacher "running the show." Once again, past experience contradicts these people's views. Children tend to learn more in smaller classrooms that allow for more individualized help. Private schools have never deviated from this policy even though they have never strayed too far from the basics.

It would seem that many school systems have destroyed the true spirit of the back-to-basics movement. Although the progressive movement of the sixties may have swung the pendulum too far towards permissiveness, forcing students to march single file through school corridors will not improve their knowledge of the basics. The need for the basics in the schools is a definite one, yet the basics must be taught in a humane atmosphere, where art and music contribute to the total growth of the student. There is a lot more to living the good life than knowing how to balance a checkbook.

Roger Rapoport is a young free-lance writer who special-
izes in education and science, especially medicine, health,
and ecology. The following investigation of the job market
for college graduates is excerpted from *Esquire*.

# New Myth on Campus
## Roger Rapoport

In the union bookstore at Berkeley, the student government is sponsoring a show by makeup artist Tory Jeffrey, "creator of the
Mary Quant face." Jeffrey is a short man in a green shirt and he chats
pleasantly as he applies Greasepot to the lips, Blushbaby over the cheeks
and Jeepers Peepers around the eyes of one student after another. There
are about a dozen women lined up, waiting patiently for Jeffrey to work
on them. There are even a couple of curious men students on the edges of
the crowd. "If we had brought him here a year or two ago, he would have
been laughed off campus," says Margot Robb, the bookstore's supply-de-
partment manager. "But the kids are worrying about jobs this year.
Makeup is selling, nylons are selling, clothes are selling. They know these
things really count with recruiters. I guess that's why we've become the
top Mary Quant account in the Bay Area, outside of I. Magnin in San
Francisco."

Not far away, in his Eshleman Hall office, Willis Shotwell has just
finished what he figures to be his thirty-fifth phone call of the day, and is
preparing to see the first of ten students who have appointments with him
this afternoon. He works in the Office of Student Advising and Assistance
with premed, prelaw and pre-graduate-school students. He used to be Coordinator of Facilities and Regulations, and was known for his zeal in
prosecuting student radicals. By the Fall of 1973, Shotwell's office had run
out of students to prosecute, so he switched jobs. He estimates he sees an
average of sixty students a week. "I'm a lot more popular now than I used
to be, but I'm exhausted," Shotwell says. "We've got four thousand prelaw students here at Berkeley and they all seem to think they're going to
make it into law school. It's hard work getting them straightened out. The
competition is fantastic. This year Boalt Hall Law School had thirty-eight
hundred applications for two hundred ninety places."

The figures are prophetic. According to the American Council on
Education, twenty-four percent of all American freshmen want to be doctors, lawyers or teachers, apparently because—against all evidence—they
think those professions are "secure." Of course there *is* a shortage of doc-

tors in certain areas of the country, according to the A.M.A., but you can't become a doctor if you don't get into medical school, and at the moment there are 41,000 applicants competing for 14,400 medical-school places. There are also 86,000 applicants for 38,500 law-school openings and equivalent proportions of applicants to many other graduate-program places. Although in the last few years more students have gone to careers that aren't so difficult to crack—business management, allied health fields, accounting, et cetera—the *ideal* is still medicine, law or teaching, areas that combine practical skills and earning potential with "altruistic" aims. It's as if the illusion of the utopian Sixties had been replaced by the illusion of the pragmatic Seventies.

And the job market shows no sign of improving. Last year there were 117,000 positions available to the 231,000 certified elementary and secondary-school teachers looking for work, and the U.S. Office of Education predicts that by 1980, universities will be producing 50,500 Ph.D.'s annually and only one fifth of them can expect to find university jobs. The American Bar Association reports that there were 16,000 jobs for the 29,-000 lawyers admitted to the bar last year. Nixon Administration studies predict that about 9,800,000 college graduates will enter the labor force during the 1970's, but only 6,600,000 jobs requiring more than a high-school education will be waiting for them.

The economic rate of return on investment in higher education is only about eleven percent, according to Clark Kerr's Carnegie Commission on Higher Education. "Education may not 'pay off' as much and as certainly as we once thought," Kerr admitted recently. Kerr, the "father of the multiversity," is now earning his living studying colleges rather than running them; some members of his staff are former teachers and administrators who fled academe in the face of shrinking undergraduate enrollments.

Some students are no longer buying the higher-ed illusion. A drop of roughly ten percent in the proportion of high-school graduates attending college between 1968 and 1974 has left about 680,000 vacancies on American campuses. Schools as diverse as Wisconsin, Southern Illinois, Indiana State and Antioch have fired both tenured and non-tenured faculty in the last several years. An advertisement for an assistant professor's job in the English department at Missouri Southern State College recently drew 253 applications from candidates at 101 different schools. Ninety-one applicants were Ph.D.'s. The job paid $10,500 to $12,000.

The decrease in undergraduate enrollment has to do with the ending of the draft, the greater earning potential of blue-collar jobs like plumbing and electrician work (an electrician can expect to average $20,000 a year after five years as an "apprentice," whereas college professors can only expect to earn $18,000 annually after twenty years on the job), and the trend to "stop-out," what the Carnegie Commission calls the period of drifting that many high-school and college graduates go through these days before deciding what they *really* want to do.

However the mass of students still are plugged into the current illusion, and a good part of its pervasiveness is due to a simple lack of information. The rest of its pervasiveness is due to the efforts of hard-sell admissions officers.

"When enrollments began to fall off, many schools took a note from business and increased their sales-recruiting force," explains Ted S. Cooper, executive director of the National Association of College Admissions Counselors. Getting the names of prospects is crucial. For a time, one Oregon school offered its students cash bounties for new recruits. Other schools turned to the alumni—who they traditionally resist when the latter try to high-pressure them into admitting unqualified applicants.

Obviously, this kind of recruiting pressure means reasonably qualified students no longer have to sweat out admission. With the exception of schools like Harvard, they can attend any university or college they can pay for. The University of Southern California, for example, filled its freshman class last fall by accepting seventy-five percent of all applicants. Attitude and emphasis, however, are another matter.

Professor Mark Green, who taught organic chemistry at the University of Michigan last year, laments that "the classes were jammed with premed kids only interested in getting A's. Instead of having a faculty teaching chemistry you end up with one that exists to judge people's credentials to get into medical school." Throughout the premed course, Green said, the pressure of competition led to systematic cheating. Some premed students found the identity of unknown compounds without bothering to experiment. They simply bought information from chemistry-store employees who prepared the test compounds for the student labs. Steve Nissen, who worked as a Michigan chemistry grader and tutor last year: "The premed kids are very candid. They told me they were willing to lie, cheat, steal, sabotage or do anything else it takes to get into medical school." The day after exams were handed back, Nissen recalls, an average of fifty people would line up at his office door, all clamoring for a few extra points. Many had made crude attempts to change wrong answers and tried to bluff their way to better grades. "It makes you wonder about the kinds of people who are going to become doctors," Nissen, who is now enrolled at the University of California's Irvine medical school himself, observes.

Premed students simply won't take no for an answer. A Stanford survey shows many of those turned down for med school hope to reapply. About 1700 rejected American applicants have enrolled at the University of Guadalajara medical school in Mexico, where tuition is $4,000 a year, despite the fact that severe restrictions make it difficult for most Guadalajara graduates to practice in this country. Within four years, if the current enrollment rate keeps up, the school will be graduating more American medical students than any medical school in the United States.

Although Ph.D.'s in the physical and life sciences can find work in government and industry, eighty-five to ninety-five percent of those taking humanities doctorates have gone into college teaching, which is one of the hardest hit areas today. English departments find the problem particularly serious. Even the Berkeley English department, which ranks second only to Yale, is having trouble placing its graduates. In 1973, twenty-four of the fifty-five graduates searching for college teaching jobs found them. By last May only fifteen of sixty-two Berkeley candidates had been hired. And that is a better record than most departments can claim.

Dismal employment prospects have dissuaded some Berkeley English students from finishing their theses. One explains: "I've been on my last chapter for two years. I don't want to finish because that would mean giving up my teaching-assistant position here and force me to begin repaying four thousand dollars' worth of student loans. Of course, the fact that I haven't finished my thesis hurts my chances of getting a tenured job elsewhere. But without some guarantee of employment I'm afraid to complete the thing and lose my Berkeley job. I may be here forever."

Although Berkeley took only forty new graduate English students this fall, applications keep coming in at the rate of about five hundred a year. "People are programmed to get degrees," a graduate student admits. "We all think we're the best and that, somehow, people will beg for us when we get out."

Predictably, this vocational pressure has worked to reverse innovations that were supposed to improve the quality of American education. In 1969 nearly a third of Harvard Law School's freshman class elected to take the pass/fail option. Last winter, the alternative grading system was dropped due to a lack of student interest. "The problem," according to David Hollander, a 1974 Harvard law graduate, "is that students began to realize that taking courses pass/fail hurt their employment prospects. Now everyone *wants* those grades."

Of course you really can't expect colleges caught in a zero-growth situation to warn undergraduates off because they aren't likely to get into graduate schools or find jobs. They can't just declare a "holiday" like Roosevelt did with the banks when *their* spiral got out of hand. The only thing colleges are able to do is wait and hope for things to change, and keep on doing what they were taught to do.

Phyllis Zagano was a lecturer at the State University of New York at Stony Brook when she set out to investigate the business of selling term papers. The result produced the following essay, first printed in *The Chronicle of Higher Education*. Although the voice is informal, Zagano presents the facts objectively, withholding her own judgment until the end.

# Hey Kid, Wanna Buy a Used Term Paper?
## Phyllis Zagano

The term-paper companies that gained considerable notoriety in the early 1970's are neither gone nor forgotten. Ready-made term papers, once hawked from dingy storefronts near college campuses, are now offered for sale through the mails. Affluent students can purchase by mail papers that are written to their specifications.

During the past few months, I've completed the same procedure any enterprising student with a Master Charge card can go through if he's unwilling to write an assigned paper. All it takes is a few weeks and between $14 and $35 to get any assignment, no matter how specialized, written by someone else.

Just days after I wrote to Research Assistance, Inc., in Los Angeles, I held in my hands Volume 6 of the "Nation's Most Extensive Library of Research Material"—184 closely typed pages of merchandise with a table of contents running from Advertising to Women Studies (*sic*). I had over 6,000 titles from which to choose. I chose two: No. 1439, "The Treatment of Death by Emily Dickinson" ("Contends that the poet's attitude toward death influenced her use of words in unconventional ways. Quotes from poems and critics. f.n. Bib. 5pp.") and No. 3473, "American Literature from Colonial Times to the 1860's" ("Reviews several books to illustrate their contrasting of Civilized [Old World] and Wilderness life [New World] 5pp."). Each retailed for $13.75. The unimpressive results seemed to be photocopies of papers previously submitted elsewhere. One had handwritten corrections and comments on it. But, undaunted, I continued with my plan.

Professors Miriam Baker and Peter Shaw, of the Stony Brook English Department, had both agreed in advance to read "my" papers. Well, I got the papers back the other day, and it seems that the classic rip-off can be a rip-off itself. Shaw gave me a C-minus. Baker failed me. Baker, an assistant professor of English and a Dickinson scholar, wrote that "the writer failed utterly to make any genuine statement about the poet as an artist and instead falls back on commonplace and genuinely erroneous biographical ideas." An undergraduate who doesn't know anything about Emily Dickinson doesn't have to pay $13.75 for erroneous biographical ideas. He can make them up on his own.

All was not lost. I still had the C-minus from Shaw, an associate professor of English and the author, most recently, of *The Character of John Adams*. The paper managed a C-minus only because it was marked as a freshman paper.

In essence, what I did was pay a company $28.20 ("Include 70¢ extra for postage and handling") to help me pass two courses. While I really managed to pass only one, there are thousands of students across the country who regularly make use of these services and regularly pass courses using bought papers.

You really *can* get through school on a credit card. And it's not illegal.

Both New York and California have laws that regulate the sale of term papers—but just the sale. I purchased my papers from a Los Angeles firm that is prohibited by California law from selling papers that will be presented for academic credit in the State of California. I'm in New York, and there is nothing outlawing my action. I am bound only by my own college's regulations (if I am caught). New York has a similar law, which classes the sale of term papers as a Class B misdemeanor. But a law firm specializing in criminal law has advised me that it would be difficult, if not impossible, to prove that Research Assistance, Inc., is doing business in New York.

The country's first legislation outlawing the sale of term papers came in North Carolina in 1969. Since then, several other states besides New York and California—among them, Illinois, Massachusetts, Connecticut, Pennsylvania, and Maryland—have acted to try and prohibit an activity that seems tantamount to fraud.

The state legislatures are still at it. In Washington State, the Subcommittee on Postsecondary Education of the House of Representatives' Higher Education Committee has drafted a law it hopes will end the state's problem with plagiarism. The law has passed the House, and is awaiting action in the Senate. Washington is the home of several typical term-paper mills, as well as of Research Unlimited, a more specialized firm.

Research Unlimited set up offices there in 1972, shortly after term-paper laws were enacted in its home state, Illinois. Its brochure offers a complete line of individually written academic assignments, including doctoral dissertations: "In the case of larger and more complex projects, such as theses and dissertations, we offer a complete service, beginning with the proposal and ending with the abstract. In addition to preparing all of the written texts, we compile and assemble the bibliographic material required and perform any statistical analysis that may be involved." I found out about Research Unlimited through an ad in *The New York Times Book Review*. The Washington law is similar to those in other states; it will prevent such companies only from doing business within the state. It won't prevent their moving to another state, or advertising and doing business by mail in states where laws have yet to be enacted.

While the Washington State law is constitutionally defensible, the nationwide pastiche of laws has not been effective in dealing with term-paper companies. Probably the only thing that can put an end to them is a national law.

It's fraud. It's fraud and conspiracy to commit fraud through interstate commerce. Injunctions have come out of the courts against term-paper companies based on common-law fraud principles. And there is nothing constitutional about fraud.

Those who say it is up to the university to protect itself against plagiarism are begging the question. The recommended remedies—specialized assignments, more in-class writing, more examinations—forget that it is the nature of the true scholar to find a topic and deal with it in writing. The university is interested in fostering scholarship, and it is hampered by the fact that honest students are competing against professionally written material that has been tailor-made and is therefore untraceable.

Congress should be willing to protect the reputation of an educational system it pours so many millions of dollars into. After all, while I've completed a process that is seemingly illegal, it turns out that, in the State of New York at least, I can't even get myself arrested for it.

# PART

## *Writing About Ideas, Issues, and Values*

# FIVE

Ideas are abstract. To write effectively about abstractions requires all the writing skills you've developed so far: describing, narrating, reporting, informing, evaluating, and interpreting. But several new techniques are called for. These new skills are often described as expository methods. That word *expository* sometimes frightens students. Perhaps it suggests hospitals or mortuaries more than writing, but it simply means "to set forth" or "explain." Expository writing is not limited to abstractions, of course. An essay on the development of nuclear power, an analysis of the rotary engine, a description and interpretation of political unrest in Mongolia—each involves the skills of exposition because each attempts to explain. But expository methods are most essential when you explore complex subjects involving attitudes, opinions, values, or philosophical concepts. The techniques discussed in this unit should help in that endeavor, first, as you look into a subject and come to an understanding of it and, second, as you search for a form in which to express your understanding.

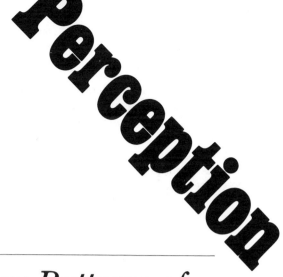

# 23 *Expository Patterns of Perception*

You have reached the point in your study where you must deal with abstract concepts—with ideas that may by their nature seem vague and unwieldy. You have already learned to describe a tree or a person's face. You can report on factual events or draw a reasonable inference. But how can you write about larger questions, about social issues or human values, without drifting off into obscure generalities? How can you bring it all down to the human level and explain it to others?

Here is how one student recently attempted to write about urban violence:

> Concern for the survival of mankind comes with faith in others. War and pollution illustrate Americans' lack of concern and siege of apathy regarding the rest of the world. How can we expect them to react differently to the horrible violence that plagues their cities at home? Both subjects suggest eventual extinction of the human race. If the people of this nation had faith and trust in each other, they would realize that survival should be a mutual goal of all nations and all peoples everywhere.

The question is, Have we learned anything about urban violence? I think the answer is no. This student has attempted to deal with a complex issue by using impressive-sounding generalities: *the survival of mankind, war and pollution, extinction of the human race.* In some way, all of this, along with urban violence, is to be resolved by *faith* and *trust.* It sounds so noble. But vague abstractions offer no meaningful suggestions on how to deal with the immediate problem. We have learned nothing about the causes or consequences of inner-city violence. Nor do we understand its history, the psychology behind its perpetrators, or the effect on its victims. Thoughts fly off at random, without shape, design, or consequence. Quite clearly, the student has not known how to focus ideas.

I have argued that perception is the key to good writing and clear thinking. Through our perceptions we must find order and pattern in the world. Nowhere is that more true than in dealing with abstractions where we must deliberately seek out categories and components that allow us to infer relationships or form meaningful judgments. The conventional strategies of exposition serve as guidelines for helping us do that: *comparison* and *contrast, classification, definition,* and *analysis.* Each of these alone or in combination provides us with a valuable method for organizing ideas in our minds—and eventually in our essays.

## Comparison and Contrast

To *compare* is to show similarities. To *contrast* is to show differences. Note that in both cases I've used the phrase *to show.* Because the use of comparison and contrast provides the opportunity to be specific, it has proved to be one of the most successful methods of writing about abstractions. But to use it in writing, you must first see it in your subject.

Do you want to understand the feminist movement? One way might be to compare it to other social revolutions—perhaps to the effort black people have exerted in America to achieve equal levels of human rights.

Comparison

Both women and blacks have been arbitrarily limited to certain occupations and social roles because of an inherited characteristic: sex and color.

Both have been considered less intelligent than white males and both at times have been denied the right to education.

Both have been "honored" for stereotyped qualities: blacks, for physical ability and cheerfulness; women, for virginity and motherhood. As a consequence, both blacks and women have often attempted to live up to the stereotype.

Aristotle once said that to see relationships is one of the highest acts of human intelligence. By comparing, we draw together like qualities from things or concepts that may have previously seemed unlike.

Contrast often proves equally instructing. Again consider the feminist and black movements for equal rights.

Contrast

Although often disagreeing on means, blacks have tended to support the goals of equal rights fully; women, however, have been divided to the extent that some have formed opposition groups to
resist equal rights.

The black movement has produced a charismatic leader in Martin
Luther King, Jr., a single person who represented and expressed
the highest ideals; the women's movement has tended to remain
fragmented.

Pressure for change has always begun first among blacks and been
followed shortly thereafter by women. (Is there a cause-and-effect
relationship?)

Comparison and contrast, together or singularly, can lead to insight.
You'll recall that contrast, opposition, and contradiction are some of the
qualities reporters seek out in any subject. The same could probably be
said of a State Department analyst studying military spending in Bulgaria
or a business executive studying market trends. Comparison and contrast
are perceptual strategies that clarify, as the concept of male is clarified by
female, and female by male.

# Classification

To *classify* is to arrange persons, places, ideas—almost anything—in
groups or categories according to certain characteristics. The goal of classification is to understand the whole of something by understanding an arrangement of its parts.

Actually, classification is something you do almost every day without much conscious thought. When you trudge down to the Laundromat
to wash your clothes, you sort bright colors into one pile, white clothes
into another; or you make a separate grouping for synthetic fibers and another for cottons. Whatever your categories, you do it because to mix
them randomly might mean that some clothes would be ruined. The purpose determines the way you classify, and you can apply the same principle to complex questions and issues. A concept won't be "ruined" by
mixing all the parts, but any attempt to understand it may be confused.

When we classify, then, we determine the qualities that any particular item or concept must have to fall within a particular *class*. The items
in the class, selected according to purpose, constitute a *subclass*. If you
decided to write a humorous essay on the sexual attractiveness of males to
college females, you might come up with the following:

    *class:* potential college lovers
    *subclass:* party boys, jocks, fire eaters, brains, duds

On the other hand, if you wanted to write a serious essay on the same subject, your subclass would be quite different:

*class:* potential college lovers
*subclass:* those who are afraid of commitments; those who are chauvinistic; those who need mothers; those who possess maturity and sensitivity

A further step in classification occurs when you identify the distinguishing characteristics of any one item in the subclass:

*subclass:* those who possess maturity and sensitivity
*distinguishing characteristics:* respect for self, openness to the needs of others, spontaneity, numerous interests, sense of humor, creativity

But how does all this help in working with abstract subjects? First, it provides you with a means of narrowing any broad subject to a more specific and manageable topic. Second, the classes or subclasses you arrive at may form various portions of your paper (in other words, all this helps you organize the body of the essay). And, third, the technique of classification itself may serve as a method of introduction. Here is how business major Sheri Martin introduced a paper on economic systems:

> The relationship between the economic system of a country and the amount of government regulation of that system depends upon five different organizational structures: communism, socialism, fascism, regulated capitalism (as in the United States), and pure capitalism. In a short paper of this nature, I cannot treat all of these. Instead, I will attempt to outline the contrasting functions of government in two seemingly similar systems: regulated capitalism and pure capitalism. I will try to show that those functions are actually as unlike as day and night.

Economics (a difficult, abstract subject) has been classified into five methods of organizing the economic structure of a society. Sheri then narrows her proposed topic to two of those structures. By attempting to *see* (intellectually) a subject's various subclasses according to a defined purpose, you can clarify the resulting order and begin the process of understanding. For both writer and reader, classification serves to focus perception.

# Definition

Classification may reduce a subject from a general concept to more specific categories, but unless we all agree on the meaning of those categories, clarity may still be absent. You've probably all had the experience of arguing with someone, perhaps in a heated and emotional exchange, only to discover you were using the same word to mean different things.

Without definition, communication may not occur. *Capitalism,* for example, is still a general term. *Regulated capitalism* is a rather specialized term, one that may not be familiar to many readers. Here's how Sheri Martin continued the second paragraph of her paper on economic systems:

> Capitalism is one of the oldest economic systems in the world. In essence, it is characterized by a free market with private ownership of production and means of distribution. When two tribal farmers in West Africa meet in a market to sell and exchange goods based on their own needs and desires, without regulation by any other authority, they are engaging in a primitive form of capitalism. But regulated capitalism is very different. It is characterized by private ownership and imposed government restrictions. The restrictions theoretically prevent any one person or company from dominating the free market or prevent monopolies, like utilities, from earning an unfair profit. By contrast, socialism means that the government not only regulates the market, it may actually own much of the production and means of distribution, retaining all profits for itself.

Sheri has used several conventional methods of defining. She has *described* the basic qualities of both systems. She has given a specific *illustration* of one system and an *example* of the other. And she has *contrasted* the second system to something it is not.

As senses shape experience, so words shape our thoughts. Failure to define words leads to faulty thinking. But we are dealing here with something more than mere definition of specialized terms (as important as that is). Definition is inherent in the very notion of understanding ideas in themselves. Concepts such as *liberalism, imagination, faith, human nature,* as well as *capitalism,* may require extended definition—the pursuit of meaning through a complete essay or even a book. Definition means clarification through precision; it means getting at the nature or basic qualities of a concept. The need for definition, then, begins inside ourselves as we first approach a subject. Later, as we begin to write, the need becomes public, to communicate and explain what we have learned.

# Analysis

To analyze a chemical compound, a short story, a political campaign, or the nature of the good life means to break a subject into parts for individual study, much as you would for classification. But where classification stops with identifying the parts, analysis proceeds to evaluate their relationship.

Here, in simple outline, is the analytic process:

Consider the subject as a whole, as an idea, argument, issue, or whatever in its full context. General definition is essential at this point.

Divide the subject into its various components as you would in classification (that is, as determined by your purpose).

Consider each part separately. If the subject is too large, this is the point to narrow your focus and deal primarily with only one or two components (each of which might need further definition). Some narrowing of the subject will probably be inevitable.

Evaluate the relationship of each part to every other part. The compare-and-contrast strategy will often prove helpful at this stage.

*or*

If you've narrowed your focus to a single component, consider how it relates to the subject as a whole.

Interpret your findings. What do you now know about the subject from having studied the parts and their relationships? (Students often omit this final phase, but analysis is of little value unless you draw the subject together again and form an overall assessment.)

You can see that analysis makes use of other expository methods: classification, comparison and contrast, and definition. By drawing them all together and by discovering relationships, you will find that analysis becomes one of the single most important intellectual strategies you can learn. For further clarification, analysis is traditionally divided into three related but somewhat different approaches, each of which is determined by your purpose.

## Item Analysis

If your purpose is to understand the organization of the United States Government, you could divide it into the Congress, President, and

Supreme Court. Each item could then be considered separately. What is the composition of the Congress? Why is it divided into a Senate and House of Representatives? What is the responsibility of each? How are members selected? Next you could consider the presidency and the Supreme Court in their selected functions. By the end of this stage you would have completed a description of the parts and their individual characteristics (as in classification). In the next phase, you would consider relationships. What is the responsibility of the president to the Congress and to the Supreme Court? How is the court affected by the Congress and the president? Finally, in light of your findings, you would draw all information and interpretation together again to consider what you now know about the subject as a whole.

Obviously, this example suggests that you plan to write a book—or several books. But even if you narrowed your focus to one particular element of governmental structure that would be manageable for a short essay, the method of item analysis would be the same: to divide into parts and to study each item separately.

## Process Analysis

If you wanted to understand relationships that are part of a chronological sequence, you could trace and evaluate the process. This text is an attempt to work with a process of writing. In preparing it, I first spent a number of years mulling over actual steps the mind goes through as it explores a subject, as words are put on paper for the first time, and as the mind reshapes and refines those words. I attempted to break down my own process into steps and phases. I read about how others had described such steps in their writing. I attempted to see how each related in sequence. I have to admit that no new discovery resulted. *Perception, audience, form, first draft, rewriting* and *editing* turned out to be a process long known by professional writers and many teachers of writing. But for me it was an invaluable insight. By identifying the steps in the process and their relationship, the subject of writing as a whole seemed clarified. Analysis helped me understand why some methods of teaching writing might have disastrous consequences when taught out of sequence. It helped me see that the expository methods I'm discussing in this chapter are actually ways of looking at and thinking about a subject that can later become ways of organizing the same subject on paper. To analyze a process, then, is to explore the way the mind and the world works—in its actual sequence.

## Cause-and-Effect Analysis

A process may involve both causes and effects. Any time events occur in sequence, the possibility exists that one may have caused the other. But this type of potential relationship is fraught with danger. We must always distinguish between necessary factors and incidental factors. If $X$ precedes $Y$, is it necessarily the *cause* of $Y$?

I have relatives, for example, who lived in Kansas when the first atomic bomb was dropped on Hiroshima, Japan. They heard the announcement on the radio and moments later the sky turned greenish-black, the winds howled, and a tornado swept down upon them, barely missing their house. My relatives were convinced that what they were experiencing was caused by the atomic bomb. It was not an unnatural fear, nor was it an unnatural link for the mind to make. Tolstoy talks about how serfs on his estate believed that the spring winds were caused by new buds on oak trees. Yet, in both cases, either a coincidence or incidental relationship was incorrectly perceived as a cause. This type of fallacy has been so common throughout history that logicians have given it a fancy name—*post hoc, ergo propter hoc*. It simply means, "after this, therefore because of this"—after my cat ate raw liver, she climbed a tree; therefore, my cat climbs trees because she eats raw liver. These examples may seem silly, but when a doctor is confronted with a symptom, a cause must be determined and the consequences of error could be fatal.

How then can we be reasonably sure of a cause-and-effect relationship? In the scientific laboratory, two rules have been devised as tests:

1. Without $X$ there would be no $Y$.
2. Whenever we find $X$, we will find $Y$.

One or the other of these two conditions (some would say both) must be met for a cause to be considered reasonably certain. Yet in dealing with the complexities outside the laboratory, such a formula, valid as it may be, can lead to distortion and oversimplification. Without Hitler there might not have been the Second World War, but we cannot therefore say that Hitler was the sole cause of war. Literally thousands of other factors played a significant role. Causal analysis, then, requires caution and a concern both for finding the *necessary factors* (as opposed to incidental ones) and a *sufficient number of factors* (as opposed to a single or simplistic one).

## How Do Expository Strategies Relate to "The Writing Process"?

A few years ago I was asked to observe a student teacher in a local high school. The young man had been a superior college student and received almost straight $A$'s in English. I watched as he described various techniques in expository writing. He outlined each concept clearly on the blackboard. He answered questions well. Everything about the class seemed to go satisfactorily until he gave the assignment: "Write a one-page essay using the method of extended definition." The students suddenly looked blank. They left the room downcast and confused. And as might be predicted, the papers they submitted the next day were awkward, contrived, and vacuous. Both the students and the young teacher felt disappointed.

The problem did not lie in the student teacher's explanation or in the expository method. It lay in the assignment. To ask someone to write according to a predetermined form is to reverse the normal process of writing. Form depends upon the subject. No professional writer sits down and says to himself or herself, "Now I'm going to write a 'compare and contrast' article for *National Review.*" Instead, the writer begins with a subject—with the nature of the good life or prison reform or the Far Right Movement in California politics. In the process of studying the subject, the writer uses not only the methods described in this chapter—comparison and contrast, classification, definition, analysis—but all the other methods covered in this book. He or she looks for *who, what, where, why,* and *when;* for the human examples that will make the subject come alive and seem relevant; for *change, conflict, characterization;* and for possible leads that will make an imaginative introduction. The writer *evaluates* and *interprets.* Each of these alone or in combination may be used as part of an expository essay. Each is a means to an end—to explain a subject to an audience. But remember that, in themselves, they are only methods. They do not constitute knowledge. For that you must turn to personal experience, interviews, and reading, where you will use your perceptive powers to seek out the facts, the details, the *substance* that leads to understanding.

Here is an outline of steps you might want to take in studying an idea, issue, or value and of the various methods that might be useful in preparing to write on it:

| Perception Process | Method |
|---|---|
| 1. Begin with an overview of the subject as a whole. | *Define* the terms of the concept with a dictionary. Use an encyclopedia or general article to explore the background if necessary. Consider various ways the subject can be *classified.* What are its major categories? How can you narrow the subject to one specific component or subclass that might be treated in a short essay? |
| 2. Form a question or series of questions on the narrowed subject. | Further *define* the specific terms and components you plan to write about. If possible, use the technique of *comparison* and *contrast* |

| | to focus your purpose more clearly and to form specific questions for inquiry. |
|---|---|
| 3. Investigate for details. If possible, locate original sources to interview. Read several articles or a relevant chapter from a book. | Look for 5 *W*'s and 4 *C*'s. Collect specific examples to make the subject as concrete as possible. *Analyze, interpret,* and *evaluate* what you discover. |

Methods of exposition, like other methods of writing, are *means* not *ends*. Chapter 24 will show how a professional writer has used many of these techniques in an expository essay, but it must be remembered that the *product* you'll see there evolved from a *process* much like the one described here.

### EXERCISES

1. Classify one of the following items. Assume your purpose is to write a humorous essay.

> male chauvinists
> college professors
> TV advertisements for toilet paper
> fraternities or sororities
> roommates

2. Classify the same subject again with a serious purpose—an intention to write an essay that is critical of the subject.

3. Although no definition may be totally adequate, consider the following. In what way is each satisfactory (if it is), and in what ways unsatisfactory? What methods of definition are used? What additional methods might extend the definition and make it more complete?

> a. Americans seem to live and breathe and function by paradox; but in nothing are we so paradoxical as in our passionate belief in our own myths. We truly believe ourselves to be natural-born mechanics and do-it-yourselfers. We spend our lives in motor cars, yet most of us—a great many of us at least—do not know enough about a car to look in the gas tank when the motor fails. Our lives as we live them would not function without electricity, but it is a rare man or woman who, when the power goes off, knows how to look for a burned-out fuse and replace it. We believe implicitly that we are the heirs of the pioneers; that we

chap 24

have inherited self-sufficiency and the ability to take care of ourselves, particularly in relation to nature. There isn't a man among us in ten thousand who knows how to butcher a cow or a pig and cut it up for eating, let alone a wild animal. By natural endowment, we are great rifle shots and great hunters—but when hunting season opens there is a slaughter of farm animals and humans by men and women who couldn't hit a real target if they could see it. Americans treasure the knowledge that they live close to nature, but fewer and fewer farmers feed more and more people; and as soon as we can afford to we eat out of cans, buy frozen TV dinners, and haunt the delicatessens. Affluence means moving to the suburbs, but the American suburbanite sees, if anything, less of the country than the city apartment dweller with his window boxes and his African violets carefully tended under lights. In no country are more seeds and plants and equipment purchased, and less vegetables and flowers raised.

—John Steinbeck, *America and Americans*

b. Being an artist means, not reckoning and counting, but ripening like the tree which does not force its sap but stands, confident in the storms of spring, without fear that after them may come no summer. It does come, but only to the patient, who are there as though eternity lay before them so unconcernedly still and wide. I learn it daily, learn it with pain to which I am grateful. Patience is everything.

—Rainer Maria Rilke, *Letters to a Young Poet*

c. The term "concept" has a multitude of meanings. Most of us have used or applied it in a myriad of ways, and among these uses there may not be a great deal of obvious similarity. For example, "concept" is commonly used as a synonym for idea, as when we say, "Now he seems to have the concept," in reference to someone who has finally caught onto a message. Or we may talk of an abstract state of affairs, such as freedom, and call it a concept. On other occasions, a concept seems to be akin to a mental image, as in the case of trying to conceptualize (visualize) an unfamiliar object or event from a verbal description. Undoubtedly, each of these examples captures in part the meaning of "concept." But clearly, it would be difficult (or impossible) to formulate an unambiguous definition from them.

In experimental psychology the term "concept" has come to have a rather specialized meaning, which may not encompass all its various ordinary uses. Psychology is the scientific investigation of the behavior of organisms, which includes as a sub-area the

From Lyle E. Bourne, Jr., *Human Conceptual Behavior*. Copyright © 1966 by Allyn and Bacon, Inc., Boston. Reprinted with permission of the publisher.

study of how organisms (human beings and lower animals) learn and use concepts. In such an undertaking, explicit, communicable definitions of terms are an absolute necessity. "Concept" is no exception.

As a working definition we may say that a concept exists whenever two or more distinguishable objects or events have been grouped or classified together and set apart from other objects on the basis of some common feature or property characteristic of each. Consider the class of "things" called dogs. Not all dogs are alike. We can easily tell our favorite Basset from the neighbor's Great Dane. Still all dogs have certain features in common and these serve as the basis for a conceptual grouping. Furthermore, this grouping is so familiar and so well defined that few of us have any difficulty calling a dog (even an unfamiliar dog) by that name when we encounter one. There is then the concept "dog"; similarly, the class of all things called "house" is a concept, and the class of things call "religion."

—Lyle E. Bourne, Jr., *Human Conceptual Behavior*

4. Discuss with others in your class the steps you would follow in analyzing one of the following. Decide first whether you would be performing an item analysis, process analysis, or cause-and-effect analysis. Follow the steps on page 244. What types of questions would you need to ask at each stage of the analysis? How much "narrowing" of the subject would you need to do before beginning to write a paper on one of these subjects?

| | |
|---|---|
| cheating in college | stereo equipment |
| a successful football game | the American dream |
| happiness | changing a flat tire |
| English grammar | atomic power plant |
| the college administration | human sexuality |

5. Can you identify relationships between the expository methods described in this chapter and the various methods of perception covered in previous units?

**SUGGESTED WRITING ASSIGNMENT**

Write a four-to-six page expository essay on an idea, issue, or value. Follow the steps below:

1. Select a subject from the following list (or choose a similar type of concept about which you feel a personal concern):

| | | |
|---|---|---|
| consumerism | self-discipline | marriage |
| American heroes | campus area landlords | grades |
| pornography | sexism | cheating |
| environmentalism | TV violence | community service |

2. Because, by its nature, an expository essay should explain a subject to further an understanding of it, your purpose is to some extent predetermined. However, here are some questions you might want to consider in order to help you focus your purpose more clearly:

a. What are the causes of . . .?
b. What are the effects of . . .?
c. What is the common perception of . . ., and is it right or wrong?
d. What is the value of . . .?
e. What changes have occurred in . . .?
f. Who is affected by . . .?
g. Who is responsible for . . .?
h. How effective is . . .?
i. How does it work?
j. How could it be improved?

With such questions in the back of your mind, consider how you might involve the concept of *comparison* and *contrast*. Then write out a statement of purpose:

I want to understand more about the effects of a single parent family on children by comparing it with the traditional family.

I want to understand more about the current attitudes toward having sex before marriage by contrasting such attitudes to those held in the 1950s.

I want to understand more about loneliness by comparing and contrasting the loneliness of teen-agers with the loneliness of the aged.

(Naturally, not all topics will involve comparison and contrast.)

3. Classify the various categories of your subject according to the purpose you have for studying it. Use your classification to narrow the subject to a manageable topic for a short paper. Here is an example:

*abstract issue:*   racism
*purpose:*   to understand Northern racism better by comparing it with racism in the South.
*possible categories:*
       racism in education
       racism in social life
       racism in job opportunity
       racism in housing
*select one category and consider its various components:*
       racism in social life
          dating
          attending parties
          among strangers

outside the classroom

in the dorms

*select one or two components for study*

4. As a first step in studying your subject, prepare an *extended definition* (of at least a paragraph):

    a.  Find the denotation of the general concept.

    b.  Describe the basic qualities of the specific components about which you plan to write.

    c.  If possible, find an illustration or several concrete examples to clarify.

    d.  If necessary, tell what your subject is *not,* or *contrast* your subject to an opposite or decidedly different component.

5. As you study and think about your narrowed subject, continue to look for comparisons and contrasts.

6. Look for relationships.

7. Before you begin to write an actual essay, read Chapter 24 on *audience* and *form.*

# 24 *Shaping the Formal Essay*

Expository writing has no prescribed form. Too bad. It would be so much easier if I could tell you to write first this, then that, or the other. But the concept of exposition suggests only a purpose: to explain. It does not include the shape or form in which you will achieve such a goal. As in most other types of writing, *subject, audience, context,* and *purpose* must guide you. Over the years, however, some traditions have developed, and many instructors will expect you to adhere fairly closely to them, at least in the beginning stages.

## Audience and Context

Expository essays may be written for national audiences in national magazines, they may take the form of specialized studies for scholarly journals, or they may be written—as they often are—for a college assignment. Obviously, the needs and expectations of all those varying audiences will differ. It is exactly the differences you must keep in mind. Specialized terms and professional jargon may be satisfactory in many circumstances, whereas simple terms and careful definitions of abstract concepts may be the crux of your paper for another audience. *You* must be the one who asks yourself the needed questions: What experience does my audience have with the subject? What level of vocabulary can I expect my audience

**253**

to recognize? What terms and concepts should I be sure to define? What, exactly, does my audience need to know?

A recognition of your audience also forces you to consider the tone of your paper. Tone was earlier defined as the attitude an author takes toward his or her material. Sarcasm may be effective in some cases. Anger or hostility may work in others. But for most expository essays, you will be expected to write in a straightforward, serious, and impartial tone. You should at least give the impression of objectivity. As Erich Fromm expressed it, "Objectivity does not mean detachment, it means respect; that is, the ability not to distort and falsify things, persons and oneself." A tone that shows "respect" will probably be the most convincing of all.

Finally, like tone, the voice you write in will be determined in part by audience and context. Some college instructors may want a strictly formal voice with complete absence of the personal "I." Others may feel the personal voice should be used in a paper dealing with values or in one that tries to persuade a reader to accept a certain argument. When context, however, is outside the college classroom, voice may be prescribed by a company's individual policy or by the journal to which you plan to submit your essay. Again, *you* are responsible for knowing your audience and making the determination in advance.

## The Introduction

As in earlier forms of writing, the imaginative lead may be an effective means of capturing your reader's attention while creating a sense of immediate involvement. Professional writers almost always use a lead. But an expository essay also requires a formal introduction. Such an introduction may contain any or all of the following elements:

1. *A general overview of the subject, usually in a sentence of two.*

The United States has been in the foreign aid business since the end of World War II. Last year alone we spent more than $143 billion, supposedly in an attempt to help underdeveloped nations.

The overview presents the reader with a broad picture so that more focused details of the essay can be seen in perspective.

2. *A brief review of the historical or cultural context.*

Since 1965 two national commissions have studied the effects of explicit televised violence on children. Both commissions came to the same conclusion: televised violence can teach, influence, and legitimatize antisocial behavior. The U.S. Surgeon General has presented testimony to the United States Senate that "the overwhelming consensus and the unanimous Scientific Advisory Committee's report indicate that televised violence, indeed, does have an adverse affect on certain members of our society . . ." Yet as recently as 1975 NBC presented a prime time film, *Born Innocent,* that depicted an explicit rape of a young girl with a broom handle. Three days later in San Francisco, three girls, ages 10 to 15, committed a similar attack on a nine-year-old child.

As no idea, issue or value exists in a vacuum, the historical context prepares us to understand attitudes or events that influence the subject you plan to write on.

3. *A definition of the concept that will be expounded upon in the essay.*

In 1886, Thomas Henry Huxley defined education as "the instruction of the intellect in the laws of Nature, under which name I include not merely things and their forces, but men and their ways ..." Today, however, we define education as a process involving compulsive attendance at an institution for twelve years. Only a fool believes that education means learning.

By beginning with a definition, you immediately begin to focus the subject.

4. *A classification of the subject.*

There are two kinds of happiness. First is the happiness based on consumption and possession. The second, by contrast, is based on giving and sharing.

Classification directs the reader's attention to the specific categories or components you plan to discuss. The example given here also has the happy advantage of comparing and contrasting.

## The Thesis Statement

A formal essay may also require a *thesis statement,* usually as the concluding sentence of the introduction. The concept sometimes sounds frightening, but it simply requires you to summarize the dominant idea of your findings in a single sentence. It should be a simple, unadorned statement of the argument you plan to support with evidence and reason. Traditionally, a thesis statement focuses and further restricts the subject, it states the purpose or direction of the paper in precise words, and, if possible, it indicates something about the writer's attitude toward the subject.

> The pollution problem in Lake Angelo can be solved only through the combined efforts of the city government and the Forystal Mining Company.

*Subject of paper:* the pollution problem in Lake Angelo.
*Restriction of subject:* how the problem can be solved.
*Purpose of argument:* to demonstrate that a combined effort of two organizations can solve it.
*Attitude of writer:* This is the only way the problem can be solved.

In some ways the thesis statement is similar to a 5 *W* lead, except that instead of merely gathering important facts together, it shapes those facts and gives them a purpose or direction or meaning. A weak thesis statement will usually be caused by a failure to narrow the subject, by a failure to use precise language, by a failure to suggest a single dominating purpose to the paper, or by a sentence structure that is too complex and therefore confusing.

*Subject too broad:* Pollution must be solved.

*Imprecise language:* The pollution problem around here can be solved in a couple of good ways.

*No clear purpose:* Lake Angelo is full of pollution from the Forystal Mining Company because of years of chemical dumping even though the city has been aware of it.

*Too complex:* Although it is now evident that only by working together can progress be made, the Forystal Mining Company, having spent twenty years dumping chemical waste in Lake Angelo without a sense of guilt, has been made recently aware of the bad public relations and wants to solve the problem, the same problem the city itself wants to solve, although to date conflicting proposals and bureaucratic bungling have prevented them from joining forces.

Here are four guidelines to keep in mind as you shape a thesis statement:

1. Use a simple declarative sentence.
2. Use language with precise denotations.
3. Narrow the subject to the single, most important idea in your paper.
4. Clearly indicate the purpose or argument of the essay.

So far so good. But when should you write the thesis statement? Many argue that a thesis must be formulated *before* you begin a first draft. It may take several hours of thinking, writing, and rewriting. You have already studied your subject, asked questions, and narrowed your focus. You should now have at least a general idea of what you want to write about. Rather than begin randomly, however, formulate a thesis statement to help you organize before you write. This formulation forces you to identify the dominant argument or purpose. It forces you to shape your own attitudes toward that idea if you have not already done so. It forces you to be precise about what you want to say. This is the essence of what we mean when we say, "Good thinking." Unless you put yourself through such a process, you may find your essay drifting off on irrelevant byways or surveying six ideas at once or beginning with attitude *A* and ending with argument *B*. The thesis statement is important to a reader, but even more important to the writer. It requires you to organize previously unorganized ideas.

On the other hand, not everyone's mind works alike. I have to confess I've seldom been able to write a thesis statement in advance of a first draft. I usually don't know what my argument is until I've reached my conclusion. And at times I've been fortunate to find new insights only because I allowed myself to follow an "irrelevant" byway. Although it will not be true for all, the effort to compose a thesis statement in advance may block creativity and inhibit the potential for discovering ideas in the course of the writing. So here's the result. If you don't form a thesis statement before the first draft, you *will* probably wander around and write a disorganized essay, and you *will* be envious of those who seem to have more structured minds. But if that's the kind of person you are, don't worry about it. Just don't submit your first draft (which you shouldn't be doing anyway). Use that draft as a time for exploration. Afterward, look over what you have written and force yourself at *that* point to identify your thesis. Write it up in a simple statement. Then reorganize and rewrite your essay to correspond to your newly perceived purpose. A thesis statement written after the first draft serves the same function as one written before the first draft. It defines and clarifies. It helps determine organization and gives a sense of direction to the essay. Only after years of frustration did I realize that the reader doesn't care *when* you organize, only *that* you organize.

---

**THE FORMAL INTRODUCTION**

Any Combination of the Following:
 —General overview of the subject
 —Review of the historical or cultural context
 —Definition of the basic concept
 —Classification of the subject
Plus:
 —A Thesis Statement
 • Restriction to one narrow component
 • Purpose or argument made clear
 • Attitude of writer suggested
 • All in a simple focusing sentence

---

# The Body of the Essay

Obviously, the rest of your paper will be shaped by subject and purpose. No single pattern exists to guide you. But it may be helpful to recall some organizational forms used by professional writers (see Chapters 15 and 21).

If your subject involves conflicting ideas or deals extensively with comparison and contrast, one of the two "contrast designs" may be appropriate:

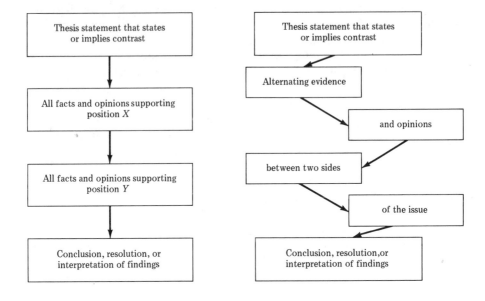

If your study has led you to make a discovery or arrive at a solution to a problem or perhaps has suggested a new interpretation, then the "literary design" may prove the most useful:

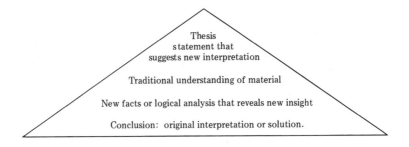

The literary design suggests another pattern you've already worked with: organizing from *the least important material to the most important*. You'll remember that a news report used the opposite format. But unlike the time-pressed reader of reports, the reader of an expository essay usually plans to complete it. By saving the strongest material for the end, you'll leave that reader with a persuasive and powerful conclusion.

The most traditional method of organizing a formal essay, however, is identical to the design used for a "Dramatic Statement or Bold Generalization." Because a thesis statement is similar, it is easy to see why the "I" pattern has always worked so well.

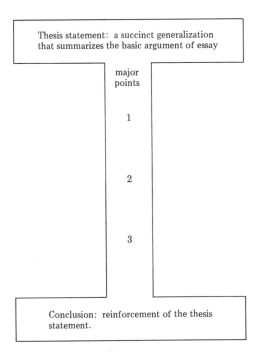

The interior organization of the "I" form usually follows two traditional patterns. The first simply requires a logical narrative, description, or analysis of your findings; in other words, a presentation of your evidence, again usually moving from least important to most important. The other method is used when your approach to an idea, issue, or value involves "taking sides," that is, when you plan to argue that one position or solution is better than another. In such a case, you might want to group your material into two parts. First, draw together all the reasonable (or not so reasonable) arguments against your thesis. Present them fairly and without show of bias on your part. Then, in the second half of your paper, group all arguments that favor your position. Make sure that the essay is equally balanced, approximately half on opposition ideas, half on supporting ideas. That way no one can accuse you of "weighting" the argument unfairly. But by saving the position you favor until last and then following it with a strong restatement or reinforcement of your thesis, you will have a subtle psychological advantage.

## A Professional Model

No single example can illustrate the variety of forms open to you, but the following essay, by Warren Boroson, a New York writer and editor, demonstrates how some of the methods discussed in this unit can be combined into an interesting article that deals with an abstract concept. This essay first appeared in *Money,* which suggests the type of audience Boroson had to keep in mind as he wrote.

# The Workaholic in You
## Warren Boroson

*Introduction classifies two types of people who work hard.*

Lots of Americans work hard and play hard. But some just work, either from the unquenchable love of it or from a compulsion beyond their control. Work lovers—the unquenchables—provide society with many leaders in business, politics, science and the arts. Those who overwork out of compulsion—the work addicts, or workaholics, of this world—are in trouble. Their addiction can lead to deadend careers, to poor health, even to early death. They are so emotionally dependent on work that without

*Thesis*

it they start coming unglued. Though the purebred workaholic is rare, there is a little of him in almost everyone. It is well to know the warning signals and how to cope with them.

*Contrast emphasized through example*

Confusing workaholics with work lovers is a bit like confusing winos with oenophiles. Mark Twain was a work lover. In 1908, when he was nearly 73, he said he hadn't done a lick of work in over 50 years. Wrote Twain: "I have always been able to gain my living without doing any work; for the writing of books and magazine matter was always play, not work. I enjoyed it; it was merely billiards to me."

*Contrast stressed again through analogy*

Psychiatrist Carl Jung once said that the difference between the recondite prose of James Joyce and the poetry of Joyce's insane daughter was that he was diving and she was falling. The work lover is diving. He works hard and long by choice. When he want to, he can stop without suffering acute withdrawal pains. When the work addicts go on vacation, however, it is not the natives but the tourists who are restless.

The work lover's work is also his play. The work ad-

Adapted from the June 1976 issue of *Money* magazine by special permission; copyright © 1976 by Time, Inc.

dict's motives are mixed. In many cases, he is seeking the admiration of other people because he doesn't approve of himself. As Dr. Alan McLean, an IBM psychiatrist, points out, the healthiest people usually have various sources of satisfaction: they are lawyers, say, but they are also spouses, parents, friends, citizens, churchgoers, art lovers, stamp collectors, golfers and so forth. If such people lose their jobs, or if their work becomes less satisfying or its quality starts deteriorating, they have not lost their sole interest in life, the only prop to their self-esteem. Many compulsive workers, according to cardiologist Meyer Friedman of San Francisco, co-author of the bestselling book *Type A Behavior and Your Heart* (1974), "want status, and their status depends on what other people think of them." Eventually, many addicts manage to labor under the delusion that they are indispensable.

*First major point analyzes underlying cause of problem.*

*In-text documentation*

Guilt propels some workaholics. Several years ago, a theological seminary in the East had a problem with guilt-ridden students who kept working even when the school closed for vacations. To get them out, the school was finally forced to turn off the electricity and water and change all the locks during vacation periods.

*Specific illustrations*

Because of their diligence, work addicts in corporations tend to keep getting promoted; but a lack of imagination keeps them from reaching the top rungs. They make great salesmen and terrible corporation presidents. "Workaholics rarely become famous," says Dr. Frederic Flach, a New York psychiatrist who has treated many people with work problems. "Because they lack creativity, they rarely make an original contribution to the welfare of mankind. They usually end up in upper-middle management, giving grief to everyone around them."

*Description of major consequence*

Continual work, Dr. Flach notes, "violates one of the basic rules of coming up with original solutions—to move into another area and let the problem simmer." He adds that one reason workaholics work ten to twelve hours a day is that "they are not good at finding ways to think about something in a new fashion." Work addicts, says Robert F. Medina, an industrial psychologist in Chicago, like "the sureness and safety of processing endless details. Creativity is a little too scary. It looks like idleness to them."

*Analysis of experts*

. . .

*Second major point: effects of being a workaholic clarified by further classification*

While work addicts work hard, they tend to die easily. Time and again, researchers have found that the compulsively hard-working person is particularly prone to heart disease in middle age. Dr. Friedman and his cardiologist co-author, Dr. Ray H. Rosenman, divide the world into two working types. Hard-driving people are classified as Type A and low-pressure people as Type B. Both types can become workaholics, but in different ways. The Type-A person is excessively ambitious and competitive, and frequently hostile; he feels pressured by deadlines. Cardiologists have found that he is two to three times as likely to have a premature heart attack as a Type B, who is not so competitive and hard driving.

Type-B workaholics are civil service types who lose themselves in dull paperwork or other routine activities. Wayne Oates, a Louisville psychologist, thinks that a Type B work addict, unlike the individualistic Type A, tends to identify with the company he works for and "not have any selfhood of his own. The company is a flat earth to him. Everything beyond it is dragons and disaster."

. . .

*Continued contrast between work lover and workaholic*

Sometimes a work addict can persuade himself as well as other people that he is really a work lover, the way an alcoholic can persuade himself and others that he doesn't have a drinking problem because all he drinks is vintage cognac. Reading someone's basic motives can be difficult. But it's very likely that a work lover—unlike a work addict—has a job that offers freedom and diversity; he is well recognized and amply rewarded for his efforts. An obscure middle-aged heart surgeon or social reformer who works as hard as Dr. Denton Cooley or Ralph Nader is more likely to be a self-destructive work addict than those two men are. Nader scoffs at the notion that his

*Notice integration of summary and quotation.*

ceaseless toil makes him a workaholic. "You wouldn't ask an Olympic swimmer or chess player why he works 20 hours a day," Nader says. People don't understand Nader "because we haven't a tradition which explains me."

Without being workaholics, most people experience the addict's symptoms from time to time. "Anyone who's been busy and active," says Dr. Flach, the New York psychiatrist, "has a tendency to get locked in, to become de-

*General description of various*

pendent on his work." Examples are accountants in March and April, salesclerks during the Christmas rush, *situations and examples that seem "workaholic" on surface . . .*

air traffic controllers all the time. When they are no longer so busy, they may suffer from a mild version of "postpartum depression like women who have just given birth."

Some people work too long and hard at times because they fear being fired or are bucking for promotion or cannot do their jobs as well as they know they should. Other people sometimes lose themselves in work to escape emotional problems—the loss of a loved one, a financial setback or some other worry. They use work to keep from breaking down completely. Occupational therapy is, after all, one of the very best painkillers and tranquilizers.

*. . . but contrast to true workaholic clarifies.*

These people differ from chronic addicts in that once they have stopped working for a while, their pain begins to ebb, their spirits perk up, and they are back to normal. But someone who has been temporarily habituated to hard work would be best advised to unwind slowly. People who suddenly switch from hard work to idleness tend to develop a variety of physical and psychological illnesses, heart disease in particular. Social psychologist Jerome E. Singer of the National Research Council in Washington, D.C., mentions how people often die shortly after retiring from important posts.

. . .

*Third major point: solution proposed*

Jerome Singer recommends that hard-working people generally avoid making abrupt major changes in their work habits. People who work frenetically all year long may suffer if they suddenly flop down on a beach in Hawaii for a few weeks. Instead, Singer suggests that hard workers would be better off taking frequent short vacations or easing into long vacations by cutting down gradually on their work.

*Example*

Recognizing the value of vacations, many companies (General Motors, for one) now require all employees to take the vacations they are entitled to instead of accumulating them from year to year. Dr. Nicholas A. Pace, medical director of GM's New York executive offices, adds that employees who try not to take vacations "don't get brownie points any more. They're just looked upon as damn fools." But a vacation need not be long to be therapeutic. Dr. John P. McCann of the Life Extension Institute in New York, which gives physicals to executives, points out that for many people even a one-day vacation may constitute a refreshing change of pace.

*Opinions of experts*

The ideal vacation, in the opinion of Dr. Ari Kiev, a New York psychiatrist and author of *A Strategy for Handling Executive Stress* (1974), is a foil to a person's occupation. Someone who does close, detailed work all year long, like an accountant, might take up something less exacting, like sailing. (Says Dr. Howard Hess: "A Caribbean vacation is not the solution to everyone's problems. Just mine and yours.") A person who sees in himself symptoms of workaholism should try developing interests outside of his job. Dr. Flach recommends returning to the hobbies of your adolescence—photography, stamp collecting or what have you. "Your early interests," he believes, "are perhaps the closest expression of you as a person." Wayne Oates suggests renewing old acquaintances, making new friends and reading books you don't have to read, like mysteries. It may be easier for those further along the path to addiction to switch to hobbies that, like work, have well-defined goals, such as woodworking or sports.

. . .

*Specific illustration*

The incipient addict with the hard-driving personality of a Type A should consider slowing down the general pace of his life. Dr. Friedman, a type A himself (complete with heart attack), deliberately began dressing informally. He spent lunch hours examining the stained glass windows in a nearby cathedral; he began rereading the seven parts of Marcel Proust's interminable *Remembrance of Things Past*. He now avoids cocktail parties: "I found that all you do at them is shout, and no one cares whether you leave or stay." And he keeps away from "people who readily bring out my free-floating hostility, because I've never been able to convince those sons of bitches about anything and they've never been able to convince me."

*Conclusion illustrates theme with irony.*

To get advice from other well-known people who are reputed to work very hard, I wrote Harold S. Geneen, president of ITT, actor Elliot Gould, film director Robert Altman, Governor Jerry Brown of California, and Dr. De-Bakey, among others. A spokesman for ITT apologetically reported that Geneen could not reply because he had been very busy with management meetings recently and was out on the golf course. The others did not respond at all. Presumably they were too busy working.

This essay has obviously involved a good deal of investigation into primary and secondary sources. Such research into "outside" opinions is not a requirement for the typical expository essay. Yet I've found that few student writers have studied long enough, thought deeply enough, or known enough life experience to sit down and write about an abstract idea, issue, or value off the top of their heads. Much of the bad writing in college occurs for the simple reason that the writer has nothing to say. If the body of even a short essay is to have substance, then you might be best advised to investigate one or two sources at a minimum, if for no other reason than to stimulate your own thinking on the subject.

## The Conclusion

As the conclusion is the last contact you'll have with a reader, you'll want to leave a strong impression. The following are some of the ways to *fail:*

- Don't have a conclusion at all; let the reader guess.
- Apologize for not having done better.
- Repeat everything you've said in the same words.
- Ignore the evidence in your own paper.
- End by saying, "In conclusion . . ."

But it's easier to say what you should not do than to clearly state what you should. A good conclusion grows naturally out of the argument or evidence of your paper. In that sense, every good conclusion is in some way original and cannot be demonstrated to you in advance. If you're not feeling very original, however, here are some tried and true methods you might consider.

1. Generalize on the significance of the evidence you've presented. Don't merely make a list of all your points; rather, reflect on the meaning of them. Draw reasonable inferences from the overall pattern of information or ideas you've worked with.

2. If it is called for, offer a solution. Be modest and admit that it may not be the only answer, but, at the same time, be firm and assert that it represents a good start toward resolving the issue.

3. Consider the consequences and suggest who may be affected or what the future will hold (but beware of the overgeneralization: "Mankind will destroy itself if . . .").

4. Use a striking quotation that reinforces your ideas but do not substitute the quotation for your own judgment. The final paragraph must still be written in your words and reflect your assessment. A quotation should be used only to add strength or support.

5. If the paper is long, make an emphatic restatement of your central idea. Don't, however, merely repeat your thesis statement word for word from the introduction.

No matter what method you use, base your final paragraph on the evidence presented in your essay. If possible, try to relate your conclusion to your opening, some element of your lead, your general introduction, your thesis statement, or your title. And be especially conscious of word order in the final sentence, where a short, emphatic statement or an especially strong phrase will be most effective.

# The Function of Expository Writing

For your audience, expository writing serves an immediately apparent function: it learns something it didn't know before. But what does this do for you? Why is expository writing so emphasized in college? As surprising as it may seem, training in exposition is training in self-expression, in how to discover and set forth *your* ideas. It demands that your mind engage all its resources in a self-disciplined effort at understanding not only the concrete world about you but also the ideas and values abstracted from that world. The strong emphasis upon expository writing, then, results from the desire to prepare you for a real world where the ability to narrow a subject to a single component, classify it, analyze it, and clarify it is one of the most valued qualities. Indeed, it is this type of self-disciplined intelligence that we must clearly associate with an educated man or woman. But if by this point you feel self-expression has become lost amid the jargon, the forms, the various techniques, it may be good to remind yourself again that all of it is only a means to an end. "One must, of course, master technique," Pablo Casals has said, but "at the same time, one must not become enslaved by it. One must understand that the purpose of technique is to transmit the inner meaning, the message of the music."

## EXERCISES

1. Consider the following thesis statements. In what way is each too broad for a 1,000-word essay? Suggest ways each could be rewritten to narrow the focus and make it more precise.
   a. Dumping chemicals is dangerous to human health.
   b. Blacks are still treated unjustly in America.
   c. The Supreme Court has ignored the wishes of the American people.
   d. Drug laws reflect the interests of drug companies.

2. Consider which of the following thesis statements are effective. Which would give the reader a clear indication of what to expect in the essay that follows? If you find one that is inadequate, identify the problem.
   a. Limited opportunities for entrance into medical schools cause premed students to cheat for the sake of higher grades.
   b. Television series on single-parent families create misleading myths.
   c. I believe there are six types of students in college today.
   d. Effective comedy requires an element of surprise and a sense of timing.

   e. The central idea of a paper can usually be expressed in a single sentence.

   f. Because of its cathartic effect, art can be a central tool in the treatment of mental illness.

   3. Read one of the essays included at the end of this unit. Consider the following questions: 299-305

   a. What methods does the writer use to shape the introduction?

   b. How does the writer organize the body of the essay?

   c. What combination of expository methods is used in the body of the essay to clarify and explain?

   d. Is the conclusion effective? Can you identify any particular method discussed in this chapter as part of the conclusion, or is it unique to the particular way the writer has treated the subject?

   4. What method of analysis have you used in studying the end-of-unit essay?

# 25 *The Art of Coherence*

As writers, we want our work to express a sense of wholeness. We want it to sound as if every idea relates meaningfully to the next, as if a sense of movement and design sweeps the total collection of ideas to an inevitable conclusion. To cohere means "to stick together." *Coherence* is that quality in prose that helps the reader (and writer) see relationships—between each sentence, each paragraph, each idea.

## Transitions

If ideas are to be connected, the best method is to connect them as each link in the logical chain with a clear and simple term—a word that joins thought or contrasts thoughts (if that is what is called for); a word that clarifies time or context in which thoughts occur; a word that links thoughts in sequence when they need to be understood in one specific order. Here is a portion of an essay on I.Q. testing in which the writer clarifies the movement between each phase of development:

> ... Such care is rarely possible under customary conditions in group testing.

Shows further      *Moreover,* the very intention of the I.Q. test is fre-

From *Writing College English: An Analytic Method* by Walter Dubler and Eve Zarin. Copyright © 1967 by Walter Dubler and Eve Zarin. Reprinted by permission of Holt, Rinehart and Winston.

*development of idea from previous paragraph*

*Shows movement toward negative interpretation of that idea*

*Clarifies movement toward second negative point*

*Transition to next major development*

*Places idea in a context*

*Leads to contrasting interpretation*

*Shows movement toward a judgment*

*Shows link to further development of that judgment*

*Identifies sequence of ideas moving toward conclusion*

quently misinterpreted. Many teachers laud its accomplishment in revealing a student's general intellectual ability. *But* such a test is really capable of revealing no more than a student's skill in performing a number of tasks at the particular time that he is taking the test. John Dobbin and Henry Chauncey, two experts in the field, have stated that "no intelligence test opens the window in the student's skull through which psychologists and scientists can ascertain the amount of latent brightness or intelligence he has. *Nor* can any test trick a person psychologically or otherwise into revealing how much brilliance or stupidity he possesses."

*But* if poor administration of I.Q. tests and misinterpretation of their intentions are severe hindrances, these are but minor considerations alongside what has become the most pernicious effect of these tests: the effect on the student himself. *Too often,* the result of such tests is not the establishment of a measuring device, *but* the creation of a label. A student is labeled "slow," "average," or "bright," and once given this label, he is rarely able to divest himself of it. What others think of him becomes inextricably linked with his own self-image, *and the result* is to make of the I.Q. test a self-fulfilling prophecy. As one teacher has admitted: "Once you know a child's I.Q. you tend to see him through it. You adjust your teaching to his ability of level of intelligence." *Moreover,* a "bright" student, encouraged to smugness and complacency about his brightness, is as likely to suffer in the long run as a "slow" student on whose attainment a ceiling has been placed.

*Finally,* there is serious cause for . . .

We can identify four traditional types of connecting or contrasting words:

| | |
|---|---|
| *Thought-connecting:* | thus, and, therefore, also, moreover, indeed, then, in addition to |
| *Thought-contrasting:* | however, nevertheless, but, nor, on the other hand, in contrast to, regardless |
| *Time-connecting:* | now, later, in the future, at that time, previously, often |
| *Sequence-connecting:* | first, second, third, finally, most important, least important, then |

The experienced writer uses such words selectively. You would not want every sentence to connect with *and,* nor would you want to link idea after idea with *also.* But you should not hesitate to use a thought-connecting word at any stage of your writing where one idea or phase of an idea moves on to the next. The only result of overuse will be mild annoyance on the part of the reader who already sees the connection. With time you'll learn to know instinctively when such a connection is not needed. But if a necessary transtition is omitted, the result will be confusion and misunderstanding, an accusation of weak logic, and a likely rejection of your argument. The choice, then, is clear and simple: during the rewriting phase, make doubly sure that thoughts connect by using connecting words. *Show* the connection on paper. Do not assume your audience will see it as clearly as you do in your mind.

## Hooks

A more sophisticated form of transition, and one preferred by professional writers, is sometimes called a *hook.* Rather than using time-worn connecting words like *therefore* and *moreover,* the experienced writer attempts to pick up an idea or term from the final sentence of one paragraph and repeat it, either exactly or with slight variation in the first sentence of the next paragraph. Here are excerpts from a student paper illustrating the process.

The characteristics necessary for a successful man-woman relationship are not easy to define. All people have different personalities and, thus, different needs and desires. However, there are "ingredients" basic to every such relationship. *Friendship,* trust, loyalty, love, and respect will be found in any thriving man-woman relationship.

*The word friendship is picked up from the final sentence and introduces the next paragraph.*

*Friendship* is the basic bond between any two people . . .

*Friendship and relationship combine to hook the second and third paragraphs together.*

. . . Without *friendship,* a successful *relationship* will not evolve.

A meaningful *friendship,* however, does not constitute a good man-woman *relationship;* as the friendship deepens, a mutual trust must appear. . . .

*This time the student develops a variation.*

. . . The situation is worsened by the fact that the *distrust* is not unwarranted.

Such *unfaithfulness* can easily destroy a relationship . . .

. . . Most *loves* cannot fully recover from an act of disloyalty.

*The hook here is widely separated but still holds the paragraphs together.*   When a man-woman relationship begins as a friendship and deepens into a friendship containing mutual trust and faithfulness, the liking for one another evolves into *love* . . .

Although this student has depended primarily upon repeating the same words, she might also have used whole phrases, concepts, or images. Hooks provide a deep, psychological link between paragraphs and will usually seem less obtrusive than a more conventional use of *but* and *however,* although at times the combination of hooks and conventional transitions will serve you most forcefully.

During the rewriting phase especially, study the relationship between paragraphs, and question yourself on which method or combination of methods might be most effective. But remember that the purpose is not merely to link paragraphs; it is to link ideas—to show how one thought relates to another.

# Repetition

The more experienced writer knows that the potential for understanding an idea increases if the idea itself is repeated. The challenge is to repeat without seeming to do so. Direct restatement of an idea over and over is dulling, not enlightening. But selected repetition during the development of an idea reinforces the concept in the mind of the audience.

Repetition is a more sophisticated form of coherence derived from a basic principle in art. A dancer establishes a movement, then repeats it. A musician establishes a musical theme, varies it, expands upon it, and then repeats it. The writer attempts the same thing. We see it most clearly in rhymed poetry where sounds repeat. Indeed all art is based on pattern rhythm or repetition. Here, for example, is D. H. Lawrence using just such devices to capture your emotion:

> Never shall I forget the deep singing of the men at the drum,
> swelling and sinking, the deepest sound I have heard in all my life,
> deeper than thunder, deeper than the sound of the Pacific Ocean,
> deeper than the roar of deep waterfall: the wonderful deep sound
> of men calling to the unspeakable depths.
>
> *—The Phoenix*

Repetition used by an essayist may not seem as obvious, but it is nevertheless there. Here is a passage on the subject of laughter by Henri Bergson. We can find both repetition of key words and repetition of grammatical structures. I've marked them with four types of symbols: circles, arrows, dotted lines, and brackets.

      The first point to which attention should be called is that the comic does not exist outside the pale of what is strictly (human.) A landscape may be beautiful, charming and sublime, or insignificant and ugly; it will never be laughable. You may laugh at an [animal] but only because you have detected in it some (human) attitude or expression. You may laugh at a hat, but what you are making fun of, in this case, is not the piece of felt or straw, but the shape that (men) have given it—the (human) caprice whose mold it has assumed. It is strange that so important a fact, and such a simple one, too, has not attracted to a greater degree the attention of philosophers. Several have defined (man) as "an [animal] which laughs." They might equally well have defined him as an [animal] which is laughed at; for if any other [animal], or some lifeless object, produces the same effect, it is always because of some resemblance to (man,) of the stamp he gives it or the use he puts it to.

Bergson uses a sequence-connecting word at the beginning of the paragraph (*The first point*) and later a thought-contrasting transition (*but*). Yet he clearly achieves a more significant level of coherence through an amazing number of repetitions and variations. Four types of repetitions are interwoven, and yet no single one of them seems particularly noticeable. To the ear of the imagination, however, they establish an idea by reinforcing it: *laugh, laughable, laughed at.*

How can the inexperienced writer work toward achieving this kind of subtle coherence? Probably through two methods. First, in the rewriting or editing phase, make sure once again that in every sentence you are as specific as possible, as concrete as possible. Do not substitute weak or vague terms like "it" or "things" for the name of the idea itself—*laughter, human, animal.* The repetition of the noun is more effective. Second, read each paragraph aloud. Listen for repetitions. Your ear is often a better guide than your eye. If the same word occurs again and again and annoys the ear, replace it with a variation. But if a key word occurs only once, find ways of working variations into the passage so that, at appropriate intervals, the word is reinforced in the reader's mind.

## Tags

Other repetitions, called *tags,* may occur at more widespread intervals. Each time an idea or information from the same source is used in an essay, that source should be newly identified. This may be especially necessary in complex papers where ideas from several sources are blended or where your reactions and comments on a source might be confused with the source itself. Indeed, in a long passage of summarized material from a single source, even when no ideas from others intervene, the source should probably still be tagged so that the reader is never in doubt as to whose ideas he or she is reading.

A full identification of a source should be given the first time it's used. Afterward, the name of the source and perhaps some other identifying characteristic should be tagged or "touched upon" as a reminder.

| | |
|---|---|
| *First reference* | Harold J. Crawford, director of Educational Services at the Burrows Institute for Radical Studies in Seattle, writes in the April 1979 *Atlantic* . . . |
| *Same page, second reference* | Crawford, who has been at the Burrows Institute for seventeen years, does not believe that . . . |
| *Next page, fourth paragraph* | Yet this idea cannot be entirely supported even by Harold Crawford, who has observed . . . |
| *Three pages later* | Crawford's essay in *Atlantic* also contests the basic premise of other radicals who argue that . . . |

Each tagged reference to a source strengthens a paper by keeping all ideas clearly labeled and identified for the reader.

## Parallelism

Chapter 17 described parallel sentence structure as a means of emphasizing related ideas through related grammatical forms. Here is how Henry Fairlie, writing in *Harper's,* gives coherence to an entire paragraph through such a technique:

But behind all these attitudes, and many more that could be called in evidence, lies the central lack of belief that sustains them all. We no longer believe in the mission of our civilization. We once believed that it should explore, so that we could see Lindbergh as a hero, but we no longer do: Hillary was not a hero. We once believed that it should go to the bounds of the earth, but we do not believe in it going to the boundaries of the universe, and so we regard our astronauts as little more than acrobats. We once believed that it should teach and hear, so missionaries such as Livingstone and Schweitzer were heroes, but now when we read that some missionaries have been massacred we tend to think that they may have deserved it. We once believed in our science, so that in the Golden Age of Physics, men such as Einstein and Rutherford and Bohr were heroes, but now we do not believe in it, and out of all the scientific advances of recent years not one scientist's name is a household word. We used to think that our civilization should be guarded, and even that at times it should advance, so that our soldiers were heroes, but now we think of our generals only as stupid and knavish and war-hungry. We used to believe that our civilization should act with great authority in the world, so that we found heroes among our politicians to speak for it, but now we regard our politicians only as petty and self-serving. We once believed that our writers and artists should speak of and to the common values of our civilization and be bearers of it, so that we found heroes among them even down to the 1930s, but now we think that our writers and artists should stay on the margins and entertain us.

Fairlie has also used balanced sentences with contrasting clauses to make his argument more convincing, but it is the parallel repetitions that give coherence: *We once believed . . . We once believed . . . We once believed. . . .* Such parallel structures are like drops of intellectual glue that hold concepts together. In spite of the author's using half-a-dozen names and more than a dozen examples in a single paragraph, the reader is never for a moment confused or lost.

Parallel structure and other techniques for developing coherence go beyond craftmanship. Joyce Cary, a novelist, has written that "almost all use of language is art, and particularly all communication between us, all communication that not only gives facts, but also puts some valuation on the facts, is art." To show a relationship through transitions, hooks, repetitions, tags, and parallelism does more than help the reader follow your ideas. When done well, it creates a psychological sense of unity; it sweeps the reader along in a rhythmic flow that begins to give feeling and emotional force to an otherwise objective argument. The result is at once both clarity and strength. The audience responds as it does to other forms of art, with a sense of total involvement in the experience.

### EXERCISES

1. The following two student paragraphs have had all transitions removed. Consider where *thought-connecting, thought-contrasting, time-connecting,* or *sequence-connecting* transitions might be used, both to clarify and to improve the flow of the sentences.

a. House Bill 115 passed, repealing the old Revised Code on March 14, 1978. The bill was presented to Governor James A. Rhodes. The governor had vowed not to sign the bill before it came out of committee. The bill remained unsigned. It was returned to the House of Representatives, where it had originated. The bill became law with a three-fourths vote of the General Assembly.

   b. In Cambridge, Massachusetts, the head of the city council, Walter Sullivan, described the hitchhiking problem. "The city is flooded with them. They're causing accidents and holding up traffic." The council passed a resolution to provide fines for motorists who picked up hitchhikers. The hitchhikers go free. Piogo Teixeria, a graduate of MIT, claims the new law will not be enforced. Teixeria claims the law threatens commuting students in a college town. The mayor, Alfred E. Vellucci, picks up hitchhikers often. Vellucci says that when he was a youth he used to hitchhike.

   2. Here are a series of sentences representing the conclusion of several paragraphs. For each, write the beginning sentence of the next paragraph, using some type of paragraph *hook,* or *hook* plus *transition.*

   a. They told us, "To hell with France." They wanted some land, not France. And they engaged in a bloody battle.

Example: That *battle* began on the twenty-fourth of August.

   b. Marriages crumble, finally, when each blames the other for failing to embody the original visions that impelled their unions. "Why did I have to choose you?" they ask.
   c. And because a joyful life is one of constant, meaningful intercourse with others in a meaningful environment, equal enjoyment does translate into equal education.
   d. They have a satirical sense of humor. One elephant that I rode on, for example, deliberately turned and stomped through the Maharajah's flower beds.
   e. From every window and doorway, in back and front yards, on the stoops and hanging on the fences that lined the way, the people looked out and down upon the procession.

   3. Identify and discuss the various types of repetition and parallelism that give coherence to the following paragraphs. Read one aloud and listen to the rhythms. How do the rhythms enhance the effect? What role do "theme and variation" play in coherence?

   a. She will be reared, as her brother will be reared, with a combination of loving warmth, firm discipline, household responsibility and encouragement of independence and self-reliance. She will not be pampered and indulged, subtly taught to achieve her ends through coquetry and tears, as so many girls are taught today. She will view domestic skills as useful tools to acquire, some of which, like fine cooking or needlework, having their own intrinsic pleasures but most of which are necessary repetitive work best gotten done as quickly and efficiently as possible. She will be able to handle minor mechanical breakdowns in the home as well as her brother can, and he will be able to tend a child, press, sew, and cook with the same easy skills and comfortable feeling his sister has.

—Alice S. Rossi, "Equality Between the Sexes:
An Immodest Proposal," *Daedalus*

b. In a word, we have lost our sense of history. In our schools the story of our nation has been displaced by "social studies"— which is often the story only of what ails us. In our churches the effort to see man *sub specie aeternitatis* ["under the appearance of eternity"] has been displaced by a "social gospel"—which is a polemic against the supposed special evils of our time. Our book publishers and literary reviewers no longer seek the timeless and the durable, but spend much of their efforts in fruitless search for à la mode "social commentary"—which they pray won't be out of date when the issue goes to press in two weeks or when the manuscript becomes a book in six months. Our merchandisers frantically devise their semi-annual models which will cease to be voguish when their sequels appear a few months hence. Neither our classroom lessons nor our sermons nor our books nor the things we live with nor the houses we live in are any longer strong ties to our past. We have become a nation of short-term doomsayers.

—Daniel J. Boorstin, *Democracy and Its Discontents*

c. It took hundreds of millions of years to produce the life that now inhabits the earth—eons of time in which that developing and evolving and diversifying life reached a state of adjustment and balance with its surroundings. The environment, rigorously shaping and directing the life it supported, contained elements that were hostile as well as supporting. Certain rocks gave out dangerous radiation; even within the light of the sun, from which all life draws its energy, there were short-wave radiations with power to injure. Given time—time not in years but in millennia—life adjusts, and a balance has been reached. For time is the essential ingredient; but in the modern world there is no time.

—Rachel Carson, *Silent Spring*

*Rewriting*

# 26 *The Challenge of Simplicity*

Theodore M. Bernstein, an editor of *The New York Times,* recounted the story of a plumber who cleaned drains with hydrochloric acid and wrote to a chemical research bureau inquiring about its safety. The bureau wrote back, "The efficacy of hydrochloric acid is indisputably established but the corrosive residue is incompatible with metallic permanence." The plumber, impressed by such a response, thanked the bureau for its approval. Another letter arrived: "We cannot assume responsibility for the production of a toxic and noxious residue with hydrochloric acid. We beg leave to suggest to you the employment of an alternative procedure." More proud than ever, the plumber again expressed his appreciation. In desperation the bureau called in an older scientist, who wrote a third letter to the plumber: "Don't use hydrochloric acid. It eats the hell out of pipes."

*Jargon* has its rightful place in the language: to communicate specialized concepts to other specialists. Every profession and occupation needs a specialized vocabulary. Linguists must talk of *deep structures;* mechanics need to discuss *carbon buildup;* government officials must consider *systems management.* Yet it is not just a matter of knowing your audience. Most audiences, even those trained in the specialities you may be writing about, usually prefer clear, concrete communication. Einstein was admired for his ability to write about scientific complexities with simplicity. Freud, who probably contributed more jargon to the twentieth cen-

**277**

© 1974 United Feature Syndicate, Inc.

tury than any other individual, at least had the courtesy in his own writing to define his terms.

The problem with jargon arises when we use it pretentiously for the sake of impressing rather than communicating or when it is used to obscure meaning, to hide ignorance through lack of precision. Yet all of us want others to think we are intelligent and wise. We seek praise and reputation. We sometimes believe that if our writing sounds obscure, others will think us profound. We may fear simplicity. Only dullards are simple. Those who are knowledgeable, we believe, impress us with their vocabulary. Why, all we need do is listen to our own professors:

> ... the most basic problem that arises in connection with knowledge utilization may be those that stem from the social and organizational character of educational institutions. . . . Public schools display a myriad of normative and other regulatory structures that promote predictability, as well as a host of adaptive mechanisms that reduce external uncertainties.

Quite impressive! But sad, nevertheless. Sad because this professor (of education, no less) is not honestly trying to inform us of anything. His real subject is himself. "Look at me," he says. "Just look at all the big words I know." And too often it happens to us all, especially when we begin to write expository prose about abstract issues or values. We shift to a serious tone, we adopt a formal voice, and before the old electric typewriter even begins to warm up, we're writing as this student did:

> The choice of exogenous variables in relation to multicollinearity is contingent upon the derivations of certain multiple correlation coefficients.

Pretentiousness, affectation, overabstraction, circumlocution—the names for such gobbledygook could fill a small dictionary. Those who admire language, those who respect it, have been railing against the pseudo-intellectual misuse of it for generations. Here is Sir Arthur Quiller-Couch writing in 1923:

> If your language be jargon, your intellect, if not your whole character, will almost certainly correspond. Where your mind should

Reprinted from "Masters of Babble" by permission of James P. Degnan.

go straight, it will dodge: the difficulties it should approach with a fair front and grip with a firm hand it will be seeking to evade or circumvent. For the style is the man, and where a man's treasure is, there his heart, and his brain, and his writing will be also.

And a woman's too, we might add.

The product of writing is a social act. Like other social acts it imposes obligations. In the case of expository prose, our responsibility is to explain or set forth clearly so that the reader understands. The use of jargon or other outlandish abstraction becomes an evasion of that responsibility. That is why Quiller-Couch makes language a moral issue. The use of clear, straightforward prose means that you face up to your responsibilities, your obligation to communicate what you know.

Some of the most famous, or infamous, uses of language to avoid responsibility came from government officials during the Vietnam War. Generals described weapons that were intended to kill people as *antipersonnel devices. Protective reaction* was a military phrase meaning that we bombed "them" before they bombed "us." Concentration camps were termed *relocation centers.* Each of these is an example of a *euphemism,* that is, of a substitute for a straightforward, simple term. Certainly not all euphemisms are immoral. We call undertakers *morticians,* and we substitute *making out* for *fornication:* we elevate janitors to *maintenance engineers,* and we promote old people to *senior citizens.* But euphemisms do lead us astray from reality in the same way that jargon obscures reality through inflated words.

Unfortunately, we can sometimes lead ourselves astray just by using too many words, by circling about a subject without ever quite touching upon it. Here is a student example of *circumlocution:*

> The actualization of an objective decision to follow the rules was not something they really felt was something compelled by their hearts. Often times, a person agrees with the legal legitimacy of something but it is against his ethical values to go ahead with it. Having been confronted with these postulates and their modifications or contingencies, it soon becomes difficult determining exactly what our response should be.

The consequence of inflated language is now apparent. When we substitute jargon, pretentious abstractions, euphemisms, and circumlocutions for precision, we run the risk of concealing our meaning—or lack of meaning—even from ourselves.

When Thoreau wrote his famous advice, "Simplify, simplify," he was speaking of our lives, but the advice applies no less to our writing. Most social issues and moral values are complex. To explain complexity in simple prose is not a fault; it is a mark of achievement. Yet few of us can sit down to the first draft and say, "Now I am going to write a coherent, simple sentence." What we can do is return to those first rough scribblings and ask, "Do I know what I'm trying to say?" and "Can the reader follow it?" Both questions are important. Unless you have discovered and explored your ideas fully, demanding exactness of yourself, all the tinkering in the world will fail to patch over your own confusion. Once you feel confident that you do understand your own ideas, then you are obligated to question whether the reader can.

Your goal should be to find the simplest language possible while still conveying the seriousness and full weight of your intentions. Neither of the following examples would serve:

> The high-level government representative indulged in a special purchase of verduous flora for a close relative.

> The guy got his mom some flowers.

The first is pretentious; the second sounds like Dick and Jane. Somewhere in the middle we might try:

> The senator bought roses for his mother.

If you have plowed your way through earlier chapters in this book on rewriting and editing, you should be fully prepared to handle the extra demands complex ideas may put upon your writing: eliminate extra words; whenever possible use concrete images instead of abstractions; trust the simple sentence, build paragraphs around a single idea; and so on. To simplify essentially means to be straightforward (avoiding circumlocutions and overblown abstractions) and to be exact (to convey a precise meaning, usually through concrete nouns or active verbs). But to that list of techniques, we must add an earlier concept: *honesty*. Not just honesty of perception, but honesty in the manner of presentation. Your goal should be to present what you know in your own voice as an expression of your own imagination and intellect, avoiding the temptation to write as you think others are praised for writing—profoundly, elegantly—choosing instead to be responsible above all for clarity and precision.

### EXERCISES

1. Consider the actual meaning of the following, and try writing a simple version for each:
   a. He established an objective and pursued the ultimate achievement of success with diligence.

   Example: *He set a goal and worked hard to achieve it.*

   b. From the director of the CIA: "I wish to restrict lateral input of outside retirees into positions that could be filled within our own ranks. Therefore, effective immediately, the further hiring of annuitants is prohibited."

c. The neoclassical postulate of rationality and the concept of the entrepreneur as the profit-maximizing individual, should, I think, be replaced by a sociological analysis of the goals of the firm in relation to its nature as an organization within the sociopolitical system.

d. "Thirdly, the aim [of this book] is not to set forth a list of abstract properties of human knowledge but to assist the reader in effecting a personal appropriation of the concrete, dynamic structure immanent and recurrently operative in his own cognitional activities . . ."

e. From a student paper: "Legalization of euthanasia is, retrospectively, a barbaric liability hung upon the corporate neck of civilized society today. It manifests our egocentrical natures and ignores out inherent rights constitutionalized in 1884."

2. The following words and phrases have become the overused, empty, pretentious, or jargonish vocabulary found in almost everybody's writing. Find a simple word or phrase as a replacement for each:

| | |
|---|---|
| *utilize* | *in today's society* |
| Example: use | Example: today |
| *subject area* | *come in contact with* |
| *in the last analysis* | *in accordance with* |
| *fully recognize* | *absolutely essential* |
| *input/output* | *in the case of* |
| *the end result* | *in the field of* |
| *the final solution* | *factor* |
| *parameters* | *maturation* |
| *wholly justifiable* | *socioeconomic considerations* |
| *bottom line* | *delivery system* |

# 27 *Proofreading and Mechanics*

She was the first one to complete her course evaluation, and she flipped it defiantly on the table in front of me:

> I think you where unfare. every paper I wrote you just bers cut up for commas; and spellings. Grammer. You nver paid attention to my ideas not once so you don't worsb where a hipocrit because you kep't saying the content was the most important think. But when came to my papers it was picky picky like all the other english teacher.

I sometimes wonder how she might have felt had she bought a new Pontiac and found the heater connected to the air-conditioner, the left rear door handle broken, and both windshield wipers missing. Would she have considered such problems "picky"? Or would she have felt General Motors had been irresponsible?

In your papers the ideas you express do constitute the most important element, but, as in judging automobiles, the overall product, not just engine size, determines quality. The problem seems to arise when, in our role as writers, the ideas we discover seem stimulating and the pleasures of learning overshadow hours of painful reading and note-taking in the library. We think our readers should feel equally excited, equally pleased. In the burst of energy it takes to pull together a major paper, such details as spelling and punctuation seem trivial. I used to think so as a student. But the role of the reader is obviously different. The reader has no way of approaching a paper for anything other than what he or she reads on the page. If the reader must study every sentence twice because punctuation is confused or omitted or must pause to decipher words because spelling is erratic, attention is unavoidably diverted from meaning to mechanics. Worse, the reader becomes annoyed and irritated. Like the owner of a carelessly built car with a hidden rattle, the reader of a carelessly constructed paper may well overlook strong points and become obsessed with distracting errors.

The solution is time-consuming but simple. By summoning up a final effort, by proofreading your manuscript for every detail, details that are *your* responsibility, you insure that the reader will focus on the more important element—your ideas. This final but mandatory phase in editing contains several basic components. You will probably find it necessary to edit for *grammar, usage, spelling,* and *punctuation* before you type your final draft. Attention to *manuscript form* and *proofreading* will then become the last steps you take in the writing process.

The following chapter constitutes an outline of only the most basic elements you should be familiar with. It can never substitute for a full review of grammar and mechanics found in any major handbook.

# Grammar

Elementary grammar must be mastered because grammar affects meaning. It may seem annoying when an instructor tells you that your pronouns fail to have a clear reference, but it simply means that in some way you have not communicated successfully. Surely you wouldn't say, "John bought herself a car." You knew from the first words you formed as a child that *he's* were different kinds of people from *she's*. Attention to grammar then is little more than attention to the arrangement of words and phrases for the purpose of making them express what you intended to express all along.

### Subject-Verb Agreement

Singular subjects take singular verbs; plural subjects take plural verbs.

John *loves* Jill and Mary.
Jill and Mary *love* John.

Most of us already know the rule, but most of us also make mistakes from time to time. A problem can arise from confusion about the subject itself. Here are some clarifications:

1. *Collective nouns take singular verbs:*

The committee *is* being formed.
The government team *is* in trouble.
Politics *is* a noble profession.

2. *Compound subjects connected by* and *take plural verbs:*

Dotty, Betty, Gloria, and Jane *are* feminists.
The registrar and I *are* having a disagreement.

3. *Compound subjects connected* by either ... or, neither ... nor, *or* not only ... but also *take a verb that agrees with the nearest part of the subject:*

Neither your mother nor my friends *believe* that you will fail.
Neither my friends nor your mother *believes* that you will fail.

4. *A subject composed of a complete clause usually takes a singular verb:*

Whether it rains before breakfast *is* of no concern.

5. *Some words that refer to a plural subject actually take a singular verb (either, neither, everyone, everybody, anybody, and nobody):*

Everyone *loves* a parade.
Nobody that I know *wants* to see the film again.

## Pronouns and Antecedents

Pronouns also need to agree in person, number, and gender with the term to which they refer.

*A third person antecedent takes a third person pronoun:*

The *girls* rode bicycles to school; *they* all got wet.

*A singular antecedent takes a singular pronoun:*

*Roger* ran his boat aground where *he* had first sighted the marker.

*A masculine antecedent takes a masculine pronoun:*

*Mark Twain* was born at an early age; *he* said so himself.

And so on. Few people have problems with pronoun agreement unless the pronouns are separated by too many intervening words or clauses, in which case the solution is usually to repeat the antecedent instead of using a pronoun.

But many of us have problems with *unclear antecedents*. We write too quickly, knowing full well in our minds what we are referring to when we use *it* or *they* or *those*. But the reader, without benefit of insight into our mind, may feel confused unless an antecedent is clearly indicated:

Steven told his roommate that *his* cat died.

Whose cat? Steven's? Or his roommate's?

He searched the parking lot but *it* couldn't be found.

The parking lot couldn't be found?

> Botesius destroyed cities, plundered and pillaged the farms, raped helpless women, and then committed himself to the church. *This* was the cause of his downfall.

Which of all those actions does *this* refer to?

As the writer, you know what you mean. But editing is the point in the process where you must read as if you were the reader. Will your reader understand? Not unless each pronoun refers to a specific antecedent.

## Misplaced Modifiers

A clause or phrase must modify the word that its position in a sentence suggests it's supposed to modify. When it doesn't, the result can be puzzling:

> Walking along the sidewalk, the falling safe almost struck me.

> Being bright orange, I loved the sunset.

> I wanted a roommate to share expenses with my own moral values.

In the first sentence, the safe seems to have been walking along the sidewalk before it mysteriously fell on the writer. In the second sentence, the writer has turned orange. In the third, the writer apparently has expensive moral values. And yet we know that no such nonsense was intended. The solution is to be more specific . . .

> *As I* walked along the sidewalk, the falling safe almost struck me.

or to rearrange the sentence structure . . .

> I loved the bright orange sunset.

or to pull related phrases more closely together . . .

> I wanted a roommate with my own moral values to share expenses.

## Tense Consistency

In general, the reader will more clearly follow an argument if verb tenses are consistent. When you begin in the past tense, make every effort to stay with it unless you have a logical reason for shifting to the present tense. If you begin in the present tense, try to remain in the present. Naturally, occasions arise when shifts in tense are necessary. It is the accidental shifts that cause confusion:

> If my own small experience *is* any guide, the main difficulty in approaching the problem of juvenile delinquency *was* that there *was* very little evidence about it. It *is* unknown, for instance, what the

> actual effects of prison sentences *were* on the delinquent. Statistics *will be* few and not generally reliable. The narcotics problem alone *was* an almost closed mystery.

By this point the reader's mind is reeling. Past, present, future—just where are we? In the above example, the writer begins in the present and seems to be referring to a current situation. The complete paragraph, then, should probably take a present tense:

> If my own small experience *is* any guide, the main difficulty in approaching the problem of juvenile delinquency *is* that there *is* very little evidence about it. It *is* unknown, for instance, what the actual effects of prison sentences *are* on the delinquent. Statistics *are* few and not generally reliable. The narcotics problem alone *is* an almost closed mystery.

Here are a few general principles regarding verb-tense consistency:

1. If possible, use the same tense throughout an entire paragraph.

2. If possible, use the same tense throughout an entire essay. (Obviously there may be occasions when you are describing a movement from one time period to another in which a shift in tense is both normal and necessary.)

3. When a shift in verb tense is essential, signal the reader by moving to a new paragraph or by using a strong transition.

4. Use the present tense in statements that express general philosophical concepts, religious principles, or timeless truths.

## Person Consistency

For the same reason that you would hold to a consistent verb tense, logic requires that you hold to a specific use of *person* (first person *I, we* or *us;* second person *you;* third person *he, she, it,* or *one*):

> If *we* are unable to function under periods of relatively normal stress, *a person* may revert to actions and thoughts that *you* used in childhood. *He* may withdraw into himself, he may cry, and sometimes *you* can actually see him begin to have a temper tantrum.

Shifts of person distract the reader and disrupt the unity. In general, the same person should be used throughout a paragraph, and, if possible, throughout an essay. Many instructors will object especially to use of the second person *you* because, as in the above example, the reader may not have seen or felt the qualities being attributed to him or her. Other instructors may object equally to use of the first person *I* because it often misleads an inexperienced writer into discussing himself or herself more than the subject. The third person is probably the safest of all forms, especially in expository writing.

*One* who is unable to function under periods of relatively normal stress may revert to actions and thoughts that *he* or *she* used in childhood. *The person* may withdraw into himself or herself, may cry, and sometimes may actually have a temper tantrum.

## Sentence Fragments

Although we use sentence fragments frequently in informal conversation, they may create problems in writing. Encountering a sentence fragment is like reaching the bottom of a staircase and stepping off again as if expecting another step. The sudden jolt makes us realize that something anticipated was missing. When a writer begins a sentence with a capital letter, we set off anticipating a complete thought. The fragment itself may make perfect sense within the context, but the jolt to our expectations disrupts the flow of the reading.

| Sentence Fragment | Revision |
| --- | --- |
| We all hurried back to the hotel for our bags. *Thereby missing the parade.* | We all hurried back to the hotel for our bags, thereby missing the parade. |
| | *or* |
| | We missed the parade because we all hurried back to the hotel for our bags. |
| I had to make a decision before the end of the term. *To become an economics major or a used-car salesman.* | I had to make a decision before the end of the term: to become an economics major or a used-car salesman. |
| | *or* |
| | Before the end of the term I had to decide whether to become an economics major or a used-car salesman. |
| The idea is an old one. *Imitating the writing of others to improve your own.* | The idea is an old one: imitate the writing of others to improve your own. |
| | *or* |
| | Imitating the writing of others to improve your own is an old idea. |

Most fragments are grammatically or logically connected to sentences that precede or follow, and so most can be eliminated either by joining the fragment to the related sentence with proper punctuation or by rewriting both sentences so that the fragment is incorporated into the appropriate structure.

However, sentence fragments may be effective even in formal prose if used sparingly and with a sense of control.

Should we allow ourselves to be dominated by foreign oil interests? *Absolutely not.*

She began to write poetry for one reason. *To save her life.*

*Of course!* The answer seemed so simple after all.

## Usage

By custom and long tradition some forms of words and phrases have been accepted as correct or socially acceptable in formal writing. Errors may be considered signs of ignorance. One could raise an argument over whether it should be so, but it is so. Here is a brief list of some common problems young writers often face in *usage.*

### Contractions

Contractions like *hasn't, can't, you're,* and *didn't* were once strictly forbidden in formal expository prose. In recent years, books, popular magazines, and even a number of prestigious scholarly journals have shifted toward acceptance. In general, however, contractions are acceptable and effective for personal essays and other types of informal prose, but too casual for a serious expository paper on an idea or value or for a scholarly research paper.

### Double Negatives

The old admonishment that two negatives in a sentence equaled a positive may have been logically true, but, in terms of communicating, a double negative succeeds well: *I don't have no pencil* leaves little doubt in the reader's mind about whether you have a pencil. The problem is that a double negative is socially unacceptable. Here are some of the worst offenders:

> *can't hardly* tolerate [for one *can hardly* tolerate]
> *can't help* but understand [for *can't help* understanding]
> *did not have scarcely* any [for *had scarcely* any]

### Frequently Confused Words

As all of us grow up in a different cultural environment with exposure to different dialects, it's only natural that we use words differently. Indeed, part of the richness of our language comes from the variance in dialect and usage. But in the professional world you'll likely be entering after college, a certain conformity is expected. Here's a brief list of problem terms you'll want to master:

## Affect, Effect

Cobalt did not *affect* [influence] the cancer.

The doctor did not *effect* [bring about an improvement] in the patient's health.

Note that the two are not interchangeable: you cannot *effect* [bring about] the cancer, nor can you *affect* [influence] an improvement in the patient's health.

*Effect* may also be used as a noun, as in: The *effect* [consequences] of the cancer was visible in his face.

## All ready, Already

They were *all ready* for the exam when the lights went out. [That is, they were *totally prepared.*]

They had *already* left the party. [That is, the action was *completed.*]

## Among, Between

He was chosen from *among* sixteen candidates [more than two].

I had to choose *between* them [only two].

## Data

The data *are* prepared for tomorrow's conference. [*Data* is plural, but in informal writing it now seems acceptable to use it as singular.]

## Differ from, Differ with

Cats *differ from* dogs [expresses unlikeness].

Politicians *differ with* politicians [expresses disagreement].

## Inside of, Outside of

The dance was held *inside* the building [omit the *of* as unnecessary].

We decorated the *inside of* the gymnasium [used correctly when *inside* or *outside* is a noun].

## Is, Be

Gloria *is* an engineer [standard verb form in formal English].

She *be* here on time [used by some black speakers in place of *is* or to imply *usually;* the form is acceptable in spoken or casual English, but not accepted by standard social conventions].

## Its, It's

*It's* a real pleasure [a contraction of *it is*] when you open a book to *its* final page [a possessive pronoun for book].

## Their, There

*Their* dog was on the loose [shows possession—somebody owns the dog].

Several books were over *there* on the table [refers to place].

## Unique

He was *a most unique* character. [Wrong. *Unique* means one of a kind; it does not mean interesting or unusual].

> The statue was *unique* in the world of art. [Right. The statue was the only one like it in the world].

**Would of, Had of**

> I *would of* gone if I *had of* known. [In the first case, the *of* is a mistake made by the ear, for we often say *would've,* a contraction of *would have;* in the second case, the *of* is simply colloquial and unnecessary].
>
> I *would have* gone if I *had* known.

**Etc.**

> The term is an abbreviation of *et cetera,* meaning "and so on." It seems acceptable usage in business and technical writing, but it should be avoided in essays and formal prose because it suggests that the writer was too lazy to list the other details he or she had in mind. If more examples are worth mentioning, then list them. Otherwise don't.

If usage is a serious problem for you, you will find no recourse but to purchase a good reference book. Two works have become classic for clarity and usefulness:

> H. B. Fowler, *Modern English Usage*
> E. B. White and William Strunk, *The Elements of Style*

# Spelling

English is made up of words and derivitives from Anglo-Saxon, Latin, French, and several other languages. Our spelling is a hodgepodge of conventions and illogical formulas that seldom apply in all cases. We have only two solutions: memorization and the dictionary. If spelling errors seem more than a matter of a word here or there, then you must accept the need for double-checking every word about which you have any doubt at all. Remember to do it in the final editing stage, not while you are writing the first draft. But don't ignore the problem and hope the reader will be forgiving. Many people, rightly or wrongly, consider spelling errors a mortal sin.

Here's a list of frequently misspelled words. *Memorize* their correct spelling. In the long run, it will save frustrating minutes searching through the dictionary.

| | |
|---|---|
| all right [*not* alright] | neither [*not* niether] |
| a lot [*not* alot] | occurred [*not* occured] |
| adapt [*as distinct from* adopt] | occurrence [*not* occurence] |
| biennial [*not* biannual] | professor [*not* proffesor] |
| chief [*not* cheif] | perseverance [*not* |
| column [*not* colume] | perseverence] |

conscience [*as distinct from* conscious]
council [*as distinct from* counsel]
explanation [*not* explaination]
high school [*not* highschool]
idea [*as distinct from* ideal]
judgment [*not* judgement]
loose [*as distinct from* lose]
maintenance [*not* maintainance]
manageable [*not* managable]

research [*not* reaserch]
responsible [*not* responsable]
rhythm [*not* rythm]
site, cite, sight [*three distinct meanings*]
sophomore [*not* sophmore]
subtle [*not* sutle]
their, there, they're [*three distinct meanings*]
truly [*not* truely]
weird [*not* wierd]
whether [*as distinct from* weather]

As a student, I didn't exactly hate dictionaries, but I found them tedious and annoying. Rather than pause, lug one down from the shelf, make space amid a clutter of papers, search, and return it to the shelf, I chose to ignore words I knew I had misspelled. It was just too much effort. Then I discovered a dictionary was never meant to sit on a shelf. A dictionary should lie flat next to your writing pad or typewriter. That simple discovery meant that, with hardly a pause, I could flip easily to a new page and check a word in a matter of seconds. Afterward, I learned to leave the dictionary open, ready for the next flip of a page. Both my attitude and my spelling have improved.

# Punctuation

The goal of punctuation is simply to provide symbols that tell your reader how you want your sentence to be read. The "rules" are actually customs we all agree upon, in the same way we agree to drive on the right-hand side of the road. When you break custom, you may feel daring, but you take an undeniable risk.

## Commas

1. *Use commas to separate clauses, especially in long sentences:*

We worked for several hours debating the proposition, a motion to repeal the rights of homosexuals, but it became clear we would never agree.
*In a short sentence, you may omit the comma if the rhythm seems more effective without it:*
We debated the proposition but we could not agree.

2. *Use commas to separate items in a series:*

His laughter was obnoxious, offensive, and hysterical.
*The final comma may be omitted although it's best to read the*

*sentence aloud and determine whether the omission will lead to confusion.*

3. *Use commas to set off long introductory phrases or clauses.*

With the worst of her ordeal yet to come, Barbara decided to forgo her lunch.
In addition to other errors, he committed a crime against nature.

4. *Do not use commas to connect two independent clauses (this is often termed a "comma splice").*

We watched the boat come in, the people on the dock laughed at us.
*Complete thoughts should obviously be separated with a period.*

5. *Do use a comma to connect independent clauses already joined by a conjunction such as* for, so, but, and, nor, *and* yet:

Professor Harris was unprepared for the question, and his students were unprepared for the answer.
I knew that she was attracted to me, but I could not find the courage to ask her out.

## Semicolons

1. *Use a semicolon to separate two independent clauses that show a close relationship (an independent clause is one that could stand alone as a separate sentence; the semicolon draws such clauses together to emphasize the relationship).*

All of us supported the political activity; all of us did not support Mr. Arnold.

2. *Use a semicolon to separate independent clauses that are connected with a conjunctive adverb* (however, consequently, therefore, moreover, and then) *or by a modifier* (in fact, in the first place, on the other hand, for example):

His argument was based on emotion; *however,* it could have been based on appeal to reason.
The antique clock turned out to be the most valuable item in her collection; *in fact,* we were offered over five thousand dollars for it.

3. *Use a semicolon in a series where other internal punctuation is also used.*

We found several items for sale: sombreros, for only two dollars; ruanas, for about fifteen dollars; and estrebos, a type of brass stirrup, for about one hundred dollars.

## Colons

*Use a colon to set off the introductory portion of a sentence from items in a series or from a directly related statement or clause.*

He developed three theories: the theories of magnitude, of discrepancy, and of middle-ends.

*Note that the clause preceding the colon must always form a complete sentence.*

I had something important to say to him: "You have changed my life, but not my mind."

# Quotations, Ellipsis, and Brackets

1. *Use quotation marks for speech or for material taken directly, word for word, from a printed source:*

According to the *Times* report, "A toehold of the antidemocratic left at Berkeley has become an established beachhead in both universities and the larger society."

2. *When you wish to* omit *a word or phrase from a quotation, use an ellipses (three dots with a space between each dot):*

According to the *Times* report, "A toehold of the antidemocratic left . . . has become an established beachhead in . . . universities. . . ."

*Note that when the omission occurs at the end of the sentence, a fourth dot is added for a period.*

3. *When you wish to* add *a word or phrase to a quotation to clarify some aspect of it, use square brackets—not parentheses. As many typewriters do not have a bracket key, you must draw them in with dark ink.*

Mark Twain once said, "I believe that the impact of a single book for good or harm is shown in the effects wrought by it [*Don Quixote*] and by *Ivanhoe*."

*If this quotation were used without the editorial insertion in square brackets, the reader would not know what it referred to.*

# Punctuation Inside Quotations

1. *Periods and commas always go inside quotation marks:*

The Surgeon General reports that "cigarette smoking may be dangerous for your health."
Since the *American Journal of Psychiatry* first observed that

there "is no evidence for neurosis in guinea pigs," we have turned to other mental health problems.

*2. Colons, exclamation marks, and question marks are located inside the quotation when they form an original part of the quotation:*

J. D. O'Hara raises a serious issue: "Do we feel that the nation's oil companies alone can solve the problem?"

*But colons, exclamation marks, and question marks are located outside the quotation when they represent your punctuation rather than the author's.*

Did Richard Nixon really say, "Your president is not a crook"?

She made herself quite clear by stating, "I believe in the right to censor schoolbooks for children"!

*Note that, in such cases, the author's original, terminal punctuation is omitted. Your punctuation marks the end of the sentence.*

## Titles

*1. Use quotation marks for titles of short works:*

*Magazine articles:*    "A New Look at China"
*Short stories:*    "Young Goodman Brown"
*Poems:*    "To His Coy Mistress"
*Chapters:*    "The Social Effects of the New Deal"
*Song Titles:*    "Do You Keep Your Chewing Gum on the
    Bedpost Overnight?"

*2. Use underlining for titles of major works or works that enclose shorter works:*

*Magazine titles:*    Harper's
*Books:*    Twenty Ways to Better Health
*Plays:*    Death of a Salesman
*Record Albums:*    Beethoven's Pop Hits
*Government Documents:*    The Congressional Record
*TV and Film Titles:*    Gone with the Wind

*In printed material,* italics *serves the same function as underlining.*

*3. Never use both quotation marks and underlining on the same title unless the title contains an inner title of its own:*

Dr. Harris's first essay, "A study of Walt Whitman's Leaves of Grass" received an enthusiastic response.

*4. Do not underline or place quotation marks around the title of your own paper. However, your title may include the title of another work:*

Moral Turpitude in Shakespeare's Macbeth

# Manuscript Form

Preparing a manuscript to look professional is not difficult. The following method is not the only way, of course. Many businesses, professions, and professors will require that you follow a particular style sheet. But the form described here is one followed by experienced writers in general and should serve you well.

```
                HOW TO PREPARE YOUR MANUSCRIPT

                            by

                      Oliver Whiplash


        The first page of an essay should look like

    this.  Manuscripts should be (1) typewritten, (2)

    double spaced with wide margins; and (3) typed on

    one side of the paper only.

        The title, in all capital letters, is centered

    about one-third to one-half way down the page.  The

    word by should fall two spaces below the title; and

    your name, two spaces below that.

        Most teachers prefer a left margin of at least

    1½ inches and a right margin of about one inch.  Try

    to leave a one-inch margin at the bottom as well.
```

Whiplash -2-

Do not number the first page, but number all other pages at the top, either in the middle or at the right-hand margin.

The second and all succeeding pages of a professional looking manuscript should look like this. Attach all pages together with a paper clip. If you submit loose papers and pages become lost, you must assume the responsibility. For extra safety, type your last name at the upper left of each page or beside the numeral.

No matter how good a typist you are, you should always proofread your final copy. Use dark ink and make corrections clearly. Few teachers will expect you to be a perfect typist, and few will object to a few, clear corrections.

Finally, don't conclude by signing your name or adding a "P.S." to explain why the paper is late. When you come to the end, simply stop.

## Proofreading

The term *proof,* when used by publishers, refers to a trial sheet of printed material that is checked against the original manuscript and on which corrections are made. To *proofread,* then, is to look for any kind of mistake that may have been made in transferring your essay from the last rough draft onto a typed page. This is not the place to make your original inspection for errors of *grammar, usage, spelling,* and *punctuation.*

Those items should have been corrected in rough draft. But obviously spelling or punctuation errors may have crept in again during typing. Even worse, words and phrases may have been omitted accidentally. No matter what the error, it remains your responsibility to make a final check, line by line, and to correct the smallest mistake, especially if you have someone else type your paper for you.

How do you proofread effectively?

1. Read what you've actually written, not what you think you've written. This may require a minimum of several hours to several days to pass so that the paper can "cool" and you can develop some objectivity about it.

2. Read aloud. The ear will catch missing words or phrases. Sometimes the ear will detect incorrect punctuation because rhythms will seem awkward.

3. Check for spelling errors by skimming from right to left or bottom to top. That way the mind can focus on words alone without becoming absorbed in the context.

Does it all seem petty? Surely no more so than our expectations that a doctor will not leave a pair of scissors inside a patient after surgery or that a plumber will not leave a pipe disconnected or that a lawyer will not omit your name from your rich uncle's last will and testament. Mistakes always occur. All of us are guilty. But for a teacher to demand high standards is no more than your employer will some day demand and no more than you yourself expect from others.

## Editorial Checklist for Part Five
*Writing About Ideas, Issues, and Values*

_____ Have you explored all the different strategies of perception to gain insight into your subject?

—who? what? where? why? when?

—change? conflict? consequences? characterization?

—comparison and contrast?

—classification?

—definition?

—analysis?

_____ Have you narrowed your subject?

_____ Have you attempted to make abstractions as concrete as possible?

_____ Have you investigated primary or secondary sources?

_____ Have you distinguished between objective facts and inferences or opinions?

_____ Have you looked for relationships?

_____ Does your introduction provide a general overview? a brief historical or cultural context? a definition? or a classification of the subject?

_____ Have you provided a focusing or thesis sentence that narrows the subject? indicates the purpose? and suggests your attitude?

_____ Have you designed each paragraph around a single unit of thought?

_____ Have you read aloud and listened to the rhythms?

_____ Have you eliminated unnecessary words and used active verbs?

Pamela Drake, a freshman English major, has combined several expository techniques in her look at the challenge to conventional marriage patterns. She defines, compares, contrasts, and analyzes.

# The Option of Marriage or Cohabitation

## Pamela J. Drake

*" . . . a contract of true love to celebrate."*
—William Shakespeare, The Tempest

Within the last decade, more and more couples who seem to be candidates for marriage are opting to live together without participating in official ceremonies. *Marriage,* of course, is the legal union of a man and woman, but *living together* is a less clearly defined concept. In general, it seems to refer to the cohabitation of an adult man and woman who have made an emotional and physical commitment—but not a legal one. *Living together* sounds tempting. It seems to promise the possibility of a free-spirited relationship, yet the social and legal atmosphere still prevelent in this country make *living together* a trying situation that may not be worth the price.

According to Lewis B. Smedes in *Sex for Christians* (1976), our social ideal of marriage is based on the model of the marriage between God and his people. It is a picture of a solemn vow of enduring partnership and one in which fidelity is measured in terms of creative love for his partner. But it is interesting to note that this definition of marriage would then encompass and seem to sanctify the committed couple who are only living together. In fact, in the emotional realm, committed couples, whether married or not, are far more similar than different. The same intensity of commitment can easily exist when made privately as when made publicly. Frank Corona and Lynn Winters, both graduate students at the University of New Mexico, see their relationship as close and committed even though they have not taken the final legal step. "We share our joys, problems, and goals, like any happily married couple, and experience a warm, loving closeness," Frank relates. "We're both adults, and, for now, this suits us. Since we've made a conscious decision not to have children, our present arrangement is the best." In the *Marriage Option* (1977), the Rev. David Sammons supports the notion that a deep commitment is possible in a cohabitation situation. He suggests we need to relax our social judgments and allow natural evolution "from casual to committed relationships and a *de facto* state of marriage to continue without feeling a need to moralize or disapprove because it does not fit a traditional model."

The social acceptability of marriage, however, is an obvious and ancient custom. The rituals surrounding a marriage are many, and they serve to encourage and celebrate the occasion. In *Marriage and Family Interaction* (1971), Robert R. Bell of Temple University, suggests that because no society has ever existed without controls over some areas of human behavior, marriage has become one of our society's important areas of controlling social behavior. For that reason the social acceptability of *living together* is not assured. No matter what their commitment, young people choosing to live together find people around them may be confused, hurt, or angry. Their relationship suggests that society has lost some of its social control. Some people believe that, like the domino theory, if control is overthrown in one area of life, it will lose credibility in all areas. The family of the cohabiting couple may feel ashamed or embarrassed, adding more stress to the situation. Kathy Benson, University of New Mexico freshman, states that "when I talk about my brother, who is living with his girlfriend, I feel on the defensive, like I have to make people believe that he's a great guy *anyway*. But I'm not even very sure how *I* feel about the whole situation."

One factor that may change the social respectability of marriage is the soaring divorce rate. In 1977 there were 1,090,000 divorces in the United States. The rise in divorce may be due, in part, to a shattering of the illusion that seems to surround marriage—the so-called perfect-love myth. After marriage, one is supposed to live happily ever after. But women especially have been kept ignorant of the sacrifice involved, the money problems, and the problem of losing a personal identity—of being absorbed into the husband's name and world. For the woman, a legal marriage may signal the end of personal growth, for all of her attention must be given to the care and support of others.

By contrast, when discussing a positive aspect of *living together,* Edna J. LeShan, in her pamphlet "Mates and Roommates: New Styles in Young Marriages" (1971) relates that one girl found that the best thing about living together was knowing that both partners had a lot of growing to do, so if growing apart occurred, the final legal commitment of marriage had not yet been made.

Recently, however, the social aspects of marriage versus living together have become secondary to the myriad legal aspects. A person may feel that where love is concerned, a "little piece of paper" means nothing. But *Newsweek* (April 30, 1979) claims that lawyers now believe recent legal decisions should cause more and more unmarried couples to draw up prenuptial or "living-together contracts," just as binding as the marriage contract. Because neither marriage nor cohabitation can be assuredly "forever," the legal tangles involved in ending either relationship must be considered. Presently, there are more definite guidelines and laws concerning marriage and divorce than laws concerning living together and moving apart. U.S. laws regard marriage as a legally binding contract. When one is signing documents, receiving benefits after a spouse's death, or receiving compensation after separation, legal marriage expedites the proceedings.

No clear obligations exist for the separated couple who have merely lived together. The *Marvin* v. *Marvin* case in Los Angeles, in which Michele Marvin sued actor Lee Marvin for half of his earnings during the six years they lived together without being wed, is a landmark case. Although she did not receive all that she asked for, Michele Marvin was awarded a settlement of $104,000. Columbia University law professor Ruth Bader Ginsburg was quoted in *Newsweek* as saying that the *Marvin* v. *Marvin* case "illustrates the further breakdown of the legal line between the married and unmarried union."

Being married, or living together, without commitment is a sham. When one is considering the human beings involved, the level of commitment, not the paper, *is* most important. But the problems that can arise from social and legal pressures may be as damaging to those who live together as traditional problems are to those who marry. Within the present system, it may still be more advantageous for a committed couple to marry. The social and legal problems involved in living together seem to outweigh whatever free-spirited ideals may be involved. If a commitment truly exists, then a marriage contract—with all its formality and ritual—probably remains the best way for a man and woman to share a life together.

Nancy Weinberg is an assistant professor at the University of Illinois School of Social Work. In the following essay from *The New York Times*, Weinberg uses both definition and contrast to argue her point.

# Disability Isn't Beautiful
## Nancy Weinberg

The law barring Federal agencies and holders of Federal contracts from discriminating against the physically handicapped has not been actively enforced during its three years of existence. And though the handicapped are legally entitled to the same protection as other minority groups, they continue to be a target of discrimination while the Government acts as if they were different from other minorities.

Three characteristics define a minority. The first is easy identification. Recognition of a physically disabled person is usually simple on the basis of appearance alone. However, the physically disabled may attempt "to pass" by concealing their handicap. Deaf people, for example, will sometimes avoid using manual communication, especially in public. This refusal to use manual communication is similar to hair-straightening, skin-bleaching and other examples of minority members' attempts to deny their identity.

Another feature of a minority group is the negative prejudgment made about the behavior and abilities of its members. When able-bodied individuals are surveyed and asked to describe a disabled person or another able-bodied person, their descriptions of the former are more negative than those of the latter. Blind persons, deaf persons and individuals confined to wheelchairs are all viewed as less intelligent, less happy, less popular, less likeable, and less self-confident than the able-bodied.

The final feature of a minority group is the threat, real or imagined, that it poses to the comfort of the majority. The physically handicapped threaten the social comfort of the able-bodied. Research indicates that the able-bodied feel more uncomfortable and show greater physiological stress when interacting with a disabled person than with an able-bodied person. In addition, possibly to avoid further tension, people interacting with the disabled tailor their opinions so they are in closer agreement with the disabled and terminate their interactions with the disabled sooner than with others.

As well as meeting the three defining characteristics of a minority group, the physically handicapped experience disadvantages that other minorities do not face.

People in racial and ethnic minorities grow up with other members of those minorities. They learn from others in their group how to deal with the majority culture.

In contrast, a child born with a handicap is generally brought up around the nonhandicapped. The child has little opportunity to learn coping skills from others with similar handicaps. He or she is soon socialized to have the same values about the importance of physical perfection as the rest of society. (When able-bodied children and disabled children are asked to arrange pictures of children with and without handicaps from "most liked" to "least liked," both groups order the pictures in the same manner, with the able-bodied child always being liked best.) The sense of pride in a certain identity that can be fostered when people of the same religious or ethnic group come together is absent. There is no natural grouping to support a "disability is beautiful" movement.

Finally, even when people with disabilities are given opportunities, they are often unable to take advantage of them because of physical barriers: steps and curbs, inaccessible elevators, narrow corridors, revolving doors, a lack of accessible public transportation and a lack of accessible housing. According to a Government report, 20 million people with handicaps are "built out of normal living by unnecessary barriers."

The physically handicapped have the liabilities of a minority group. Shouldn't they be given the rights of a minority group? The answer is affirmative. It is time the action was also.

---

Susan Brownmiller is best known for *Against Our Will* (1975), a feminist study of rape and its many amplifications. Brownmiller was a feminist leader throughout the 1950s and 1960s before it was socially acceptable to be so. She has worked as a newswriter for ABC television and as a free-lance writer. The following essay was originally printed in *The New York Times*.

---

# Understanding Rape
## Susan Brownmiller

The difference between human beings and cows, someone once told me, is that cows may have a genealogy but only human beings have a history. When I first became concerned with rape as a human phenomenon, the idea seized my mind that rape must have a history, too.

Written history records ideas and material changes that are the product of human effort. If rape was something other than a blind act of instinct, if it was, as I came to believe, a deliberate conscious crime of man against woman, then a documented record of its evolution could be pieced together.

For surely a crime that begins in the mind, not in the nether regions of "lust," would have undergone changes in perception, and might undergo further changes, in the story of civilization.

Biblical references to rape provided the first clues. Rape sneaked its way into man's law as a criminal act under very special and restricted circumstances: when the victim had been a betrothed virgin.

The nature of the unpardonable crime was not that it was an act of violence against a young girl's body, but that it was a crime against her father's honor and estate. The heinous act that could not be forgiven was the theft of a father's daughter's virginity, the ruination of her pristine state and, thus, her fair price on the marriage market.

Cases in which a married woman had been forcibly ravished were not considered rape; this was adultery and both participants were deemed equally guilty in the eyes of the Hebrew patriarchs.

Deuteronomy's covenants were echoed in medieval English law. The rape of a high-born, propertied virgin brought penalties like death or blinding and castration, but the law historian Brachton allowed that the rapist could be redeemed in a singular manner: the victim might marry her violator to save him from his awful fate. Such a marriage naturally brought with it a transfer of lands and property from her name to his. Heiress-stealing (forcible abduction and rape) had quite a vogue in the Middle Ages.

Not until the 13th-century Statutes of Westminster did English law formally extend its concept of criminal rape to include the forcible violation of wives, widows, nuns, and even prostitutes.

Under the rule of Edward I, the Crown acknowledged—by taking charge of prosecutions—that the public safety of all women, not merely the protection of landed virgins, had become a matter of state concern. In theory, at least, rape had won its proper place in legal thinking.

The violation could now be seen from the vantage point of its original intent—as an act of physical violence against a female body, and not dependent on such "property" concepts as virginity, chastity and marriage. I did say "in theory."

The history of rape in war has even sorrier origins, for the violating of women after a battle was traditionally justified as the first fruit of victory. "To the victor belongs the spoils." It was perfectly lawful in ancient times to take and use captured women as slave-concubines. Indeed, the relevant passages in Deuteronomy were often cited by upholders of slavery in 18th-century America as moral justification for their own systematic sexual abuse of black women.

As late as the 17th century, according to the Dutch jurist Grotius, some nations still permitted their armies to rape freely on enemy territory. But the more civilized nations, he went on, now had rape prohibitions in their military codes.

I'm afraid, however, that the stern injunctions always read better on paper than they worked out in practice. Rape in war has continued unchecked: for instance in Bangladesh, Cyprus and Vietnam. And the legal machinery designed to bring a military rapist to justice functions poorly when the victim is an "enemy" woman who—if she survives the assault— does not speak the language of her aggressor-assailant.

Rape in war is an important part of the anguished, hidden history of women, yet most historians tend to discount or slough off the special fate of female noncombatants when they make their solemn assessments of the times that try men's souls. Rape usually crops up in history books when the author is trying for a little color, a paragraph of bright writing. But documentation of mass rape in warfare has survived despite the historians' lack of interest.

Sworn depositions, eyewitness accounts, medical affidavits and the like have been preserved from conflicts as dimly remembered as the Wars of Religion in France (a Catholic priest sorrowfully described to his diary the gang rape by Catholic soldiers of a Huguenot woman) and the Battle of Culloden (the lairds of Scotland meticulously kept their painful records).

Housed in the National Archives in Washington are six notarized affidavits from women of Hunterdon County, New Jersey, who were raped by British soldiers "sometime in December last past," 1776. The youngest was thirteen years old. Another was "five months and Upwards Advanced in her Pregnancy."

World War II offers an impartial bonanza of rape documentation from Allied and Axis sides. To match depositions from Russian women who were raped by the German Army on the road to Stalingrad there are depositions similar in content, similar in tone, from German women who were raped by the Russian Army on the road to Berlin. Has the Rape of Nanking slipped into metaphor? Read the typed transcripts of the International Military Tribunal for the Far East, held at Tokyo, for an idea of its actual dimensions.

Unpleasant to face, agonizing to come to terms with on an emotional level, the historical record must not be ignored. Accepting the history of rape is the first step toward denying rape a future.

# PART

## *Formal Analysis*

In good speaking, should not the mind of the speaker know the truth of the matter about which he is to speak?

*—Plato*

The voice of the intellect is a soft one, but it does not rest until it has gained a hearing. Ultimately, after endless rebuffs, it succeeds. This is one of the few points in which one may be optimistic about the future of mankind.

*—Sigmund Freud*

# 28 *Developing an Awareness of Critical Thinking*

The winter sun had almost set and my office was growing dark when he knocked. I had been holding conferences with freshmen for several hours and their faces had begun to blur. He was a young black man who had just received his first *F* on a literature exam. He sat across the desk twisting the paper in his hands. "All you want us to do is repeat what you think," he began. "My ideas are just as good as yours."

Outside my window the lights came on in the gymnasium across the street. My wife would be expecting me home for dinner. I took a deep breath and tried to explain that his ideas might indeed be as valid as mine but that he must demonstrate their validity. He could not simply assert, as he had, that Robert Frost's poem, "Stopping by Woods on a Snowy Evening," dealt with a ghost. That might be true, I said, but he must point to specific evidence in the poem that would show me how he had come to such a conclusion.

"That's how I felt," he said. "That's what the poem made me feel."

I spent fifteen minutes going over the poem with him. Where did he find evidence that the speaker of the poem was a ghost? Where did he find "church bells tolling for the dead"? (A line that did not appear in the poem.) His anger grew. My frustration increased. I was beginning to think all freshmen were alike. Finally, he blurted out, "All you whities think you own the truth. Well, I got a different message than you did—I felt it, and that makes it true."

I was furious that race had been brought into the issue. It was a direct blow to my self-image. I handed back his exam and told him to leave. I even suggested several places he might take his truth. Afterward, I regretted my anger, but I knew that in both of us emotion had won out over reason.

The nature of truth has long presented us with one of our most complex intellectual challenges. Are all ideas equally true? Is there such a thing as truth at all? If so, how can we know it? If not, by what method can we determine even the probable truth of anything? Those who are most confident about the existence of something called Absolute Truth (a truth that is eternally undeniable and undebatable) usually depend upon intuition and faith for their conviction. The problem is that Absolute Truth known through faith cannot be demonstrated to others. You either believe or you don't believe. By contrast, when we use *reason,* we ask that the truth of something be demonstrated through evidence or argument. In its simplest form, I might make a comparison to the concepts of *telling* and *showing* that have been emphasized in earlier chapters. You may *tell* me you perceive or possess the truth, but logic requires that you *show* me both the evidence and the method of reasoning you used to arrive at your conclusion.

Reason or logic, then, becomes a method of seeking probable truth through inference or interpretation of observable facts—something you began working with in Part Four. Reason may also be a system of argumentation that considers the relationship between various elements of abstract concepts—something you began working with in Part Five. To think critically means to apply the basic process involved in logical reasoning. Before we pursue it further, however, we need to identify some of the problems that interfere with reasoning. The incident with my student reveals several. I was tired and quick to anger. I had begun to classify all freshmen as the same. He was convinced that all professors were the same and that racial bias had influenced my judgment. I felt that he must use logic to demonstrate the truth; he felt that emotion evoked by poetry contained its own truth. Both of us ended up *feeling* we were in the right. But sometimes feelings can be seriously wrong.

## Emotional Blocks to Reason

I recently spoke to an all-male audience of college students on the surprising growth of women's athletic abilities. Among dozens of other facts, I pointed out that twenty years ago in the 100-meter dash the fastest woman in the world was 11.88 percent slower than the fastest man. By the end of 1976, this margin had been reduced to 9.62 percent and was continuing to decrease as more women entered physical training earlier. In fact, the women's marathon record (26-mile run) is 2 hours, 35 minutes, 15 seconds—a mark that would have beaten every man at the Olympic Games through 1924 and won the bronze in 1948. In other words, all evidence tends to show that, with better training and positive encouragement, women can and will close the gap on such male bastions as physical strength and endurance. My all-male audience responded with uncomfortable silence. Finally, one young man blurted out, "Well, women will never be able to play football!" The others in the room nodded in vigorous agreement and relief. The matter seemed to be settled. When we are emotionally committed to something, contradictory data are easily ignored.

The emotional support we attach to our race, ethnic group, culture, or religion will often overpower the logic of mere reason. It seems normal in human nature to believe that *our* way of living makes sense whereas others have funny habits. It seems normal to believe in our own superiority. The Indian word *Cheyenne,* for example, means "the people," a term that obviously suggests that other tribes, such as Sioux and Blackfoot, were something less than people. Hitler manipulated just such an attitude to persuade a nation that Jews were an "inferior" race deserving barbaric treatment. Americans, too, are not immune. Racist attitudes separating blacks from whites or Chicanos from whites can cause people to act in ways that they would normally condemn in others. We create such strong stereotypes in our minds that, when presented with facts to the contrary, we may tend to assume the facts are inaccurate and the stereotype true. One of the most recent examples occurred during the Vietnam War. Day after day television reports and newspaper photos showed Vietnamese women crying over the dead bodies of their children or husbands shredded with pain over the caskets of their wives. Yet many continued to insist that Orientals did not value human life as we did. Even on the most everyday level we tend to see our city or neighborhood as better than others; we tend to believe that the way we eat or the clothing styles we wear are "normal." Once we become emotionally committed to our private or cultural truths, logical reasoning is blocked. Yet for some twenty-five hundred years, logic has been the primary method accepted by the Western world for determining truth. If we are to function successfully in such a world, we must recognize how emotion sways our thinking and affects our judgment.

---

*What role does emotional bias or culturally trained attitudes play in each of the following statements?*

1. In the 1830s Mormons adopted polygamy as a form of marriage. They were driven from New York to Illinois to Missouri. Finally they sought exile in the deserts of Utah. Even there federal troops sometimes engaged them in battle. The U.S. Congress refused to grant statehood to Utah until the Mormons ceased their "immoral practices."

2. Baby girls should be dressed in pink; boys, in blue.

3. From a United States Senator: "The problem with trying to deal with the Soviets is that you can never trust them. Deceit and secrecy are part of their heritage—right back to the czars."

4. Do you know who won the Polish beauty contest? Who? No one.

5. A wife should be subordinate to her husband. As St. Paul writes in Ephesians 5:23–4, "Wives, submit yourselves unto your husbands . . . for the husband is the head of the family even as Christ is the head of the church."

6. The proper way to cut your meat is to hold your fork in your left hand and your knife in your right hand. Cut off a single bite. Place your knife at the top of the plate. Shift your fork to your right hand and eat. Repeat the process for the next bite.

---

# Intellectual Laziness

Some problems to clear reasoning derive less from emotional blocks than from lazy thinking. We prefer simple ideas over complex ideas. Truth always seems more evident if we don't bother to consider details or consequences.

An *oversimplification* is caused when we fail to investigate an idea thoroughly. In 1978, for example, the governor of Ohio ran for reelection after more than one-third of the state's public schools systems faced bankruptcy. Many schools had actually closed their doors. The governor campaigned on a banner of "no new taxes." He argued instead that because inflation was soaring, the state would collect more taxes anyway and the problem would take care of itself. The reasoning sounds clear. As inflation goes up, people would spend more money to buy goods and thus pay more sales tax. The extra income would go to the schools. But the problem had been oversimplified. For one thing, the governor failed to account for the fact that inflation would also drive up the cost of running the schools. In fact, school costs were already rising faster than inflation. The oversimplification appealed to voters, however, and the governor was reelected.

Simplification may be a valuable approach to any subject if by simplifying we clarify. But when we *over*simplify we distort and mislead. Instead of telling the truth, we lie. Here are several types of oversimplifications that sound logical and convincing but ignore the complexities of human nature.

## Faulty Cause and Effect

Alcoholism is caused by the availability of alcohol.

Rome fell after the introduction of Christianity; therefore, Rome fell because of Christianity.

Naturally, if alcohol did not exist, we would not have alcoholism, but the fact that it does exist does not make it the singular cause of the disease because not everyone who drinks alcohol becomes alcoholic. Nor does the fact that Christianity preceded the fall of Rome mean that it caused such a fall. In fact, the notion that "Rome fell" is itself an oversimplification.

### Overgeneralizations

Democracy is the best form of government.
People on welfare are lazy.
Poor students are a result of poor teachers.

Overgeneralizations usually depend upon a stated or implied *always, never, greatest, best,* or other superlatives that claim a truth without exception. We can criticize the above examples by observing that, for nations with no heritage of self-government, democracy may *not* be the best form of government, nor are *all* welfare recipients necessarily lazy, nor can *all* poor students blame their teachers. In each case, the writer should qualify his assertion: democracy is *often* the best form of government; *some* people on welfare are lazy; poor students *may* be a result of poor teaching.

### Hasty Conclusions

My friend scored 100 on an I.Q. exam. It's obvious his abilities are only average and he should become an auto mechanic.

I knew two girls who married in their sophomore year; the only reason a girl goes to college is to find a husband.

When a judgment is made too early in the reasoning process or before all evidence has been examined, it is called a hasty conclusion. An I.Q. of 100 indicates the score on a single type of examination. Your friend may be a creative genius in music or painting or sculpture, but none of those is tested on I.Q. exams. Nor can the marriage of two girls be considered adequate evidence to conclude that *all* girls seek marriage when they attend college.

### Undefined Abstractions

"Coke is the real thing."

Sam Smith is neurotic.

Just what is a *real* thing? Is it conceivable that Pepsi is an *imaginary* thing? And what is *neurotic?* The term is often used to mean that someone acts in a way that seems "strange"—but strange according to whose standards? So many mental conditions have been grouped under neurotic that the American Psychological Association no longer recognizes the term as describing a meaningful medical condition. It seems to mean whatever we want it to mean. Without precise definition, the reader can rightly suspect that we don't really know what we're talking about.

Clear reasoning requires hard work, time, and careful attention to details. Some people are upset by complexity and leap at the first solution or easiest answer. But the successful writer builds an argument slowly, with arduous attention to word choices and concrete evidence. He or she works to clarify and simplify, not to oversimplify.

---

*Consider the various types of oversimplifications you find in the following:*

1. From the Hartford, Connecticut, sheriff: "Marijuana should never be legalized. Of twenty heroin addicts now in my jail, eighteen of them started on marijuana. That's 90 percent!"

2. Laurie Lee Schaefer, Miss America for 1971, ate Campbell's Tomato Soup when she was a little girl. Look at Laurie Lee today!

3. Two hospital studies have shown that for pain other than headaches, Excedrin is more effective than aspirin.

4. Why, I would never promote fluoridation. Fluoridation was tried in Cleveland in 1843, and not *one* of those people is alive today.

5. The Marines will make a man of you.

6. From a student paper: "The issue of interracial marriages is frequently judged by today's society. But times are changing and each generation should accept new ideas. When society is against a couple's marriage, they will have a closer bond of love between themselves. They won't argue as much. If all marriages were interracial, there wouldn't be any discrimination."

7. Without a college education, you can't find a good job.

8. If guns are outlawed, only outlaws will have guns.

9. The governor of Ohio was reelected in 1978 because he oversimplified the school taxing issue.

---

# False Modes of Argument

An argument is a course of reasoning aimed at swaying or influencing the audience to believe in the truth of something. Obviously, the various modes of arguing are many, but several methods can present particular problems in that they may seem to offer forceful reasoning while actually failing to demonstrate the truth they proclaim.

## The False Analogy

An analogy is a good way of showing a relationship and leading a reader from something known to something unknown. If I tell you that learning to write is like learning to swim because both require practice and repetition, you may understand more about writing *if* you already know something about swimming. And my reasoning may be accurate if the likeness is close enough to make my conclusions "highly probable." But, by definition, an analogy contains differences as well as similarities. If we should decide that the differences are greater than the likeness, we must call it a *false analogy*. A few years ago the Shell Oil Company ran a commercial on television that concluded with the analogy: "If Shell Oil Company can make such high quality of components for airplanes, think how good its gasoline must be." The problem, of course, is that even if Shell builds quality airplanes parts, there is no guarantee that another branch of the same company a thousand miles away, under different management, and pursuing a different manufacturing process in refining gasoline from oil, will also make a quality product. The only valid connection is the corporate name, not the quality of the product; therefore, the analogy is false.

Even when an analogy is successful in clarifying or explaining, it still constitutes only a comparison. In itself, it does not *prove* anything.

## Name-Calling

Individuals often attempt to discredit an opponent's argument by attacking the person rather than the person's logic. We can all think of blatant examples of name-calling: *nigger, wetback, women's libber, commie,* and so on. Name-calling arouses negative emotions that overpower reasoning and evidence. For some, even the name of an opposing group may take on such ugly connotations that a speaker need but mention it to deride an argument as a whole. A New York journalist recently began his daily newspaper column with, "The liberals are at it again . . ." Presumably, the term *liberal* will strike such chills in a conservative reader that no matter what position a person might hold on an issue, the position will be emotionally rejected.

## Appeals to Emotion

Name-calling is only one direct form of appealing to emotions. In the late 1970s, possession of the Panama Canal was returned by treaty to Panama. Arguments abounded that America had "bought it," that American lives had been sacrificed in building it and operating it, that it constituted American territory and could not be "given away." These appeals to loyalty, fear, religion, decency, family unity, and so on seem to trigger automatic reactions in many people. A skilled writer or speaker can sway whole nations by such tactics, even though logic and evidence can demonstrate the argument is false.

## Misleading Statistics

In an age when presidents carry Gallup Polls in their pockets to demonstrate the popularity of their politics, the danger of arguments founded on statistics needs to be especially noted. Because mathematics seems "scientific," we tend to be swayed by numbers, any kind of numbers, as if numbers in themselves always constituted proof. A college professor recently talked about how a committee he served on had reached a deadlock and could not make a decision about whether to include a proposed course for the new curriculum. The professor broke the deadlock by announcing that 62 percent of the students favored such a course. The committee immediately voted its approval. Later, the professor admitted that the statistic was invented, yet it had exercised more influence than all the previous argument.

Had the statistic been taken from a valid survey of student opinion, we would still need to know when the poll was taken, the size of the sampling (just how many students were actually questioned), the wording of the questionnaire, any biases it may have contained, and how the statistic was mathematically arrived at. Without such data even valid statistics may be misleading. The American Medical Association, for example, has announced that the average American smokes a pack of cigarettes a day. But what exactly does average mean? If only two of your ten best friends smoked five packs of cigarettes apiece each day, the average for all your friends would be a pack a day, even though eight of them did not smoke at all.

Can such a statistic have the weight of proof? No. It *can* be offered as evidence, but it must always be evaluated as carefully as any other form of evidence or argument.

## Syllogisms

The heart of reasoning lies in clear relationships. A well-reasoned argument demonstrates how relationships are sound, whereas a weak argument either blurs relationships (as in name-calling and appeals to emotions) or attempts to establish a relationship that is questionable (as in false analogies or the misuse of statistics). A syllogism is a form of argument that moves from a proposition (called a major premise) to a second proposition (called the minor premise) and then to a conclusion deduced from the relationship.

| | |
|---|---|
| *All men are mortal* | (major premise) |
| *John is a man* | (minor premise) |
| *Therefore John is* | (conclusion, deduced from the relationship |
| *mortal* | of the major and minor premise) |

A syllogism reasons from the general (all men) to the specific (John). This so-called *deductive reasoning* requires that the initial generalization be either self-evident or of such a nature that we can agree upon its truth without further need for evidence. The second premise in the chain—and any others that follow—must be more specific and verifiable. If the conclusion then seems to illustrate a proper relationship between or among the premises, we can claim that the conclusion is true.

But this pattern of argument can create problems:

*All voters are good citizens*
*John votes.*
*John is a good citizen.*

Here all the requirements seem to have been met. We can say that this syllogism is valid insofar as it follows the prescribed form. Yet the conclusion is false. For it to be true, each step in the chain must be true, and the major premise or generalization in this case cannot be accepted as self-evident. All voters are not necessarily good citizens. A Mafia hit-man is not a good citizen even though he votes regularly for Republican candidates. Therefore, the fact that John votes does not necessarily make him a good citizen.

The danger of the syllogism, then, lies in the fact that it can present a valid form of argument even while leading to a false conclusion:

All dogs have four legs.    All men have facial hair.
My cat has four legs.    My mother has a moustache.
Therefore my cat is a dog.    My mother is a man.

A short chapter like this cannot pursue the hidden complexities of syllogisms. But you should be aware that a reasonable sounding argument may not at all be reasonable. Each component of the argument and each relationship must be tested and held accountable in its own right for the conclusion to be true.

---

*Consider the various problems found in the following arguments:*

1. Seventy-one percent of all business transactions today occur over the telephone or via computers. Businessmen don't need to write letters anymore; therefore, colleges ought to cease requiring composition courses.
2. From a student paper: ''To be a science fiction writer you have to be a little wacko, for the science portrayed in such works is usually fantastic and without a sound basis in fact.''
3. King James of England said that as the monarch is the head of the state, democracy is demonstrably false. James argued that if you cut off the head of a body, the other organs cannot function, and the body dies. Similarly, if you cut off the head of a state, the state may flop around for a while, but it is due to perish in time or become an easy prey to its neighbors.

---

Emotional blocks, lazy thinking, syllogisms that seem logical but are not—the list begins to seem endless. Yet if we want to write clearly and persuasively, to think clearly and soundly, we need at least an elementary grounding in the all-too-human problems that interfere. Our hope must be that even if such problems cannot be eliminated, by knowing they exist we can triumph over them. Ultimately, a sensitive perception of facts, details, emotions, and ideas is not enough for the writer. The successful writer must also perceive reasonable relationships among those facts, details, emotions, and ideas.

### EXERCISES

1. Because the emotional attachment to values learned through our family, our ethnic group, our social class, and our culture are so strong

and so prevalent, politicians and advertisers often appeal directly to emotions rather than to logic. Consider the type of emotion each of the following seeks to arouse. Why is it so powerful? Why wouldn't logic be better? Where does the illogic lie in each statement?

    a. A vote for Governor Brown is a vote for freedom, integrity, and efficiency in government.

    b. If he kissed you once, will he kiss you again? Take Certs, the breath mint, and be sure.

    c. From an advertisement for 7 Up: "It's the same thing, only different."

    d. From a speech by an individual running for city coroner: "I was born here and have lived here all my life. I went to Abraham Lincoln High School, and some of you probably still remember the home run I hit in the Medfield game."

    e. Look, Mommy, no cavities!

    f. A man running for state senator attacks his opponent: "Senator Hale has supported legislation that would encourage voter fraud. If elected, I promise to oppose any new attempt at instant voter registration."

    g. In a 1939 *Saturday Evening Post:* "Thousands of physicians smoke Luckies."

    h. The Great Silent Majority is concerned with law and order.

2. The following paragraphs were written in freshman composition classes at one of the nation's largest universities. Evaluate each for its logical problems.

    a. College is a beneficial experience to everyone who attends it. It is a start of a better life that gives a person an opportunity to pursue a meaningful and challenging career. A college graduate does not have to take a job he won't enjoy just for the purpose of money. College also enhances a person's personality in that one meets many different types of people with varying personalities. College also puts a person into a position of responsibility by making a person learn how to take care of himself.

    b. Have you ever heard of a vice-president's taking over because the president was pregnant? Well, if a woman became president, there would be a good possibility that you would hear this. It would be kind of difficult for her to refrain from sexual intercourse with her husband for four years and then, if reelected, for four more years. It would seem apparent through the four or eight years she would become pregnant. After she had her baby, she would become the president again, but couldn't you picture the same thing happening again? Having the vice-president take her place and then her coming back would cause chaos because anything the vice-president passed that she disagreed with, she would try to change. So why don't we let women stay out of politics, so when she becomes pregnant she won't upset the whole diplomatic structure of the country?

c. You should not wear a watch if you are honestly concerned about your health. A survey was conducted by the American Heart Association to relate the incidence of heart attack to personal actions or qualities. It was found that people who wore watches had a higher rate of heart attacks than those who did not. Time is important to fast-paced, high-pressured people, where promptness is a must to be successful. A high-pressured life-style also raises blood pressure, which leads to an increase in the chances of heart attack and slows the pace of life down to a new healthier level.

d. The recent sexual revolution of our times has caused some turmoil in our country, yet I'm a firm believer in premarital sex. Sex has been spoken of, in the past, only in harsh whispers or behind closed doors. This reluctance to discuss sex openly has caused certain people to lead sheltered lives and may also result in sexual inhibitions. Knowledge of one's body and that of the opposite sex brings about a greater feeling of sexual security. To acknowledge to your sexual partner the realities of how sex should be properly executed and to give them the freedom to explore bring about a better relationship. Knowledge has a tendency to take away the fears surrounding sexual intercourse. Fears of pregnancy are almost nonexistent with modern devices for birth control, for both men and women. Public awareness of these controls is also readily available. This relationship, having been established, will give proficiency in sexual intercourse with your future mate and provide the knowledge to inspire warmth and response in your mate through personal experiences.

3. Consider each of the following statements. Which follow a valid pattern of deductive reasoning? Which lead to a true conclusion?

a. The University of Southern California defeated Oregon State in football by 31 to 7. UCLA defeated that same Oregon State team by 14 to 7. The University of Southern California can obviously defeat UCLA.

b. All teen-agers have pimples. My sister has pimples. Therefore, my sister is a teen-ager.

c. A student should not be required to take classes he or she is not interested in when he or she gets to college. College students are legal adults and should be allowed to choose their own curriculum.

d. Most professors have Ph.D.'s. If all students were required to stay in college until they obtained a Ph.D., we would no longer need professors.

e. It is no longer important to have heroes in today's contemporary society. The last heroes we had like Martin Luther King and John F. Kennedy ended by getting shot.

4. Consider the following dialogue and determine its relationship to logical thinking. Does it express the limits of logic?

Master Joshu was asked: "What is the ultimate principle of Zen Buddhism?"
He replied: "The cypress tree in the courtyard."
"You are talking," another monk said, "of an objective symbol."
"No, I am not talking about an objective symbol."
"Then what is the ultimate principle of Zen Buddhism?"
"The cypress tree in the courtyard," answered Joshu again.

# 29 *Critical Reading*

Do you have a right to happiness? A strange question? But what if you encountered an essay by C. S. Lewis that claimed you had no right to happiness at all? And what if the essay presented evidence and seemingly reasoned argument? At first you might feel skeptical, even hostile. Of course you have a right, you might think, especially in America, where the Declaration of Independence names the pursuit of happiness as a basic principle. But perhaps you've only been enculturated with such notions. And what about all this evidence and argument in the essay? Is it logical? Is it valid? Can you be convinced in spite of your own inclinations? Your increasing perceptual skills must now be applied more critically to what you read.

Serious reading goes beyond entertainment. A chemist reads a scholarly journal to learn about a new discovery in organic neurology. An engineer reads about developments in architectural glass for sun control. A mother reads about a psychiatrist who claims children under five must be disciplined with physical punishment. How can any of them evaluate what they read except by considering it logically, analyzing its content, and judging its validity? Such a process requires *critical analysis*— a formal strategy that is both a method for perceiving and evaluating as well as a technique for writing. This chapter deals with analysis as a method that develops critical reading skills. The next chapter offers a traditional structure used for writing an analysis.

# The Strategy of Reading Critically

Analysis is a process in which you divide a subject into its various parts. By studying each of the parts and their relationship, you hope to understand more about the subject as a whole (see Chapter 23). But before you can actually analyze something you read, you must learn a particular method of reading that prepares you for each of the steps analysis will demand.

## Understand the Content

The need to comprehend content sounds self-evident, but it is neither so easy nor so commonly accomplished as we might like to believe. Every college instructor is aware that perhaps one-fourth of the problems on essay exams can be traced to a student's failure to read or understand the question. Critical reading is a strategy—a method of approaching your reading so that you increase comprehension.

1. Underline key sentences and circle key words. Read each paragraph as a unit of thought. Look for the most important sentences and underline them—especially those that express the theme and the major points used to support the theme. Circle words used in special ways or words you don't know or words that are repeated for emphasis.

2. Take notes in the margins. Try to summarize each major point in a few words directly beside the key sentence that makes the point. Try to use your own words for your summary. Being able to put an idea into your own words helps you understand and remember it. Number the notes in the margin so that at a glance you can tell how many major points an author has made.

3. For every major word you don't know, use a dictionary. (Alas, how many times have you heard that commandment. But you live in a world of words. Ideas are expressed in words. If you don't know the language, you are a prisoner of ignorance.) Write a brief definition in the margin by the word you've circled. Writing the definition helps you remember it.

4. Finally, once you've completed the reading, write a brief summary in your own words, *objectively* and *fairly* restating the author's theme, major points, and conclusion. (Do not interpret or make hasty judgments at this point.) Use your marginal notes to aid you in writing your summary. The summary helps draw together the author's ideas. Until you've written the summary, you may *think* you know what you've read but you can't be sure. The summary is excellent mental work for preparing to take an exam or to write a paper as well as to reinforce comprehension.

## Evaluate the Content for Logic

Once you've objectively understood the content, you're in a good position to scrutinize the author's theme more critically. When you read about Arab oil sheiks buying American factories, does the author appeal to your logic or to your emotions? Is more than one side of the issue presented? Are both sides given fair and equal treatment? Is the content based on opinion? Evidence? Logic? Are the Arab sheiks presented as stereotypes? Is the author's argument based on overgeneralizations? Cultural or racial bias? Is the conclusion based on evidence or logical argument presented in the body of the work?

Here is where you'll want to challenge each major point separately, then compare each point to the others, then to the basic theme itself—all to determine logical relationships. If you've numbered each point in the margins, your work will proceed quickly.

## Evaluate Yourself for Emotional Blocks

If you find you are easily convinced by the author's position, is it because you're already biased in favor of such ideas? If you are unconvinced, is it because you have a closed mind? In addition to considering the author, the audience, and the work, you must consider your relationship to it. If an author proposes a socialistic form of government for the United States, do you disagree because of fear of change? Or because of unexamined values and beliefs adopted from your parents? Is it possible you have misjudged the work because of a hasty conclusion? Or do the ideas sound perfectly logical to you because they conform to the values you want to believe in regardless of their logic? You cannot be sure you have treated your author's material with fairness and objectivity until you can be sure of your own emotional biases.

## Consider the Author and the Historical Context

Although it will not always be possible to find out who the author is or to discover what original audience the work was intended for, every effort should be made to see the work in its original historical context.

1. Who is the author and what is his or her authority to speak on the subject? Sometimes the author's experience and credentials will be identified on the dust jacket or last page of a book. Articles in magazines may identify the author at the bottom of the title page or on the last page of the essay. In some cases, you'll need to do a little research. Almost all libraries contain reference books that identify authors and provide a guide to their backgrounds.

Why do you need to know about the author? Because evaluation of source affects the worth of the information. In 1978, for example, a book was published claiming to document an authentic account of cloning—an actual human being had been cloned from the cells of another human being and was alive and well. The author asserted that his story was true. But who was the author? He turned out to be a science fiction writer who had previously written fictional accounts of cloning. Could his claim for truth now be taken seriously? Perhaps. But his authority to document a scientific experiment of such magnitude had to be considered somewhat less reliable than had he been a noted scientist.

2. What is the historical context? Where and when was the work originally published, and who was the probable audience? No poem, essay, or book exists in a vacuum. It grows out of that complex relationship of *subject-audience-context-purpose.* The more you can know about each element, the better you can make reasonable judgments. Every era, for example, tends to promote its own generally accepted assumptions. A writer may reflect on the values of his day or may attack them. Either way, an understanding of those cultural values would help you evaluate the argument. And if you can discover the audience or purpose for which a work is written, you can often understand why it takes the form it does, why it uses emotion or logic or a complex vocabulary or a simple vocabulary, and so on.

---

Reading and critical reading are different acts. Most reading is done for pleasure—a process of absorbing information without serious thought. But critical reading is an intense, concentrated form of evaluating what the author tells you. Here is an outline summary of the critical reading process:

**UNDERSTAND THE CONTENT**
—Underline key sentences; circle key words.
—Take notes in the margin.
—Use a dictionary.
—Write a brief summary of the main idea, major points, and conclusion.

**EVALUATE THE CONTENT**
—Look for logic; look for appeals to emotion.
—Look for both sides of an argument.
—Look for evidence, logical analysis, reasoning.
—Look for meaningful sources to support claims of fact. (If an author claims that 10,000 people died last year from smoking marijuana, where did he or she find this information? From U.S. Government research laboratories in Washington? Or from a pamphlet left on his or her doorstep by the ''I Hate Marijuana Society''?)

**EVALUATE YOURSELF**
—Beware of your own biases for and against certain ideas.
—Evaluate whether your reactions are caused by enculturated attitudes.
—Look for immediate denials or approvals; then evaluate whether you've

made a hasty conclusion or reacted according to the cultural assumptions of
your own era.

**CONSIDER THE AUTHOR AND HISTORICAL CONTEXT**
—What is the author's authority to speak on a subject? (Personal experi-
ence? Scholarly study? Research?)
—What is the motive behind the author's essay? (Self-serving? Results of sci-
entific inquiry? Propaganda?)
—Who was the original audience for the work? (Where was it first published?
In a book? In a magazine? As a lecture?)
—What were the biases of the original audience?
—Do any elements in the historical period in which it was written explain ele-
ments of the work itself?

## The Strategy at Work
Here is how you might apply these guidelines to a specific reading:

# We Have No "Right to Happiness"
## C. S. Lewis

who?

"After all," said Clare, "They had a right to
happiness."

We were discussing something that once
happened in our own neighborhood. Mr. A. had
deserted Mrs. A. and got his divorce in order to
marry Mrs. B., who had likewise got her divorce in order to marry Mr. A. And there was
certainly no doubt that Mr. A. and Mrs. B.
were very much in love with one another. If
they continued to be in love, and if nothing
went wrong with their health or their income,
they might reasonably expect to be very happy.

It was equally clear that they were not
happy with their old partners. Mrs. B. had
adored her husband at the outset. But then he
got smashed up in the war. It was thought he
had lost his virility, and it was known that he
had lost his job. Life with him was no longer
what Mrs. B. had bargained for. Poor Mrs. A.,
too. She had lost her looks—and all her liveli-

By permission of Curtis Brown, Ltd., London, as Agent for the Estate of C. S. Lewis.

ness. It might be true, as some said, that she consumed herself by bearing his children and nursing him through the long illness that overshadowed their earlier married life.

You mustn't, by the way, imagine that A. was the sort of man who nonchalantly threw a wife away like the peel of an orange he'd sucked dry. Her suicide was a terrible shock to him. We all knew this, for he told us so himself. "But what could I do?" he said. "A man has a right to happiness. I had to take my one chance when it came."

*Basic theme*

I went away thinking about the concept of a "right to happiness."

*① Happiness depends upon luck*

At first this sounds to me as odd as a right to good luck. For I believe—whatever one school of moralists may say—that we depend for a very great deal of our happiness or misery on circumstances outside all human control. A right to happiness doesn't, for me, make much more sense than a right to be six feet tall, or to have a millionaire for your father, or to get good weather whenever you want to have a picnic.

*② a "right" is guaranteed by law*

I can understand a right as a freedom guaranteed me by the laws of the society I live in. Thus, I have a right to travel along the public roads because society gives me that freedom; that's what we mean by calling the roads "public." I can also understand a right as a claim guaranteed me by the laws, and

*Correlative: "related to" > a law may guarantee you a right to divorce and remarry, but happiness is not a part of it*

correlative to an obligation on someone else's part. If I have a right to receive £100 from you, this is another way of saying that you have a duty to pay me £100. If the laws allow Mr. A. to desert his wife and seduce his neighbor's wife, then, by definition, Mr. A. has a legal right to do so, and we need bring in no talk about "happiness."

*③ But there may be a "natural law" that guarantees happiness (?)*

But of course that was not what Clare meant. She meant that he had not only a legal but a moral right to act as he did. In other words, Clare is—or would be if she thought it out—a classical moralist after the style of Thomas Aquinas, Grotius, Hooker and Locke.

*Natural law is "norm" against which man-made laws can be tested*

*Maxim: "succinct rule or principle"*

*American Declaration of Independence based on same idea*

*Natural law does not guarantee pursuit of happiness by immoral means*

*only by lawful means*

*Tautology: "the same sense in different words"*

*U.S. Declaration means equal right of all men to pursue happiness, not just those of a special class*

She believes that behind the laws of the state there is a Natural Law.

I agree with her. I hold this conception to be basic to all civilization. Without it, the actual laws of the state become an absolute, as in Hegel. They cannot be criticized because there is no norm against which they should be judged.

The ancestry of Clare's maxim, "They have a right to happiness," is august. In words that are cherished by all civilized men, but especially by Americans, it has been laid down that one of the rights of man is a right to "the pursuit of happiness." And now we get to the real point.

What did the writers of that august declaration mean?

It is quite certain what they did not mean. They did not mean that man was entitled to pursue happiness by any and every means—including, say, murder, rape, robbery, treason, and fraud. No society could be built on such a basis.

They meant "to pursue happiness by all lawful means"; that is, by all means which the Law of Nature eternally sanctions and which the laws of the nation shall sanction.

Admittedly this seems at first to reduce their maxim to the tautology that men (in pursuit of happiness) have a right to do whatever they have a right to do. But tautologies, seen against their proper historical context, are not always barren tautologies. The declaration is primarily a denial of the political principles which long governed Europe: a challenge flung down to the Austrian and Russian empires, to England before the Reform Bills, to Bourbon France. It demands that whatever means of pursuing happiness are lawful for any, should be lawful for all; that "man," not men of some particular caste, class, status or religion, should be free to use them. In a century when this is being unsaid by nation after nation and party after party, let us not call it a barren tautology.

But the question as to what means are "lawful"—what methods of pursuing happiness

*But question*
*not solved*

④ *Is argument for*
*"Right to Happiness"*
*based on right to*
*sexual happiness?*

are either morally permissible by the Law of Nature or should be declared legally permissible by the legislature of a particular nation—remains exactly where it did. And on that question I disagree with Clare. I don't think it is obvious that people have the unlimited "right to happiness" which she suggests.

For one thing, I believe that Clare, when she says "happiness," means simply and solely "sexual happiness." Partly because women like Clare never use the word "happiness" in any other sense. But also because I never heard Clare talk about the "right" to any other kind. She was rather leftist in her politics, and would have been scandalized if anyone had defended the actions of a ruthless man-eating tycoon on the ground that his happiness consisted in making money and he was pursuing his happiness. She was also a rabid teetotaller; I never heard her excuse an alcoholic because he was happy when he was drunk.

A good many of Clare's friends, and especially her female friends, often felt—I've heard them say so—that their own happiness would be perceptibly increased by boxing her ears. I very much doubt if this would have brought her theory of a right to happiness into play.

Clare, in fact, is doing what the whole Western world seems to me to have been doing for the last forty-odd years. When I was a youngster, all the progressive people were saying, "Why all this prudery? Let us treat sex just as we treat all our other impulses." I was simple-minded enough to believe they meant what they said. I have since discovered that they meant exactly the opposite. They meant that sex was to be treated as no other impulse in our nature has ever been treated by civilized people. All the others, we admit, have to be bridled. Absolute obedience to your instinct for self-preservation is what we call cowardice; to your acquisitive impulse, avarice. Even sleep must be resisted if you're a sentry. But every unkindness and breach of faith seems to be

*Western world*
*believes sex should*
*be treated*
*differently from*
*all other impulses*
*—all is forgiven*
*in the name of sex*

condoned provided that the object aimed at is "four bare legs in a bed."

It is like having a morality in which stealing fruit is considered wrong—unless you steal nectarines.

And if you protest against this view you are usually met with chatter about the legitimacy and beauty and sanctity of "sex" and accused of harboring some Puritan prejudice against it as something disreputable or shameful. I deny the charge. Foam-born Venus . . . golden (Aphrodite). . . Our Lady of Cyprus . . . I never breathed a word against you. If I object to boys who steal my nectarines, must I be supposed to disapprove of nectarines in general? Or even of boys in general? It might, you know, be stealing that I disapproved of.

The real situation is skillfully concealed by saying that the question of Mr. A.'s "right" to desert his wife is one of "sexual morality." Robbing an orchard is not an offense against some special morality called "fruit morality." It is an offense against honesty. Mr. A.'s action is an offense against good faith (to solemn promises), against gratitude (toward one to whom he was deeply indebted) and against common humanity.

Our sexual impulses are thus being put in a position of preposterous privilege. The sexual motive is taken to condone all sorts of behavior which, if it had any other end in view, would be condemned as merciless, treacherous, and unjust.

Now though I see no good reason for giving sex this privilege, I think I see a strong cause. It is this.

It is part of the nature of a strong erotic passion—as distinct from a transient fit of appetite—that it makes more towering promises than any other emotion. No doubt all our desires make promises, but not so impressively. To be in love involves the almost irresistible conviction that one will go on being in love until one dies, and that possession of the be-

*[margin notes, left column:]*

Analogy: all other impulses are sinful except sex

Those who disagree are called prudes

Aphrodite: "greek goddess of love"

⑤ Real question not related to sex but to human decency, to honesty, and to acting in good faith

Sexual motive used to condone dishonesty

Sex seems to promise eternal happiness

loved will confer, not merely frequent ecstasies, but settled, fruitful, deep-rooted, lifelong happiness. Hence *all* seems to be at stake. If we miss this chance we shall have lived in vain. At the very thought of such a doom we sink into fathomless depths of self-pity.

Unfortunately these promises are found often to be quite untrue. Every experienced adult knows this to be so as regards all erotic passions (except the one he himself is feeling at the moment). We discount the world-without-end pretensions of our friends' amours easily enough. We know that such things sometimes last—and sometimes don't. And when they do last, this is not because they promised at the outset to do so. When two people achieve lasting happiness, this is not solely because they are great lovers but because they are also—I must put it crudely—good people; controlled, loyal, fair-minded, mutually adaptable people.

*Long-lasting happiness based on being mutually adaptable; not on sex*

If we establish a "right to (sexual) happiness" which supersedes all the ordinary rules of behavior, we do so not because of what our passion shows itself to be in experience but because of what it professes to be while we are in the grip of it. Hence, while the bad behavior is real and works miseries and degradations, the happiness which was the object of the behavior turns out again and again to be illusory. Everyone (except Mr. A. and Mrs. B.) knows that Mr. A. in a year or so may have the same reason for deserting his new wife as for deserting his old. He will feel again that all is at stake. He will see himself again as the great lover, and his pity for himself will exclude all pity for the woman.

*Sexual happiness is illusory*

Two further points remain.

One is this. A society in which conjugal infidelity is tolerated must always be in the long run a society adverse to women. Women, whatever a few male songs and satires may say to the contrary, are more naturally monogamous than men: it is a biological necessity. Where promiscuity prevails, they will therefore always be more often the victims than the culprits. Also, domestic happiness is more necessary to

*⑥Sexual infidelity adversely affects women because women are more monogamous than men*
*Monogamous: > "marriage to one person at a time"*

*Domestic happiness more important to women (?)*

them than to us. And the quality by which they most easily hold a man, their beauty, decreases every year after they have come to maturity, but this does not happen to those qualities of personality—women don't really care two-pence about our *looks*—by which we hold women. Thus in the ruthless war of promiscuity women are at a double disadvantage. They play for higher stakes and are also more likely to lose. I have no sympathy with moralists who frown at the increasing crudity of female pro-vocativeness. These signs of desperate compe-tition fill me with pity.

*Conclusion*
*If right to happiness regarding sexual happiness is allowed, will it not spread to other impulses?*

Secondly, though the "right to happiness" is chiefly claimed for the sexual impulse, it seems to me impossible that the matter should stay there. The fatal principle, once allowed in that department, must sooner or later seep through our whole lives. We thus advance to-ward a state of society in which not only each man but every impulse in each man claims carte blanche. And then, though our technolog-ical skill may help us survive a little longer, our civilization will have died at heart, and will— one dare not even add "unfortunately"—be swept away.

*Carte blanche: ) "unrestricted power to act"*
*Will lead to death of civilization*

At this point, several questions, perhaps even several challenges, to C. S. Lewis's argument may have arisen, but the first step in critical read-ing is to make sure we have objectively and fairly comprehended the au-thor's ideas. We must suspend for the moment our questions and criticism. Now is the time for jotting down notes or summarizing the essay as a whole.

Here is how you might write a brief summary:

In C. S. Lewis's essay "We Have No 'Right to Happiness,' " Lewis argues that happiness depends upon luck, and luck cannot be guaranteed by man-made law. He acknowledges that "natural law" might guarantee such a happiness, but decides that, as conceived of by the men who wrote the Declaration of Independence, "natu-ral law" only guarantees the equal right of all men in all classes to pursue happiness—not necessarily to find it. Lewis believes that those who claim a "right" to happiness primarily mean sexual hap-piness. He thinks that in the Western world all is forgiven when sex is involved, but he believes that a sexual motive does not con-done dishonesty, ingratitude, or infidelity. Sex, he claims, promises only illusory happiness. Finally, he argues that sexual promiscuity is more harmful to women than men because women are more naturally monogamous and because they need domestic happiness more than men. He concludes by saying that if such impulses toward sexual "carte blanche" are allowed, other passions and impulses will be more tolerated, and the heart of our whole civilization will begin to die.

Now we are ready to analyze the content. Analysis is a process of dividing the essay into its major parts, questioning each part for its logic and validity, and then evaluating the relationship of the parts to the whole. Here are the types of questions you would want to ask about C. S. Lewis's arguments (do not confuse this stage with the writing stage—that will come later):

*Major point number one:* Does happiness depend upon luck? Lewis argues here by analogy. What are the analogies and are the relationships valid?

*Major point number two:* Lewis focuses on the concept of a "right." He uses examples to show how a legal right functions and argues that such rights cannot apply to a concept like happiness. Do the examples effectively support his contention?

*Major point number three:* Lewis attempts to distinguish between man-made laws and "natural law." He argues that natural laws do exist. If you don't understand the concept of "natural law" where could you find out what it means? What is his support? He argues that the Declaration of Independence was based on natural laws but that the statement about happiness needs to be understood in its historical context. What is the context and does his interpretation seem reasonable? What is the complete wording of the first one and one-half paragraphs in the Declaration of Independence?

*Major point number four:* What type of reasoning does Lewis use when he decides that Clare means "sexual happiness"? How does he relate that to what the "Western world believes"? Can an argument have a probable truth even if there is a flaw in the method of arriving at the conclusion?

How does he come to his statement about what people like Clare really meant when they asked us to treat sex like all other impulses? Does his analogy with fruit and nectarines effectively support his argument?

*Major point number five:* By extending the analogy of the fruit, Lewis tries to clarify the question as one of morality rather than sexual happiness. Does the analogy remain valid? What is the relationship of the next several paragraphs arguing that sexual happiness is only illusory anyway?

*Major point number six:* What kind of argument is Lewis using

when he points out that sexual infidelity affects women worse than men? What does he mean by "biological necessity"? What kind of reasoning or evidence does he supply to support his idea that domestic happiness is more important to women than to men? The sentence on domestic happiness ends with the word *us*. In the context, what could that suggest about Lewis's assumptions?
*Conclusion:* Lewis generalizes from the preceding argument and tries to show how the breakdown in one area of morality will lead to a breakdown in others. Does the generalization seem to follow from his preceding six major points? Does it support his thesis, "We Have No 'Right to Happiness' "?

No analysis is complete at this point. You must still consider your own emotional relationship to the argument as well as the author and historical context. Some of Lewis's ideas may seem convincing; some may seem illogical. They may even anger you. But to what extent are your feelings due to your own biases or to the cultural assumptions of your particular generation? Can reasons be found outside the reading itself that might help us to judge more temperately the overall worth of Lewis's argument?

A check in *Current Biography* (available in most libraries) would show that Lewis was a professor of Medieval and Renaissance English at both Oxford and Cambridge. Born in 1898, he published widely, especially fiction and essays dealing with moral values. This particular essay was first published in *The Saturday Evening Post,* December, 1963; and although John F. Kennedy was assassinated in November of that year, the December issue was already on the newsstand. The turmoil in American culture that dominated the sixties had barely begun. Civil Rights marches were limited to a few Southern states. The Martin Luther King and Robert Kennedy assassinations, the Vietnam War, the shooting of students at Kent State, the feminist movement, and the whole long Watergate affair were all ahead. In other words, the essay came at the end of a fairly stable period in American history before we were shocked into challenging some of our longest-held cultural values. Could any of Lewis's ideas be more clearly understood by knowing that the article *preceded* cultural changes that shaped the values of the 1970s and 1980s?

Having now considered the man and the historical context, having accounted for our own prejudices if any, and having scrutinized each part of the essay for logic and evidence, we can feel reasonably confident that an overall assessment can be made: What are the strong points and weak points? Where is Lewis's argument most convincing? Where does this argument appear to fail and why? What is the ultimate value and worth of the essay in terms of the ideas it offers for consideration?

The critical voice is sometimes mistaken as negative voice. Actually, to be critical means to discriminate with exactness. Hence a critical analysis must discriminate between good and bad. It praises as well as condemns. If we are exacting, we will usually discover that an author is seldom wholly right or wholly wrong. We will not slant our own judgment to one side or the other, but toward fair and balanced understanding. The conclusion of a critical analysis should assess the work in its fullness.

By its nature the critical reading process is slow and methodical. It takes effort and self-discipline. But when objectivity is maintained, the close scrutiny of detail pursued, and relationships evaluated, it can lead to insight that is balanced, rewarding, and reasonable.

### EXERCISES

1. Consider the editorial positions put forth in the following television debate between Arthur Peterson, a professor of political science, and Robert N. Shamansky, a lawyer. Each speaker was allowed only three minutes. The broadcast occurred a few weeks after 911 members of a U. S. religious group committed mass suicide in Guyana, South America. Analyze the basic theme of each speaker, the logical development of it, and the types of argumentation each is using:

> *Peterson:* . . . it is easy to see why President Carter sidestepped the hard question of governmental intervention into the practices of religious cults. His own wife, Rosalynn, his Vice-President Mondale, his cabinet member Califano, and his Ambassador Andrew Young warmly embraced Jim Jones and approved some of his ideas. Obviously they would all like to forget the long, sad story of their endorsement of this madman.
>
> . . . nowhere has the Supreme Court held that the First Amendment freedom of religion protects leaders who indulge in inhuman beating, denial of personal liberty, and the kind of mental torture which was for years commonplace in the cult of the People's Temple.
>
> . . . just as it was necessary for the Justice Department to intervene during the nineteen fifties and sixties to protect the *civil* rights of voting and education against their denials by certain Southern States so it is now necessary for the Justice Department and the FBI to intervene where religious cults deny basic *human* rights of personal dignity and bodily security. The concept of religious freedom as a so-called preferred freedom is a mischievous concept if by it we violate the tenets of reasonableness and common sense and destroy the ability of the government to maintain a peaceful and orderly society.
>
> *Shamansky:* . . . [The Jonestown massacre was] so hideous that [our] first impulse is to demand, "Why didn't someone do something about it? Where were the FBI and State Department?" But

shock and outrage are not good emotions for judging a situation like this where there is a great temptation to look for a scapegoat. It is vital that we remember that all of our respected religious groups started out as small cults breaking away from older established groups; and that the very first phrase of the First Amendment to the U.S. Constitution says, "Congress shall make no law respecting an establishment of religion . . ."; and that the Reverend Jim Jones, leader of the People's Temple fought racism, helped the elderly, the needy, drug addicts and prostitutes, and opposed the Vietnam War.

Unfortunately . . . he also became a bisexual, sadistic, Communist and undoubtedly insane at the end. Very few People's Temple members objected to their church, and there was little, if anything, in public to condemn until the ghastly end. Even the brave Congressman Ryan apparently thought things were generally satisfactory at Jonestown, except for those few who chose to leave with him. Those tragic people in that South American jungle had deliberately put themselves beyond the protection of American law.

The point is . . . it would be unfair to expect Federal and California public officials to disregard the constitutional rights which every American religious group possesses. . . .

—Eyewitness News
WBNS-TV
Columbus, Ohio

2. Study the following paper written by a freshman in a political science course. As the essay was written in class, no opportunity was available for bringing in concrete evidence. Analyze it only for the logic and soundness of the argument.

We owe allegiance to the state, namely the United States of America, because we live here. We are part of the country. People can choose where they want to live and we have chosen to live here. The nation protects each person's individual liberties and thus demands certain duties from its people. Everyone has human rights—freedom of speech, religion, and the press. We can choose what area we want to live in and how we want to live our life. The list goes on and on. As our country gives us so much, we should be loyal to it.

In past years, many times when war was announced, that was it. A person's responsibility was now to the state and no one could take time to do what they wanted unless, of course, it was for the good of the war. When farmers fought during a war, their responsibility was often to themselves as well as to the state. They worked the land and it was theirs. The land was their life. They fought to protect it and to keep it free. People were impassioned during these

wars to fight with all they had, in hopes that future generations
would be free. It was an honor to go into battle and something
that men and boys often looked forward to. There wasn't much of
a question whether or not a person would go to war at that time,
like there was during the Vietnam War—it was a person's privilege
and responsibility.

Responsibilities that are greater than our responsibilities to
the state are to yourself, your family and friends and your religion.
You have to think of yourself because if you don't, no one else
will. If you don't save yourself, you won't be any good to yourself
or to anyone else. If your family and friends were killed, and you
could have helped prevent it, but didn't what good would it be to
be free? What would be the use of winning a war if you had nothing to live for?

A country grants each person certain civic rights that he possesses from the day he is born. It offers its citizens protection
when they are away from it and privileges when they are at home.
In turn, each citizen owes allegiance to his country. It is his duty
to support his government, obey its laws, and defend his country.

## SUGGESTED WRITING ASSIGNMENT

Select one of the readings at the end of the unit to critique. Underline key ideas; look up words you are not familiar with; evaluate the content for soundness of argument; and because each reading involves
controversial material, be sure you consider your own position on the
issues involved before you draw a hasty conclusion.

# 30 *The Structure of Formal Analysis*

Analysis is a process, a method of thinking and perceiving. Even when it moves from the thinking phase to the writing phase, analysis remains a way of organizing (and of clarifying) ideas. In this chapter I'm going to describe a conventional organization that has proved its effectiveness over many generations. The guideline may well sound as if we have fallen into the trap of naming the ten elements of beauty or whatever. But there are no rules, only method. A conventional form is not like a glass bottle into which you pour the milk of your observations. Instead it is a pattern of movement like a dance step. At first you may feel as if you're being asked to follow cut-out footprints pasted on the floor. The movements may feel awkward. You may feel inhibited. But with practice and experience you'll find the organization is merely a guideline. You may continue to follow it mechanically and dully, or you may bring to it your own spirit and liveliness, investing it with style, grace, and originality.

## The Formal Introduction
In Chapter 29 you needed an objective understanding of the essay by C. S. Lewis before you could analyze it. So, too, does your reader need an objective overview of a subject before you plunge into smaller details. A formal introduction usually includes three elements:

## Name of Author and Work

Give the full name of the author and the essay or book you plan to discuss. (You'd be surprised at how many inexperienced writers forget to do this.)

In C. S. Lewis's essay "We Have No 'Right to Happiness,' " Lewis argues that . . .

According to Richard Poirier's "Learning from the Beatles" (*Partisan Review,* 1967), contemporary criticism fails to account for . . .

Martin Luther King's "Letter from Birmingham Jail" (April 16, 1963), is a major document explaining the nonviolent philosophy behind King's campaign for . . .

Each of these examples identifies author and title, then leads the reader toward the next step.

## Characterization of the Whole

Although your audience may have read the work you are analyzing, you should not expect others to have memorized it or to have studied it as closely as you. You'll want to provide a brief summary of the article or book in its historical context. Knowledge about the author and his or her qualifications to speak—or about the cultural era out of which the work arose—can sometimes contribute to a general understanding. You may even want to note briefly the publishing history of a work if it is especially interesting or perhaps the reaction of critics when the work first appeared.

The summary itself is most important. No matter what your ultimate judgment, give fair hearing to the author at this point. Present his or her ideas accurately and without bias. As briefly as possible, give at least the basic theme and the author's conclusion. If the work is long and complicated, you may want to go into more detail and review some of the major points as well.

This combination of historical context and brief summary is common courtesy to the reader. It provides us with a context in which to follow your more detailed analysis. Here is how sophomore Ann Max introduced her subject, using a rather full characterization:

*Identification of author and her credentials*

*Overview of author's argument*

*Title and source of publication*

*Summary of the essay*

Ellen Willis is a free-lance journalist and reviewer for such major publications as *The New Yorker* and *The New York Review of Books.* In 1970 she attacked the conventional understanding of the consumer as a victim of the sellers and the advertisers.

In "Women and the Myth of Consumerism," first published in *Ramparts* (June, 1970), Willis argues that the theory of the advertisers using depth psychology to convince women to buy a product is not only a false theory, but one that confuses cause and effect. The true

*Basic theme*

*Judgment (must be supported later)*

*Historical context*

*Focusing sentence*

purpose behind advertising, she claims, is merely capitalistic exploitation, which she finds normal and inoffensive in a capitalist society today. What does disturb her is that advertising creates images that reflect "women as they are forced by men in a sexist society to behave." But her presentation is marred by her angry and bitter tone in the essay. *Ramparts* was a semirevolutionary magazine that grew out of the cultural upheaval of the late sixties and early seventies. Willis obviously assumed that her readers already held anticapitalist, antisexist, anti-just-about-everything attitudes. The result is interesting but contains serious oversimplifications and unsupported assumptions.

Ann Max took the time to find out about both the author and the magazine in which the author published. Ann summarizes the basic thesis, then moves toward a focusing of how she plans to criticize the work.

### The Focusing (or Thesis) Sentence

If you plan to analyze an entire essay, you must focus on how you propose to do it. If the subject is too complex to analyze the whole, then the focusing sentence should indicate how you've narrowed your subject. The reader needs to move from the general overview of the work to the more specific direction you plan to take in your paper.

Virginia Smith's argument is logical and effectively argued, but she fails to account for a great number of scientific studies that provide evidence on the other side of the issue. For example . . .

Professor Harris's thesis is flawed by several dramatic breakdowns in clear reasoning. First . . .

John Binder's book is especially important to the young person seeking direction and meaning to life. Perhaps his most important point is . . .

You might think of a formal introduction as following the same pattern used in the Panoramic Scene (described in Chapter 10). Begin with a broad overview that provides a general background; then move in closer, looking at major details—the theme and the conclusion; and finally, focus in (or narrow the subject) to the elements you find most important for analysis.

## Objective Analysis

Most of your paper should present a detailed analysis of the single theme or major components of the work you have focused on:

First, objectively *describe* the specific portion of the work you plan to deal with. Your formal introduction gives only an overview. Here we need details. What is the major point the author is making? Use your own words to summarize. Back up your summary with a short but significant quotation.

Second, *analyze* the idea for its logic, its evidence, its soundness, and its relationship to other ideas.

Third, *interpret* your own findings. If you are dealing with more than one point, limit your interpretation to the first element. Save final judgment until you have analyzed each of the author's ideas or themes you plan to cover.

Do not assume that your paper must follow the sequential organization of the original essay. Do not assume that you should discuss every argument in the original. In Chapter 29, I found six major elements in C. S. Lewis's essay on happiness. For the sake of understanding Lewis's logic, I needed to question each point in my mind. But I would not want to write on each point. As in any other paper, the subject must be narrowed and only the most significant elements discussed. A formal critique on "We Have No 'Right to Happiness' " might focus on only one or two of Lewis's concepts. Your analysis will almost always seem more effective if you go into detail on a single but significant theme rather than attempt to discuss each phase of the original.

However, for each theme or argument that you do discuss, repeat the three steps listed here: *describe, analyze, interpret.* Be sure to include quotations and examples from the work itself to make your own paper as concrete as possible—that is, to provide evidence that supports your own analysis. Here is an excerpt from freshman Tony Ludlum's critique of a single portion of John Locke's "Second Treatise of Civil Government." In a brief introduction, Tony narrowed his subject to the section of Locke's argument that deals with establishment of government. Then he began the body of his essay:

*Description of the author's major point.*

After proposing that the natural condition of man is one of freedom and equality, Locke argues that freedom is limited by the "law of Nature" which is, as he defines it, "reason." This law teaches us that our liberty is not absolute. We may not, for example, kill or steal, unless it is to punish an offender of this law of nature.

For the law of Nature would, as all other laws that concern men in this world, be in vain if there were nobody that in the state of Nature had a power to execute that law . . .

*Student integrates summary in his own words with selected quotations from the author.*

Locke then decides that in the perfect state of Nature, since all are equal, each of us has the right to prosecute the law, although punishment too must be guided by reason. Locke concludes this portion of his essay by saying that it is not his intention to describe the "particulars of the law of Nature" but "it is certain there is such a law," one that is clearly understandable to rational creatures.

*Analysis begins by questioning—in this case, student focuses on a key term.*

But is there? Apparently reasonable men in the eighteenth century believed there was. The Declaration of Independence mentions the same phrase. If a whole culture believed something to be true, maybe you can get away with such a statement so that there is not any need to go into detail or define it. But even if for the time being we suspend our twentieth-century doubts

*Student recognizes that historical factors may influence even reasoned belief.*

and accept such a law, how can it be so clear that Nature's law is reasonable? Or that it is so reasonable that it can even be clearly "executed" by men even when it is not defined. However, Locke doesn't claim that the law is reasonable. He claims that the law *is* reason. I guess my problem with this is that I end up going in a circle:

*Student focuses on logical relationships in author's argument.*

the law of nature is certain, the law is reason; if we are reasonable we will understand the law; if we are not reasonable we will supposedly not understand it nor even know that it is certain. Locke's use of the term cleverly says, in effect, if you believe me and accept what I say, you are a reasonable man, but if you don't accept what I say, or doubt my "certainty," you are unreasonable.

*Interpretation of relationship by student leads to first tentative conclusion.*

Also since the rest of his argument in the essay depends upon this one concept, the reader is placed in a bind. Believe and you will be saved. Don't believe and you are not worth saving. For a reasonable man, this sounds like a strangely unreasonable argument.

## Conclusions

Conclusions are sometimes difficult to generalize upon, for every good conclusion flows naturally from the evidence or argument presented in the body of the paper. But several important points about the conclusion to a formal analysis can be made. Analysis is meaningful only when the parts are joined together again with the whole. To have looked in detail at a single theme or even at each major argument is not enough. You must show your reader how it all relates to the whole.

Do the parts depend upon rational arguments? Upon emotion or unclear thinking? Upon an historical or cultural value? Where is the work sound and meaningful? Where is it less effective?

As we noted earlier, the point of critical analysis is not to attack everything you read with a negative voice. The goal is to discriminate between that which is valuable and that which is not. Although the examples I've given in this chapter have focused on weaknesses, a good critical argument may focus on strengths. Your conclusion should give appropriate hearing to both.

Finally, it is equally important that you take care that your conclusion does not reflect a personal bias or stereotype or emotional argument of your own. Judgment should be based on reason, on critical thinking, not on personal opinions such as "I don't like this book because I don't like cats."

---

### THE STRUCTURE AS OUTLINE

Here is how we might informally outline the structure of formal analysis:

Introduction
- —name of author and work
- —general overview of the subject and summary of the argument
- —focusing (or thesis) sentence

Body
- —objective description of major point
- —detailed analysis of logic and relationships
- —interpretation
- —repetition of description, analysis, and interpretation if more than one major concept is to be covered

Conclusion
- —overall interpretation of findings
- —relationship of findings to the subject as a whole
- —critical assessment of the value, worth, or meaning of the work, both negative and positive

---

Critical analysis does not guarantee you will discover the truth. Yet it can provide the concrete evidence that permits you to demonstrate (to *show*) you have used logical reasoning to arrive at a conclusion. Should your reasoning be faulty, the process also allows someone else to pinpoint precisely where you have erred. Thus analysis is a method that permits verification by a second observer. In that sense, both you and the reader can feel more confident about the probable truths revealed by the process.

## Writing the First Draft

Did Tony Ludlum or Ann Max write a successful analysis in their first draft? The answer is simply no. The first draft for almost all of us remains a time of exploration, a time of crossing out and starting over. As E. M. Forster once said, "How do I know what I think until I see what I say?"

By studying the subject and taking notes before you begin to write (as described in Chapter 29) and by using the guideline described here as "the traditional structure of written analysis," your first draft might flow more simply and clearly than if you plunge in without preconceived direction. But for some students, obsessive concern with form will actually block ideas. The form must be thought of as a guideline only, not a God-given standard. Your personal experience with the subject, filtered now through reason, must still be the main focus as you face the blank page. You must be willing to follow new ideas as they occur, not force ideas to fit the form. Write the first draft as quickly as possible, absorbed in the subject. Use the form in the rewriting phase as a check against what you have written. For example, you may find you have failed to describe certain parts of the essay before you analyzed the detailed points. The formal guideline should remind you that your reader needs that description. Go back and work it in. In other words, use the first draft as you have in the past—to experiment and explore. Use the formal guideline to clarify and organize, either before or after the first draft, depending upon your own personal needs. But do use it because the audience for critical writing will expect a clear and logical form.

## Exercises

Study the two student analyses that follow. Both critique the same essay but use distinctively different methods. Which do you consider the more effective? Does either approach seem more convincing? Can you anticipate how a combination of the approaches might work? Can you find logical problems that might raise a challenge to either student's arguments?

---

The first essay, by Jan Kuntz, a freshman nursing major, considers the basic logic found in a pamphlet attacking sex education in the public schools.

---

# A Critical Analysis of ''A Letter to Landers''
## Jan Kuntz

*Author and title blended with context in which work first occurred*   "A Letter to Landers" by Wallis W. Wood, National Coordinator of THE MOVEMENT TO RESTORE DECENCY, asserts sex education in U.S. schools will promote immoral and corruptive behavior among young

Reprinted by permission of the author.

people. The essay (published by Hall Syndicate: Chicago, Illinois) was a response to an article in which Ann Landers, a nationally known columnist, endorsed sex education courses in the nation's schools. Wood contends these courses will attack society in three major areas by damaging family relationships, by destroying religious beliefs, and by corrupting young minds. Although the author presents some valid points, many of his arguments are grossly distorted. The result is a work based on oversimplification and faulty assumptions.

*Summary of article and focusing sentence*

Wood first claims sex education will have disastrous effects on school-age children. He states that "public discussion of sexual intimacies will always promote immoral behavior." He concludes that "this is especially true for the young." Wood follows up this reasoning by stating that an emphasis on sex will eventually lead students to experiment sexually. He cites an observation by Dr. Otis Gay, a member of the County Health Department in Huntsville, Alabama. Dr. Gay concluded Huntsville's sex education program was a failure because it "actually caused among students an incitement to experiment."

*First major point presents unbiased summary of author's position.*

But does sex education necessarily yield sex? Wood apparently believes so because his entire argument is based on this assumption. However, Wood's argument on this point travels in a straight line. First, he states, that sex education is disastrous. Then he says it will promote immorality. Finally, he concludes it will lead to sexual experimentation. This pattern leads the reader to believe the three terms are equal. Perhaps a more harmful breakdown on this point is that Wood's argument relies on his own undocumented assumptions. The only evidence supporting the causal relationship between sex education and sex is Dr. Gay's comment on Huntsville's sex education program. Not enough information is given on this case to accept it as valid in general. It doesn't really prove that the program caused some students to experiment. The case is a single instance based on one person's opinion.

*Analysis begins by questioning author's logic.*

*Is this argument as clear as it could be?*

Wood also examines the Swedish experience with sex education. Sweden began the sex education movement and established mandatory sex courses in its schools about twenty years ago. Wood lists some statistics concerning Sweden's present social conditions—"Health officials have acknowledged that venereal disease in that unhappy country is now 'catastrophic.' ... Sweden now

*Second major point again presents summary of author's views.*

has the highest rate of alcoholism in the world, the highest rate of divorce, and the highest rate of suicide in the Free World." Wood realizes sex education couldn't be responsible for all of these conditions, but he states it "contributed mightily." He concludes by citing that "the King's personal physician, Dr. Ulf Nordwall, and 140 other physicians and teachers officially petitioned the government to get sex instruction out of the schools, because of the hysteria it has caused."

*Analysis of second point questions logical relationships.*

Note the direction Wood's argument has now taken. He now contends sex education will create more social harms besides illicit sex. Using the Swedish experience, Wood links such social harms as alcoholism, divorce, and suicide with sex education programs. Again he fails to establish a valid causal link. Does he really expect people to believe sex education will increase the suicide rate in the United States? Wood uses ambiguous terms such as "catastrophic" or "contributed mightily." Wood doesn't note a source to which his statistics on Sweden can be attributed. His example of the Swedish experience lacks thorough documentation of facts. The ambiguous terms need to be replaced with some numerical values so the harm can actually be measured. Most of this argument fails because Wood doesn't recognize that many other factors influence social conditions—sex education is not the only factor. Wood finally appeals to the king's physician to save his argument, but he doesn't state if this official is really knowledgeable on the subject to give a valid criticism. Because Wood does not cite any sources, you cannot be sure that the "hysteria" referred to matches the previous described social harms.

*Third major point*

Toward the end of the essay, Wood implies the American press covered up the sex education programs so that these courses could be integrated in the schools with little opposition. Wood contends the issue has gained publicity only because parents discovered the truth about these programs and rebelled against them. He further states that "there are no demonstrable benefits from such courses" and that there isn't a "single community where school sex instruction has improved sexual behavior."

*Analysis questions author's interpretation.*
*Is the statement "he cannot prove . . ." supported with evidence or logic?*

Wood has again made hasty assumptions with no facts to support him. He accuses the American press of failing to report the facts, but he cannot prove this is actually what occurred. I find myself questioning his judgments of these programs. Are they his own hastily drawn conclusions based on bias, or are they substantiated facts? I can only assume that these statements are the author's because they are not documented.

*Conclusion begins with interpretation of findings.*

Obviously, the scope of this problem has been greatly distorted by the author's own view. Wood consistently draws hasty conclusions on little amounts of facts or, in some cases, none at all. Most of his arguments fail because he doesn't show a cause-effect relationship. Wood does not actually prove the sex education courses will definitely lead to increased sexual activity or serious social harm. I cannot accept many of Wood's arguments because it appears his own interpretations have colored his points in the essay.

*Is the final sentence as clear or forceful as it could be?*

---

John Restrepo, a freshman political science major, has taken a different approach, evaluating the reading for the validity of its evidence rather than for the validity of its logic.

---

# A Little Distortion Never Hurt Anyone—Much
## John Restrepo

*Identification of author and authority to speak on subject are blended with title of essay and general description of its basic argument.*

Wallis W. Wood, national coordinator of the National Committee of the Movement to Restore Decency, takes a firm stand against sex education in the schools in his essay "A Letter to Landers." According to Woods, the purpose of the Movement to Restore Decency is to preserve decency in the home, school, and church. Wood believes that one of the most important responsibilities of parents is to educate their children. The parents must be concerned with their young, and the young must trust their parents. With increasing sex education in the schools, parents are failing to fulfill their duty. Promoters of sex education believe it should begin in kindergarten and continue through the twelfth grade. Teachers and parents have always encouraged homework, and Wood pointedly questions what will happen when children do "homework" for a sex class. He believes that more than likely it will lead to experimentation, which in turn will lead to a higher rate of divorce, venereal disease, and illegitimacy. In Wood's viewpoint, sex courses have "the po-

*Focusing sentence raises a single issue.*

tential for destroying the religious beliefs and ideals of an entire generation." Wood's views seem one-sided, but he supports his ideas with evidence. Where did Wallis Wood get his evidence and how valid is it?

*First major point described.*

Wood's first questionable reference concerns the comments of Dr. Mary S. Calderone, executive director of SIECUS (Sex Information and Education Council of the U.S.) in *McCall's* (January, 1968). Wood claims that *McCall's* refers to Calderone as the "commander-in-chief" in this "war for sexual liberation." But I question

*Analysis begins by comparing quotations to original source.*

where Wood came up with such a label. Dr. Calderone has been interviewed in only one article in *McCall's* from 1960 to 1980, and nowhere in that article were such terms used. Wood also claims that Calderone considers children abnormal if they do not reject their parents' values and standards. Yet in the article nothing is mentioned about parents except that if they are not going to tell their chil-

*"In reality"?*

dren about sex, someone is going to have to. In reality, SIECUS consists of thousands of members ranging in age

*Is this alternative view of SIECUS supported with evidence?*

from eighteen to eighty-five. Its members travel all over the world, not "promoting sex," as Wood states, but informing and assisting churches, schools, and health centers with the planning of sex education courses to suit their needs.

The January 1968 *McCall's* describes Dr. Calderone as a conservative even though she feels sex education is important in today's society. She claims that sex education began in the school as a result of parents' failing to tell their children about "the birds and the bees." In her opinion the schools took over the parents' responsibility only because they were not doing it.

*Second major point described. Note how student integrates quotation and summary.*

Wood also attacks Dr. Calderone in the field of religion. He claims that Calderone was once asked by a group of students at a boy's school "whether or not premarital sex was right." Wood quotes her as replying, "Nobody from on high determines this. You determine it. . . . I don't believe the old 'Thou shall not's' apply anymore." Wood feels it is this type of attitude that is going to be responsible for destroying the morals of an entire generation of young people. But Woods does not indicate where

*Is student justified in saying, "As he well knows"?*
*Analysis again compares sources.*

this quotation comes from. And as he well knows, the January 1968 *McCall's* article explains the position SIECUS holds in regard to sex education and religion. SIECUS recognizes that there are strong ties between the two. SIECUS is very much in favor of teaching sex in the

*On basis of first two major points, student offers tentative interpretation.*

church and the aspects of religion that deal with sex in schools. The *McCall's* material directly contradicts the supposed quotation from Dr. Calderone. I can't say that Wood has misquoted her because he does not give his source for me to check, but I can say that substantial doubts must be raised about the accuracy of Wood's claims.

*Third major point*

*Quotation compared to alternative source*

A third contradiction in Wood's essay is found in a quotation from a Dr. Kirkendall, director of SIECUS and a professor at Oregon State University. Wood claims that Kirkendall believes the way to begin a sex education course is to "just sneak it in." I can't claim that this quotation is incorrect because again Wood offers no source for me to check. But in an article for *Reader's Digest* (June, 1968), Dr. Kirkendall describes his philosophy. He indicates that he favors educating the parents before the children. The parents need to be taught so that they can assist their children at home and perhaps influence them with the appropriate religious beliefs. Kirkendall believes that this strategy will help parents realize they need to work together with the schools in sex education. I have to admit that after reading Kirkendall I don't believe that he gives much credit to the intelligence of parents. He seems to believe that in all cases the schools can do a better job than the parents. But the whole idea of educating the parents before educating the children would seem to contradict Wood's claim that Kirkendall wants to "sneak it in."

*Conclusion begins by interpreting evidence found in 3 major points.
Student begins to question relationship of findings to the whole.*

*Final assessment of the work.*

The majority of Wallis Wood's essay appears to be his own personal opinion. Even when he has noted sources for his information, there seems to be a conflict between what he claims articles contain and what they actually contain. This holds true for three examples at least. I was unable to locate some of the other sources he mentioned. But can we trust his representation of the goals of sex education when he has so badly distorted or misused the facts available to him? Even if his goal of "decency" can be applauded by all, his means for achieving it is deceptive and untrustworthy.

### Editorial Checklist for Part Six
*Formal Analysis*

_____ Have you written a complete, formal introduction, including _____name of author_____title of work_____general overview of subject_____a focusing (or thesis) sentence?

_____ Does the body of your paper provide an objective description of each major point as well as analysis and interpretation?

_____ Do you have a conclusion in which you interpret your overall findings and show the relationship of your findings to the subject as a whole?

_____ Have you assessed both the positive and negative values of the work?

_____ Have you made any effort to investigate the author's authority to speak on the subject?

_____ Have you evaluated your own biases and tried to prevent them from intruding into your argument?

_____ In rewriting, have you kept the needs of your audience in mind by attempting to use clear transitions or hooks between paragraphs to insure logical coherence?

_____ Have you made each paragraph develop a single idea through evidence, examples, or argument?

_____ Have you eliminated unnecessary words and used active verbs?

Nick Thimmesch is a journalist who has reported for the *Des Moines Register,* the *Davenport Times, Time* magazine, and *Newsday.* In the following essay from *Newsweek,* he makes a strong plea against abortion. Is his argument based on logic? On emotion? Read the article critically and consider where it is effective and where it might be weak.

# The Abortion Culture
## Nick Thimmesch

A journalist often gets caught up in events flaring into instant print and broadcast—a Watergate, feverish inflation, a fretful fuel crisis. We grab at these, try to make some sense out of it all and soon turn to what's next. Occasionally we come on to something that strikes the core and won't go away. For me, it has been the question of the value of human life—a question embracing abortion, letting the newborn die, euthanasia and the creeping utilitarian ethic in medicine that impinges on human dignity. It's all reminiscent of the "what is useful is good" philosophy of German medicine in the '30s—a utilitarianism that sent 275,000 "unworthy" Germans to death and helped bring on the Hitler slaughter of millions of human beings a few years later.

Now super-abortionists and others who relish monkeying around with human life cry that this is scare stuff inspired by hysterical Catholics waving picket signs. Not so. There is growing concern among Protestant and Jewish thinkers about "right to life" and the abortion-binge mentality.

Fetal life has become cheap. There were an estimated 1,340,000 legal and illegal abortions in the U.S. last year. There were a whopping 540,245 abortions in New York City in a 30-month period under the liberalized state abortion law. The abortion culture is upon us. In one operating room, surgeons labor to save a 21-week-old baby; in the next, surgeons destroy, by abortion, another child, who can also be reckoned to be 21 weeks old. Where is the healing?

Look beyond the political arguments and see the fetus and what doctors do to it. An unborn baby's heartbeat begins between the 18th and 25th day; brain waves can be detected at seven weeks; at nine to ten weeks, the unborn squint, swallow, and make a fist. Look at the marvelous photographs and see human life. Should these little human beings be killed unless it is to save the mother's life?

Other photos show this human life aborted, dropped onto surgical gauze or into plastic-bagged garbage pails. Take that human life by suction abortion and the body is torn apart, becoming a jumble of tiny arms and legs. In a D and C abortion, an instrument slices the body to pieces. Salt poisoning at nineteen weeks? The saline solution burns away the outer layer of the baby's skin. The ultimate is the hysterotomy (Caesarean section) abortion. As an operation, it can save mother and child; as an abortion it kills the child. Often, this baby fights for its life, breathes, moves and even cries. To see this, or the pictures of a plastic-bagged garbage can full of dead babies, well, it makes believers in right-to-life.

It's unfair to write this way, cry the super-abortionists, or to show the horrible photos. But Buchenwald and Dachau looked terrible, too. Abortions are always grisly tragedies. This truth must be restated at a time when medical administrators chatter about "cost-benefit analysis" factors in deciding who lives and who dies.

The utilitarian ethic is also common in the arguments of euthanasia advocates at work in six state legislatures. Their euphemisms drip like honey (should I say, cyanide?) just as they did in Germany—"death with dignity," the "good death." Their legal arguments fog the mind. Their mentality shakes me. One doctor, discussing the suicide-prone, wrote: "In such instances, positive, euthanasia—a nice, smooth anesthetic to terminate life—appears preferable to suicide." Dr. Russell Sackett, author of the "Death with Dignity" bill in Florida, said: "Florida has 1,500 mentally retarded and mentally ill patients, 90 percent of whom should be allowed to die." The German utilitarians had concluded the same when they led the first group of mental patients to the gas chamber at the Sonnestein Psychiatric Hospital in 1939. It bothers me that eugenicists in Germany organized the mass destruction of mental patients, and in the United States pro-abortionists now also serve in pro-euthanasia organizations. Sorry, but I see a pattern.

Utilitarianism isn't all abortion or euthanasia. Utilitarians ran the experiment in which syphilitic black men died through lack of penicillin. There are also experiments on free-clinic patients, students, the institutionalized. Senate hearings revealed that two experimental birth-control drugs were used on the "vulnerable" for purposes other than those approved by the Food and Drug Administration.

This monkeying around with people is relentless. Some medics would like to sterilize institutionalized people from here to breakfast. Psychosurgery is performed on hundreds of Americans annually, not to correct organic brain damage, but to alter their behavior. This chancy procedure, a first cousin of the now discredited prefrontal lobotomy that turned 50,000 Americans into human vegetables, is performed on unruly children and violence-prone prisoners.

Experimenters produce life outside the womb—combining sperm and ovum—and dispose of the human zygotes by pouring the solution down the sink drain. Recently scientists debated guidelines for experimenting with the live human fetus. To those considering the fetus as an organ, like, say, a kidney, Dr. Andre Hellegers of Georgetown University pointed out that fetuses have their own organs and cannot be considered organs themselves. How does one get consent from a live fetus? he asked. Or even from its donors—the parents who authorized the abortion?

Once fetal experimentation is sanctioned, are children to be next? Farfetched? No. In the New England Journal of Medicine, Dr. Franz Ingelfinger recently advocated removing the World Medical Association's absolute ban on experimenting with children and mental incompetents.

We can brake the tendencies of technocratic-minded doctors and administrators coldly concerned with "cost-benefit analysis." There was no such brake in Germany. After the first killings at Sonnestein, respected German doctors, not Nazi officials, killed 275,000 patients in the name of euthanasia. Many were curable. Eventually the doomed "undesirables" included epileptics, mental defectives, World War I amputees, children with "badly modeled ears" and "bed wetters."

The worst barbarisms often have small beginnings. The logical extension of this utilitarian ethic was the mass exterminations in slave-labor camps. In "A Sign for Cain," Dr. Frederic Wertham tells how death-dealing technicians from German state hospitals (and their equipment) were moved to the camps in 1942 to begin the big job.

Could the "what is useful is good" mentality lead to such horror in the U.S.? Not so long as I am allowed to write like this—which German journalists couldn't. Not so long as right-to-life Americans can dispute—which Germans couldn't. The extremes of the utilitarian mentality rampaging today through medicine, the drug industry and government will be checked by our press, lawmakers and doctors, lawyers and clergymen holding to the traditional ethic. The Germans weren't blessed that way.

E. G. (''Bud'') Shuster has been a congressman from Pennsylvania's 9th District since 1972. Shuster earned a Ph.D. from American University and serves as a trustee of the University of Pittsburgh. In Congress he serves on the Surface Transportation Subcommittee and chairs the National Transportation Policy Commission. In the following essay, excerpted from *Motor Trend,* Shuster uses various analogies to argue against mandatory seat belts. Consider each of his arguments carefully.

# Should Seat Belts Be Mandated by Law?
## Bud Shuster

The Swedish car manufacturer Volvo found in a recent study of 28,000 auto crashes that the fastening of both shoulder and lap belts increases your chances of surviving an accident tenfold.

A General Motors study estimates that 7700 lives can be saved each year if only three-quarters of us would buckle up.

The U.S. Department of Transportation estimates that between 10,000 and 15,000 lives can be saved each year if we *all* use safety belts.

The statistics make a telling point, one that should be central to the driving experiences of Americans: Seat belts save lives.

There are those who take this point one step further and add: "If seat belts save lives, then the government should make the wearing of them mandatory."

I disagree.

I think that any person who operates or rides in a motor vehicle and who fails to use the safety belts provided by the manufacturer is foolish. But I also think that, in a free society, people have a right to do dumb things. And I further believe that legislation is a totally inappropriate remedy for this particular type of foolishness. Highway fatalities and injuries are a bad problem for our society—but they will not be solved by passing a bad law.

In order for a law to be appropriate it must do three things: fit the situation or ill that it is intended to correct; be effective in correcting it; and not create additional problems which outweigh the intended benefits. A mandatory safety-belt usage law would satisfy none of these requirements.

As a general rule, we make behavior subject to criminal liability only if it adversely affects other members of the society. If others' rights are

Reprinted by permission of *Motor Trend* magazine.

not impaired by an individual's behavior, we do not hold the individual guilty—even if he does something which is harmful to his own health or well-being.

We allow individuals to take all sorts of liberties with their health. As a society, we tolerate smoking, drinking, overeating, overconsumption of caffein and any number of other excesses visited upon individuals by themselves. But no one seriously expects to pass laws prohibiting smoking—except as it infringes upon the rights of non-smokers. No one that I know has proposed a law to limit our caloric intake, although obesity contributes to heart disease and other illnesses. The government tried to curb drinking during Prohibition, and it was a disaster . . . and I defy anyone to legislate a sudden stop to the consumption of caffein in this coffee-, tea- and cola-saturated society.

All these are matters which the individual should share only with his conscience. For the government to pass laws prohibiting self-destructive behavior is, in effect, for the government to say, "We know what is good for you." There is, I think, a direct analogy here to the use of safety belts.

I submit that the failure to wear safety belts does not harm society at large, any more than the aforementioned abuses. Of course, it can be said that injuries resulting from an accident in which the passenger was not wearing a belt have effects beyond the individual himself—after all, someone will have to pay for the cost of his medical care and tend to his children if he is left impaired.

But I feel very strongly that these are matters for which the individual, and not the state, must assume responsibility.

There should be a distinction drawn, when considering legislation, between those actions by an individual which directly risk the safety and welfare of other members of the society, and those actions which affect primarily the individual, with only indirect consequences to the rest of the community. Legislation should not be a bludgeon employed by the government to eradicate every evil; rather, it should permit the government's intervention in human affairs only when absolutely necessary, and for very particular remedies. It is inappropriate to make a criminal offense of an action which risks the safety of only the individual, if by doing so he does not *directly* risk the safety of others.

And it seems obvious that the failure to wear safety belts does not cause such a direct risk. The wearing of safety belts, after all, does not decrease the chances of an accident. It only decreases the chances of an injury to the individual wearer. A driver's failure to fasten his safety belt will not impair his ability to drive the car—and forcing a bad driver to wear a safety belt won't make him any less of a threat to the other motorists.

So it is clear, then, that legislation is not the right solution to the problem at hand. But let's assume for a moment that Congress passed a law making it mandatory to wear safety belts. Would it work? Could it, as I asked previously, be effective?

It's apparent that enforcement of such a law would be difficult at best. Proponents of this legislation often draw an analogy between it and drunk-driving laws: If a car were stopped and the driver were found not to be wearing a belt, a penalty would result.

But there is no analogy, really. Drunk driving contributes to speeding, weaving and other infractions that alert authorities to the need to stop the car in question. Safety belts do not cause such recklessness. So how could the "offense" be checked out?

Do we expect policemen, observing a flow of traffic, to be able to spot each driver or passenger not fully harnessed? Or would we resort to sophisticated monitoring devices? And how would detection be possible at night?

I know for certain that the American people will not stand for the interruption of their driving by buzzers and bells telling them to buckle up. The outcry against mandatory seat-belt interlock devices—which I opposed on the floor of the House in 1974—was too great.

The difficulty of enforcement raises another very serious question.

During the debate on safety belt legislation in the British Parliament on March 1 of this year, the Minister for Transport claimed that he would be satisfied with a wearing rate of 80% resulting from the law he proposed. I expect that proponents of a similar law in this country would likewise be happy with 80% compliance, given the enforcement problem.

But in a nation with over 100 million registered autos, that means that roughly 20 million persons a day would be violating the law!

I can only ask what it would do to respect for the law in general if so large a number of citizens regularly disobeyed a law. There are few things more disruptive to the lawful order of society, and to relations between citizens and authorities, than the passage of a bad law easily ignored. Again, I point to Prohibition as an example.

As one who has authored several pieces of highway safety legislation, I realize the crying need for people to use safety belts. I know that, as a nation, we have not done nearly enough to promote their usage, and I accept the notion that government has a responsibility to join in the fight—not through coercive and unworkable legislation, but through persuasion and education.

Some more feasible means of reaching our goal of universal safety belt usage, by the enlistment of all sectors of the public, should be explored. They include:

• Educational programs in schools and educational aids at licensing and renewal time.

• A major media campaign, wherein all broadcast and print media would flood the public with information on the value of safety belts, both in "public service" formats and during news programs.

• Legislative endorsements—resolutions in the national and state legislatures promoting seat belt usage, with concurrent publicity.

• A road sign program to remind motorists to buckle up—for example, access ramps to major highways could be marked with signs saying "Please fasten safety belts before entering roadway."

• Development of more comfortable belts by manufacturers, facilitating their use.

Along with these measures, research should continue into alternative means of preventing auto injuries. Passive restraints, such as air bags, should be developed and marketed so that their reliability is improved and their cost brought into reasonable equivalence with that of safety belts.

In this election year, we are hearing much about the evils of big government and regulation from Washington of our daily lives. It's well to remember that big government will continue to exert ever-greater influence on us as long as we relinquish to it our responsibility for our own health and safety. For this reason, I say we should let every individual make the wise choice to wear a safety belt.

# PART

---

*Critiquing the Arts*

---

# SEVEN

The activity of art is based on the fact that a man receiving through his sense of hearing or sight another man's expression of feeling, is capable of experiencing the emotion which moved the man who expressed it.

—Leo Tolstoy

# 31 *Developing an Awareness of the Arts*

Thomas Carlyle, one of the major nineteenth-century men of letters, once wrote that "the tragedy of life is not so much what men suffer, but rather what they miss." Unfortunately, what seems so often missing from our twentieth-century world is an appreciation of the arts. In a technological age where value seems determined by what can be measured and weighed or bought and sold, the intangible, the imaginative, the dreamlike, or what exists solely because of its beauty seems at best of secondary importance. But psychologist Carl Jung has pointed out that our overemphasis on rationality has resulted in a dangerous moral and spiritual disintegration.

It may sound odd at first to insist that feelings need to be developed and educated with as much attention as we give to the mind. Yet training that focuses exclusively upon analysis of objective facts and upon logic is training that educates the intellect while leaving emotional and moral development in a primitive state, rather like an athlete who concentrates his attention on developing a single set of muscles, his biceps, perhaps, until they bulge and ripple—all in grotesque proportion to the rest of his body. Through much of this book we have been exercising our perception in objective ways, attempting to hold back private emotions, to eliminate personal feelings. In dealing with fact and reason, that is the only way probable truth can be found. But there are other kinds of truths.

# The Education of Emotion

Over three hundred years ago Pascal wrote that "the heart has its reasons which reason cannot know." Most of us live most of our lives in a world dominated by emotion that we seldom understand: we fall in love, we pursue each other sexually, we hate, we are horrified by the evil we think we detect in others, we admire the nobleness in some, we weep at loss, and we celebrate—sometimes just because we are alive. It is exactly this chaos of emotion that logic teaches us to avoid. By contrast, the artist attempts to deal with it, not by avoiding it, but by giving it shape and form. All art is primarily an expression of feelings structured according to the private vision of the artist. This ordering of feeling is the key to the way art educates our emotions.

If it is good art, we share the emotion; we experience it as real. We can even experience feelings we might never encounter in our own lives: the tragic fall of a great man, the sacrifices of idealistic lovers. Through such experiences we expand our potential for human sympathy. But we also have the opportunity to stand back from the feelings expressed by the artist—as we seldom do from our personal emotions. This standing back allows us to contemplate both our experience and the form of the artist's vision. As the mind finds meaning only in form, not in chaos, it is the shaping of art that allows us to interpret the experience, to uncover its significance, to question whether it reveals some important truth about human nature. Art then, not only communicates emotion; it translates feelings into ordered patterns that help us understand emotion—and thus our humanness.

# Training Perception

As is true of all knowledge, our understanding and appreciation of the arts begins with sensuous perception. Above all else, art is a concrete medium. Although it may sometimes express "ideas," it does so first through forms that reach out to our sight, hearing, or sense of touch. We listen to a rock band, but we also physically feel the beat of the music. We look at shadows and texture on a bronze sculpture by Henry Moore, but we also touch the sweep of motion with our hands. We read flat symbols on a page in a novel, but our imagination transforms them into visual images, sound images, smell images. In a novel like *The Red Badge of Courage,* Stephen Crane evokes every possible sense experience in order to involve us both physically and emotionally. Art *is* sensuous experience.

Study the photos of the two famous works of sculpture on page 361. You *see* them of course, but *what* do you see? Both reach out to your sense of sight, but in different ways, for each artist has formed his material differently. Each is the product of an artist's interpretation of his or her own experience and emotions—in the one case, chiseled in stone, and, in the other, cast in bronze. What do you *see,* and what different kinds of responses do you feel?

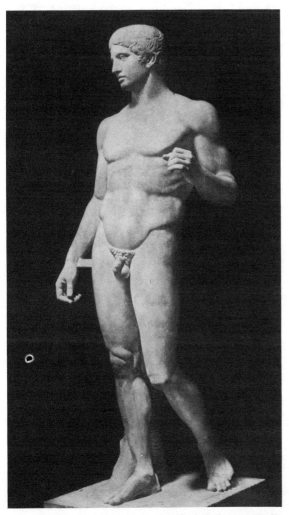

*Polyclitus. Doryphorus ("Spear Bearer"). Roman copy of original of c. 450–440 B.C. Marble, height 6'6''. National Museum, Naples.*

*Alberto Giacometti. Walking Man. 1947–1948. Bronze, 26½ x 11½ x 5''. Hirshhorn Museum and Sculpture Garden, Smithsonian Institution.*

Here are two student responses:

Student A

The Roman statue looks like a real person. The other looks like the artist wasn't very good and didn't know how to make a man. He's probably just a beginner and the first one's by his teacher. I like the Roman because he looks like an OK guy, but I think the other one is dumb.

Student B

Doryphoros stands like some sort of ideal male figure. The lines of his chest, his abdomen, the strength in his biceps, his calves, his powerful thighs make him seem like some adolescent's dream of an ideal athlete. The face is serene, composed, confident. Each line in his hair is defined but casual. He just radiates strength and greatness. He is all confidence, but not proud or arrogant. Maybe he is even supposed to be a god of some kind. Could any male be this physically beautiful?

The Giacometti, on the other hand, is strung out. Literally. This guy looks like he has been shredded by pain. Every nerve shows, and every nerve seems to twist and strain in agony around his body. His face is compressed, almost shrunken; he doesn't seem to have any real human character like the Roman figure. The Giacometti doesn't even have genitals. He has no manhood. The first lifts my spirit and makes me feel anything in life can be faced; the second gives me a tragic, almost hopeless sense of loss. I guess the Roman man is a hero in the noblest sense, while the Giacometti statue is more like today's view of ourselves. We are no longer the gods we once were.

Student A fails to see anything with his senses and as a result he fails to feel or experience either work of art. His eyes scan the surface quickly.

One figure looks real. The other looks odd. The student leaps to a hasty conclusion: one work is made by a teacher, the other by a learner. And having reached a conclusion, he sees no need to think about the matter further. The Roman sculpture, because it's familiar, is "OK," whereas the other, because it's unfamiliar, is "dumb." The problem with Student A is that his senses have never been trained to look for anything in a work of art that does not leap out at him. He expects art to come to him on his own terms. He expects it, like television, to entertain without any exertion of intellect or imagination. He has not yet learned that art demands active involvement from the audience. True art does not entertain passively. It engages you in an experience that requires your full participation.

Student B has the advantage. She becomes excited about both works of art because she sees details that lead her to both pleasure and understanding. She engages her perceptions fully, not just scanning the surface, but studying the lines and forms of each figure. Various details *suggest* qualities of human experience—nobility, strength, beauty, in one case, and pain, weakness, and loss of character in the other. From these different feelings she interprets the experience that each work of art communicates. Although they reflect different views of man, Student B finds value in both. She does not limit her appreciation only to that which is common and familiar; she explores each artist's vision in search of new aesthetic pleasure, new knowledge. She has perceived that it is the small details in art that communicate, and, from the way the details are shaped and formed, she comes to an interpretation.

# From the Literal to the Suggestive

All works of art begin with a literal, sensuous experience. The first step in developing an increased appreciation of the arts is to become *sens*itive to the actual picture or sound or shape the artist has created. The sense experience evokes our physical emotions. This is where feeling begins.

But a good work of art, through any number of techniques, may also suggest something larger than itself—may suggest something more than the literal sense experience. Doryphoros is literally a stone figure of man. It may suggest to us certain "heroic" or "godlike" qualities. No sign on the pedestal tells us we should see these attributes. We infer them from the shape of the stone. To put it another way, the details of the carving can be thought of as similar to the "facts" you have been searching for in other types of writing. From the facts you *infer* certain conclusions. The process of interpretation from objective facts or from artistic forms is almost identical, except that in art the forms may be ambiguous, and you may need to be more open-minded to various levels of suggestiveness.

Study the following poem by William Stafford. What do you see in it literally? What is the actual sense picture the poet draws for us in words? What type of feelings do the images evoke? And do any qualities of the poem suggest anything beyond the literal?

## Traveling Through the Dark

Traveling through the dark I found a deer
dead on the edge of the Wilson River road.
It is usually best to roll them into the canyon:
that road is narrow; to swerve might make more dead.

By glow of the tail-light I stumbled back of the car
and stood by the heap, a doe, a recent killing;
she had stiffened already, almost cold.
I dragged her off; she was large in the belly.

My fingers touching her side brought me the reason—
her side was warm; her fawn lay there waiting,
alive, still, never to be born.
Beside that mountain road I hesitated.

The car aimed ahead its lowered parking lights;
under the hood purred the steady engine.
I stood in the glare of the warm exhaust turning red;
around our group I could hear the wilderness listen.

I thought hard for us all—my only swerving—
then pushed her over the edge into the river.

Here are two in-class student responses:

## Student A

This poem doesn't seem to
have much meaning. I don't
get much out of it except that
the deer got hit by his car and
he threw it into the river,
probably so the game warden
wouldn't find it because it is
against the law to kill a deer
except during hunting season.
The guy is probably afraid he
will have to go to jail or pay a
fine and the people with him
tell him to just hide it. I like
poems that deal with emotion.
This one just seems to tell a
story.

## Student B

It describes a scene where he
has found a dead deer on a
narrow river road. He stops
his car and in the light from
the tail lights he discovers
that the deer is pregnant. By
touching the doe's stomach, he
can feel the live fawn inside
but knows that it will never be
born. For a moment he hesi-
tates but knows that if he
doesn't push the deer off the
road into the river, another
car might swerve to miss it
and plunge into the river killing the people. After thinking
about all involved, he chooses

human life and pushes the deer off the edge of the road.

So much is happening here that I don't know where to begin. It's like two kinds of death and two kinds of life are being considered. "I thought hard for us all—" he says. The doe is dead, but the fawn is alive. Life *inside* death. But someone else driving along the road might be killed. The wilderness listens for his answer. What kind of life will he choose? The pain is enormous, like why do you have to choose at all? Maybe the title sums it all up. He has been traveling through the dark on the side of the mountain. Also in a different way through his whole life. Now he is confronted with a choice that seems terrible to him, but he makes the choice—human life over animal life. The poem leaves me with an empty feeling, as if such choices should not have to be made.

Student A has found little of value in "Traveling Through the Dark" because he fails to see the literal image for what it is. He believes the car in the poem has struck the deer, but the first line clearly says that the speaker "found" a deer on the road. Later the student asserts that other people are with the speaker in the poem, but no such people exist. The student even ignores or misses a central point: the doe contains a living fawn. Like the first student who observed the photos of sculpture, Student A has only scanned the surface. Because he sees no details, he sees nothing of significance and finds himself forced to "invent" a meaning. He speculates that the speaker in the poem may be avoiding the law to escape paying a fine. But the law is never mentioned in the poem, and the student offers no evidence that might support such an interpretation. This is not inference from fact, nor interpretation from sense details. It is guesswork. The result can only lead Student A to decide the poem lacks emotion. He has not worked from the literal to the suggestive. He has invented a poem and then invented an interpretation. No wonder he finds no feeling in it.

Student B, however, describes in detail the visual images, sound images, and touch images he sees in each line. He identifies the dilemma that actually exists by quoting the line, "I thought hard for us all." Having read the literal poem, the student goes on to contemplate the various ideas it suggests to him. First, he considers the paradox of life-in-death; second, he observes that we travel through life in darkness until confronted by such paradoxes; third, he questions why we should be faced with such choices at all. Throughout his comments, Student B continues to keep in mind the emotions stirred by such problems: pain, emptiness, terrible choices. Student B looks at the actual ordering of images, considers the feelings and questions they evoke, and allows the details to suggest several levels of significance we might find in the work.

## The Humanistic Heritage

In both of these examples—responses to sculpture and poetry—the students who failed to exert effort, who failed to look and thus failed to feel, are left exactly where they began. They may be intelligent, but their intelligence remains limited to obvious surfaces. They do not question; they do not grow. Their lives are unchanged. They remain content to hibernate in their familiar caves, comfortable but dull, preferring only those experiences with which they are already accustomed and which demand nothing of their imagination.

The students who looked intently at sense details, however, and who allowed the details to suggest qualities of experience and emotion, found themselves contemplating aspects of human nature in terms that expanded their consciousness of life itself. The artist's vision presented them with a context for raising questions of values: Is it truth? Does it clarify an aspect of the human condition? Does it show the consequence of human choice and behavior? Do we know something more about ourselves than we did before? For these students, intelligence and emotion interact. Through art, they discover a unity between knowledge of fact and feeling about the fact. They participate in the education of the whole person, not just the mind. As a result, they find themselves linked to a great humanistic heritage, no longer limited to an isolated narrow world of here and now, but joined in spirit to ever-enlarging circles of human experience. Here is how Leo Tolstoy expressed it:

> Art is a human activity consisting in this, that one man consciously by means of certain eternal signs, hands on to others feelings he has lived through, and that others are infected by these feelings and also experience them ... it is a means of union among men joining them together in the same feelings, and indispensable

for the life and progress towards well-being of individuals and of humanity.

The development of artistic appreciation begins then (as we began this book and as we have begun each new unit) by urging you to seek out the concrete details, the shapes and forms that they take, and by letting them suggest to you both feelings and ideas.

### EXERCISES

1. Study the eighteenth-century portrait of King Louis XIV of France on page 369. Look at each detail closely: the various lines and suggested movements in the painting, the pose of the figure, the expression on the face, the clothing and background. If we assume the artist has attempted to portray the spirit and character of the king, not just photographically reproduce him, how do the details suggest such qualities? What feelings does the painting evoke? What could you infer about the king and his era from the painting?

2. Consider Pablo Picasso's portrait of a Spanish poet done in our own century (page 368). Again, look at the details closely, at the various lines and shapings. If the work seems distorted, can you suggest any reasons for it? Does the face seem to be in motion? Is the expression stable or shifting? Which are you most aware of: the character of the woman or the vision of the artist?

3. Compare the two portraits. What can you learn about two different visions of the world?

4. Here is a well-known poem by Ezra Pound. The simplicity of it may be deceiving. Consider how the various sensory images build toward and contribute to the feeling that is achieved by the end. How would you describe the feeling?

The River-Merchant's Wife: A Letter

While my hair was still cut straight across my forehead
Played I about the front gate, pulling flowers.
You came by on bamboo stilts, playing horse,
You walked about my seat, playing with blue plums.
And we went on living in the village of Chokan:
Two small people, without dislike or suspicion.

At fourteen I married My Lord you.
I never laughed, being bashful.
Lowering my head, I looked at the wall.
Called to, a thousand times, I never looked back.

At fifteen I stopped scowling,
I desired my dust to be mingled with yours
Forever and forever and forever.
Why should I climb the look out?

At sixteen you departed,
You went into far Ku-to-yen, by the river of swirling eddies,
And you have been gone five months.
The monkeys make sorrowful noise overhead.
You dragged your feet when you went out.
By the gate now, the moss is grown, the different mosses,
Too deep to clear them away!
The leaves fall early this autumn, in wind.
The paired butterflies are already yellow with August
Over the grass in the West garden;
They hurt me. I grow older.
If you are coming down through the narrows of the river Kiang,
Please let me know beforehand,
And I will come out to meet you
                  As far as Cho-fu-Sa.

*Pablo Picasso. The Poet Jaime Sabartés. Royan, 22 October 1939. Oil,
18⅜ x 15¼". Private Collection, Paris.* © *S.P.A.D.E.M., Paris/V.A.G.A.,
New York.*

*Hyacinthe Rigaud, Louis XIV, Louvre, Paris.*

5. Telling stories is one of the most natural things people do. Stories can be as long as *War and Peace* or as short as a few paragraphs. Here's a short one by Susan Fromberg Shaeffer, which tries to take you from where you are in an everyday world into something you don't expect. Read carefully. Be prepared to let your imagination go with the story.

# The Taxi

## Susan Fromberg Schaeffer

There was a taxi driver who had one story he liked to tell over again, and over again: "One day in December, it was unusually warm and unusually beautiful; there were no clouds in the sky, and patches of blue sky were fallen to the curbs in small puddles left from the old melted snow. Everyone was walking and the cabs were empty as coffins. It wasn't until two o'clock in the morning that it began to rain, and even then it was a light rain, so there would be no fares for that day. I am a night owl and a late riser and so is my wife, so I went out to get some cigarettes. Most of the stores were closed; I got into my cab and began driving around.

"I had not gone more than two blocks when a man flagged me. Even from a distance, I could see he was elegantly dressed. The street lights glinted from his brown leather coat and his attaché case, and when he got in, I could see his coat had a heavy beaver collar. He had on some very thin leather gloves made of an even lighter shade, and the stitches in them were lighter still. The man wanted to go into Manhattan: we drove to One Hundred and Sixty-fifth Street, and I waited; then he wanted to go to the Island, and I waited; he went into a house that was huge, half the size of our block and with a porch supported by great white columns. He came back; he got in; he smiled. Then he gave me his address in the city; he said he had to pick up his suitcase; he was going to the airport. When we got to Eighty-sixth and Central Park West, I was to wait again. By this time the meter read almost sixty dollars, and I thought, what makes me think he will ever come back? But when I opened the door to look out, the doorman came over and told me not to worry about him, he was always good for his money.

"We drove out to the airport. He had nothing to say; he stared ahead, his perfect marble face diminished in the mirror, seeming not to breathe, nostrils of marble. Some seagulls cast dim shadows over the silvery marshes as we drove in the gray light; there were some shrieks; it was five in the morning. When we got to the terminal, my eyes, used to the dark, kept closing and closing, uncontrollable blinks. He got out, handed

"The Taxi" originally appeared in *TriQuarterly* 35, © 1976 TriQuarterly. Reprinted by permission.

me some money, took his case, said keep the change, and left. Then I counted my money. One hundred eighty dollars! A one-hundred-dollar tip! It was a miracle I didn't get killed driving home to tell my wife. Naturally she wanted to know where I'd been. Naturally she didn't believe me. I showed her the money; she still didn't believe me.

"I got angry. Who knew, it was possible two such things could happen, twice in one night. I got back in my cab. From its window, I could see my wife, in her blue terry-cloth robe, watching through the dust-streaked windows of her apartment. She was a good housekeeper, but the snows when they melted were too much, even for her. I remember pulling away from the curb as if I were leaving a dock. The streets were empty. No elegant man at all. But on the front seat was a black attaché case. I didn't stop driving, but opened it with one hand, and guided the steering wheel with the other. There was a gleam even before the lid lifted. Inside was a solid gold head, like the man's, but eyeless, and with real hair growing out of its metal scalp. By now, it seemed to be shoulder length.

"I pulled over against the curb to look closer at it, but the curb vanished to mist. It was obvious the head wanted to keep going. I began to drive and it began to look pleased. The more we drove, the less scenery there was, and the more pleased it was. I kept thinking it would tell me something soon, tell me where we were going. Its gold lips never moved, its hair kept growing, and I kept one hand on a cheek, steadying it, as if it were a sick cat, or a child, frightened. But when there was no scenery at all, only the pull of the road, its lips seemed to turn up at the corners, or so it seemed to me then. There was never a problem with engines, or tires, or gas.

"It was the radio that spoke to me first. My daughter had gotten a scholarship to college; my wife, her insurance; it was thought she would marry again. Naturally, she would buy a new robe. I didn't have to hear this, and I know it would be smooth, like silk, or else fuzzy, like velvet. My son was growing up to look more and more like his father, and fighting in the playgrounds. The gold hair spilled over the seat and onto the floor near the accelerator pedal. The meter has long ago lost its ability to register the fare for the miles that we cover, but still it keeps on, like an electrified heart. It clicks. It clicks. I keep waiting for the gold head to speak to me, for the gold lips to part, but so far it has said nothing, although it seems that now, when I drive, I have to place my hand on the cheek differently, which may mean it has changed its position and is now staring at me."

    a. How would you describe the literal happenings of the first half of the story? What happens in the second half? Is Schaeffer still creating sense pictures for us? In what way are they different?

    b. Authors, like painters and sculptors, work through form to shape emotional experience. Do you find the two parts of the story create different feelings? How would you describe them?

c. Can you find any clues that suggest whether the second half of the story is meant to be seen as a fantasy that occurs only within the mind of the taxi driver? Or should we accept the "reality" of the fantasy and consider the possibility that it is not just a dream but something that happens beyond everyday comprehension?

d. Which interpretation would make the story more interesting? Which would demand more imaginative participation from the reader?

e. If it is possible to understand this story in at least two different ways, can you consider why an author would want to be so ambiguous? Why not make clear the exact "message" instead of creating such difficulties for the reader?

f. Although you may never be able to decide what the story means, does it lead you to question or contemplate any aspect of human experience?

## 32 *Reading for Literary Significance*

As a sophomore in college I enrolled in a Victorian literature class. I was fascinated by my professor's enthusiasm for poetry and equally enthralled by his gymnastics. I remember how he once climbed upon a windowsill and sat precariously balanced, waving one arm and reading poems by Christina Rossetti. On another occasion he bounded up the center stairs of the classroom, reciting and acting out "The Charge of the Light Brigade." But the day I remember most clearly is the day I decided not to become an English major.

I had spent the night before looking over poems by Gerard Manley Hopkins. Although none of them made much sense to me, I pushed my way through half a dozen and went to class confident I had fulfilled the assignment. Then the lecture began. My professor perched himself cross-legged on a table and announced, quite to my discomfort, that the sweeping flight of a bird in Hopkins's "Windhover" was a symbol for Christ. Image by image, line by line, he worked his way happily through the poem pointing out metaphors, subtle connotations, and historical allusions. By the end of the hour his face was red and puffed with pleasure while I sat crushed by my own inadequacies. I had seen no Christ symbol. Indeed, I wasn't even sure I had seen a bird. It was obvious that others "saw things" in poetry that I didn't.

Not until I began graduate studies seven years later did I return to English literature, knowing then that what had happened to me was not all that unusual with students. I had looked at Hopkins's poems, all right, but I had not really read—not for significance and insight. I had skimmed hurriedly in much the same way one glances through a newspaper, looking for information, willing to be entertained if that should happen, hoping the "meaning" would leap out at me. Admittedly I felt puzzled by strange language and odd sentences, but not so much that I was willing to reread. I had not even looked up in a dictionary the term *windhover*. How could I have known the poem was about a bird if I didn't know the title named the bird? Nor had I paid attention to the dedication, *To Christ Our Lord,* printed in bold italics directly under the title. After all, who reads dedications? The fact was I hadn't read at all.

The process of critical reading outlined earlier in Chapter 29 should give you the advantage over me. The strategy of reading described there is similar to the one you must use in reading for more than surface effects. Because a poem or novel or play may deal with so many complex levels (with emotion, fantasy, reality, myth, and alas yes, with symbols), we cannot outline the same straightforward steps we used for reading prose essays. Each work of art is unique, and each may present us with new demands. But we can illustrate a similar approach that at least introduces the essential concept of reading with an engaged imagination.

## The First Reading

Almost all art forms, and especially literary forms, must be experienced more than once. You should not expect to appreciate fully a poem or play or even a novel the first time you read it. A poem must be read many times. A play should be read at least twice, with parts of it several more times. And although a novel may be too long, or your time too limited, to read twice through, key sections will often require rereading. There is no escape from this fact: art demands your participation, your committed involvement. Because art forms are often subtle or ambiguous, because they often work on more than one level of understanding, because indeed they are often obscure, you must be willing to *study* the work. The most serious mistake young people make about art is to believe it does not require at least as much study and attention as a good problem in geometry.

Here are eight primary steps to serious reading:

1. Read slowly. If you roller skate through an art museum you won't see the paintings. Literature must be read at a slower pace than other forms of writing. Do not "speed-read" or skim. An author uses words as his or her basic tools. Every word counts for the author, as every color and line are meaningful for the painter. To feel the full effect, you must be conscious of words themselves; you must allow sounds, images, and connotations to set up reverberations. If you have been trained to look only for facts, you must slow down and be willing to experience feelings.

2. Read with pen in hand. Underline key phrases, key speeches by major figures, key statements by the narrator. Take notes on ideas or questions (do not trust your memory). Circle words used in special ways or repeated in significant patterns. Look up in the dictionary words you do not know or words you think you know but that seem to have special weight or placement—the author may be using them in new ways. *You cannot expect to understand literature if you do not know the meaning of the words.*

3. Be willing to read aloud. Words have sounds and sound is sensuous experience. Poetry, especially, needs to be listened to as well as read. Drama is by its nature a spoken medium. Even key passages from novels may become clear only when read aloud. James Joyce's *Finnegan's Wake,* for example, looks like nonsense on the page, yet, when listened to, its words become transformed into a hilarious, sensuous, flowing Irish brogue.

4. Begin each new novel, play, or poem without predetermined bias. If you decide in advance that all good art uses realistic settings and promotes your personal moral values, you close out the possibility of new experience. You do not have to, nor should you, enjoy every work of literature you read. But you should be willing to recognize that the imagination is limitless. No matter how comfortable you may be with certain traditional forms and ideas, a new form or experiment in writing may offer you as much or more imaginative pleasure than the old. A first reading is almost never the time to pronounce final judgment.

5. Ask silent questions of the material as you read. Do not read passively, waiting to be told the "meaning." Most authors will seldom pronounce a moral. Even if they do, a work of literature is always more than its theme. Use the questions devised by reporters: *Who, What, Where, When, Why,* and *How.* You should usually be able to answer the first four questions after one reading—they form the surface of the work. *Why* and *How* may take more study—such questions probe the inner levels.

6. Look for those qualities that professional writers look for in real life: *conflict, contrast, contradiction,* and *characterization.* Most fiction and drama are built around one or all of these elements. Poetry, too, may use such devices, but in more subtle ways.

7. Look for rhythm, repetition, and pattern. Successful works of literature incorporate such structural devices in the language, in the dialogue, in the plot, in the characterization, and elsewhere. Pattern is form, and form is the shaping the artist gives to his or her experience. If you can identify the pattern and relate it to the content, you'll be on your way to insight.

8. Finally, do not force an interpretation. Because of the Western world's tradition of "interpreting" art, we often feel pressured to find instantaneous meaning: we search desperately for moralistic

tags or simplistic messages or profound symbols. The truth is that a good work of literature comes to us by indirection, implication, suggestion, and feeling. The good author finds life too rich and complex for simplistic "messages." The good reader will wait patiently for understanding to grow out of various readings and rereadings.

The first reading must be thoughtful, but you must resist the temptation to plunge ahead with analysis. Read for the total feeling; read for an understanding of the work as a whole, before you return for more in-depth considerations.

Here is a very short story by Sherwood Anderson on which you might try applying some of these eight basic steps:

# The Book of the Grotesque
## Sherwood Anderson

The writer, an old man with a white mustache, had some difficulty in getting into bed. The windows of the house in which he lived were high and he wanted to look at the trees when he awoke in the morning. A carpenter came to fix the bed so that it would be on a level with the window.

Quite a fuss was made about the matter. The carpenter, who had been a soldier in the Civil War, came into the writer's room and sat down to talk of building a platform for the purpose of raising the bed. The writer had cigars lying about and the carpenter smoked.

For a time the two men talked of the raising of the bed and then they talked of other things. The soldier got on the subject of the war. The writer, in fact, led him to that subject. The carpenter had once been a prisoner in Andersonville prison and had lost a brother. The brother had died of starvation, and whenever the carpenter got upon that subject he cried. He, like the old writer, had a white mustache, and when he cried he puckered up his lips and the mustache bobbed up and down. The weeping old man with the cigar in his mouth was ludicrous. The plan the writer had for the raising of his bed was forgotten and later the carpenter did it in his own way and the writer, who was past sixty, had to help himself with a chair when he went to bed at night.

In his bed the writer rolled over on his side and lay quite still. For years he had been beset with notions concerning his heart. He was a hard smoker and his heart fluttered. The idea had got into his mind that he would some time die unexpectedly and always when he got into bed he thought of that. It did not alarm him. The effect in fact was quite a special thing and not easily explained. It made him more alive, there in bed, than at any other time. Perfectly still he lay and his body was old and not of much use any more, but something inside him was altogether young. He was like a pregnant woman, only that the thing inside him was not a baby but a youth. No, it wasn't a youth, it was a woman, young, and wearing a coat of mail like a knight. It is absurd, you see, to try to tell what was inside the old writer as he lay on his high bed and listened to the fluttering of his heart. The thing to get at is what the writer, or the young thing within the writer, was thinking about.

The old writer, like all of the people in the world, had got, during his long life, a great many notions in his head. He had once been quite handsome and a number of women had been in love with him. And then, of course, he had known people, many people, known them in a peculiarly intimate way that was different from the way in which you and I know people. At least that is what the writer thought and the thought pleased him. Why quarrel with an old man concerning his thoughts?

In the bed the writer had a dream that was not a dream. As he grew somewhat sleepy but was still conscious, figures began to appear before his eyes. He imagined the young indescribable thing within himself was driving a long procession of figures before his eyes.

You see the interest in all this lies in the figures that went before the eyes of the writer. They were all grotesques. All of the men and women the writer had ever known had become grotesques.

The grotesques were not all horrible. Some were amusing, some almost beautiful, and one, a woman all drawn out of shape, hurt the old man by her grotesqueness. When she passed he made a noise like a small dog whimpering. Had you come into the room you might have supposed the old man had unpleasant dreams or perhaps indigestion.

For an hour the procession of grotesques passed before the eyes of the old man, and then, although it was a painful thing to do, he crept out of bed and began to write. Some one of the grotesques had made a deep impression on his mind and he wanted to describe it.

At his desk the writer worked for an hour. In the end he wrote a book which he called "The Book of the Grotesque." It was never published, but I saw it once and it made an indelible impression on my mind. The book had one central thought that is very strange and has always remained with me. By remembering it I have been able to understand many people and things that I was never able to understand before. The thought was involved but a simple statement of it would be something like this:

That in the beginning when the world was young there were a great many thoughts but no such thing as a truth. Man made the truths himself and each truth was a composite of a great many vague thoughts. All about in the world were the truths and they were all beautiful.

The old man had listed hundreds of the truths in his book. I will not try to tell you of all of them. There was the truth of virginity and the truth of passion, the truth of wealth and of poverty, of thrift and of profligacy, of carelessness and abandon. Hundreds and hundreds were the truths and they were all beautiful.

And then the people came along. Each as he appeared snatched up one of the truths and some who were quite strong snatched up a dozen of them.

It was the truths that made the people grotesques. The old man had quite an elaborate theory concerning the matter. It was his notion that the moment one of the people took one of the truths to himself, called it his truth, and tried to live his life by it, he became a grotesque and the truth he embraced became a falsehood.

You can see for yourself how the old man, who had spent all of his life writing and was filled with words, would write hundreds of pages concerning this matter. The subject would become so big in his mind that he himself would be in danger of becoming a grotesque. He didn't, I suppose, for the same reason that he never published the book. It was the young thing inside him that saved the old man.

Concerning the old carpenter who fixed the bed for the writer, I only mentioned him because he, like many of what are called very common people, became the nearest thing to what is understandable and lovable of all the grotesques in the writer's book.

## Beginning with the Literal

If you're like most of us, you've probably read Anderson's story too quickly. I point no finger of guilt here because in searching for a story to print as an example, I, too, read it hurriedly. "Ah," I said to myself, "here's a short, simple story with few complications. Just the thing for a brief example." Had you asked me about the story after my first reading, I probably would have said something like, "Well, it's about an old man who sees everyone as grotesque." But I would have felt uncomfortable in my answer. Something about my first reading left an ache about the old man, about something lost and something gained. Vague feelings I could not identify. My summary-type statement about the story would have seemed strangely inadequate for the feelings it aroused in me. Was there more to it than I had noticed? Had I really understood it at all? I began asking questions of myself, trying not to make hasty interpretations or judgments, but to *see* the literal level of the story:

> *Who*      Who is the main character? The old man or the narrator? What is the role of the carpenter? What qualities about characterizing does Anderson use: physical details? actions? speech? background? other's responses? a self-created environment? And which are important in this particular story?

*What*    What actually happens in the story? Is there anything
that could be called a plot? Is there a turning point or crisis? Any real conflict within the old man? With others?
Any contrast between beliefs and actions? Is there a key
scene where the action seems most revealing or
important?

*Where*   Where does the story take place? A large city? A small
town? Can we tell? Is it important? Does the old man's
bedroom have any significance?

*When*    Do we know the time period in which the events occur?
Should we ask when this particular event occurs in terms
of the old man's life? Would it make a difference?

*Why*     In some works, like *Hamlet,* the question "why" may be
the central focus of the story: Why does Hamlet delay in
killing his uncle? Is there a "why" in Sherwood Anderson's story? Does it relate to the old man? Or to the
narrator?

*How*     How is the work put together? It may be too soon to answer this question. A second reading will probably be necessary to consider how each of the main elements
relate—narrator, characters, plot, language, sense details,
and so on.

Did I really ask myself such questions? Yes and no. Even after years
of experience at reading literature, the questions hover in the back of my
mind, although most of them have become more intuitive than conscious.
For the beginning student, however, it seems to me that these questions
do need to be consciously considered. Many will be rejected as inapplica-
ble to any one particular work, but those that suggest possibilities must be
followed up. And if you do not work with such questions consciously, the
chances are you'll forget some, perhaps the very ones that might have
been most important.

The point is to understand the literal story. It makes no sense to
pursue a "deeper" meaning if you haven't understood the surface. In
Chapter 29, I encouraged you to write out a brief summary after reading
an essay. You may want to perform a similar act after reading a literary
work. A poem, especially, cannot be dealt with intelligibly until you have
understood its literal level. Writing a paraphrase—a type of summary in
which you rephrase the sense of the work in your own words, not just
generalizing from the whole, but holding fairly close to an image-by-image
or stanze-by-stanza rewriting—is one of the oldest and most useful techniques for aiding comprehension. You must remember, of course, that a
paraphrase is not the poem. Your rephrasing only helps you understand
the surface of the work. Many other levels must still be explored.

It's obviously time for a second reading. Let me urge you to turn
back at this point and read "The Book of the Grotesque" one more time.

If you didn't underline and take notes the first time, do so now, asking all the questions we've been considering.

## Contemplation of the Major Elements

The second reading is the real beginning of your critical study. By the time you've finished a second reading of a poem you should have completed your paraphrase of it. A novel or short story is too long to consider writing a detailed paraphrase of it, but you should have taken thorough notes either in the margins or on separate cards. Here is a reproduction of my own notes, exactly as I took them on my second reading of Anderson's story.

---

relationship
Writer — old — young inside — "pregnant w/ youth"
carpenter — is he example of grotesque? How?
Dream not a dream? Key event?
    — the young in him drove grotesques before him
Narrator's statement
    — many thoughts, no truths
    — many made truths out of the thoughts
    — all were beautiful until adopted by
        individuals as their truths
    → which turned them into grotesques
Writer in danger of becoming a grotesque
    — the young in him saves him
                3rd tag of this idea
what is there about the young that saves the old man?
    — youth has innocence? No fixed truths?
    — open to experience?
Relationship to truth ??
    — are all truths beautiful until they
        become obsessions? My truth vs.
        your truth? Makes each of us
        grotesque

---

Your notes might look quite different. You may have focused on different points or seen other important ideas that I missed. But from my notes you can tell that I was beginning to consider the major elements or parts of the work and how they related to each other. If the first reading is to get a feeling for the whole of it, the second reading should begin the process of looking consciously at the details. A scholar of literature might be sensitive to hundreds of different elements, but every beginning student should at least know the following:

## Fiction

- Almost all novels and short stories are written about characters, so *character* itself becomes the key quality to look for. Who is the major character? What is his or her basic quality: courage, innocence, pride, greed? Does the character change during the story? Is the character faced with conflict from external forces? From internal forces?
- Who tells the story may be a key element in understanding both the character and the events. *Point of View* can come from the character's own eyes, from a narrator, or from another character. Can you speculate on why the point of view would make any difference in the story?
- Some fiction, but not all, has *plot*. A plot is more than just a series of events or actions; it also involves consideration of why such actions occur. What you need to consider most carefully is the relationship between the plot and the character. Does the character cause events to happen, or does the action bring about changes in the character?

## Drama

- Most plays are built around *character,* so the same basic element is our first consideration. But drama may also have specific types of characters that function in traditional ways. The main character is called a *protagonist*. A *foil* is a character who helps us understand the basic qualities of the main character, usually by exhibiting opposite traits.
- As drama is constructed around the spoken voice, *dialogue* must be considered a prime element. Dialogue involves two or more speakers. In many plays, however, a character may talk aloud to himself in a *soliloquy*. The soliloquy tells us what the character is thinking about and may be a major clue to understanding ideas or actions expressed in the play.
- Like fiction, plays usually have a plot, but the action or movement of drama is often formally divided into *acts* and *scenes*. The divisions may give insight into the way the author has shaped his or her material. Even more important, many plays are traditionally built around a structure that moves from *exposition* (The situation at the opening), through *rising action* (a

series of complications that increase tension) to the *climax* (a crucial moment for the main character where his or her fate is often decided), and a *falling action* (the final moments of the play where the new situation is established as resolution to the drama).

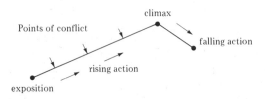

### Poetry

- The poet has the widest range of options and, for that reason, may deserve the most concentrated attention. The most basic element of poetry is the language itself, the *words*. Every word counts. A good dictionary is mandatory. Both *denotation* and *connotation* must be considered.
- *Images* are the imaginative sense-pictures the poet creates with words. You must open yourself to seeing, hearing, touching, feeling, and tasting the images.
- *Rhythms* of various kinds affect the experience of any one poem. A poet may use meter, the formal counting of stressed and unstressed syllables; or the poet may achieve rhythm through such devices as parallel structure, line length, and even rhyme.
- Most poets use *figurative language, metaphors, similes, analogies,* and *symbols*. In some way these elements may be the most difficult to analyze but you must recognize that they are not exclusive to poetry and certainly nothing to be afraid of, for we use all of them every day in normal speech. A poet merely uses them with more precision and control.

A brief list like this cannot pretend to do justice to the many basic elements, subtleties, and variations found in literature. Only a specialist would recognize and appreciate them all. But you should be aware that the artist does use such devices. Even though, on first reading, a good story or poem may seem unified and indivisible, on a second or third reading, with concentrated attention, you can begin to identify *how* the writer has shaped such elements to form the total effect. Once you've made that step, you are in a position to question how the parts relate. In seeing relationships, you move toward the goal of serious reading: an understanding or insight into the significance of the work.

# Moving to the Suggestive

After rereading, after questioning, after note-taking or paraphrasing, you should be ready to consider the work on its suggestive levels. Indeed, by this point you've probably already begun to interpret relationships and to see values in Sherwood Anderson's story that could not have been appreciated on the first reading. I, for one, was genuinely surprised at how much more complex and richly textured the story was than I first thought. After a second reading I could *not* say, "Here's a story about an old man who sees others as grotesque." Such a shallow response would be seriously inadequate.

How to see and interpret relationships, however, is not something that can be clearly illustrated in a text. A relationship is something that must be perceived inside your mind. It is an inner process for which we have no real mechanism of instruction. But we *can* identify two phases of the process that a good reader will work his or her way through when contemplating a work of art.

## Searching for the Pattern

Even if the author provides a direct expression or generalized statement about the significance (as Anderson does), that expression or idea must be seen in relation to the characters, actions, and events. The reader must look for repetitions or variations of concepts, speeches, words, actions, feelings, or whatever. For example, you might consider why Anderson tags the word *young* three times in the story. Its repetition suggests that we should be considering its relationship to the "old" man and to his "truth." The story seems to center around those elements—hence we have the beginnings of a *pattern.* Only in looking at all the possible *connections* can you work toward an underlying significance.

## Relating to the Emotion

All this effort will be wasted unless you can perceive a relationship of the parts to the whole, to the total experience of the work, and to the feelings it evokes. Students often complain that to criticize a poem or a story is destructive. And, indeed, any critical approach that tears apart without joining together again may leave a negative impression. But the point of critical reading is not "to tear apart." When we read for significance, we study the details only to see their relationship to the whole. It is the total effect, *the feeling captured in form,* that we want to appreciate. The final step in serious reading, then, is to draw together all that we have seen and to consider its relationship to the human emotion the art expresses.

**A SUMMARY OF BASIC STEPS IN READING FOR SIGNIFICANCE**

*Read Fiction, Drama, and Poetry More than Once*

—Read first for the total experience of the work.

—Read slowly for the words, feelings, emotions, and ideas.

—Underline key passages, phrases, and words. Take notes on ideas and questions.

—Look up important words in the dictionary.

—In poetry and drama especially, read aloud.

—Be open to new possibilities; do not reject that which cannot be understood instantly on first reading.

*Ask Silent Questions*

—Who, What, Where, When, Why, How?

—What is the conflict, contrast, contradiction?

—Is there a pattern? A design? A significant repetition?

*Consider the Major Elements*

—Study the character, his or her basic qualities, conflicts, and growth.

—Consider the actions, the movement, or plot.

—Always, always attend to the words themselves.

*Contemplate the Relationships*

—How do each of the parts relate to each other?

—How does the whole of it relate to the central feeling the work expresses?

---

With a head full of feelings and ideas, a page full of notes, and a text underlined and marked, you're now ready to write. Only when you've engaged yourself in this type of thorough involvement with art can you expect to develop a written critique with any depth. The next chapter will discuss the actual job of getting it down on paper.

**EXERCISES**

1. Read the following poem by D. H. Lawrence. Use the techniques discussed in this chapter. Read it once for the total impression, for the feeling. Then reread aloud, slowly. Circle key words. Use a dictionary for every word you are unsure of. Consider both the denotation and the connotation within the overall context.

# Piano

## D. H. Lawrence

Softly, in the dusk, a woman is singing to me;
Taking me back down the vista of years, till I see
A child sitting under the piano, in the boom of the tingling strings
And pressing the small, poised feet of a mother who smiles as she
    sings.

In spite of myself, the insidious mastery of song
Betrays me back, till the heart of me weeps to belong
To the old Sunday evenings at home, with winter outside
And hymns in the cozy parlour, the tinkling piano our guide.

So now it is vain for the singer to burst into clamour
With the great black piano appassionato. The glamour
Of childish days is upon me, my manhood is cast
Down in the flood of rememberance, I weep like a child for the
    past.

a. Now that you've read the poem several times, write a prose
    paraphrase. A paraphrase is a retelling in your own words,
    moving almost line-by-line or stanza-by-stanza (not just
    summarizing the whole of it).
b. Consider now some of the following questions:

    —How does the imagery (the sensuous pictures) in the
      poem contribute to its effect?
    —What do you know about the speaker of the poem?
      About his feelings, his sensitivity, his present attitude as
      well as his past experience?
    —Is there any element of conflict in the poem? Is it
      important?

c. Now that you've studied the poem, can you draw together your
    various experiences with it? How would you describe the
    emotion the poet is trying to express? A poem does not need to
    have a "meaning" as such; it may only communicate an
    experience. Which does this poem seem to present? What is its
    ultimate significance? Is it successful or does it fail? Consider
    the details in the poem that would support your answer to each of
    these questions.

2. Here are two other simple poems you might want to read closely. Move slowly through the steps that might apply to each poem. Do not rush to judgment. Remember that it may take time for a poem to grow on you.

# A Blessing
## James Wright

Just off the highway to Rochester, Minnesota,
Twilight bounds softly forth on the grass.
And the eyes of those two Indian ponies
Darken with kindness.
They have come gladly out of the willows
To welcome my friend and me.
We step over the barbed wire into the pasture
Where they have been grazing all day, alone.
They ripple tensely, they can hardly contain their happiness
That we have come.
They bow shyly as wet swans. They love each other.
There is no loneliness like theirs.
At home once more,
They begin munching the young tufts of spring in the darkness.
I would like to hold the slenderer one in my arms,
For she has walked over to me
And nuzzled my left hand.
She is black and white,
Her mane falls wild on her forehead,
And the light breeze moves me to caress her long ear
That is delicate as the skin over a girl's wrist.
Suddenly I realize
That if I stepped out of my body I would break
Into blossom.

# in Just-

## E. E. Cummings

in Just-
spring     when the world is mud-
luscious the little
lame balloonman

whistles     far     and wee

and eddieandbill come
running from marbles and
piracies and it's
spring

when the world is puddle-wonderful

the queer
old balloonman whistles
far     and     wee
and bettyandisbel come dancing
from hop-scotch and jump-rope and

it's
spring
and
    the

        goat-footed

balloonMan     whistles
far
and
wee

3. The Parable of the Good Samaritan is familiar to most readers. But consider it for its basic literary elements.

# The Parable of the Good Samaritan
## New Testament, Luke 10:30–37

And Jesus said, A certain man went down from Jerusalem to Jericho, and fell among thieves, which stripped him of his raiment, and wounded him, and departed, leaving him half dead.

And by chance there came down a certain priest that way; and when he saw him, he passed by on the other side.

And likewise a Levite, when he was at the place, came and looked on him, and passed by on the other side.

But a certain Samaritan, as he journeyed, came where he was; and when he saw him, he had compassion on him,

And went to him, and bound up his wounds, pouring in oil and wine, and set him on his own beast, and brought him to an inn, and took care of him.

And on the morrow when he departed, he took out two pence, and gave them to the host, and said unto him, Take care of him: and whatsoever thou spendest more, when I come again, I will repay thee.

Which now of these three, thinkest thou, was neighbor unto him that fell among the thieves?

And he said, he that showed mercy on him. Then said Jesus unto him, Go, and do thou likewise.

a. Who is the major character?
b. What kind of conflict is involved?
c. Is there a pattern or repetition that helps suggest the theme or meaning of the parable? If you changed the story so that no repetition occurred, would it have the same meaning or impact?
d. If the story were told from a different point of view (from the Samaritan's or the victim's), what would be the effect on the overall meaning of the work?

# 33 *The Formal Critique*

Until now I have discussed your audience as someone outside yourself, as a reader real or imagined, to whom you wanted to communicate. In studying art, however, you, too, form a part of the audience. First, you are audience to the creative work of someone else—to a symphony, a poem, a painting—before you are a writer about that work. Second, even though the paper you produce will be nominally addressed to a reader other than yourself, you'll find that during the actual process of writing, you continue to respond and react to the art. The writing process becomes a method of clarifying and discriminating for yourself, for your own understanding, not just for your imagined reader. In other words, writing about literature or music or art becomes in a genuine sense an exploration of your own experience, both emotional and intellectual. As the artist has given form to his or her feelings, so you must give form to yours, for your own benefit as well as the benefit of another reader.

## The Other Reader

What does the audience for a formal critique want and expect? The concept of a *literary critique* does not include the notion of fixed form so much as the idea of a serious examination of a specific work of art, including an assessment of its value. The form is flexible, but your reader will expect more than just a "review," more than just a retelling of the plot. You'll be expected to use your analytical abilities to separate the work into its major components; to narrow your focus to the one or two elements you feel are most significant; and to look in detail at how they are constructed, how they relate, and how they work toward (or fail to work toward) the overall value of the work—toward the expression of feeling, meaning, significance, or whatever.

The best critique will not only analyze a portion of a work in some detail, but it will also communicate a sense of the feeling that a work imparts to a reader. For that reason it presents added complications. Your reader will probably be expected to use a personal voice yet retain an objective tone—that is, you must write in a natural way so that your own feelings and human sympathies are not inhibited, but you must do so while scrutinizing the work with a critical eye. If you are too cold and analytical, you may lose the human feeling the art is primarily concerned with. If you become too personal, your own feelings may overshadow the story or poem. Keep this in mind: the experience and emotions you are to write about are the ones expressed by the art. If the art is successful, those feelings become your feelings, but the subject of your paper must be the play or the poem or story—and how the artist has shaped his or her work in such a way that it evokes that feeling. The reader wants to know about the emotion rendered by the art, but the reader seldom cares whether the emotion reminds you of your grandfather or the time you visited Mississippi. This balancing act forces you to struggle with your own feelings but to share them with the reader through an objective examination of the work itself.

## The Critical Process

Critical perception can be divided into four phases:

| | |
|---|---|
| *description:* | What do you see? |
| *analysis:* | How is it put together? |
| *interpretation:* | What does it mean? |
| *assessment:* | What is its value or worth? |

The four phases represent a logical progress you should follow, both in observing a work of art and in writing about it. First, look at the whole; then look more closely at the details; then interpret what you find; and, finally, form a judgment.

Many students mistakenly believe that if a story or a poem has been read by a class as a whole or even discussed in class, they need not guide the reader through each of these steps. Instead, they plunge immediately into analysis; or, worse, having completed the analysis in their minds, plunge directly into interpretation. Even though the reader may have knowledge of the work being discussed, such abrupt leaps create a sense of disjointed confusion. You should not assume your reader has experienced the work as you have, even on the literal level. You have used your eyes; the reader has used his or hers. When studying a work of art and when writing about it, demand of yourself the discipline required to move the mind through each phase of the critical process.

# The Formal Introduction

The introduction to a formal critique must provide the reader with an essential overview before you consider the small details:

1. Name the author and the work.
2. Summarize the literal level—what the work is about as a whole.
3. Provide a focusing or narrowing of the subject. Describe or imply what specific element you plan to examine.
4. Give a general indication of the larger significance you plan to lead the reader toward.

Here is an example from a paper by Christopher McCrystal:

*Title and author*       In the short story "Angel Levine," Bernard Mala-

*Student general-*   mud interweaves Jewish traditions and history with his
*izes on the*   own expanded vision of compassion. Manischevitz, a tai-
*whole.*   lor, suffers the agonies of Job in a large city ghetto; his

*Briefly sum-*   establishment burns to the ground; his customers sue
*marizes the lit-*   him; his back aches excruciatingly; his wife takes to her
*eral story*   bed with a seemingly incurable illness. "My Dear God,
  Sweetheart," he prays, "did I deserve that this should
  happen to me?" With wonderful irony, God sends help
  in the form of Alexander Levine, a black Jewish angel.

*Begins to focus*   It is the conflict between Manischevitz's expectations
  about the world, about the angel, and ultimately about

*Subject nar-*   God that sets up the resolution. By studying this con-
*rowed and sig-*   flict, we should see more clearly into Malamud's vision
*nificance implied*   of the true meaning of compassion.

Although an introduction *can* be written without including a sentence that suggests the ultimate significance or judgment you plan to arrive at, by including it, you establish an element of interest at the beginning—you say, "Here reader, is why this whole thing is important"—and you prepare the reader for your conclusion. In doing so, you will make the critique seem more unified and complete. But we need a reminder. Introductions often can't be written until you've completed your first draft. If you're like me, you'll need to explore ideas in a rough form before you can return and write a clear introduction of the kind I've presented here.

# The Body of the Critique

Most of your essay should present a detailed analysis of the work or of the major elements of the work you have focused on. Each step of your discussion should repeat the analytic process:

> First, *describe* the specific element of the story or poem or play you plan to focus on. Use your own words to introduce your point; then provide a quotation, paraphrase, or description directly from the work.

> Second, *analyze* that particular component. Show how the image works or what the character says or how the plot turns. This is the place for details.

> Third, *interpret* your findings. Limit your interpretation to the single element you are dealing with, or show how it relates to other elements, but save your overall assessment for the end.

Repeat the three steps for each phase of the work you deal with: *describe, analyze, interpret.* Be sure to include quotations and examples from the work as evidence to support your ideas.

Here is Jim Havens, a freshman, writing about a long poem, "Stages on a Journey Westward," by James Wright. In his introduction Jim has already narrowed his focus to the images in the poem that suggest death, and he has implied that the real subject of the poem is the dying of the American dream. In the body of his paper he looks in detail at each of the images.

*Description of the literal level in student's own words*

In the first stage of Wright's work, he recalls the start of his trip westward by painting for the reader a scene of horses wandering into a barn to relax and eat.

*Quotation to reinforce student's description*

I began in Ohio.
I still dream of home
Near Mansfield, enormous dobbins enter dark
    barns in autumn,
Where they can be lazy, where they can munch
    apples
Or sleep long.

*Analysis begins—in this case, by considering how individual words suggest a particular feeling.*

But if we probe further in Wright's word choice, we discover a possible foreshadowing of death. A "dobbin" is a term that is used for old workhorses that are really no longer of use for labor, a horse that is ready for the glue factory. The use of the word *dark* itself suggests death.

*Student admits that interpretation must await more evidence.*

*Description of literal level again: blend of paraphrase and quotation*

*Analysis of various images*

*Interpretation shows relationship of images to earlier points.*

*Transition; student will repeat same process for second stage of poem.*

*Autumn* is the figurative season for dying. *Apples* are the Biblical symbol that calls to mind the death of paradise for mortal man. Nothing at this point in the poem confirms this image of death. But as we move toward the next lines in the poem, the dark foreshadowing seems to continue.

Wright describes his memories of his father (or perhaps night dreams of his father) prowling, waiting in bread lines, wearing blue rags, leading a blind horse. He recalls how in 1932, "grimy with machinery," his father sang to him of a goosegirl while outside the house slag heaps were piled. In German folk tales the goosegirl was a Cinderella figure. Nineteen-thirty-two was the time of the Great Depression: poverty, hunger and degradation. The slag heap suggests the plight of the common worker. It was a pile of waste material that was separated during the smelting of iron. All of these negative images reinforce the foreshadowing of death we saw in the first lines. The suggestion is that the American dream of justice and individual dignity seemed to be coming to an end, as it surely must have seemed in 1932. Like the goosegirl story, the American dream was only a fairy tale.

In the second stage of his journey, Wright moves further west, to Minnesota, where a series of new images build upon this theme of death. . . .

Jim Haven's interpretation might be disputed by another reader who saw no death images at all in the poem. But by demonstrating that a repetition (a pattern) of words and images suggests death or dying, Jim hopes to lead even the unconvinced reader to his conclusion. Does that mean his interpretation is "right" and someone else's is "wrong"? No. It means that an effective work of art may have several interpretations so long as each provides specific, concrete evidence from the work and so long as the overall context of the work supports it.

## The Conclusion

As assessment is part of the critical process, you must arrive at a final judgment. Like all conclusions, yours must grow out of evidence and ideas you've developed in your paper. This is not the point to intrude with an irrelevant or personal opinion:

I just didn't like this play because it was about sex and I don't like stories about sex.

If indeed the work has been poorly accomplished, your analysis should demonstrate it, and your conclusion should be strong, but it should be based on the argument you've presented:

> In *A Farewell to Arms,* Hemingway's hero hasn't really learned very much at all. If all the old values are no longer meaningful, we are left with the question, "How can I lead my life?" But Hemingway's vision is incomplete, for it fails to give us any answers. Hemingway implies, as I've tried to show, that values can be found in a return to sensations. But sensations are structureless, like a bunch of building blocks without any foundation. In terms of the current generation, *A Farewell to Arms* tells us what we already know, but it ends where it should begin.

If the poem or story or play has been successful, however, your conclusion should note it with equal forcefulness:

> The unity of the poem depends on the recurrence of light and dark images, to which Tennyson has given particular attention. Throughout the poem, the words *day* and *dark* have appeared again and again. The light and dark contrasts become symbolic of man's belief or doubt in God. They create a tension of opposites until they are brought together and seen as a balancing rather than a conflicting force. Tennyson's brilliance has been in leading us to see that faith swells not from "the light alone" but from the "darkness and the light."

A study of literature goes beyond merely increasing our appreciation of an art form. It increases our sensitivity to emotions and to the shades of human experience. It heightens our awareness of subtlety and ambiguity, of form and symbol, of line and color, of language itself. It develops our hearts and our minds.

## THE STRUCTURE AS OUTLINE

Introduction
   —name of author and work
   —brief summary of the work as a whole
   —focusing sentence
   —general indication of overall significance

Body
   —literal description of first major element or portion of the work
   —detailed analysis
   —interpretation
   —literal description of the second major development
   —detailed analysis
   —interpretation (including, if necessary, the relationship to the first major point)
   —and so on

Conclusion
   —overall interpretation of the elements studied
   —relationship to the work as a whole
   —critical assessment of the value, worth, meaning, or significance of the work, both positive and negative

## EXERCISES

Study the student critique that follows. In it, Diane Key, a sophomore biology major, has attempted to analyze Sherwood Anderson's story. The approach she has used is only one of many; you may have seen the story in a different light. But consider where Diane's effort is successful and where it might be strengthened.

# Truth in the Grotesque
## Diane Key

*Analyze the components of Diane's introduction.*    The title of a short story by Sherwood Anderson, "The Book of the Grotesque," appropriately depicts the overall significance of the story. At first glance, the plot seems bizarre. Anderson takes his readers through the story by introducing us to a writer, an old man past sixty. The writer employs the services of a carpenter to raise the writer's bed so that he can see out the window. As the writer lies in his elevated bed one night, many

Reprinted by permission of the author.

strange thoughts and feelings overtake him. Although the old man has a weak heart and would not be alarmed if death came to him in the near future, he feels at odds with death; he feels as if a youth or young woman lived within him. Even though awake, the writer experiences a dream or vision caused by the young thing inside his body. An hourlong procession of grotesque figures appears before the old man's eyes. Because he is a writer, the old man later writes a book describing his dream and its significance. The book contains hundreds of truths and describes how these truths can turn people into "grotesques." The narrator of the story foresees the possibility that the old man may also become grotesque if the old man becomes obsessed with his book, but the young thing inside him saves him from such an outcome.

*Consider how Diane moves from concrete details to what they suggest and how they may relate to the larger theme.*

Anderson puts a great deal of stress on the writer's age. Besides using the word *old* to describe him, Anderson indicates that he has a "white mustache," he has "some difficulty in getting into bed," he is "past sixty," "he would die some time unexpectedly," and "his body was old and not of much use any more." Old age suggests brittleness, conformity, death, and finality. In a sense, these words and images are like truths. A truth according to its dictionary definition is fact or actuality. A fact is rigid, incapable of being changed, and is clearly defined. A truth is an absolute—there is no gray between the black and white.

*What expository technique does Diane use here?*

In conflict with the finality of his age, however, the writer senses a contrasting feeling:

> ... something inside him was altogether young. He was like a pregnant woman, only that the thing inside him was not a baby but a youth. No, it wasn't a youth, it was a woman, young, and wearing a coat of mail like a knight.

*Discuss how the student moves through description, analysis, and interpretation in this paragraph.*

The word *pregnant* holds special significance, as does the observation that the sensation felt like a young woman, someone capable of giving new life. We can even note that a coat of mail is *flexible* armor. These three concepts suggest birth, newness, and pliability. In fact, they are antonyms of the connotations of old age. Old age can be equated with rigidity and truth. Youth, on the other hand, is equated with flexibility, with that which is not absolute and can be changed. How does this all relate to the procession of grotesques that passes before the writer's eyes? It could be possible that as each person seizes a truth and tries to live his or her life according to its standards, he or she becomes cast into a mold that is unnatural and restricting. He or she is distorted into something other than human. "The grotesques were not all horrible. Some were amusing, some almost beautiful," states the narrator. But the grotesques are like the truths they embrace. Some of the grotesques are hideous when people try to live accordingly, like the truths of poverty and carelessness. Others are handsome, such as the truths of courage and thrift. The word *old,* therefore, suggests the inflexibility of "truth" and the "truth's" distortion of people. As the writer is old, he is in danger of becoming a grotesque as his acquaintances have. But the old writer embodies the conflicting force of youth. "It was the young thing inside him that saved the old man."

*Did you see the carpenter's role as Diane does? If not, is her interpretation convincing?*

One begins to wonder when the writer first realized the young force within himself. I feel that the old man's discovery began soon after the carpenter's visit. Here again words and images are suggestive that the carpenter aided the writer in seeing his vision of the grotesques and in finding the youth within him. By means of the carpenter, who is a builder, the old man's bed was raised. The carpenter brought the man's bed to the level of the window so the old man could see the tree, which might suggest life, growth, and youth, or, at the very least, something outside the confines of the old man's age. The carpenter is a grotesque himself because he is obsessed with the truth of war and death. Unknowingly, by serving as an example, the carpenter stimulates the old man to see the procession of grotesques later. This is not to say that the carpenter enlightened the writer. On the contrary, Anderson writes, "The plan the writer had for the raising of his bed was forgotten and later the carpenter did it in his own way and the writer, who was past sixty, had to help himself with a chair when he went to bed at night." It was the writer's plan to raise the bed and it was the writer who had to help himself. Active participation on the part of the writer was required if he was to recognize the youthful element in his life.

*Consider how Diane assesses the overall value of the story?*

Perhaps Sherwood Anderson's story suggests that we should keep our youthful attitudes along with their flexibility. We should not be rigid and unbending; we should not try to live our lives solely by a single truth. A single truth, no matter how appealing, is always a distortion. We must not accept only the black and white, but live and experience the vast area of gray also. Yet there is a danger of excess in following this vision too. Without some kinds of truths, our lives would be meaningless. What we need is to live somewhere between an unyielding framework and total license. Sherwood Anderson's old writer has found that middle ground and is all the more human because of it.

## SUGGESTED WRITING ASSIGNMENT

Read one of the poems or stories included at the end of this unit. Write a formal critique on it. Narrow your subject. Do not attempt to deal with every aspect of a poem or story. Use the guidelines in this chapter for organizing your essay.

## Editorial Checklist for Part Seven
### *Critiquing the Arts*

_____ Have you looked at the literal level of the work—the sensuous level—and let yourself respond to it?

_____ Have you studied the work before writing about it? _____taken notes?_____defined key words?_____read aloud?_____read more than once if possible?

_____ Have you asked silent questions? Who, what, where, when, why, and how?

_____ Have you looked for contrast, conflict, and characterization?

_____ Have you looked for patterns and relationships?

_____ Have you named the author and the work in your introduction?

_____ Have you provided a *brief* summary of what the work is about as a whole?

_____ Have you focused on one element or theme?

_____ Have you described, analyzed, and interpreted that element or theme?

_____ Have you come to a conclusion that shows a relationship to the whole? That assesses the value, worth, or significance? Both positive and negative?

_____ Have you read your own work aloud for rhythm and emphasis?

_____ Have you edited for unnecessary words and strong verbs?

## A Sampler of Poetry and Stories

# During Wind and Rain
## Thomas Hardy

They sing their dearest songs—
He, she, all of them—yea,
Treble and tenor and bass,
   And one to play;
With the candles mooning each face . . .
   Ah, no; the years O!
How the sick leaves reel down in throngs!

They clear the creeping moss—
Elders and juniors—aye,
Making the pathways neat
   And the garden gay;
And they build a shady seat. . . .
   Ah, no; the years, the years;
See, the white storm-birds wing across!

They are blithely breakfasting all—
Men and maidens—yea,
Under the summer tree,
   With a glimpse of the bay,
While pet fowl come to the knee. . . .
   Ah, no; the years O!
And the rotten rose is ript from the wall.

They change to a high new house,
He, she, all of them—aye,
Clocks and carpets and chairs
   On the lawn all day,
And brightest things that are theirs. . . .
   Ah, no; the years, the years;
Down their carved names the rain-drop ploughs.

Reprinted from *Collected Poems* by Thomas Hardy (New York: Macmillan, 1953).
Reprinted by permission of the Macmillan Publishing Co., Inc.

# from A Street in Bronzeville
# The Mother
## Gwendolyn Brooks

Abortions will not let you forget.
You remember the children you got that you did not get,
The damp small pulps with a little or with no hair,
The singers and workers that never handled the air.
You will never neglect or beat
Them, or silence or buy with a sweet.
You will never wind up the sucking-thumb
Or scuttle off ghosts that come.
You will never leave them, controlling your luscious sigh,
Return for a snack of them, with gobbling mother-eye.

I have heard in the voices of the wind the voices of my dim killed children.
I have contracted. I have eased
My dim dears at the breasts they could never suck.
I have said, Sweets, if I sinned, if I seized
Your luck
And your lives from your unfinished reach,
If I stole your births and your names,
Your straight baby tears and your games,
Your stilted or lovely loves, your tumults, your marriages, aches, and your
    deaths,
If I poisoned the beginnings of your breaths,
Believe that even in my deliberateness I was not deliberate.
Though why should I whine,
Whine that the crime was other than mine?—
Since anyhow you are dead.
Or rather, or instead,
You were never made.
But that too, I am afraid,
Is faulty: oh, what shall I say, how is the truth to be said?
You were born, you had body, you died.
It is just that you never giggled or planned or cried.

Believe me, I loved you all.
Believe me, I knew you, though faintly, and I loved, I loved you
All.

# What Were They Like? (Questions and Answers)
## Denise Levertov

1)  Did the people of Viet Nam
    use lanterns of stone?
2)  Did they hold ceremonies
    to reverence the opening of buds?
3)  Were they inclined to rippling laughter?
4)  Did they use bone and ivory,
    jade and silver, for ornament?
5)  Had they an epic poem?
6)  Did they distinguish between speech and singing?


1)  Sir, their light hearts turned to stone.
    It is not remembered whether in gardens
    stone lanterns illumined pleasant ways.
2)  Perhaps they gathered once to delight in blossom,
    but after the children were killed
    there were no more buds.
3)  Sir, laughter is bitter to the burned mouth.
4)  A dream ago, perhaps. Ornament is for joy.
    All the bones were charred.
5)  It is not remembered. Remember,
    most were peasants; their life
    was in rice and bamboo.
    When peaceful clouds were reflected in the paddies
    and the water-buffalo stepped surely along terraces,
    maybe fathers told their sons old tales.
    When bombs smashed the mirrors
    there was time only to scream.
6)  There is an echo yet, it is said,
    of their speech which was like a song.
    It is reported their singing resembled
    the flight of moths in moonlight.
    Who can say? It is silent now.

# The Pennycandystore Beyond the El
## Lawrence Ferlinghetti

The pennycandystore beyond the El
is where I first
> fell in love
>> with unreality
Jellybeans glowed in the semi-gloom
of that september afternoon
A cat upon the counter moved among
>> the licorice sticks
> and tootsie rolls
and Oh Boy Gum

Outside the leaves were falling as they died

A wind had blown away the sun

A girl ran in
Her hair was rainy
Her breasts were breathless in the little room

Outside the leaves were falling
> and they cried
>> Too soon! too soon!

# Sonnet LXXIII
## William Shakespeare

That time of year thou mayst in me behold
When yellow leaves, or none, or few, do hang
Upon those boughs which shake against the cold,
Bare ruined choirs where late the sweet birds sang:
In me thou see'st the twilight of such day
As after sunset fadeth in the west,
Which by and by black night doth take away,
Death's second self that seals up all in rest:
In me thou see'st the glowing of such fire
That on the ashes of his youth doth lie
As the death-bed whereon it must expire,
Consumed with that which it was nourished by:
> This thou perceivest, which makes thy love more strong
> To love that well which thou must leave ere long.

# Lullaby
## Leslie Silko

**I**

The sun had gone down but the snow in the wind gave off its own light. It came in thick tufts like new wool—washed before the weaver spins it. Ayah reached out for it like her own babies had, and she smiled when she remembered how she had laughed at them. She was an old woman now, and her life had become memories. She sat down with her back against the wide cottonwood tree, feeling the rough bark on her back bones; she faced east and listened to the wind and snow sing a high-pitched Yeibechei song. Out of the wind she felt warmer, and she could watch the wide fluffy snow fill in her tracks, steadily, until the direction she had come from was gone. By the light of the snow she could see the dark outline of the big arroyo a few feet away. She was sitting on the edge of Cebolleta Creek, where in the springtime the thin cows would graze on grass already chewed flat to the ground. In the wide deep creek bed where only a trickle of water flowed in the summer, the skinny cows would wander, looking for new grass along winding paths splashed with manure.

Ayah pulled the old Army blanket over her head like a shawl. Jimmie's blanket—the one he had sent to her. That was a long time ago and the green wool was faded, and it was unraveling on the edges. She did not want to think about Jimmie. So she thought about the weaving and the way her mother had done it. On the tall wooden loom set into the sand under a tamarack tree for shade. She could see it clearly. She had been only a little girl when her grandma gave her the wooden combs to pull the twigs and burrs from the raw, freshly washed wool. And while she combed the wool, her grandma sat beside her, spinning a silvery strand of yarn around the smooth cedar spindle. Her mother worked at the loom with yarns dyed bright yellow and red and gold. She watched them dye the yarn in boiling black pots full of beeweed petals, juniper berries, and sage. The blankets her mother made were soft and woven so tight that rain rolled off them like birds' feathers. Ayah remembered sleeping warm on cold windy nights, wrapped in her mother's blankets on the hogan's sandy floor.

The snow drifted now, with the northwest wind hurling it in gusts. It drifted up around her black overshoes—old ones with little metal buckles. She smiled at the snow which was trying to cover her little by little. She could remember when they had no black rubber overshoes; only the high buckskin leggings that they wrapped over their elk-hide moccasins. If the snow was dry or frozen, a person could walk all day and not get wet; and in the evenings the beams of the ceiling would hang with lengths of pale buckskin leggings, drying out slowly.

She felt peaceful remembering. She didn't feel cold any more. Jimmie's blanket seemed warmer than it had ever been. And she could remember the morning he was born. She could remember whispering to her mother who was sleeping on the other side of the hogan, to tell her it was time now. She did not want to wake the others. The second time she called to her, her mother stood up and pulled on her shoes; she knew. They walked to the old stone hogan together, Ayah walking a step behind her mother. She waited alone, learning the rhythms of the pains while her mother went to call the old woman to help them. The morning was already warm even before dawn and Ayah smelled the bee flowers blooming and the young willow growing at the springs. She could remember that so clearly, but his birth merged into the births of the other children and to her it became all the same birth. They named him for the summer morning and in English they called him Jimmie.

It wasn't like Jimmie died. He just never came back, and one day a dark blue sedan with white writing on its doors pulled up in front of the boxcar shack where the rancher let the Indians live. A man in a khaki uniform trimmed in gold gave them a yellow piece of paper and told them that Jimmie was dead. He said the Army would try to get the body back and then it would be shipped to them; but it wasn't likely because the helicopter had burned after it crashed. All of this was told to Chato because he could understand English. She stood inside the doorway holding the baby while Chato listened. Chato spoke English like a white man and he spoke Spanish too. He was taller than the white man and he stood straighter too. Chato didn't explain why; he just told the military man they could keep the body if they found it. The white man looked bewildered; he nodded his head and he left. Then Chato looked at her and shook his head. "Goddamn," he said in English, and then he told her "Jimmie isn't coming home anymore," and when he spoke, he used the words to speak of the dead. She didn't cry then, but she hurt inside with anger. And she mourned him as the years passed, when a horse fell with Chato and broke his leg, and the white rancher told them he wouldn't pay Chato until he could work again. She mourned Jimmie because he would have worked for his father then; he would have saddled the big bay horse and ridden the fence lines each day, with wire cutters and heavy gloves, fixing the breaks in the barbed wire and putting the stray cattle back inside again.

She mourned him after the white doctors came to take Danny and Ella away. She was at the shack alone that day when they came. It was back in the days before they hired Navajo women to go with them as interpreters. She recognized one of the doctors. She had seen him at the children's clinic at Cañoncito about a month ago. They were wearing khaki uniforms and they waved papers at her and a black ball point pen, trying to make her understand their English words. She was frightened by the way they looked at the children, like the lizard watches the fly. Danny was swinging on the tire swing in the elm tree behind the rancher's house, and Ella was toddling around the front door, dragging the broomstick horse Chato made for her. Ayah could see they wanted her to sign the papers, and Chato had taught her to sign her name. It was something she was proud of. She only wanted them to go, and to take their eyes away from her children.

She took the pen from the man without looking at his face and she signed the papers in three different places he pointed to. She stared at the ground by their feet and waited for them to leave. But they stood there and began to point and gesture at the children. Danny stopped swinging. Ayah could see his fear. She moved suddenly and grabbed Ella into her arms; the child squirmed, trying to get back to her toys. Ayah ran with the baby toward Danny; she screamed for him to run and then she grabbed him around his chest and carried him too. She ran south into the foothills of juniper trees and black lava rock. Behind her she heard the doctors running, but they had been taken by surprise, and as the hills became steeper and the cholla cactus were thicker, they stopped. When she reached the top of the hill, she stopped too to listen in case they were circling around her. But in a few minutes she heard a car engine start and they drove away. The children had been too surprised to cry while she ran with them. Danny was shaking and Ella's little fingers were gripping Ayah's blouse.

She stayed up in the hills for the rest of the day, sitting on a black lava boulder in the sunshine where she could see for miles all around her. The sky was light blue and cloudless, and it was warm for late April. The sun warmth relaxed her and took the fear and anger away. She lay back on the rock and watched the sky. It seemed to her that she could walk into the sky, stepping through clouds endlessly. Danny played with little pebbles and stones, pretending they were birds, eggs and then little rabbits. Ella sat at her feet and dropped fistfuls of dirt into the breeze, watching the dust and particles of sand intently. Ayah watched a hawk soar high above them, dark wings gliding; hunting or only watching, she did not know. The hawk was patient and he circled all afternoon before he disappeared around the high volcanic peak the Mexicans call Guadalupe.

Late in the afternoon, Ayah looked down at the gray boxcar shack with the paint all peeled from the wood; the stove pipe on the roof was rusted and crooked. The fire she had built that morning in the oil drum stove had burned out. Ella was asleep in her lap now and Danny sat close to her, complaining that he was hungry; he asked when they would go to the house. "We will stay up here until your father comes," she told him, "because those white men were chasing us." The boy remembered then and he nodded at her silently.

If Jimmie had been there he could have read those papers and explained to her what they said. Ayah would have known, then, never to sign them. The doctors came back the next day and they brought a BIA policeman with them. They told Chato they had her signature and that was all they needed. Except for the kids. She listened to Chato sullenly; she hated him when he told her it was the old woman who died in the winter, spitting blood; it was her old grandma who had given the children this disease. "They don't spit blood," she said coldly, "The whites lie." She held Ella and Danny close to her, ready to run to the hills again. "I want a medicine man first," she said to Chato, not looking at him. He shook his head. "It's too late now. The policeman is with them. You signed the paper." His voice was gentle.

It was worse than if they had died: to lose the children and to know that somewhere, in a place called Colorado, in a place full of sick and dying strangers, her children were without her. There had been babies that died soon after they were born, and one that died before he could walk. She had carried them herself, up to the boulders and great pieces of the cliff that long ago crashed down from Long Mesa; she laid them in the crevices of sandstone and buried them in fine brown sand with round quartz pebbles that washed down from the hills in the rain. She had endured it because they had been with her. But she could not bear this pain. She did not sleep for a long time after they took her children. She stayed on the hill where they had fled the first time, and she slept rolled up in the blanket Jimmie had sent her. She carried the pain in her belly and it was fed by everything she saw: the blue sky of their last day together and the dust and pebbles they played with; the swing in the elm tree and broomstick horse chocked life from her. The pain filled her stomach and there was no room for food or for her lungs to fill with air. The air and the food would have been theirs.

She hated Chato, not because he let the policeman and doctors put the screaming children in the government car, but because he had taught her to sign her name. Because it was like the old ones always told her about learning their language or any of their ways: it endangered you. She slept alone on the hill until the middle of November when the first snows came. Then she made a bed for herself where the children had slept. She did not lay down beside Chato again until many years later, when he was sick and shivering and only her body could keep him warm. The illness came after the white rancher told Chato he was too old to work for him any more, and Chato and his old woman should be out of the shack by the next afternoon because the rancher had hired new people to work there. That had satisfied her. To see how the white man repaid Chato's years of loyalty and work. All of Chato's fine-sounding English talk didn't change things.

## II

It snowed steadily and the luminous light from the snow gradually diminished into the darkness. Somewhere in Cebolleta a dog barked and other village dogs joined with it. Ayah looked in the direction she had come, from the bar where Chato was buying the wine. Sometimes he told her to go on ahead and wait; and then he never came. And when she finally went back looking for him, she would find him passed out at the bottom of the wooden steps to Azzie's Bar. All the wine would be gone and most of the money too, from the pale blue check that came to them once a month in a government envelope. It was then that she would look at his face and his hands, scarred by ropes and the barbed wire of all those years, and she would think 'this man is a stranger'; for forty years she had smiled at him and cooked his food, but he remained a stranger. She stood up again, with the snow almost to her knees, and she walked back to find Chato.

It was hard to walk in the deep snow and she felt the air burn in her lungs. She stopped a short distance from the bar to rest and readjust the blanket. But this time he wasn't waiting for her on the bottom step with his old Stetson hat pulled down and his shoulders hunched up in his long wool overcoat.

She was careful not to slip on the wooden steps. When she pushed the door open, warm air and cigarette smoke hit her face. She looked around slowly and deliberately, in every corner, in every dark place that the old man might find to sleep. The barowner didn't like Indians in there, especially Navajos, but he let Chato come in because he could talk Spanish like he was one of them. The men at the bar stared at her, and the bartender saw that she left the door open wide. Snow flakes were flying inside like moths and melting into a puddle on the oiled wood floor. He motioned at her to close the door, but she did not see him. She held herself straight and walked across the room slowly, searching the room with every step. The snow in her hair melted and she could feel it on her forehead. At the far corner of the room, she saw red flames at the mica window of the old stove door; she looked behind the stove just to make sure. The bar got quiet except for the Spanish polka music playing on the jukebox. She stood by the stove and shook the snow from her blanket and held it near the stove to dry. The wet wool smell reminded her of new-born goats in early March, brought inside to warm near the fire. She felt calm.

In past years they would have told her to get out. But her hair was white now and her face was wrinkled. They looked at her like she was a spider crawling slowly across the room. They were afraid; she could feel the fear. She looked at their faces steadily. They reminded her of the first time the white people brought her children back to her that winter. Danny had been shy and hid behind the thin white woman who brought them. And the baby had not known her until Ayah took her into her arms, and then Ella had nuzzled close to her as she had when she was nursing.

The blonde woman was nervous and kept looking at a dainty gold watch on her wrist. She sat on the bench near the small window and watched the dark snow clouds gather around the mountains; she was worrying about the unpaved road. She was frightened by what she saw inside too: the strips of venison drying on a rope across the ceiling and the children jabbering excitedly in a language she did not know. So they stayed for only a few hours. Ayah watched the government car disappear down the road and she knew they were already being weaned from these lava hills and from this sky. The last time they came was in early June, and Ella stared at her the way the men in the bar were now staring. Ayah did not try to pick her up; she smiled at her instead and spoke cheerfully to Danny. When he tried to answer her, he could not seem to remember and he spoke English words with the Navajo. But he gave her a scrap of paper that he had found somewhere and carried in his pocket; it was folded in half, and he shyly looked up at her and said it was a bird. She asked Chato if they were home for good this time. He spoke to the white woman and she shook her head. "How much longer," he asked, and she said she didn't know; but Chato saw how she stared at the box car shack. Ayah turned away then. She did not say good-bye.

### III

She felt satisfied that the men in the bar feared her. Maybe it was her face and the way she held her mouth with teeth clenched tight, like there was nothing anyone could do to her now. She walked north down the road, searching for the old man. She did this because she had the blanket, and there would be no place for him except with her and the blanket in the old adobe barn near the arroyo. They always slept there when they came to Cebolleta. If the money and the wine were gone, she would be relieved because then they could go home again; back to the old hogan with a dirt roof and rock walls where she herself had been born. And the next day the old man could go back to the few sheep they still had, to follow along behind them, guiding them into dry sandy arroyos where sparse grass grew. She knew he did not like walking behind old ewes when for so many years he rode big quarter horses and worked with cattle. But she wasn't sorry for him; he should have known all along what would happen.

There had not been enough rain for their garden in five years; and that was when Chato finally hitched a ride into the town and brought back brown boxes of rice and sugar and big tin cans of welfare peaches. After that, at the first of the month they went to Cebolleta to ask the postmaster for the check; and then Chato would go to the bar and cash it. They did this as they planted the garden every May, not because anything would survive the summer dust, but because it was time to do this. And the journey passed the days that smelled silent and dry like the caves above the canyon with yellow painted buffaloes on their walls.

## IV

He was walking along the pavement when she found him. He did not stop or turn around when he heard her behind him. She walked beside him and she noticed how slowly he moved now. He smelled strong of woodsmoke and urine. Lately he had been forgetting. Sometimes he called her by his sister's name and she had been gone for a long time. Once she had found him wandering on the road to the white man's ranch, and she asked him why he was going that way; he laughed at her and said "you know they can't run that ranch without me," and he walked on determined, limping on the leg that had been crushed many years before. Now he looked at her curiously, as if for the first time, but he kept shuffling along, moving slowly along the side of the highway. His gray hair had grown long and spread out on the shoulders of the long overcoat. He wore the old felt hat pulled down over his ears. His boots were worn out at the toes and he had stuffed pieces of an old red shirt in the holes. The rags made his feet look like little animals up to their ears in snow. She laughed at his feet; the snow muffled the sound of her laugh. He stopped and looked at her again. The wind had quit blowing and the snow was falling straight down; the southeast sky was beginning to clear and Ayah could see a star.

"Let's rest awhile," she said to him. They walked away from the road and up the slope to the giant boulders that had tumbled down from the red sandrock mesa throughout the centuries of rainstorms and earth tremors. In a place where the boulders shut out the wind, they sat down with their backs against the rock. She offered half of the blanket to him and they sat wrapped together.

The storm passed swiftly. The clouds moved east. They were massive and full, crowding together across the sky. She watched them with the feeling of horses—steely blue-gray horses startled across the sky. The powerful haunches pushed into the distances and the tail hairs streamed white mist behind them. The sky cleared. Ayah saw that there was nothing between her and the stars. The light was crystalline. There was no shimmer, no distortion through earth haze. She breathed the clarity of the night sky; she smelled the purity of the half moon and the stars. He was lying on his side with his knees pulled up near his belly for warmth. His eyes were closed now, and in the light from the stars and the moon, he looked young again.

She could see it descend out of the night sky: an icy stillness from the edge of the thin moon. She recognized the freezing. It came gradually, sinking snow flake by snow flake until the crust was heavy and deep. It had the strength of the stars in Orion, and its journey was endless. Ayah knew that with the wine he would sleep. He would not feel it. She tucked the blanket around him, remembering how it was when Ella had been with her; and she felt the rush so big inside her heart for the babies. And she sang the only song she knew to sing for babies. She could not remember if she had ever sung it to her children, but she knew that her grandmother had sung it and her mother had sung it:

> The earth is your mother,
>    she holds you.
> The sky is your father,
>    he protects you.
> sleep,
> sleep,
> Rainbow is your sister,
>    she loves you.
> The winds are your brothers,
>    they sing to you.
> sleep,
> sleep,
> We are together always
> We are together always
> There never was a time
> when this
> was not so.

# A Conversation with My Father
## Grace Paley

My father is eighty-six years old and in bed. His heart, that bloody motor, is equally old and will not do certain jobs any more. It still floods his head with brainy light. But it won't let his legs carry the weight of his body around the house. Despite my metaphors, this muscle failure is not due to his old heart, he says, but to a potassium shortage. Sitting on one pillow, leaning on three, he offers last-minute advice and makes a request.

"I would like you to write a simple story just once more," he says, "the kind de Maupassant wrote, or Chekhov, the kind you used to write. Just recognizable people and then write down what happened to them next."

I say, "Yes, why not? That's possible." I want to please him, though I don't remember writing that way. I *would* like to try to tell such a story, if he means the kind that begins: "There was a woman . . ." followed by plot, the absolute line between two points which I've always despised. Not for literary reasons, but because it takes all hope away. Everyone, real or invented, deserves the open destiny of life.

Finally I thought of a story that had been happening for a couple of years right across the street. I wrote it down, then read it aloud. "Pa," I said, "how about this? Do you mean something like this?"

> Once in my time there was a woman and she had a son. They lived nicely, in a small apartment in Manhattan. This boy at about fifteen became a junkie, which is not unusual in our neighborhood. In order to maintain her close friendship with him, she became a junkie too. She said it was part of the youth culture, with which she felt very much at home. After a while, for a number of reasons, the boy gave it all up and left the city and his mother in disgust. Hopeless and alone, she grieved. We all visit her.

"O.K., Pa, that's it," I said, "an unadorned and miserable tale."

"But that's not what I mean," my father said. "You misunderstood me on purpose. You know there's a lot more to it. You know that. You left everything out. Turgenev wouldn't do that. Chekhov wouldn't do that. There are in fact Russian writers you never heard of, you don't have an inkling of, as good as anyone, who can write a plain ordinary story, who would not leave out what you have left out. I object not to facts but to people sitting in trees talking senselessly, voices from who knows where . . ."

"Forget that one, Pa, what have I left out now? In this one?"

"Her looks, for instance."

"Oh. Quite handsome, I think. Yes."

"Her hair?"

"Dark, with heavy braids, as though she were a girl or a foreigner."

"What were her parents like, her stock? That she became such a person. It's interesting, you know."

"From out of town. Professional people. The first to be divorced in their country. How's that? Enough?" I asked.

"With you, it's all a joke," he said. "What about the boy's father? Why didn't you mention him? Who was he? Or was the boy born out of wedlock?"

"Yes," I said. "He was born out of wedlock."

"For Godsakes, doesn't anyone in your stories get married? Doesn't anyone have the time to run down to City Hall before they jump into bed?"

"No," I said. "In real life, yes. But in my stories, no."

"Why do you answer me like that?"

"Oh, Pa, this is a simple story about a smart woman who came to N.Y.C. full of interest love trust excitement very up to date, and about her son, what a hard time she had in this world. Married or not, it's of small consequence."

"It is of great consequence," he said.

"O.K.," I said.

"O.K. O.K. yourself," he said, "but listen. I believe you that she's good-looking, but I don't think she was so smart."

"That's true," I said. "Actually that's the trouble with stories. People start our fantastic. You think they're extraordinary, but it turns out as the work goes along, they're just average with a good education. Sometimes the other way around, the person's a kind of dumb innocent, but he outwits you and you can't even think of an ending good enough."

"What do you do then?" he asked. He had been a doctor for a couple of decades and then an artist for a couple of decades and he's still interested in details, craft, technique.

"Well, you just have to let the story lie around till some agreement can be reached between you and the stubborn hero."

"Aren't you talking silly, now?" he asked. "Start again," he said. "It so happens I'm not going out this evening. Tell the story again. See what you can do this time."

"O.K.," I said. "But it's not a five-minute job." Second attempt:

Once, across the street from us, there was a fine handsome woman, our neighbor. She had a son whom she loved because she'd known him since birth (in helpless chubby infancy, and in the wrestling, hugging ages, seven to ten, as well as earlier and later). This boy, when he fell into the fist of adolescence, became a junkie. He was not a hopeless one. He was in fact hopeful, an ideologue and successful converter. With his busy brilliance, he wrote persuasive articles for his high-school newspaper. Seeking a wider audience, using important connections, he drummed into Lower Manhattan newsstand distribution a periodical called *Oh! Golden Horse!*

In order to keep him from feeling guilty (because guilt is the stony heart of nine tenths of all clinically diagnosed cancers in America today, she said), and because she had always believed in giving bad habits room at home where one could keep an eye on them, she too became a junkie. Her kitchen was famous for a while—a center for intellectual addicts who knew what they were doing. A few felt artistic like Coleridge and others were scientific and revolutionary like Leary. Although she was often high herself, certain good mothering reflexes remained, and she saw to it that there was lots of orange juice around and honey and milk and vitamin pills. However, she never cooked anything but chili, and that no more than once a week. She explained, when we talked to her, seriously, with neighborly concern, that it was her part in the youth culture and she would rather be with the young, it was an honor, than with her own generation.

One week, while nodding through an Antonioni film, this boy was severely jabbed by the elbow of a stern and proselytizing girl, sitting beside him. She offered immediate apricots and nuts for his sugar level, spoke to him sharply, and took him home.

She had heard of him and his work and she herself published, edited, and wrote a competitive journal called *Man Does Live By Bread Alone*. In the organic heat of her continuous presence he could not help but become interested once more in his muscles, his arteries, and nerve connections. In fact he began to love them, treasure them, praise them with funny little songs in *Man Does Live* . . .

> the fingers of my flesh transcend
> my transcendental soul
> the tightness in my shoulders end
> my teeth have made me whole

To the mouth of his head (that glory of will and determination) he brought hard apples, nuts, wheat germ, and soy-bean oil. He said to his old friends, From now on, I guess I'll keep my wits about me. I'm going on the natch. He said he was about to begin a spiritual deep-breathing journey. How about you too, Mom? he asked kindly.

His conversion was so radiant, splendid, that neighborhood kids his age began to say that he had never been a real addict at all, only a journalist along for the smell of the story. The mother tried several times to give up what had become without her son and his friends a lonely habit. This effort only brought it to supportable levels. The boy and his girl took their electronic mimeograph and moved to the bushy edge of another borough. They were very strict. They said they would not see her again until she had been off drugs for sixty days.

At home alone in the evening, weeping, the mother read and reread the seven issues of *Oh! Golden Horse!* They seemed to her as truthful as ever. We often crossed the street to visit and console. But if we mentioned any of our children who were at college or in the hospital or dropouts at home, she would cry out, My baby! My baby! and burst into terrible, face-scarring, time-consuming tears. The End.

First my father was silent, then he said, "Number One: You have a nice sense of humor. Number Two: I see you can't tell a plain story. So don't waste time." Then he said sadly, "Number Three: I suppose that means she was alone, she was left like that, his mother. Alone. Probably sick?"

I said, "Yes."

"Poor woman. Poor girl, to be born in a time of fools, to live among fools. The end. The end. You were right to put that down. The end."

I didn't want to argue, but I had to say, "Well, it is not necessarily the end, Pa."

"Yes," he said, "what a tragedy. The end of a person."

"No, Pa," I begged him. "It doesn't have to be. She's only about forty. She could be a hundred different things in this world as times goes on. A teacher or a social worker. An ex-junkie! Sometimes it's better than having a master's in education."

"Jokes," he said. "As a writer that's your main trouble. You don't want to recognize it. Tragedy! Plain tragedy! Historical tragedy! No hope. The end."

"Oh, Pa," I said. "She could change."

"In your own life, too, you have to look it in the face." He took a couple of nitroglycerin. "Turn to five," he said, pointing to the dial on the oxygen tank. He inserted the tubes into his nostrils and breathed deep. He closed his eyes and said, "No."

I had promised the family to always let him have the last word when arguing, but in this case I had a different responsibility. That woman lives across the street. She's my knowledge and my invention. I'm sorry for her. I'm not going to leave her there in that house crying. (Actually neither would Life, which unlike me has no pity.)

Therefore: She did change. Of course her son never came home again. But right now, she's the receptionist in a storefront community clinic in the East Village. Most of the customers are young people, some old friends. The head doctor has said to her, "If we only had three people in this clinic with your experiences . . ."

"The doctor said that?" My father took the oxygen tubes out of his nostrils and said, "Jokes. Jokes again."

"No, Pa, it could really happen that way, it's a funny world nowadays."

"No," he said. "Truth first. She will slide back. A person must have character. She does not."

"No, Pa," I said. "That's it. She's got a job. Forget it. She's in that storefront working."

"How long will it be?" he asked. "Tragedy! You too. When will you look it in the face?"

# PART

## *Scholarly Research*

# EIGHT

*Whether he is an archaeologist, chemist, or astronomer, at the heart the researcher's goal is very much the same. Basically, he looks for facts that interest him and then tries to arrange them in meaningful sequence. . . . He defines what happens, then figures out where, when, how, and why it happens. His adverbial search for cause and effect, for the basic ordering in things, is primal, compelling, and satisfying, quite apart from practical considerations.*

—James H. Austin

To many young writers, a research project sounds foreboding. For those who have been through the experience, the excitement of discovery, of learning, of creative play with ideas more than compensates for the hard work. Research papers written in college tend to remain in memory long after class work and exams are forgotten. These are the paper to which the whole self is given for days or even months. These are the papers that help you discover that the merit of the mind lies not so much in what it knows, but in that it knows how to learn.

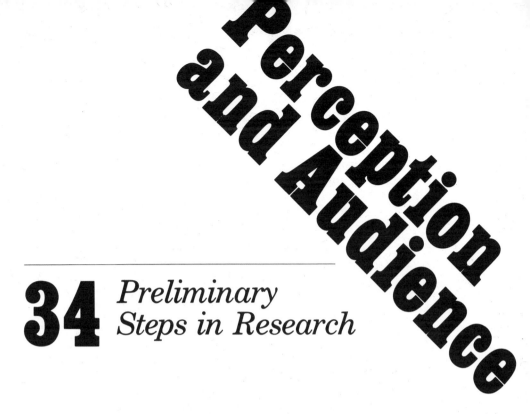
_Perception and Audience_

# 34 _Preliminary Steps in Research_

Engineering, law, business, medicine, economics, government—no matter what profession you enter, you'll probably find yourself engaged in research. The audience for the product of research is broad and varied, but in general that audience is college-educated. You should begin scholarly study with the assumption that the reader of your final product will be well-read although not necessarily on the particular topic of your study. You should assume your reader will be skeptical; you'll need to offer evidence and examples—generalizations will be shrugged off for the most part. Your reader will probably be critical; logic and close reasoning are simply expected. And you should assume your reader will probably expect an impartial, objective approach to a subject, although he or she may also expect you to exercise your own sense of judgment by evaluating, interpreting, and drawing conclusions. Most of all, you will be expected to inform and explain. The reader wants to learn.

## Prepare a Work Schedule
Research cannot be rushed. There are books to study, notes to gather, outlines to make, first drafts to cross out in favor of second and third drafts, even footnotes and bibliographies to suffer through. It all takes time, self-discipline, and planning. The first step is to organize a day-by-day schedule for yourself, as in this example:

Days 1–3

> Select a subject.
>
> Begin preliminary reading—an overview.
>
> Narrow the subject; form a question.

Days 4–5

> Locate topic in indexes, abstracts, and card catalog.
>
> Prepare a working bibliography.

Days 6–11

> Investigate sources.
>
> Gather data, ideas, facts, and information on note cards.

Day 12

> Organize note cards and outline ideas.

Day 13–15

> Write first draft.

Days 16–17

> Rewrite (several times if necessary).

Day 18

> Prepare footnotes and bibliography.

Days 19–20

> Leave unscheduled days for the unexpected or to allow time and cooling off before final editing.

Day 21

> Edit line by line.

Days 22–23

> Type final draft and proofread.

Day 24

> Celebrate.

You might need more or less time depending upon the length of the paper and upon your own personal working habits, but never underestimate the time it will take. A necessary book may turn up missing, information you've requested from a government agency may not arrive, or your roommate may use your most valuable note card for an ashtray. Build in time for the unexpected.

And build in time for relaxation. Numerous studies of the creative process show that most original ideas tend to appear in the mind when long periods of concentrated study are alternated with short periods of diversion and rest. Most documented cases of inspiration reveal that it seems to happen *between* intense work and play. No one knows why, but the unconscious elements of our mind need time to sort out and organize information. If your schedule is too tight or you find yourself working day and night, you may also find yourself overwhelmed by the material, unable to evaluate it and resorting to a so-called *cut-and-paste* product where ideas are merely strung together without thought. French scholar Jean Guitton has described the golden rule for intellectual work: "Tolerate neither half-work nor half-rest. Give yourself totally *or* withhold yourself absolutely. Never allow the two to overlap."

Psychologist Rollo May argues strongly that you must schedule one other element: *solitude.* The inner workings of the mind are a private thing. Students who surround themselves with stereo, television, and radio distract the mind from serious work. Rollo May asserts that we must teach ourselves the capacity for using solitude in constructive ways:

> It requires that we be able to retire from a world that is "too much with us," that we be able to be quiet, that we let the solitude work for us and in us. It is a characteristic of our time that many people are afraid of solitude: to be alone is a sign one is a social failure, for no one would be alone if he or she could help it. It often occurs to me that people living . . . amid the constant din of radio and TV . . . find it exceedingly difficult to let insights from unconscious depths break through. . . . [Yet] if we are to experience insights from our unconscious, we need to be able to give ourselves to solitude.

# Clarify and Define Your Subject

Once you've outlined a tentative schedule, set to work immediately. Whether you've selected a subject on your own or received an assigned subject as part of a class project, you'll need to obtain a general overview of the topic as a whole. You cannot plunge into research on educational innovations without knowing some background about, and history of, education. You cannot analyze a proposal for a guaranteed annual wage without knowing the cultural and economic context that has brought about such a proposal. Even if you already feel that you have a background in the subject, you will need to verify your understanding of terms and concepts you plan to deal with.

## Reference Tools

One of your primary goals is to seek information while wasting as little time as possible in the actual search. Reference works such as encyclopedias and dictionaries exist for exactly that purpose. They not only provide you with historical and general information, but they often also list the major sources and authorities on a subject, saving you hours of random searching in the card catalog.

## Encyclopedias

*The Encyclopaedia Britannica* is still probably the best single source for general information, especially for topics in the humanities and social sciences. Many scholars consider the ninth edition, organized alphabetically, as the best. The newest fifteenth edition provides a *Propaedia* (a single volume introduction and outline of subjects), a *Micropaedia* (a ten-volume set of short, factual articles that serves as an index), and a *Macropaedia* (nineteen volumes of articles on most fields of knowledge). Of special value is the list of major sources that often follows each article in the *Macropaedia*. Be sure to make a list of such sources for later research.

*The Encyclopedia Americana* is less exhaustive but is in some ways a better general work on the sciences. Again the list of sources at the end of articles is especially helpful. Volume 30 offers a comprehensive index and is a good place to begin a search.

Specialized encyclopedias in many ways provide even more technical coverage as well as information on major authorities and sources. *The International Encyclopedia of the Social Sciences, Grove's Dictionary on Music and Musicians,* and the *McGraw-Hill Encyclopedia on Science and Technology* are just a few of hundreds of examples. To determine whether your library has a specialized encyclopedia on your subject, consult the card catalog under your subject heading and look for the subdivision *Dictionaries,* where you'll find both encyclopedias and specialized dictionaries listed.

### Dictionaries

As all subjects involve words and concepts, do not fail to obtain exact definitions. Any specialized term or jargon will probably need to be defined in your paper itself. Know the meanings *before* you begin your research, not after.

*The American Heritage Dictionary of the English Language* is one of the best desk-sized dictionaries. In addition to extensive definitions, it often provides connotations, synonyms, diagrams, photographs, and examples of how a word is used in a sentence.

*Webster's Third New International Dictionary* is even more exhaustive, but too large for most home use. You'll find it in almost every library. It seems especially strong in scientific and technical terms. (By the way, the name, *Webster's,* is not copyrighted and is used in the titles of many dictionaries. Do not confuse this major work with many of the smaller, less beneficial dictionaries.)

*The Oxford English Dictionary* is a multivolume work detailing the history of words and can be particularly useful for understanding how the meaning of words may have changed over the years.

Again specialized dictionaries are available in almost everything from ballet to physics. They may be essential to you for highly technical subjects.

## Focus the Subject

You cannot write a successful paper on World War II. You could not even do a satisfactory job on the role of women in World War II. You *might* be able to go into some detail on the role of women in the labor force during World War II *if* you were planning to write a Master's Degree thesis. But if you are considering a smaller research paper, you must find a single element of your subject that is both appropriate for the size of paper required and for the amount of research time available to you. Failure to narrow your topic may leave you awash in a sea of general information.

This is not the time to form an actual thesis statement that might lock you into an idea that can't be proved or into a subject on which information is unavailable. But it is the time to ask questions. All the different techniques you're familiar with should now come into play. Begin with the 5 W's: *who, what, where, when,* and *why.* Consider the 4 *C*'s of observation: *change, conflict (or opposition), consequences,* and *characterization* (in the full sense of that term—*physical details, actions, speech, background, others' reactions*). And, finally, recognize that all of the expository patterns of perception may also need to be included: *comparison and contrast, definition, classification,* and *analysis.*

That may seem like a lot to keep in your head at once, but you've already practiced using most of those techniques in earlier papers. What you'll need now is time—lots of it. You cannot rush this phase or postpone it. It may be the single most crucial step you perform in preparing to engage in effective research.

Here is how you might consider the subject of women's entrance into the labor force during World War II. Begin with a general approach that has some personal interest to you. Let's say that in this case you're curious about the origins of the current feminist movement. Perhaps you could begin with one or two broad questions: Did women's entrance into the wartime labor force create new expectations and demands from women? Did it bring about any change in male attitudes? A satisfactory start, but still too general. Even more focused questions must be found:

- What percentage of the work force consisted of women before the United States' entry into the war?
- What were men's and women's attitudes toward working women prior to the war?
- What percentage of women were working by the end of the war?
- Why did this movement occur?
- What kinds of jobs did women take?
- Was there any opposition to women's entry into male jobs at that time?
- Was the working woman viewed as a temporary wartime phenomenon? By women? By men?
- Was it a temporary phenomenon? Evidence?
- Can specific consequences be determined?
- What were mens' and womens' attitudes after the war?
- Did opposition arise against women who continued to work? Evidence?
- What kind of evidence would be satisfactory? Did women speak out? Were new labor laws passed?
- Where could such evidence be found?

This is only a small beginning. But notice already how raising questions about the subject has led to raising questions about evidence. If the initial subject is a poor one or too complex, such questions will begin to identify the dangers of pursuing it further. No need wasting several weeks on a topic if evidence is not available. Only by considering in advance the types of evidence you may need and where you may have to look to find it can you begin to be somewhat confident that your research will prove successful.

One final suggestion: don't try all of this in your head. Sit down in a quiet location and write out questions as you think them. Seeing the words on paper will stimulate more questions, and it will also help you begin early to find an order or pattern to your research. Related questions can be grouped. Questions that seem to lead nowhere can be struck out. Only by doing this will you be prepared for the next two steps in the process: finding and investigating sources of information.

# Locate Primary and Secondary Sources

As most students do not attempt to locate and use primary sources, you can often impress your reader by showing a little initiative and imagination. A letter to a congressman or a company president, a telephone call to a local journalist or director of a social agency may bring in unexpected and fresh information. An interview with the curator of the local art gallery or a scientist at a major university may provide new ideas as well as human interest. Make a list of the potential primary sources, and attempt to locate at least one or two if possible:

Authorities on the topic
local or national organizations
people involved or affected by the issue
letters, journals, diaries
movies, television, records, radio
original documents

Most of your research, however, will take place in the library. Knowing that, some students head directly for the card catalog. But the experienced researcher knows that other reference tools can be far more helpful at this stage.

### Indexes

Not all information can be found in books, especially if your topic deals with current issues and ideas. *Indexes* provide author and subject listings of material found in magazines, journals, and newspapers. (A journal is usually published quarterly or biannually for a specific professional audience and tends to print articles that deal with a subject technically or with scholarly depth; *magazines* are usually published weekly or monthly and tend to print material aimed at the general reader.) Here are some of the most important indexes with which you should be familiar.

*The New York Times Index* is indispensable for research on people, events, and organizations in the news since 1851. It even offers a brief summary of the information contained in each article so that you can quickly determine whether you need to pursue it further.

The *Reader's Guide to Periodical Literature* lists articles published since 1900 in popular magazines like *Time, Redbook, Ladies Home Journal* and *Sports Illustrated.* Obviously, you probably won't find in-depth coverage in such sources. But *Reader's Guide* also lists many superior periodicals: *Atlantic, New Republic, Commonweal, Harper's* and *National Review.* If you use this index selectively, you can often find excellent material, especially on current topics and problems.

For more technical or scholarly treatment, you'll need more specialized indexes. The *Applied Science and Technology Index* lists articles in highly specialized journals and may provide you with more depth on subjects like forestry, biology, chemistry, and the environment.

The *Business Periodicals Index* covers almost three hundred different magazines and journals that deal with economics, finance management, and so on.

The *Humanities Index* will be the primary place to begin a study on the arts, literature, languages, music, and philosophy.

The *Social Sciences Index* provides author and subject headings for hundreds of magazines and scholarly journals in psychology, sociology, political science, and similar fields.

This list could continue for pages. Hundreds of specialized indexes list the works you may need to consult. You should probably begin your hunt for secondary sources in one of the general indexes such as the *Humanities Index* and then move toward more specialized indexes in your particular subject such as the *Art Index.* Within an hour or so, you'll probably find a surprising amount of material impossible to locate through the card catalog.

### Bibliographies

A *bibliography* is merely a list of books on a given subject. If you can locate one on your topic, it may save you hours. If, for example, you were considering a study of the influence of black African writing on black American writers, you might begin with *Black African Literature in English Since 1952.* This one book would provide you with a list of books on African literature in English, a list of critical articles according to subject matter, a list of anthologies of black African writing, an alphabetical listing of black African authors publishing in English, and even a list of other bibliographies on the subject. You'll find specialized bibliographies on individuals, organizations, historical events, and individual topics. Some are annotated—that is, they offer brief comments on the contents and quality of each work they list.

Two places to look for bibliographies on your subject are the *Bibliographic Index* and the card catalog under your subject with the subdivision *bibliography:* for example, *Women—Bibliography* or *Literature, Black—Bibliography.*

## The Card Catalog

Only now (after a preliminary search through indexes and bibliographies) should you turn to the card catalog for books. I make such a suggestion because too many students who begin their search at the card catalog never seem to get past it. No doubt, information from books will constitute a major part of your research, but journals and magazine articles should not be omitted. By discovering what current material is being published in periodicals and by having studied the various classifications of books on the subject as listed in a bibliography, you are in a more credible position to make meaningful selections from the card catalog.

Books are listed in a card catalog in three ways: under author, title, and subject. If you've obtained some names of authorities from your previous overview of the subject, you will want to check their work under author headings. Otherwise, subject headings will group all works on a single topic, and you'll probably find it the most productive place to begin. But note that any topic may have several related subject headings. If your subject involves changing attitudes toward marijuana, don't look solely under the heading of marijuana. You would probably also want to try *drug abuse, drugs, drug—laws and legislation,* and perhaps others. Give yourself several hours and be willing to explore.

## The Reference Librarian

What if you can't determine other headings to look under? What if you don't know where the indexes are located? Or how to read some of the codes used in bibliographies? Fortunately, every major library has a *reference librarian,* an individual specially trained in locating the right index or bibliography and in helping you make the most productive use of the card catalog. Don't be shy. You need sources on your subject, and each library may have a different system for locating and organizing reference materials. You are not expected to know already where to find such information or how to use it. Ask the reference librarian for help. That's what he or she gets paid for. The reference librarian may be your single best friend in any library.

# Prepare a Working Bibliography

During this whole process of preliminary investigation, you'll want to compile a list of possible sources for your actual research. The list is called a *working bibliography* because it is indeed one from which you work. It will seldom be identical to the final bibliography you submit with your paper.

This preliminary list should be at least two to three times as long as you expect to need. For every ten items on it, two may be checked out by other students, one may be lost, one may be stolen, and one will no doubt be at the bindery. Perhaps four will be found on the shelf. Of those, two may actually deal with your topic in a useful way. If you calculate that you need fifteen sources for your paper, then make a list of at least thirty to forty-five entries. If you stop after the first fifteen, you'll only end up returning to the library a week later and beginning the preliminary stage over again. Don't take chances or waste time. Be selective, of course, but be thorough.

Every researcher develops his or her own best method of working. Some believe the working bibliography should be placed on 3-by-5-inch cards in traditional form that can easily be transfered to your final bibliography. That has much to say for it. Time may be saved at the end. Others insist that because you don't yet know what you'll need at the end, your list at this stage does not need to be formal, only complete. Later when you decide to use a specific article or book, you can take the time to fill out a formal bibliography card.

I tend to agree with the latter point of view. Your time might be better spent at this stage making judgments about the content of books and articles rather than worrying about the mechanics of a bibliography. An informal working list should probably look like this:

Sample Working Bibliography

| | |
|---|---|
| Name the index in case you must return to check entry. | *Social Science Index* |
| Record name of author, title, name of magazine. | Frobes, Allyn, "The Disaster of CIA Involvement in Iran," *Harper's* (June, 79), 15-21. |
| List full date and page numbers. | |
| Record both volume number and page number for journals. | Greenbaum, R.A. "Who Really Controls Our Foreign Policy?" *Foreign Policy*. vol. 19, Sept. 1980, 101-117. |
| (For newspapers, the final numbers refer to page and column.) | "The Decline of American Influence in Iran," *N.Y. Times*, Sept. 19 [1978] 62-3. |
| | *Card Catalog* |
| | Zisko, Christopher, *A Ship of State Without a Captain*, N.Y.: Peabody Press, 1979 [328. 13]. |
| Record call numbers for books. | |

All this preliminary work may sometimes seem tedious and frustrating, but, without it, your research phase will consist of random guesswork and hope work. Take the necessary time now to assure yourself that your actual investigation will be focused and productive.

---

### AN OUTLINE OF PRELIMINARY STEPS IN RESEARCH

(1) Prepare a Work Schedule
   —Do not underestimate the time needed.
   —Build in unscheduled days for rest or to gain perspective on the )opic.
(2) Clarify and Define the Subject
   —Obtain an overview and historical background.
   —Check encyclopedias and dictionaries.
(3) Narrow the Subject and Place in Question Form
   —Formulate your questions in impartial terms.
   —Consider kinds of evidence that will be needed.
(4) Locate Primary and Secondary Sources
   —Consider potential organizations or authorities to contact for interviews.
   —Search indexes, bibliographies, and card catalog.
(5) Prepare a Working Bibliography
   —Obtain two to three times as many sources as you think you'll need.
   —Write down *all* information available on each source.

---

### SUGGESTED WRITING ASSIGNMENT

Write a fully developed research paper. Consult with your instructor on a recommended length. Select a subject from one of those listed below or from your own personal interests. Be sure to have your subject approved by the instructor.

1. Here are some broad subjects that might suggest topics for research:

Health Care
Theatre of the Absurd
California Migrant's Union
Women's Athletics
Extrasensory Perception
Changes in Attitudes Toward Sex
Mark Twain's Attack on Religion
Prophets: Orwell and Huxley
Motherhood or Career
Child Abuse
The Energy Crisis

The Syphilis Epidemic
Teaching Reading
Attacks on Freedom of the
   Press
Contemporary Music
   Developments
The Israeli-Arab Peace Treaty
Values found in Whitman's
   poetry
B. F. Skinner's World

2. Begin the process of narrowing and defining your subject:
   a. Study the general background in encyclopedias or specialized dictionaries.

    b. Prepare a series of specific focusing questions.

    c. Look for patterns and relationships among the questions.

    d. Consider the type and amount of evidence needed to answer those questions.

    e. Pursue the questions that seem to give direction and to limit the subject to a manageable topic for the amount of time you have available.

3. Begin the task of locating primary and secondary sources:

    a. Prepare a list of possible primary sources.

    b. Consult several indexes and prepare a list of possible secondary sources available in journals, newspapers, or magazines.

    c. If possible, find a specialized bibliography on your subject.

    d. Consult the card catalog on books available in your library.

    e. Use your focusing questions as guidelines for determining which sources might be most useful.

    f. Don't hesitate to ask the reference librarian for assistance.

4. As you locate sources, prepare a working bibliography. Some instructors will ask you to submit your working bibliography accompanied by a general statement of purpose. Be sure to keep a copy for yourself so that you can continue the investigation while the instructor evaluates your work to date.

5. Before you begin to study your sources and take notes, read Chapter 35, "Thoughtful Note-Taking."

# 35 *Thoughtful Note-Taking*

Once you learned to hold a pencil and scrawl your alphabet in shaky letters across the lined page. Each uncertain movement of the pencil was consciously made. Yet with time the instrument in your hand and the words on the page became only another extension of yourself. In the following chapters, detailed steps of formal note-taking, outlining, and documenting may at first seem equally foreign and awkward. We all know it is not knowledge of such mechanics in itself that will bring the rewards of scholarship, yet with time the mechanics become second nature—like holding a pencil. Each technique becomes only another extension of yourself, freeing you for more concentrated attention to those qualities of intellectual endeavor that do bring satisfaction.

## Preliminary Skimming

A scholarly approach to a subject requires a selective approach. You'll not want to waste time reading unrelated material. Before sitting down to a twenty-page essay, quickly study the opening paragraph and the conclusion. If you find nothing that points toward the narrowed questions you've posed for study, skim the remainder of the essay. Usually, this can be done by reading only the first and last sentences of each paragraph. If you find even a single idea that might be valuable, go back and read the whole more closely. Otherwise, in only a few minutes, you can determine that the essay has nothing of relevance and you can move on to something more important.

**430**

Skimming a book involves several additional steps. If you've already obtained an overview of your subject, you'll seldom need to read complete works; after all, you need specific information on only a narrow portion of a topic. Begin with the *table of contents*. Select from it those chapters that seem relevant, and skim each chapter in the same way you would a magazine article. Do not take notes until you are certain the chapter offers something worth your time. If none of the chapter titles seem pertinent, quickly read the *preface* and *introduction*. That's where most authors summarize their intentions, their basic thesis, and their approach to a subject. Finally, turn to the *index* at the back of the book. Search out several different headings or terms that relate to your specific topic, and check those individual pages. If nothing meaningful shows up, you've spent only a few minutes with a book that would have proved of little value in the first place. But if you find even a single potential idea, read the whole chapter in which it occurs. See the idea in the full context in which the author intended it. Then, if it proves useful, take notes.

Preliminary skimming allows you to investigate far more material than the average student who checks out a few large books and reads them cover to cover. You will be able to research five times as much material with less effort and less wasted time.

## The Bibliography Card

If, after a preliminary skimming of an essay or book, you decide it will probably contain useful information or ideas on your topic, the first step (before you begin critical reading and certainly before you begin to take an actual note) is to write a *bibliography card*. You must train yourself to take this simple step first because no matter how good your intentions, generations of experience prove that students who take their notes first may forget to record a full bibliographic entry. The failure will not be apparent until you reach the final stage of writing your paper and suddenly find yourself needing footnotes and a bibliography page. That's when your friends will see you at midnight pounding on the library door.

Don't take a chance. Use large 4-by-6-inch cards, and write down *all* necessary information. The larger the card, the less likely it will become lost.

From the title page of a book, record the following:

1. Full name of author(s) or editor(s) (last name first).
2. Full title of book, including subtitle (underlined).
3. Place of publication.
4. Full name of publisher.
5. Date of publication (use the last date given because later printings may contain revised material or new page arrangements).
6. The library call number.

author → DeMott, Benjamin    917.303 ← call number

title → Supergrow: Essays & Reports on Imagination in America

place → N.Y.: E.P. Dutton & Co., 1970 ← publisher and date

space for comments or notes on author → [Writes column on contemporary culture for Atlantic; considered authority on contemporary lit., professor at Amherst.]

For an article from a magazine or journal, record the following:

1. Full name of author(s) (last name first).
2. Title of the article (in quotation marks).
3. Full name of magazine (underlined).
4. Volume number (usually located on table of contents page).
5. Date of the magazine.
6. Inclusive pages (that is, from p. *x* through p. *y*).

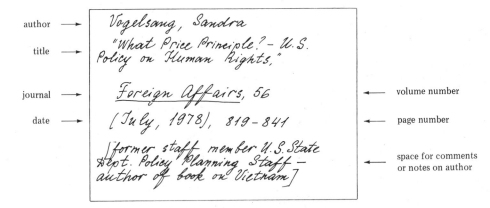

author → Vogelsang, Sandra

title → "What Price Principle? - U.S. Policy on Human Rights,"

journal → Foreign Affairs, 56 ← volume number

date → (July, 1978), 819-841 ← page number

[former staff member U.S. State Dept. Policy Planning Staff - author of book on Vietnam] ← space for comments or notes on author

Although these two formats should serve for most sources, from time to time you'll encounter a source that creates special problems in both bibliographical and footnote entries: that's when you'll need to consult a *style manual.* Two of the most widely used are Kate L. Turabian's *A Manual for Writers of Term Papers, Theses, and Dissertations* and the *MLA Handbook for Writers*. Both offer dozens of variations on foot-noting and bibliographic forms. Both are usually available in college bookstores or libraries.

## Critical Reading

Once you've located material directly relevant to your narrowed topic, you'll want to apply all the mental steps of critical reading covered earlier in Chapter 29. Approach the material as objectively as possible. Attempt to understand the author's ideas on his or her own terms. Know your own biases as best you can, and avoid making hasty judgments. But do not take notes without careful evaluation of the content: make an effort to discover who the author is and what his or her authority to speak on the subject might be; try to consider the historical and cultural context in which the work was written; and, most important, look for logic, look for appeals to emotion, look for evidence supported with valid sources, and look for sound reasoning.

## Note-Taking: The Wrong Way

Learning how to take proper and meaningful notes requires more skill than young writers may first realize—and more effort. Here are three methods you'll want to avoid.

1. Do not copy an author's ideas word for word. A note that consists of nothing but a long quotation taken directly from a secondary source may give you the impression you're busy working hard—after all, it takes a long time to copy down a page of print in longhand. With few exceptions, however, you'll seldom need a page-long quo-tation from anyone. If you do, a photocopy machine can do it faster. But that leads to negative warning number two.

2. Do not photocopy passages from secondary sources as a *substitute* for taking a note. Photocopying machines are wonderful inventions. Yet they obviously do not *digest* or *contemplate* information as you should be doing. The time saving may be dangerously misleading.

3. Perhaps equally wasteful is the method of avoiding all note-taking by underlining important passages in books or marking them with slips of paper and trying to write the first draft by spreading a dozen books about you on desk and floor, turning from first one to another and typing the paper as you go. Again, no assimilation or under-standing or the material occurs. Such a writer is not really writing, only collating.

None of these methods will accomplish your purpose. No real think-ing occurs. A machine can copy; the human brain has more potential. Unless you are summarizing or paraphrasing ideas in your own words, you are not really exerting intellectual effort; you are not grasping the meaning of ideas, evaluating, or interpreting. Note-taking must be a thinking process, not merely a recording process. As your research progresses, you must be involved in a continual reassessment and refinement of the subject. You must be alert for areas of exploration that you might not have anticipated earlier. It may be possible that the direction established by your main question will prove unfruitful. New questions will almost always appear as you move from source to source. Unless you are actively engaged in thinking about the material, questioning the material, challenging the material *as* you take notes, you are not truly engaged in research at all.

## Note-Taking: The Right Way

Correct note-taking involves a two-phase process. First comes the thinking phase. You must make repeated judgments about the worth and meaning of each idea you encounter. You must be involved in a constant process of evaluating the relationship of that idea or fact to all others you have uncovered. Train yourself to be highly selective. Take notes only on relevant ideas you have thought through or on your own ideas as they occur to you. Correct note-taking should accompany intellectual activity, not overshadow it. If you find yourself recording piles of information it may be a signal that you're depending too heavily on your sources and not assimilating or digesting material. Too many notes also have a way of pressuring you to use each and every one of them. All that effort expended on writing them down makes you feel guilty if they aren't used whether they're needed or not. The first phase in note-taking then involves the careful screening of information. You'll want to select only the most significant ideas for recording.

The second step involves the actual writing of the note on paper. Here, too, the most effective method requires experience, but it is one that can be more easily illustrated. Consider the following passage by Paul Zweig taken from an essay on heroes:

> Which is not to say that the contemporary world does not have its "heroes." For I doubt that human beings can live without some expanded ideal of behavior, some palpable image of the spaciousness of man. We want to know that our personal limitations are only a special case, that somewhere there is someone who can translate his words, thoughts, and beliefs into acts, even if we can't. Heroes in this sense represent a profoundly humanistic ideal.

© *Saturday Review,* 1978. All rights reserved. Reprinted by permission.

Here are two different student notes taken during an in-class exercise:

| Student A | Student B |
|---|---|
| Zweig believes that the contemporary world has its "heroes." He doubts that human beings can get along without some expanded ideal of behavior. All of us want to know that our personal limitations are special and that somewhere there will be someone else who can turn words, thoughts, and beliefs into acts. Heroes thus represent a profoundly humanistic ideal. | Heroes still seem necessary today according to Paul Zweig. Although each of us personally may feel small and limited, we require the knowledge that somewhere out there someone can put our ideals into action. |

Student A has seemingly rephrased Zweig's material in his own words, but a closer look reveals a serious problem. Although a phrase or two have been omitted, the expression of ideas is almost identical to the original. Only a few minor words have been shifted about. The student thinks he has paraphrased correctly, but should this note end up in his final paper, it would be considered plagiarism. Student B, on the other hand, has succeeded in taking a valid note that is accurate to the sense of the original while actually *rephrasing* the ideas in her own words.

A *paraphrase* expresses the sense of a passage in your own terms. Technically, a paraphrase is a rewording of the *whole*. In practice, it may be handled like a summary: you may condense information or extract selected ideas, so long as you rephrase them. Any time you present information from another source, the words themselves must be yours, *or* the words must be enclosed in quotation marks. If the words are not in quotation marks and are as similar to the original material as in Student A's example, plagiarism will be charged.

*Plagiarism* involves the appropriation of someone else's words or ideas as your own. The sad thing is that plagiarism may be accidental. Students may believe that because they have changed a word or two, they have written a proper note. Or students may believe that because they have documented the material by saying, "Zweig believes . . . ," they have precluded plagiarism, no matter how close their phrasing is to the original. Ignorance, however, should not be an excuse. *Even when you give credit to the source in text or footnote, the words of a paraphrase must be yours.*

Fortunately, you can almost guarantee yourself a proper note (one that is not plagiarized), as well as an accurate note, by following a traditional procedure developed by generations of students and scholars. And although the doing requires concentrated effort, the method is surprisingly simple: *do not look at the original material when writing your note.* Inexperienced writers tend to write their notes by keeping one finger in the book pointing to the original sentences while writing the note with their other hand. Their eyes move back and forth between the two. But words printed in a book, especially words you've selected as important, have a way of psychologically dominating your own vocabulary. "How can I say it any better—or any differently?" you ask yourself. You may find yourself changing small, insubstantial words while retaining the author's principal phrases.

Instead, once you've chosen a passage as relevant to your study, *turn completely away from it.* Either close the book, turn the book upside down, or move your notepaper so that the book is out of your line of sight. Now write down the idea that struck you as important. This will set in motion a train of meaningful intellectual consequences. What you'll discover is that your brain is suddenly required to recall the idea. Without the direct influence of the author's words, your own vocabulary will be all you can depend upon. Psychological studies have repeatedly shown that unless you can say something in your own words, you cannot be certain of having understood it. Once you've phrased it for yourself, you not only know that the idea is understood, but you have also made it more permanently a part of you. Recall implants the idea in your memory. Finally, you have in a sense forced yourself to think through the idea in order to phrase it, and you're in a sounder position to evaluate it or to compare it to others. Ideas of your own are likely to develop. Relationships and interpretations become possible. In other words, by the simple act of turning away from the original to write down your note, you discipline your mind and demand that it deal with the idea on its own terms. You engage yourself in the actual process of what we call "study."

One final step remains. Once you've completed your note, you must turn back and check the accuracy of it with the original (see Chapter 38 for a full discussion of accuracy). Again, an important train of consequences is set in motion. In the act of checking for accuracy, you assure yourself that your understanding of the author's idea is correct. If your note is in error, you are in an immediate position to clarify the mistake. If the note is accurate to the *sense* of the original, you can proceed with your reading, confident that when the time comes for writing your paper, you will be able to include the author's information accurately, thoughtfully, in your own words—because it already *is* in your own words.

This process of successful note-taking does not seem to come naturally to many of us. We must train ourselves, and the training is demanding. Turning away and writing an idea in your own words requires an incredible amount of concentration. You may constantly find yourself tempted to do it in the old way. What you are faced with is the question of means and ends. If your "ends," your goal, is nothing more than to slide through college and life with the least possible effort, the old method will serve you. But if you have higher goals, if training your mind is important to you, then the "means" begins with the first step. It cannot be leaped over. *Note-taking must be a thinking process, not merely an act of recording.*

## Note-Card Mechanics

Every individual tends to devise his or her own format for keeping notes, but the following points have generally proven essential:

1. Use *large* 4-by-5-inch cards that allow plenty of room for writing and then can later be shuffled easily into a sequence that will match your outline.
2. Write on one side only.
3. Record only one idea, statistic, or fact on each card.
4. *Always* identify the source and page number(s).
5. Write a brief generalization in the upper right or left corners to identify the contents of the card at a glance.

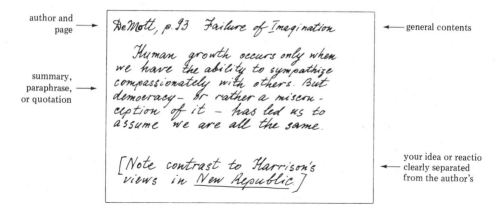

author and page →

summary, paraphrase, or quotation →

DeMott, p. 93   Failure of Imagination   ← general contents

Human growth occurs only when we have the ability to sympathize compassionately with others. But democracy — or rather a misconception of it — has led us to assume we are all the same.

[Note contrast to Harrison's views in *New Republic*.]

your idea or reactio(n)
← clearly separated from the author's

As you've already made a complete bibliography card, you need not repeat that information, but you must still take extraordinary care to label your note card accurately. The best advice is to write the author's last name and the page numbers first, *before* you take the note. Make it a habit and you'll never end up with a mystery card that provides an idea without a source or page reference.

### EXERCISES

1. The following three paragraphs express fairly complex ideas. Write a paraphrase of each (or a summary-type paraphrase where you select the most important elements to put in your own words). Use the techniques described in this chapter: (a) do not look at the original mate-

rial when writing your note; (b) attempt to recall the most important elements of the idea and express them in your own words; (c) reread the original and check the author's expression against your own to determine whether your understanding is accurate and correct to the *sense* of the original.

a. Health care has become more readily a matter of ability to pay rather than who is the client. It is an economic matter in the sense that blacks still are more likely to be sick and disabled, and less likely to benefit under quasi-universal public health programs such as Medicare and Medicaid. The rising level of living since 1940 has made it possible for all Americans to live longer and healthier lives. But the American health-care system, even when it nominally includes everyone, leaves out too many who must trade off making an out-of-pocket initial expenditure of $50, $80, or more for the doctor or the hospital stay against paying the rent or sending a child to school well fed and with a warm winter coat. This becomes the choice for blacks much more often than for whites.

—Dorothy K. Newman et al., *Protest, Politics, and Prosperity*

b. The national trend is toward vocational courses, and it is that trend which must be blamed for the new "functional literacy" credo. Clearly, those who adopt the credo are imagining that an efficient vocational course will soon be devised that will achieve functional literacy for the whole nation in a few easy lessons, preferably by the use of some as yet uninvented audiovisual machine. My sad guess is that the trend is permanent, that the humanities are simply dead and don't know it yet, that they have gone the way of the classics. My evidence is private, fragmentary, and wholly convincing, consisting of such discoveries as a bookstore humanities shelf with nothing on it but books by psychologists and doctors on how to make love. My brain is loaded with deathly detail like that, and it all adds up to a takeover—by journalists and social scientists—of great magnitude.

—Reed Whittemore, *Harper's*

c. In this final conception of conscience, Freud continued to be impressed with the importance of guilty fear and the internalized parent, but in addition he postulated that there is an internalized ideal of behavior by which we, our actual selves (our egos), judge our own behavior—and in our failures experience true guilt. Guilt, then, is a form of self-disappointment, a sense of anguish that we did not achieve our standards of what we ought to be. We have fallen short. We have somehow or other betrayed some internal sense of potential self. This is why guilt is the most internalized and personal of emotions. You-against-you allows no buffer, and no villains except yourself. Even when guilty fear is internalized, it is as if someone else were there. But guilt is like tearing apart our internal structure. This is why guilt is so painful to endure.

—Willard Gaylin, *The Atlantic*

2. Make up three sample bibliography cards from the publication data provided below. The information is listed in a jumbled sequence, and, in some cases, more information is given than you'll actually need.

a. Holmes & Meier Publishers, New York
473 pages
Printed in Great Britain
Eda Sagarra, author
*A Social History of Germany: 1648–1914*
copyright, 1977
Library call number: 301.143 Sal8

b. Bruce E. Nickerson, author
*The Journal of American Folklore*
Published for the American Folklore Society by the
University of Texas Press
"Is There A Folk in the Factory?"
Vol. 87, April–June, 1974
pp. 133–140
Journal Editor, Barre Toelken

c. "Opiate of the Masses"
March 8, 1965
*Newsweek*
Published weekly by Newsweek, Inc., Dayton, Ohio
Editor, Osborn Elliott
pp. 83–84

3. Consider the hypothetical research project described below. Following the description is a passage that offers ideas and information on the project. First, prepare a complete bibliography card based on the data provided. Second, prepare one or two sample note cards in which you select, summarize, or paraphrase relevant material. You should include only a minimal amount of direct quotation. Your note cards must be both complete and accurate, but the notes themselves should be highly

selective, with only one main idea per card. Be sure to choose only information directly relevant to your project.

Project:  *You are researching natural childbirth and decide to investigate the early uses of anaesthesia. You are specifically interested in why it became popular even though many doctors and clergy condemned its use. You discover the following passage in an essay on nineteenth-century attitudes toward childbirth.*

Publication Data:

"Temple and Sewer: Childbirth, Prudery, and Victoria Regina"
by John Hawkins Miller
in *The Victorian Family: Structure and Stresses*
edited by Anthony S. Whol
St. Martin's Press, New York, 1978

Relevant Passage (pp. 24–25):

On 7 April 1853, Queen Victoria gave birth to her eighth child; Leopold, Duke of Albany. Present in the lying-in room with the Queen were Mrs Lilly (the Queen's monthly nurse), Mrs Innocent, and Dr John Snow. This nominally spiritual and immaculate trinity might well have helped the Queen to overcome her distaste for the 'animal' and 'unecstatic' aspects of childbirth so well-represented in the confinements attended by Mrs Bangham and Sarah Gamp of Victorian fiction. During this confinement, moreover, the Queen did not have to endure the 'sacred pangs' of labour, for, as she wrote later, Dr Snow 'gave me the blessed Chloroform and the effect was soothing, quieting, and delightful beyond measure.' Her personal physician, Sir James Clark, wrote to James Young Simpson, the Edinburgh obstetrician who first used chloroform in midwifery, that the anaesthesia 'was not at any time given so strongly as to render the Queen insensible, and an ounce of chloroform was scarcely consumed during the whole time. Her Majesty was greatly pleased with the effect, and she certainly never has had a better recovery.'

While the Queen testified to the heavenly benison bestowed by the drug in relieving women of the ancient curse upon Eve (that 'in sorrow shall she bring forth'), there were members of the clergy who considered chloroform a 'decoy of Satan, apparently offering itself to bless women; but in the end, it will harden society, and rob God of the deep earnest cries which arise in time of trouble for help.' The more puritanical and abstemious also inveighed against chloroform because of its well-known intoxicating effects: 'To be insensible from whisky, gin, and brandy, and wine, and beer, and ether and chloroform, is to be what in the world is called Dead-drunk,' wrote Dr Meigs, in his *Obstetrics: The Science and the Art*. 'No reasoning—no argumentation is strong enough to point out the 9th part of a hair's discrimination between them.'

This debate was largely resolved by the women themselves— including the Queen, a lady not known for irreligion or drunkenness. It was the Queen, as Head of the Church, who effectively silenced the objections of religious leaders by legitimizing the use of anaesthesia through her own use of it in 1853, and again in 1857 for the birth of her last child. It has even been claimed by Elizabeth Longford that her 'greatest gift to her people was a refusal to accept pain in childbirth as woman's divinely appointed destiny'.

According to a story current at the time, many of the Queen's subjects were eager to learn of Her Majesty's reactions to the use of anaesthesia. John Snow, the anaesthetist, was besieged with requests from his patients for such information. One woman, to whom Snow was administering anaesthesia while she was in labour, refused to inhale any more chloroform until told exactly what the Queen had said when she was breathing it. Snow replied: 'Her Majesty asked no questions until she had breathed very much longer than you have; and if you will only go on in loyal imitation, I will tell you everything.' The woman obeyed, soon becoming oblivious of the Queen. By the time she regained consciousness, Dr Snow had left the hospital.

While we too may be curious about what the Queen said at the time, we do know that she heartily approved of the effects of the anaesthesia, and many of her subjects were persuaded, in loyal imitation, to demand it during their confinements. What was technically called 'intermittent chloroform analgesia', became more commonly known as 'chloroform *à la Reine*'.

# 36 *Organizing Complex Material*

As your research continues, you will usually reevaluate and reformulate your questions about the subject. Your insight will change and grow as unexpected ideas enter the picture. By the time you near the end of your project, you may feel overwhelmed with possibilities. How can it all be pulled together?

## Categorizing Notes

Begin by reviewing and sorting your note cards according to categories. Use the brief summaries of note contents you've jotted in the upper corner as a guideline. All cards with similar or related ideas should be placed together. For example, a study of how supersititon continues to influence our lives might break down into three groups: customs, ceremonies, and gestures. Or you might see other possibilities: fear, sexuality, and anger. The same topic might be organized around one of the 4 *C* methods: change, conflict, consequences, and characterization. Causes and effects might be grouped separately—or comparisons and contrasts. A commonly mistaken view of superstition might be sorted into one pile, whereas more accurate interpretations (that you've discovered) are collected in another. Or you might arrange note cards according to an historical sequence: the continuing evidence of superstition through the twentieth century. The possibilities are endless.

Unfortunately, no one can provide you with a simple formula. The subject itself, your powers of reasoning, and a little intuition must all interact. But the organizing is essential. Form may be "discovered" in the first draft stage of personal writings, reports, and even expository essays. The research paper is decidedly different. Complex ideas, dozens of sources, conflicting views—the research paper *must* be organized before you begin the first draft. Indeed, as you think through your ideas and consider your material, now is the time to change those questions you began with into a thesis.

## The Thesis

The concept of a *thesis statement* was introduced in Chapter 24. Essentially, it is a brief statement, usually in a single sentence, that summarizes the dominant idea of your findings. If you're not yet sure what that dominant idea is, all the more reason for pausing at this point and working on it. Indeed, you may not be able to sort those note cards at all until you have a clearly defined thesis. More than likely, however, you began to develop a thesis in your head during the time you were reading your sources—although you may not have called it such. You may simply have thought, "Here's a fascinating angle on the subject," or "Look at how all of these points are pulling together." Now's the time to shape those vague feelings into an exactly worded statement that will guide you in organizing your paper, and eventually guide the reader in reading it.

1. Narrow your topic to the *single* most important element of your subject.

2. Start writing about the one or two significant points you've discovered about that element. Use your own voice. Don't worry about being formal or writing for an audience at this stage. This one's for you.

3. Be forceful. State what you know now in such a way that if someone asked you to prove it, you could begin offering evidence from that pile of note cards you've collected.

4. Get your own attitude or opinion into it. If you think something is wrong, say so. If you think something needs to be changed, say so.

Don't worry about bias; you can return later and make it sound more objective. At this point it's more important to get yourself involved with the subject.

And what if nothing happens? You stare at the page and you have all this information but nothing seems to shape up. Then try another tack. Pretend you're sitting in a bar with a group of friends interested in the same subject you've been studying. Someone asks you to tell them about it—only the catch is that the bar closes in fifteen minutes. You have time only to summarize. Everyone looks at you, waiting. Start talking. Tell your friends about the most important ideas you've found. Talk out loud. Most of us are a lot more relaxed talking out loud than writing silently on paper. So talk. Your friends are waiting, and you've got to summarize what you now know as briefly as possible but as forcefully as possible. Try to find the three or five most important points. Then if you can, narrow it to the one or two most important points. *Talk out loud.* Finally, grab a pencil and paper and write down the single most important point you have learned. Sometimes you may have to write down all five, but that's all right, too, because now you've got five ideas on paper and you can begin working on how to generalize about them in a single sentence.

All of this is only to suggest that although most of us think of the thesis as a formal (and perhaps somewhat inhibiting) statement, it is actually only a *means,* not an end in itself—a means of helping you come to precise understanding of your own study before you begin to organize and write. Later, it may form a portion of your introduction and will serve the reader as a means of getting into the same ideas.

Here are some good and bad thesis statements. The bad ones are bad only because they couldn't help either the writer or reader get a focus on what the material is about.

| Effective Thesis Statement | Weak Thesis Statement |
| --- | --- |
| Professional basketball has been destroyed by the players' greed for million-dollar salaries. | Robert Frost writes poems that reveal some moral values. [*Which poems? Which moral values And is that good or bad? What is the purpose for telling us?*] |
| Jimmy Carter is not a populist Democrat at all; the evidence from his first term in office shows that he is a middle-of-the-road Republican. | America needs energy. Socialism may be the answer although it has not solved the problem in Europe. [*Where's the focus? Energy? Or Socialism in Europe? How do they relate?*] |

America's health care costs are continuing to inflate because three special interest groups—the physicians, the politicians, and the insurance companies—are all making a profit. The patient is the only one who pays, and no change is in sight.

Today's society is composed of a phenomenon in which we find ourselves afraid to be individuals or to be willing to challenge the conformity imposed upon us.
[*Too broad. Individualism and conformity are abstract subjects that need narrowing to specific components.*]

Notice that the last example of an effective thesis (in the left column) uses more than one sentence. Try as you might, sometimes you'll find that a complex subject needs two sentences or three or even a paragraph to state the thesis fully. The single-sentence ideal is not a holy commandment that can't be broken. The point is to design a statement that helps you organize your paper, not to terrorize yourself with a rule that can't possible anticipate every situation. Make the thesis statement work for you; don't become its slave.

## Developing a Design

No one can predict at what stage in the process a design will begin to take shape. By this point, you may already have a solid feel for how you're going to organize. If not, here's a quick review of all the different possibilities:

1. As in narration and description, almost all organizations move from either the general to the specific or the specific to the general, from most important to least important or from least important to most important (see Chapter 8 and 10 for a review).

2. An imaginative lead is effective for both reader and writer and can help the writer envision an organization. A bold statement, a dramatic scene, a statement of contrast or conflict, a question, or pileup of statistics that intrigue the reader—each can suggest a pattern for the rest of the paper to follow (see Chapters 20 and 21 for a review).

3. Definition, classification, comparison and contrast, item analysis, process analysis, or cause-and-effect analysis may also give an almost automatic shape to the material (see Chapters 23 and 24 for a review).

Here is what you must remember: the methods you used to *see* your subject, whether sensuously or intellectually, are almost always productive methods around which to design your paper. If to understand Confucianism you studied the historical and cultural development of it, then it follows that a narrative presentation may be the most effective organization.

But if you compared Confucianism to Christianity, it only makes sense that you will probably use one of the two contrast designs. And if you analyzed the demise of Confucianism under the Communist Chinese rulers, then of necessity you must break the subject into parts and move step-by-step through each one, showing how each relates and whether or not there was cause and effect.

Before you move to the outline stage, take a few minutes and draw some visual designs—boxes, pyramids, circles, or whatever. Try to see visually the pattern your material may fit into. We are visually oriented creatures. Scientists tell us that some 90 percent of all information we gather comes through our eyes. The direction and organization of your paper may become more clear if you can design a visual statement of it— if you can *see* the pattern you're about to follow.

## The Working Outline

Some instructors who want to make sure you've thought through your project may require you to submit a formal topic outline, as in this example:

**Thesis Statement:** *The decision by Harry S. Truman to drop the atom bomb on Japan was expedient but immoral.*

   I. Summary of historical events leading up to Hiroshima
  II. Truman uninformed of atomic experiments
    A. Secrecy under Roosevelt
    B. Truman puzzled by Stimson's account
 III. The alternatives as perceived by Joint Chiefs of Staff
    A. Invasion of Japan
    B. Public threat of invasion by all allies jointly
    C. Show of power with atomic bomb
 IV. How Truman made his decision
    A. Military considerations
    B. Political considerations
    C. Moral considerations
  V. Evaluation of his final decision
    A. Consequences in terms of military effectiveness
    B. Consequences in terms of political effectiveness
    C. Consequences in terms of human life
 VI. Overall assessment
    A. Politically and militarily correct
    B. Morally wrong
    C. The dilemma of choice

The assumption behind a conventional topic outline is that, at the very least, you will divide your subject into main ideas and sub-ideas, as in the above example. Some writers may go further and fill in examples or perhaps even specific details and facts.

I. Main Idea
  A. Sub-idea
    1. Example
    2. Example
  B. Sub-idea
    1. Example
      a. Specific fact
      b. Specific statistic
      c. Specific quotation
    2. Example

How much detail you go into depends upon your own personal needs and methods of working. Some students are best advised to omit nothing: only in such a way will gaps in information or logical flaws be revealed. Others work well from general subheadings or even from a casual outline that does not use Roman numerals:

—Wartime pressures, national debt, and rationing put pressure on Truman to end war.
—The alliance between Russia and the West was weakening.
—Chiang Kai-shek was more interested in consolidating his own gains on mainland China.
—After Roosevelt's death, Truman discovered he was totally unprepared for all the complexity.
—Stimson's information about a new secret weapon was more puzzling than helpful.
—The Joint Chiefs of Staff presented Truman with several alternatives but could not agree among themselves.
—And so on.

An outline is a working tool. Don't be afraid of it. Use your piles of note cards to shape each step. Be willing to revise several times. And recognize that no matter what method you use or how thorough you are, new ideas may still occur during the first draft that will cause you to break the pattern of your outline. After you finish the first draft, a second or third outline may be needed before you begin rewriting.

# 37 *Drafting and Documenting*

You've finished your inquiry, organized your ideas, and drawn up a design to follow. But certain components of a research paper tend to create problems you may not encounter in other forms of writing. The introduction, the handling of documentation in early drafts, the final organizing of footnotes, and a formal bibliography page all require extra attention.

## Leads and Introductions

Although a research paper may begin with a formal introduction, an imaginative lead always adds interest and spark. The two can sometimes be combined. Here's how a freshman nursing major drew together various elements from her research to organize an effectively unified lead and introduction:

## An Undignified Death
### Terrie Clinger

*Terrie's lead consists of three examples.*

In New Freedom, Pennsylvania, George McGraw, a fifty-eight-year-old construction worker, rushed to the hospital after being involved in an automobile accident, was released because he appeared to only suffer from a

**448**

scraped elbow. No X-rays were taken. On the way home, fragments of bone from a fractured neck and skull "sliced" into McGraw's brain and spinal cord paralyzing him for life.

In New York, a thirty-five-year-old printer who had been released from an emergency room with only pain-killers for a stomach ache died at home with massive hemorrhaging of stomach ulcers.

In Dallas, an accident victim brought in "appearing" to be dead on arrival was ignored for several hours until he caught someone's attention when he coughed. The patient survived but because of delay in treatment he suffered severe brain damage.

*Formal introduction begins with general overview.*

These three cases are almost insignificant when compared to the more than one million lives annually lost in crisis situations with approximately sixty thousand of those being preventable deaths. These losses and tragedies are a result of mishandlings due to either inadequate emergency facilities or inadequate emergency treatment.

*Historical context is established.*

Fifteen years ago, the American Academy of General Practice listed a membership of 95,526 doctors, but today the list contains only 68,326 members. Although more and more doctors are turning to specialization, more and more people are turning to the emergency room for treatment. According to Scudder Winslow, M.D., and head of New York's Roosevelt Hospital Emergency Service, the Emergency room has "simply become a substitute for the family doctor" because there are only a few general practitioners for people to turn to. Yet 90 percent of the seven thousand accredited hospitals in the United States provide emergency rooms that are poorly equipped and understaffed. This failure of hospitals and medical associations to deal with—or at times even to recognize—the emergency room crisis has led to a frightening situation that shows no signs of early solution.

*Specific focus begins to take shape.*

*Thesis stated.*

Obviously, an introduction can take other shapes, but Terrie has followed a fairly conventional and traditionally successful method.

1. An imaginative lead (dramatic statement, literary scene, contrast, question, quotation, and so on).
2. General overview of what the paper is about as a whole (in a sentence or two).
3. A brief summary of the background or historical context to orient the reader and establish the foundation for evidence that follows.
4. A focusing sentence (usually the thesis statement) that narrows

the topic or presents the dominant idea that will be explored and supported by the body of the paper.

It might be misleading, however, to leave the impression that Terrie's introduction looked like this on a first draft. Actually, it went through hours of work and half a dozen thrown-away pages. For most of us, the introduction remains the most difficult element of any paper to write. In fact, some writers avoid it entirely until the rest of the first draft is complete. If the introduction becomes hopelessly bogged down, give it up. Go straight to the body of the paper. Begin with your first example or quotation and write as fast as possible. You can return later and decide how to introduce the whole. As Ezra Pound put it, "It doesn't matter which leg of your table you make first, so long as the table has four legs and will stand up solidly when you have finished it."

## The First Draft and Preliminary Documentation

It must be stated one final time that a first draft should be written as quickly as possible. You should *see* the subject before your mind's eye; concern yourself only with ideas; save spelling, punctuation, correct usage, and all other necessary mechanics for later revisions. But research papers may create a special problem for the first draft because you are concerned not only with your ideas but also with those taken from others. You may be tempted to "sew together" your notes, moving slowly from one to the next and merely transcribing the information from note card to paper, adding here and there a transition like *also* or *therefore*. The danger in doing so is that any understanding of the subject you have gained in your research tends to be repressed for the safe ideas gleaned from books or journals. *Remember that your imagination, memory, and reasoning must form a major part of your writing. The notes exist to support what you know, not to substitute for your own insights.*

A second problem—and one that may especially slow down the inexperienced writer—involves the documentation of material taken from other sources. Should you try to write out footnotes as you go? Should you create a color code or numbering system matching the code on the page to one on each note card? For most of us, the answer is probably no. Such methods either take too much time or open the door to later confusion. In order to keep your first draft flowing with as little interruption as possible, you must use one simple technique: *as you write, include all documentation in the text itself.* The reader needs to know *who, what, where,* and *when* anyway. Other publication data can be placed in brackets immediately following the quotation, paraphrase, statistic, or whatever.

Grover Woodland, president of the American Society for Consumer Advocacy, writes in *Commonweal* that a majority of lawyers "are more interested in preserving the perks of their profession than they are in extending service to the poor." [July, 1979, p. 14]

If America is spending $53 billion a year—5.9 percent of our gross national product, 7.5 percent of all personal income—for junk food of questionable nutrition, don't we need to ask ourselves some serious questions? [U.S. Congress, House, Subcommittee on Health, *America's Health Needs,* Con. Info. Serv., Wash., D.C., 1970, p. 9]

Such a concept is totally unrecognized by Fred M. Lorch, who writes in *American Literature* that the murder of the stranger is a fictional incident and therefore does not explain why Twain deserted the war. ["Mark Twain and the 'Campaign that Failed,'" *Am Lit,* XII (Jan, 41), 454]

By handling documentation in this way, you avoid losing or confusing sources. You know at a glance where you obtained the information. And if, during rewriting, paragraphs must be shifted from one portion of a paper to another, they will carry their documentation with them. If you use a footnote numeral, any shifting of the information would take the number out of sequence and make all following numbers incorrect as well.

Retain your documentation in the text through each draft. Once you're ready to type a final copy, knowing that no more changes will be made and that each paragraph has found its proper order, each bracketed note can be numbered in sequence. As the typing proceeds, all information in brackets should be omitted and either typed at the bottom of the page in proper footnote style or saved for typing on a note page at the end of the paper.

## Footnote Forms and Traditions

More students seem to panic over footnoting than any other aspect of formal writing. Admittedly, footnote requirements seem complex. But you do not need to memorize all that complexity; indeed, you should not. Footnote requirements vary from profession to profession, from one instructor's class to another, from one style manual to another. What you do need is to determine the form expected by your reader, obtain a sample of it, and then *imitate* it to the last comma and period. If you gather *all* information needed on bibliography and note cards, you will find it is only a matter of rearranging it in varying sequences to meet the expectations of your audience.

In spite of all the variations, however, you should know that footnotes are traditionally used as follows:

1. To acknowledge indebtedness to a primary or secondary source, whether direct quotation or paraphrase is used.

2. To define specialized terms when you do not want to interrupt the flow of your text for such a definition.

3. To explain a point or provide additional background when such material is interesting but not essential to the text itself.

4. To evaluate or compare authorities.

5. To provide cross-reference to another authority or to another part of your paper.

Here is a brief sampling of footnoting forms used by most divisions of the humanities:

*Book by single author*

[1] Joyce Cary, *Art and Reality: Ways of the Creative Process* (New York: Harper & Brothers, 1958), p. 137.

[*Note that the footnote numeral is placed one-half space above the line; the first word of the note is indented like a sentence, beginning with a capital letter and ending with a period.*]

*Book by two authors*

[2] Robert M. Gorrell and Charlton Laird, *Modern English Handbook* (Englewood Cliffs, N.J.: Prentice-Hall, 1976), pp. 72–73.

*Book by more than two authors*

[3] Walter M. Cummins et al., *The Other Sides of Reality: Myths, Visions, and Fantasies* (San Francisco: Boyd & Fraser Publishing Co., 1972), p. 203.

*Book by an editor*

[4] Jonathan Baumbach (ed.), *Writers as Teachers, Teachers as Writers* (New York: Holt, Rinehart and Winston, 1970), p. 20.

*Book with second or later edition*

[5] Jan Harold Brunvand, *The Study of American Folklore: An Introduction*, 2d ed. (New York: W. W. Norton & Co., 1978), p. 267.

*Reference to one author in a collection edited by another*

[6] Philip Roth, "Eli, The Fanatic," in *The Process of Fiction*, ed. by Barbara McKenzie (2d ed.; Atlanta: Harcourt Brace Jovanovich, Inc., 1974), p. 175.

*Magazine article*

[7] Michael Daly, "The New York Scene," *The Atlantic*, September, 1978, p. 67.

*Journal article with volume no.*

[8] Abby Arthur Johnson and Ronald M. Johnson, "Reform and Reaction: Black Literary Magazines in the 1930s," *North Dakota Quarterly*, 46 (Winter, 1978), 11.

*Newspaper article*

[9] "Inflation Staggers Mexican Workers," *Chicago Tribune*, March 21, 1980, p. 1.

*Association, institution, or government agency as author*

[10] U.S. Department of Health, Education, and Welfare, *Findings on Marijuana* (Washington, D.C.: Government Printing Office, 1967), p. 4.

*Pamphlet or bulletin*

[11] *National Income* (1615 H. St. N.W., Washington D.C.: Chamber of Commerce of the U.S., 1967), p. 9.

*Biblical refer-
ence (chapter,
verse)*

[12] Ecclesiastes 12:4–6.

*Reference to a
play (act, scene,
line)*

[13] *Hamlet,* IV. ii. 25.

Footnotes may be located at the foot of each page on which the reference occurs (as in the sample research paper at the end of this unit), or they may be collected at the conclusion of a paper prior to the bibliography page.

## Sample Page of Terminal Notes

TERMINAL NOTES

[1] Joyce Cary, <u>Art and Reality: Ways of the Creative Process</u> (New York: Harper & Brothers, 1958), p. 137.

[2] Ibid., p. 141. [<u>Ibid.</u> means "<u>in the same place</u>."]

[3] Ibid., p. 32.

[4] Abby Arthur Johnson and Ronald M. Johnson, "Reform and Reaction: Black Literary Magazines in the 1930s," <u>North Dakota Quarterly,</u> 46 (Winter, 1978), 11.

[5] Cary, pp. 52–53.

[6] Johnson and Johnson, 11.

[7] "Inflation Staggers Mexican Workers," <u>Chicago Tribune,</u> March 21, 1980, p. 1.

[8] "Inflation Staggers," p. 2.

[9] Joyce Cary, <u>A House of Children</u> (Garden City, N.Y.: Anchor Books, 1962), p. 64.

[10] Cary, <u>Art and Reality,</u> p. 22.

# Bibliographic Forms

The bibliography of a research paper should list all sources (in alphabetical order according to last name) that you actually used and to which you made reference. Sources that you may have glanced at which are not refered to should *not* be included. Here is how a sample bibliography page might look. I've made comments in square brackets after certain entries to call your attention to specific details.

---

BIBLIOGRAPHY

Baumbach, Jonathan, ed.  Writers as Teachers, Teachers as Writers.  New York: Holt, Rinehart and Winston, 1970.  [The first line of a bibliographical reference is extended to call attention to the alphabetical order of the last name.  Unlike a footnote, each component of the entry is separated by a period.]

Cary, Joyce.  Art and Reality: Ways of the Creative Process.  New York: Harper & Brothers, 1958.

_____.  A House of Children.  Garden City, N.Y. Anchor Books, 1962.  [The line indicates the author is same as the one above.]

Correll, Robert M., and Charlton Laird.  Modern English Handbook.  Englewood Cliffs, New Jersey: Prentice-Hall, 1976. [The second author's name is not inverted.]

Daly, Michael.  "The New York Scene."  The Atlantic, September 1978, 66-69.  [Journal and magazine references must include inclusive pagination.]

"Inflation Staggers Mexican Workers."  Chicago Tribune, March 21 1980, p. 1.  [Alphabetize anonymous articles by title.]

Johnson, Abby Arthur, and Ronald M.  "Reform and Reaction: Black Literary Magazines in the 1930s."  North Dakota Quarterly, 46 (July, 1978), 5-8.

---

Footnotes and bibliographies may seem time-consuming and overly complex. But they add concrete support to your writings, revealing to the reader the strength of your sources and the extent of your research.

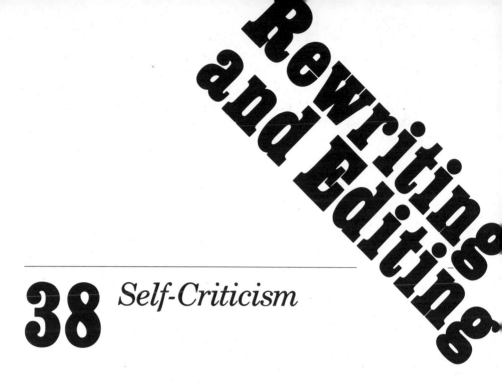

# 38 *Self-Criticism*

Writing about abstract ideas may be the most difficult of all types of writing. The problem is often that writers know precisely what they mean but fail to recognize that their words do not express their meaning. The reader, however, knows only what the words actually say; we can't look into the writer's mind. The old excuse, "I know what I meant," is never an excuse, writers are always responsible for verifying that their words express their intention. That verification occurs during both the rewriting and editing phase. It may involve the slow, thoughtful review of every word and sentence. Not just once, but several times.

## Accuracy and Precision

Several types of accuracy must be checked. Most important is the accuracy of summarized or quoted material. Not only is it a courtesy to the author you are dealing with, but it is also one of the most unbreakable rules of intellectual work: *thou shalt not misquote.* Every word inside a quotation must be accurate, and ideas rephrased in your own words must be accurate to the *sense* of the original. Here is how one student writer expressed an idea he found in Charles W. Ferguson's book *Say It with Words.* I've placed Ferguson's original material to the left for you to compare:

| Ferguson | Student Version |
|---|---|
| No generalization is wholly true, as Disraeli reminds us, including this one, but you will find it of great practical use to husband verbs. | In a chapter called "Mind Your Verbs," Ferguson shows us just how long attention has been paid to verbs: "Disraeli reminds us . . . you will find it of great practical use to husband verbs." And Disraeli was a prime minister of England in 1868! |

The error here is serious. The student believes he has quoted accurately because every word inside the quotation appears in the original. But both Ferguson and Disraeli have been misrepresented. Either from careless reading or in a careless transferral of reading notes to manuscript, the student has botched the whole idea. Ferguson is paraphrasing Disraeli as saying that "no generalization is wholly true." Ferguson offers no indication that Disraeli ever said a word about verbs.

Unfortunately, this type of thing happens all too frequently to all of us when we work under pressure. We read too quickly; we write the paper late at night, glance over it hurriedly for spelling errors, and submit it. Critical thinking, however, demands a slow, attentive concern, not only to ideas others have presented, but to the way you represent those ideas. Here is how another student described a portion of Kate Millett's work on *Sexual Politics*.

| Millett | Student Version |
|---|---|
| . . . it was the Renaissance which furnished the first applied theories of education for women. Alberti's *Della Famiglia* is fairly representative of these. The purpose of such minimal training as it recommends is merely an aesthetic and convenient docility. | Also Millett tells us that the education for women has risen as a sort of modern-day achievement of educating the lower levels of man to simply keep them content and satisfied. This is illustrated when Alberti said in *Della Famiglia,* "The purpose of such minimal training as it recommends is merely an aesthetic and convenient docility." |

Like the previous student, this one has attributed a portion of the author's ideas—this time, Kate Millett's—to someone she has referred to in her text. It was not Alberti who said, "The purpose of such minimal training . . ." Those are Millett's words. But the first part of the student's summary is also inaccurate because the student has not looked closely at his own words and considered what they mean: " . . . the education of women has risen as a sort of modern day achievement *of educating the lower levels of man ...*" Not only does Kate Millett say no such thing; it makes no sense. How can the education of women be aimed at *educating* the lower levels of man? What the student probably means is that Millett believes the education of women is aimed at *satisfying* the lower levels of man. The failure to find the precise word makes a parody of the original material.

Another type of imprecision shows up in this student's paper:

> The stock show champion was sired by a prize steer from Lyndon Johnson's ranch.

President Johnson would no doubt have been surprised that a steer could sire anything, since by definition, a steer is a castrated bull.

Accuracy and precision include historical ideas:

> ... it was Abraham Lincoln who was elected on the promise of freeing the slaves.

Lincoln, of course, promised nothing of the kind and probably would not have been elected if he had. Such a historical inaccuracy casts a dark shadow over the paper as a whole. If a writer can make this kind of error, how can we trust his or her other information to be sound?

A final illustration appears in this freshman analysis of an essay on gun control:

> The First Amendment to the Constitution gives everyone the right to bear arms.

But it is the Second Amendment, not the first, that discusses the right to bear arms. Even the second is not clear as to whether "everyone" has such a right. The precise wording of the amendment may refer only to the right to form a state militia. Did the student verify the number of the amendment or the actual wording? Obviously not.

Accuracy and precision in themselves seldom bring a writer praise; inaccuracy and imprecision will invariably bring condemnation.

## Omissions

From the writer's point of view, the omission of a portion of an argument or even a single word may be terribly difficult to spot. I've often found myself reading a sentence four times before discovering that I've left out something, a phrase or word I could swear was there in print the first three times I read the sentence. Because our mind *knows* what the sentence is supposed to say, it tends to fill in any blanks. Unfortunately, the reader cannot.

Here's a student example I received a few years ago:

> Pitcher advised the divorcing parents to explain divorce to the young child in the following manner: This method will help ease the negative impact of the divorce on the child. Pitcher's method provides divorcing parents with a format that will help minimize the effect of divorce on the child.

The *method* around which the passage focuses is strangely absent. After some questioning the student recognized she had omitted a whole page of handwritten material. As she typed her paper, two pages had apparently stuck together—a simple error that could happen to any of us. But what should *not* have happened is that the student failed to reread her paper. She knew what she had written, but she failed to verify what she had typed.

Here's a different kind of omission:

> Art is also a form of therapy. Participating in creative with other people helps to replace the loss of objects and to express their feelings openly.

As it is impossible to participate in "creative," a word must be missing. Creative *activities*? Creative *efforts*? Creative *arts*? We don't know. Neither do we know what the mention of a "loss of objects" means. It may be possible for participation in creative activities to help people express their feelings. But how does it replace a loss of objects? It turns out that the student had read a pamphlet on various mental problems that art therapists claimed to treat. Somewhere in that pamphlet, an emotional condition was defined as arising out of a loss of "objects" that were of no particular worth, but that held symbolic value for the patient. The student failed to provide that explanation. He knew in his own mind what the phrase meant. After all, he had read the pamphlet. But he failed to consider that his audience had not. A definition or explanation for specialized concepts must occur on the page, not remain buried in the writer's mind. A single missing word can make nonsense of an otherwise valid argument.

# Hidden Assumptions

We may so thoroughly believe something that we fail to realize others do not, that others might consider our beliefs only an *assumption*. If you believe that all human beings have souls, for example, you may argue that because Bob and Maria are human beings, they obviously have souls. The logic of your argument is valid so long as we all agree upon that first premise. Indeed, many reasonable arguments *must* begin with assumptions because we can't possibly know everything. But if you present an argument based on an assumption without realizing that it is an assumption, you may find yourself being challenged.

After an essay in *Fortune* described the struggle between the Environmental Protection Agency and certain large industrialists in the Southwest, a student criticized the essay with the following argument:

> The author has attempted to make us believe that Schrieber, Danforth, Holman, and other factory owners are struggling over a principle involving individual rights. But how many times has that been the rallying cry for self-interest? The Southern states used a similar justification for breaking from the Union just because they didn't want to give up slaves. Actually, the real reason Schrieber and his kind are resisting efforts to clean up the air and water is simple. They are involved in big business. Money is more important than the environment. They have to answer to their stockholders, not to the trees.

The student seems to have presented a forceful argument. The final sentence seems especially strong. He tries to discredit both the author and the industrialists by arguing that their actions are based on self-interest. But what is the student's proof? Answer: *those involved represent "big business."*

Something is missing. The proof rests on a hidden assumption that the student believes his readers share: all those connected with big business are greedy. Money, to such individuals, means more than the common good. Only if we agree with that *assumption* can we find the student's argument valid. If we question such generalities, however, we are in a position to challenge the argument as a whole. Are *all* big business men greedy? Do *all* value money over the welfare of the nation? For a writer, the danger of the hidden assumption is that you may believe you've erected a convincing and logical argument when, in actuality, you've omitted its very foundation. As a result, the whole of it may come tumbling down.

The solution to all these problems—inaccuracy, imprecision, omissions—is to read your paper with the same critical attitude you use when you read someone else's work. You must apply the same criteria of logic, clarity, and concern for detail to your own essay that you expect to find in another's. The process of self-criticism is demanding, time-consuming, and often frustrating. But as Rimbaud once said, "Excellence costs less trouble than mediocrity." You can be sure that if you don't criticise your own work, your audience will. Better to be embarrassed in private than in public.

### EXERCISES

1. Check each of the following passages—all written by students—for inaccuracy, imprecision, or vagueness due to apparent omissions or for other problems that would cause confusion for a reader:

   a. The two doctors are father and son who displayed two very interesting sides about vitamin C. The father told me that for colds, he tries to consult the patient to drink clear liquids. But his son goes much farther and tries to prevent the cold in the first place. Because a cold averages three persons per year, we know that prevention is more vital than cure. The son tries to get his patients to take massive doses of vitamin C before it gets them.

b. John Locke was not very bright if he believed in Natural Law. All scientific evidence shows that there are physical laws, but it is only a form of ego trip to believe that your personal moral values are God-given and form some kind of Natural Law or Absolute Law. John Locke was obviously enculturated into believing that the attitudes of his time were right and all others wrong. As common sense tells us that all men are not created equal, Locke was merely providing an argument that can only be described as wish fulfillment.

c. Burglars are of two varieties, the professional and the amateur. Most thieves are only interested in the merchandise they have come to steal, not inflicting bodily harm. . . . most criminals work no harder than necessary to what they want . . . it is far easier for them to abandon a house with good locks on all doors and windows and look for one less protected," according to *Safety Strategy* by Jack de Celle. And evidence shows that what they want is televisions, tape recorders, and other electrical equipment. This has probably always been true such equipment is easier to sell than say clothes.

d. Katherine Anne Porter was trying to relate war and epidemic in her essay *Pale Horse, Pale Rider,* with epidemic as the rider and war as the horse. The horse carries his rider around, allowing him to cover more territory quicker and easier. Epidemic is not caused by war but war by an epidemic. World War I was a sign of the direction man was heading toward. War, although dating back into the ancient times, is a forerunner of death. War shows all the deathly sides of human nature. It causes people to want to die, to give up their lives, their will to live. There is a close knitting parallel between war and epidemic.

# 39 *The Whole of It*

By now it is clear that rewriting and editing must be seen as more than a step in which a writer alters a few words or checks for spelling. As we approach the final draft, we must consider numerous potential techniques that might be used to create an effective, polished, and professional essay. The checklist that follows may at first seem overwhelming. Actually, it is only an outline of many concepts you've already studied. I offer it here as a reminder. Ideally, each point on it has now become, or will soon become, an intuitive part of your individual skills. As in the learning of any skill, you have begun with conscious instruction, but the goal is to absorb and synthesize through practice until the process is internalized. Not one of the rewriting and editing steps that follow will in itself turn out a good essay. Only your imagination and spirit working through each one—in your own way—will make your work effective and successful.

## A Review
For simplification I've grouped rewriting and editing into six categories. In each category I've listed the most essential questions you should be asking yourself as you edit your way through a final draft.

# Check for Concretions and Specifics

[ ] Have you used sensory details and images that help your reader *see?*

[ ] Do you *show* instead of *tell?*

[ ] Have you used strong nouns and verbs?

[ ] Have you included the elements of scene? _____ Light? _____ Time? _____ Place? _____ Character? _____ Purpose? _____ Five senses?

[ ] Have you included Actions? _____ Physical details? _____ Speech (direct quotation)? _____ Other's reactions?

## Student Draft

In starting a business a proprietor often finds it hard to get enough capital together. Sam Harris, founder of SAGA Sheet Metal, told me how hard it was for him in the beginning. Nobody would put up the capital for him to make things he knew would be successful. Finally, he had to get some funds from his father-in-law for him to start production in a small building.

## Edited Version

In starting a business, a proprietor often finds it hard to borrow money. Sam Harris, founder and president of SAGA Sheet Metal, is an example. As he guided me around several twenty-ton pressing machines in his current factory on East Los Angelos Boulevard, he told me about how hard it had been for him in the beginning. "Bankers just laughed at me," he shouted over the banging presses. "I remember one of them told me to quit dreaming and get a decent job." Harris led me into a carpeted office. Through the glass window he could look out over half an acre of metal works and foundry equipment. Two secretaries typed away behind short partitions. His desk was stacked with paper work. Harris sat down and lit a cigar. "I finally had to borrow from my wife's father—seven hundred. Just enough to set myself up in an old garage."

# Check for Word Choice and Sentence Effectiveness

[ ] Have you searched for the right word instead of the almost right word?

[ ] Are the connotations appropriate and effective?

[ ] Have you eliminated every unnecessary word?

[ ] Have you eliminated unnecessary *whos, whiches, theres,* and *thats*?

[ ] Have you eliminated clichés?

[ ] Have you read aloud and listened to the rhythms of your own sentences?

[ ] Have you avoided pretentious language? _____Jargon? _____Circumlocutions?

[ ] Have you tried to express complex ideas in simple terms?

---

Student Draft

High fidelity audiophiles show a marked inclination toward the open reel format over the cassette concept. There are reasons for this that are very important. First, the speed that the cassette tape travels is very slow, relatively speaking, while the open reel tape advances at 1-1/2 inches per second, making for a consequential compression of the audio input on the cassette tape that produces audible distortion in the woofers and tweeters.

Edited Version

Lovers of high fidelity prefer the open reel format to the cassette format. A cassette tape travels at a relatively slow 1-1/8 inches per second while the open reel travels at 1-1/2 inches per second. The music on the cassette tape must therefore be compressed into a smaller space. The result causes distortion in woofers (base frequencies) and tweeters (high-pitched frequencies).

# Check for Paragraph Coherence and Unity

[ ] Have you organized each paragraph around a central, unifying idea?

[ ] Could the reader find a sentence in each paragraph that clearly states the topic or theme of the paragraph?

[ ] Does each paragraph have a point of emphasis?

[ ] Is each idea clearly connected to the next with a direct or implied transition?

[ ] Are ideas related through "hooks"? _____ Through controlled repetition? _____ Through "tags"? _____ Through parallel structure? _____

## Student Draft

The images can be separated from the poem through analysis, but the poem is actually a "whole" that includes the images as only one part of it, and they should not really be separated. A study of Donne's imagery helps us understand Donne as a poet. He wrote it as a farewell to his wife before leaving on a diplomatic mission to France in 1612. It brings us closer to the poem. Donne does not stop with one comparison. The compass metaphor extends through the last three stanzas expanding (like a compass's legs) showing the fixed relationship of the lovers and how no matter what the distance, they are drawn back again: "Thy firmness drawes my circle just,/And makes me end, where I begunne." A circle symbolizes perfection and unity. The firmness of the imagery draws the circle of the poem and makes it end where it begins.

## Edited Version

A study of Donne's imagery helps us understand Donne as a poet and brings us closer to the poem. For example, the image of the compass, the most important image in the poem, extends through three stanzas. Donne shows us how the relationship between himself and his wife is so fixed that they are always drawn back to each other. Donne may leave her side, but like the twin foot of a compass, he but circles her: "Thy firmness drawes my circle just,/And makes me end, where I begunne." The circle symbolizes perfection and unity. In a similar way, the firmness of the metaphor completes the circle of our reading and should remind us that although such images can be separated from the poem, the poem cannot be separated from the imagery.

# Check for Logic and Accuracy

---

[ ] Have you evaluated and eliminated your own bias whenever possible?

[ ] Have you avoided arguments that depend upon emotions or stereotypes?

[ ] Have you attempted to eliminate oversimplification? _____ Overgeneralizations? _____ Undefined abstractions? _____ False analogies? _____ Name calling? _____ Appeals to emotion?

[ ] Have you checked quotations, statistics, dates, and your own statements for accuracy?

[ ] Have you considered whether your arguments are built on hidden assumptions?

---

### Student Draft

Pornography is writing, pictures, etc., intended to arouse dirty feelings. The naked body is very personal and should not be viewed by just anyone. People shouldn't share their bodies with anyone except the man (or woman) they intend to marry. Magazines such as *Playboy* are not only pornographic, but also dirty. They portray poses of women (or men) in outrageous positions that sicken everybody. The perverts that read such things are sick and should be treated by psychiatrists. Sex is really a beautiful experience to be shared privately by two people in love. Unless something is done to stop it, love will be destroyed as we know it.

### Edited Version

Pornography is intended to arouse sexual desire. Magazines such as *Playboy* show pictures of women and men in various states of nudity. Sometimes the photos show couples in simulated sexual acts involving different positions. Although some readers may not be offended, I am. I believe that sex should be shared only by two people in love and not exposed for public titillation and profit. I will attempt to show that pornography is destructive to the privacy of love that I value.

# Check for Mechanics

[ ] Have you reviewed each sentence for basic grammar and standard usage?

[ ] Have you proofread for spelling?

[ ] Have you double-checked the accuracy and form of each footnote?

[ ] Have you checked the form of bibliographic entries down to the last comma and period?

| Student Draft | Edited Version |
|---|---|
| Some cities have objected to fluridation because they consider it forced medication,Christian Scientists even object that it violates their religious freedom. "In states where the issue has been litigated" according to the Salt *Lake City Tribune*, "the highest courts have held that flouridation is mass medication and does not infringe on any constitutional rights".[1] Some people do not except this however. | Some cities have objected to fluoridation because they consider it forced medication; Christian Scientists even object that it violates their religious freedom. "In states where the issue has been litigated," according to the *Salt Lake City Tribune*, "the highest courts have held that fluoridation is not mass medication and does not infringe on any constitutional rights."[1] Some people do not accept this as final, however. |

---

[1] *Salt Lake City Tribune,* "New Court Challenge to Fluridation January 21, 1974.

[1] "New Court Challenge to Fluoridation," *Salt Lake City Tribune,* January 21, 1974, p. 1.

# Check for Form and Organization

[ ] Have you attempted to visualize the design of your paper?

[ ] Have you outlined either before or after the first draft?

[ ] If you've used an imaginative lead, does it truly *lead* into the basic theme of your paper?

[ ] Does your introduction provide a general overview of the subject in a few brief sentences?

[ ] Does the introduction provide historical or cultural context when necessary?

[ ] Does your introduction clearly focus the reader's attention toward a narrow aspect of the subject you plan to deal with in detail?

[ ] Is the body of your paper organized around a pattern? _____ From most important to least important, or from least important to most? _____ Around contrasting views? _____ According to a narrative time sequence? _____ According to a logical argument?

[ ] Does the conclusion summarize, interpret, evaluate, or assess the findings actually presented in the body of the paper?

[ ] Is your typed manuscript organized according to a standard and acceptable format?

A review of this nature can at best jog your memory. To be certain that you can apply the many points presented here, test your editing skills on the exercise that follows.

**EXERCISE**

Here are the first four pages of an actual student research paper (I've changed the name to protect the not-so-innocent). Read it through completely before you consider what suggestions you would make to the author for editing and rewriting; then use the checklists in this chapter as guides for a line-by-line editing review. When the errors or omissions are too serious to correct on the page, clearly indicate what the writer needs to accomplish to turn this into a satisfactory essay. Discuss the changes you would recommend with others in your class.

RELIGIOUS VIEWS ON EUTHANASIA

by

Clyde Careless

The theme of my paper is the many difficult decisions arising from the euthanasia conflect and not only how they affect the medical and legal professions, but also religious beliefs.

The definition of euthanasia is a Greek word for "happy death." The context it usually takes concerns "the killing either voluntarily or compulsorily of those suffering from incurable disease, old age or serious physical handicaps."[1]  It can be further broken down into two main categories passive euthanasia and active euthanasia.  Many of the religious ideas on euthanasia make use of this distinction.

---

1.  N. St. John Stevas, "Euthanasia: A Pleasant Sounding Word," America, 132 (May 31, 1975)

In the Portestant faith, alone, there is a
wide range of viewpoints.  Some Portestant theologians condemn euthanasia, like Robert M. Cooper.
Cooper is an assistant professor of ethic and moral
theology at Nashtoah House (Episcopal), Nashotah,
Wisconsin.  Cooper feels that "The evil greater than
pain is to deny that pain radically an ingredient of
the human condition."[2]

Passive euthanasia is to allow death to come
gently.  Supportive measures are not used to prolong
the dying process where there is irreversible brain
damage and intractable pain.[3]  But however, active
euthanasia involves the process in which a doctor
gives a fatal dosage of a drug to a hopelessly ill
person.[3a]

He goes on to give what he thinks is as good a

---

[2] Robert M. Cooper, Christian Century, "Euthanasia and the Notion of Death with Dignity", 90
(February 21, 1973) pp 225.

[3] Nancy Littel Fox, L.P.N., "A Good Birth, A
Good Life, Why Not a Good Death?" (New York: The
Euthanasia Educational Council Bulletin, 250 W.
57th St., New York, N.Y. 10019, 1974)

[3a] Richard Trubo, p. 89

definition of "death with dignity" as any.  Death

with dignity is lost when "pain so intense as to be

unendurable degrades the sufferer, robs him of his

dignity.[4]  Most Protestant theological leaders be-

lieve that euthanasia can be permitted under cer-

tain circumstances.  Joseph Flecther, professor of

biomedical ethics, believes that for the most part

euthanasi, direct or indirect, voluntary (suicide)

or involuntary, depends on the situation concerning

right or wrong.[(5)]  Fletcher believes that we should

forget the traditional "sanctity-of-life" ethic and

incorporate a "quality-of-life" ethic, because "per-

sonal integrity is more important than biological

survival."[6]

The Catholic views are divided.  One well-known

concept among Catholic theologians is the situa-

tional theory.  Maguire asserts that "no system of

----

[4]Cooper, p 225

[5]Flecchner, Joseph, "The 'Right' to Live and
the 'Right' to Die: a Protestant View of Euthanasia,
"The Humanist," 34 (July, 1974), 14.

[6]Daniel C. Maguire, "A Catholic View of
Mercy Killing," The Humanist 34 (July, 1974), pp
16-18.

ethics could know the morality or immorality of an

action or process without being sensitive to the

situational factors that make up the reality of the

case."[7]   This means they base their decision for

or against euthanasia on the condition of a par-

ticular case.   They don't have a fixed opinion on

the rights or wrongs of euthanasia in general.

---

[7] Daniel C. Maguire, "A Catholic View of
Mercy Killing," The Humanist 34 (July, 1974), pp
16-18.

---

Donna Pastor was a freshman speech major when she wrote the following research paper. As you read through it, consider all the various techniques Donna has used. Notice how she has begun with an imaginative lead and followed it with a formal introduction; consider whether the informality of the lead conflicts with the serious treatment of her subject; notice how definitions and background are integrated with contrasting opinions throughout her text; finally, decide whether her conclusion is soundly based on her evidence. Ask the most important questions of all: is it interesting? Do you learn something from it?

DISORDER? OR JUST DIFFERENT?

by

Donna Pastor

"Oh we get a lot of terms, and I guess we prefer 'gay people.' But we hate to be sort of set off
from everybody else--we want to be known as just
people." As the quiet young man in the jeans and
nondescript shirt speaks, my eyes follow his mouth
and I nod to let him know I'm listening. There he
sits. Gary Donn, Ohio State University student,
active member of the Columbus Gay Activist Alliance,
and self-acknowledged homosexual. A thousand images
race through my mind. Is this the sick man whose
maladjusted mind leaves him incapable of leading a
"normal" sex life? The effeminate pervert whose
abnormal longings force him to trail other men and
little boys in hopes of performing unnatural sexual

acts? Is this the fag, the queer, the fairy who provokes disgust in ordinary people? Funny, he doesn't look like it.

In fact, according to the Institute for Sex Research at Indiana University, only fifteen percent of all male homosexuals are easily recognizable.[1] Many homosexuals appear to be completely masculine, athletic types. Shirley Braverman of the Jewish Hospital School of Nursing in St. Louis reports that most homosexuals are "ordinary-looking" people with "otherwise ordinary interests."[2] The stereotype of the homosexual child molester may be similarly dispelled by evidence indicating that more male heterosexuals are interested in young girls than male homosexuals in young boys.[3] Not every homosexual lurks around schoolyards waiting to entice unsuspecting youngsters with candy and dirty pictures. The majority of homosexual child molesta-

---

[1] J. Gramick, "Myths of Homosexuality," Intellect, 102 (November, 1973), 105.

[2] Shirley J. Braverman, "Homosexuality," American Journal of Nursing, 73 (April, 1973), 652.

[3] Ibid.

-3-

tions involve relatives and acquaintances of the child.

Homosexuality as a mental illness is the most controversial aspect of the homosexual image. Is the person with an emotional or erotic preference for members of one's own sex victim of a pathologic disorder, or is he or she merely an individual exercising personal preference? Does homosexuality represent deviant behavior, or is it just another facet of human sexuality? Present opinion is greatly divided.

Sigmund Freud identifies two types of homosexuality. Facultative or situational homosexuality involves someone who has genital sex with a person of the same sex but really prefers those of the opposite gender. This is simply a matter of sexual deprivation common in prisons and on long sea voyages and is not considered a sexual disorder (mental illness). On the other hand, obligatory homosexuality deals with the person who exclusively wants relations with members of the same sex.[4] It is

---

[4] Richard Green, "Homosexuality as a Mental Illness," International Journal of Psychiatry, 10 (March, 1972), 77-78.

-4-

this type of homosexuality that has psychiatrists
puzzled.

Prior to December 15, 1973, institutional psychiatry considered homosexual behavior to be due to
something gone wrong in an otherwise normal human
being, and the American Psychiatric Association
officially spoke of "disorders." But on December
15, the American Psychiatric Association's thirteen-
member board of trustees voted unanimously to remove
homosexuality from its category of mental illness.[5] This ruling came after extensive gay
lobbying and endorsement of the change in classification by all of the American Psychiatric Association's sixty-eight district branches.[6] The new
official definition uses the term <u>sexual orientation disturbance</u> as a category for "individuals
whose sexual interests are directed toward people of
their own sex and by, in conflict with, or wish to

---

[5] R. E. Gould, "What We Don't Know About
Homosexuality," <u>New York Times Magazine</u> (February
24, 1974), 13.

[6] "Instant Cure; Controversy Over Ruling on
Homosexuality by the American Psychiatric Association," <u>Time</u>, 103 (April 1, 1974), 45.

-5-

change, [sic] their sexual orientations."[7]

When asked to clarify "sexual orientation dis-
turbance," Robert Spitzer, spokesman for the nomen-
clature committee responsible for the text of the
resolution, replied that the trustees were not defining homosexuality as either "normal" or "abnormal," but merely stating that homosexuality in
itself is not a psychiatric disorder. He added
that, even though the ruling was vaguely worded,
the American Psychiatric Association's reversal was
real, not imaginary.[8]

The December ruling generated considerable disagreement within the American Psychiatric Association itself. For the first time in the association's 129 years, enough signatures were collected
by dissenters to put a board decision to a vote of
its entire 21,000 members. The outcome is still
uncertain, but Judd Marmor, anti-illness theory
advocate and psychiatrist at the Cedars-Sinai Medi-

---

[7] Richard D. Lyons, "Psychiatrists Review
Stand on Homosexuals," New York Times, 24 (February 9, 1973), 1.

[8] Ibid., 25.

-6-

cal Center in Los Angeles, fears a repeal of the
resolution. He warned that "psychiatrists are not
immune to their culture."[9]

The American culture, according to a study of
193 cultures by Hock and Zubin, authors of Psycho-
sexual Development in Health and Disease, seems to
be in the minority in its rejection of male homosexuality. Hock and Zubin's statistics reveal that
twenty-eight percent of the cultures studied accepted male homosexuality, fourteen percent rejected
it, and fifty-eight percent demonstrated partial
acceptance. A similar study of 225 American Indian
cultures reports that fifty-three percent of them
accepted male homosexuality, whereas only twenty-four
percent rejected it. An interesting observation is
that overt homosexuality was probably practiced
more among the cowboys of the nineteenth century
"Wild West" than among any other group of United
States males.[10]

---

[9] Time, 45.

[10] Wardell B. Pomeroy, The Same Sex; an
Appraisal of Homosexuality (Philadelphia: Pilgrim
Press, 1969), pp. 4-8.

-7-

Just how did current American attitudes toward homosexuality develop? The basis for these attitudes can be traced back to Judaism five centuries B.C. When the Jews returned from exile in the fifth century before Christ their Talmudic laws on sex--including homosexuality--had become very strict. Their laws on sex became the basis for the ecclesiastical laws of the Middle Ages. In England the administration of sex laws continued to belong to the Church for many years, even after the signing of the Magna Charta in 1215. The Church's abhorrence of homosexuality was incorporated into the system of English common law, under which homosexual behavior was considered a felony. Thus the United States' legal system, which was founded on the basis of English common law, took a similar position on the matter.[11] American antihomosexual attitudes are thus reflected in both legal and theological aspects.

Most contemporary psychiatric attitudes are based on the theories of Sigmund Freud. According

---

[11] Ibid., 5-6.

-8-

to Freud's libido theory, a male child's instinctual
sex drive has to be formed during the Oedipal phase
for him to have a healthy sex life later.  The
Oedipal phase occurs between the years of six and
eight and involves the boy's desire for his mother
as his first love object. [12]  The boy goes through
a period of sexual rivalry with his father, which
ends successfully when he identifies with his father
and looks for a woman like his mother.  Failure to
solve this Oedipal conflict can take many forms,
each of which potentially forms the basis for a
variety of sexual disorders, including homosexuality.  In an "inverted Oedipal complex," the boy
hates his mother for liking his father better, so he
rejects her in favor of his father.  The father then
becomes the boy's first homosexual love object.
Freud considered all humans basically bisexual and

---

[12] Freud, along with nearly everyone else,
was less than clear in discussing female homosexuality.  He formulated complex causative theories
similar to those responsible for male homosexuality.  These models generally reversed parental
roles and cited the homosexual female's envy of the
penis as causing her to act "masculine."  Freud's
attitude now makes him extremely unpopular with the
Women's Liberation Movement.

-9-

felt that if a boy had more "passive" ("feminine") elements in his nature, he might be unable to solve his Oedipal conflict. [13]

Another of Freud's causative models for homosexuality is narcissism. This theory deals with the boy who grows up looking for an idealized image of himself, whom he will love as he would have wanted his mother or father to love him. Narcissism is especially likely to occur in the boy who is attached to his mother but whose father is absent or detached. It is also likely for this condition to cause fear of women owing to unconscious castration anxiety or to expected punishment from other men for wanting a woman sexually. [14]

Freud postulated that although humans are basically bisexual, a boy whose innate "maleness" is right will make the "correct sexual object choice." [15] Homosexuality was considered by Freud to be an arrest of sexual development. Because Freud

---

[13] Gould, 13.

[14] Ibid., 51.

[15] Ibid., 63.

-10-

saw homosexuality as a perversion, he considered it
to be incurable by treatment. Most analysts today,
however, consider homosexuality to be a neurosis,
the antithesis of perversion, and therefore treat-
able.[16]    Most of the leading modern authorities
on homosexuality who favor the sickness theory that
has been dominant in psychiatry base their theories
on Freud. The most notable of these was the late
Edmund Bergler, a Vienna-born psychiatrist, who felt
that homosexuality is a regression to the oral
stage, lowest level of psychic development, in which
the male homosexual substitutes the penis for his
mother's breast. He was convinced that "There are
no happy homosexuals."[17]

Recently, however, more attention has been paid
to nonsickness views. Supporters of theories that
consider homosexuality to be merely a normal preference within the range of human sexuality include
Judd Marmor, Alfred Kinsey, and Evelyn Hooker. Judd

---

[16] Lional Ovesey, M.D., Homosexuality and
Pseudohomosexuality (New York: Science House, 1969),
pp. 16-19.

[17] Gould, 54.

-11-

Marmor writes that "homosexuality in itself merely

represents a variant sexual preference which our

society disapproves of but which does not constitute

a mental illness."[18]  Marmor argues against the

disturbed-family causal theory, holding that many

homosexuals' families are not the classic homo-

sexual producing "type."[19]  Marmor also defends

homosexuality by citing comparative psychologist and

census-taker of animal sexuality, Frank Beach.

Beach feels that whereas many animals will at times

show "homosexual" behavior, there aren't any ex-

amples of animals that are exclusively "hetero-

sexual."  He further explains that "human homo-

sexuality reflects the essential bisexual character

of our mammalian inheritance.  The extreme modi-

ficability of human sex life makes possible the

conversion of this essential bisexuality into a

_____

[18] "Psychiatrists, in a Shift, Declare Homosexuality No Mental Illness," New York Times, December 16, 1973, p. 1.

[19] Gould, 54.

-12-

form of unisexuality. . . ."[20]  Beach adds that
both exclusive homosexuality and heterosexuality
are unique to humans.

A warning, however, comes from psychologist
Robert E. Gould, author of <u>What</u> <u>We</u> <u>Don't</u> <u>Know</u> <u>About</u>
<u>Homosexuality</u>, concerning the use of animal studies.
Gould charges that it is easy to find studies that
suggest that homosexuality is "normal" or "abnormal."  He also notes that behavior norms in animals are not necessarily applicable to humans.  He
is supported by Dr. Beach himself: "The concept of
normality is species-limited."  The higher one goes
in the mammalian scale, the less important is the
role of hormonal and instinctual drives compared to
social and cultural conditioning.[21]

Finally, Marmor contends that homosexuality and
heterosexuality are just different areas on a "broad
spectrum of human sexual behavior."  Neither type
of behavior can be considered by psychiatrists more

---

[20] Judd Marmor, "Homosexuality: Mental Ill-
ness or Moral Dilemma?" <u>International</u> <u>Journal</u> <u>of</u>
<u>Psychiatry</u>, 10 (March, 1972),  34.

[21] Gould, 63.

-13-

or less "natural" than the other because the sci-

entist must approach his data on a nonevaluative

level.[22]  Martin Hoffman, psychiatrist at the

University of California Medical School in San

Francisco, agrees that the labeling of homosexu-

ality as a "disorder," regardless of unproved causal

theories, does not result unless an "evaluative

judgment independent of the research data is inter-

posed somewhere along this line of reasoning."  He

concludes, "We cannot describe behavioral events as

examples of health or illness."[23]

Another expert important in refuting the "homo-

sexuality as a mental illness" claim is California

psychiatrist Evelyn Hooker, whose classic study con-

cludes that there is no relation between homosexual

orientation and clinical symptoms of mental ill-

ness.  In this study, thirty well-adjusted non-

treatment homosexuals were matched with thirty

heterosexuals having approximately the same age,

---

[22] Green, 94.

[23] Martin Hoffman, "Homosexuality as a Mental
Illness: Philosophic, Empirical, and Ecologic Re-
marks," International Journal of Psychiatry, 10
(March, 1972), 107.

-14-

education, and IQ.  Dr. Hooker gave all of them a battery of psychological tests and then submitted the results to clinicians for analysis.  The experts were unable to distinguish between the two groups.[24]

Well-known research psychiatrist Alfred Kinsey also raises the question of the difficulty in defining "normality" and "abnormality."  In a 1948 study, Kinsey compared the "normal" sex practices of 12,000 United States men based on years of formal education.  For example, "male mouth-female genital" contact is fairly normal (one in two) for persons with thirteen or more years of education.  But the same sex practice is considered "abnormal" for those with nine to twelve years of education (one in six) and eight or less years (one in twenty-five).  Variance in sex practices is also related to factors such as religion, age, and residence (urban or rural).  In reviewing the study, Kinsey states that:

. . . 'abnormal' may designate certain indi-

---

[24] Evelyn Hooker, "The Adjustment of the Male Overt Homosexual," _Journal_ _of_ _Projective_ _Technique_, 21 (February, 1957), 101.

-15-

viduals . . . whose sources of sexual outlet
are not as usual in the population as a whole;
but in that case, it is preferable to refer to
such persons as rare; rather than abnormal . . .[25]

He adds that many items labeled as "abnormal" or
"perversions" in textbooks occur in as many as thirty
to seventy-five percent of certain populations.[26]

A similar objection to the use of definitions
comes from P. J. O'Connor, who feels that with a
definition of psychiatric illness as "a state of
mind which causes discomfort to the patient or to
society," seventy-six percent of his homosexual subjects are neurotic.[27] Their "discomfort due to a state
of mind" is primarily anxiety. But, as O'Connor points
out, if a more severe definition of "neurotic illness" is used, then most of his group is not ill.

Concerning definitions, Franklin E. Kameny, the

---

[25] Green, 85-86.

[26] Ibid., 85-86.

[27] Graham Robertson, "Parent-Child Relationships and Homosexuality," British Journal of Psychiatry, 121 (November, 1972), 527.

-16-

man who coined the phrase "gay is good" and who is one of the driving forces in the move for homosexual freedom in the United States, wrote bitterly, "We have been defined into sickness by a mixture of cultural, theological, moral, and sociological value judgments camouflaged in the language of science."[28]

Psychiatry does not have the data on which to base judgments that homosexuality is or is not a mental illness. First of all, there are too many conflicting theories. None of them have been "proved" because valid data does not seem to be obtainable. A true cross section of the homosexual population is not possible when the number of homosexuals can only be estimated. Animal studies can support either side, and studies of psychiatric patients are one-sided. Finally, the difficulty of even defining "mental illness" makes it impossible to draw a line between what is preference and what is illness.

---

[28]Franklin E. Kameny, "Gay Liberation and Psychiatry," The Homosexual Dialectic (ed.), Joseph A. McCaffrey (Englewood Cliffs, New Jersey: Prentice-Hall, Inc., 1972), p. 187.

-17-

I realize that some will argue that it is necessary to decide whether homosexuality is a mental
illness so that homosexuals can be properly classified. But does it really matter? I tend to agree
with Franklin University psychologist and guidance
counselor Kerm Rogers. "I'm not too sure where
homosexuality belongs in terms of mental illness,"
he says. "What I worry about in treating the person
is whether he wants to adjust to his homosexuality
or to become heterosexual. Then I help him the
best I can." [29]

My mind flashes back to the image of young
Gary Donn of the Columbus Gay Activists Alliance,
sitting calmly in a lounge chair directly facing
me. Is it so important to categorize him as a
member of a stereotyped group? Isn't it better to
recognize him simply as an individual and to accept
him as different from the majority, regardless of
whether or not he's technically "ill"? I say it is.

---

[29] Interview with Kerm Rogers, guidance
counselor, Franklin University, November 16, 1975.

-18-

BIBLIOGRAPHY


Braverman, Shirley, J.  "Homosexuality."  American
    Journal of Nursing, 73 (April, 1973), 652-655.

Gould, R. E.  "What We Don't Know About Homosexu-
    ality."  New York Times, February 24, 1974,
    pp. 12-13.

Gramick, J.  "Myths of Homosexuality."  Intellect,
    102 (November, 1973), 104-107.

Green, Richard  "Homosexuality as a Mental Illness."
    International Journal of Psychiatry, 10 (March,
    1972),77-98.

Hooker, Evelyn.  "Adjustment of the Male Overt Homo-
    sexual."  Journal of Protective Techniques, 21
    (February, 1957),97-119.

"Instant Cure: Controversy Over Ruling on Homosexu-
    ality by the American Psychiatric Associa-
    tion."  Time, April 1, 1974, 45.

Lyons, Richard D.  "Psychiatrists Review Stand on
    Homosexuals."  New York Times, February 9,
    1973, p. 1.

Marmor, Judd.  "Homosexuality: Mental Illness or
    Moral Dilemma?"  International Journal of Psy-
    chiatry, 10 (March, 1972), 114-117.

Pomeroy, Wardell B.  Same Sex: An Appraisal of Homo-
    sexuality.  Philadelphia: Pilgrim Press, 1969.

"Psychiatrists in a Shift Declare Homosexuality No
    Mental Illness."  New York Times, December 16,
    1973, p. 1.

# Index

Abstraction, 17–22; undefined, 313
Accuracy, 46; checklist for, 466; in
    quoting and paraphrasing, 456–458; in
    logic, 312–317; in note-taking, 436; of
    word choice, 46–50
Actions (in description), 84
Active voice (*see* Verbs)
Adverbs, 58
Adjectives, 57–58
Agee, James, 12–13, 29
Analogies, false, 314–315
Analysis, 243–244; cause and effect,
    245–246, 392; critical, 321–325, 390;
    item, 244–245; process, 245; structure
    of in formal essay, 337–342
Anderson, Sherwood, 376
Antecedents, correct, 284–285
Arts, appreciation of, 359–367
Audience, for literary critique, 389–391;
    for objective reporting, 133–134; for
    personal writing, 31–32; importance of,
    3–4; influence on tone, 254; influence
    on vocabulary, 253; influence on voice,
    254
Austin, James H., 417

Bernstein, Carl, 177–178
Bertagnolli, Olivia, 92–93
Bibliography, 425; bibliography card,
    431–432; correct forms, 454–455;
    reference works, 425; use in research,
    425–426; working bibliography,
    426–427
Boorstin, Daniel J., 276
Boroson, Warren, 260
Bostic, Mark, 96
Bourne, Lyle E., Jr., 249
Brackets, use of, 293
Bradbury, Ray, 5, 87
Brooks, Gwendolyn, 401
Brooks, Sandra, 88
Brownmiller, Susan, 303
Bunyan, John, 224

Card catalog, 426
Carlson, Peter, 26
Carson, Rachel, 171, 223, 276
Categorizing, 442–443
Cause and effect, 245–246; faulty, 312
Change, as perception strategy, 126, 128,
    182

Character, 81–87
Character sketch, actions, 84;
    background, 85; chronological
    ordering, 75–77; first draft, 95; general
    to specific, 92–93; others' reactions,
    85–86; perception of character, 82–86;
    physical description, 83–84; scene,
    elements of, 91–92; selecting details,
    75–77; self-created environment, 84–85;
    specific to general, 94–95; speech, 84
Characterization, as perception strategy,
    86, 127, 128, 182; in fiction and drama,
    381
Chase, Alton, 223
Chronological order, 77
Churchill, Winston, 38
Circumlocution, 279
Clark, Elizabeth Breed, 169
Classification, 241–242
Cliché, 26–28
Coherence, 268–274
Colloquial usage, 36
Colons, 293
Commas, 291
Comparison and contrast, 240–241
Completeness, in paragraph, 218
Conclusions, in analytical essays, 341–342;
    in expository essays, 265–266; in
    literary critique, 393–394
Concretions, 17–22; checklist for, 463
Conflict, as perception strategy, 126, 128,
    182, 240–241
Connotation, 48; in poetry, 382
Conroy, Frank, 15–16
Consequences, as perception strategy,
    127, 128, 182
Context, 133–134
Contractions, 288
Contrast, as perception strategy, 126, 128,
    182, 240–241
Critical analysis (*see* Formal analysis)
Critical reading, for ideas and meaning,
    321–325; for literary values, 373–384
Critique (*see* Literary critique)
Crowley, Hal, 151
Cummings, E. E., 387

Definition, 242–243
Description, describing actions, 84;
    focusing, 74–77; in character sketch,
    73–78; its use in literary critique,

Description (*continued*)
390–393; physical, 83–84; selection of details, 76–77; techniques in, 74–75
Denotation, 46; in poetry, 382
Design (*see* Form)
Details, importance of, 117–118; in description, 76–77; in factual investigation, 181–182; in personal writing, 11–14
Dickens, Charles, 82
Dictionaries, use of, 291; specialized, 422
Didion, Joan, 79
Dillard, Annie, 21
Doctorow, E. L., 59
Documentation, in text, 194–196
Double negatives, 288
Drake, Pamela J., 299
Drama, basic elements, 381

Editing, 7–8, 53; for sentence emphasis, 158–163; for sentence rhythm, 155–156; for sentence variety, 156–158; for unnecessary words, 53–59; for verbs, 100–103; proofreading, 296–297; review of, 462–468; the paragraph, 220–222
Editorial checklists, for character sketch, 105; for factual investigation, 226; for critical analysis, 349; for formal essay, 298; for literary critique, 399; for personal essay, 61; for objective report, 166
Eiseley, Loren, 108
Eliot, Jane Winslow, 136
Ell, Sandie, 106
Ellipsis, 293
Emotion, education of, 360; interference with perception, 118–121; relation to form in literature, 383. *See also* Connotation
Emphasis, in paragraphing, 218–220; through balanced sentences, 160–161; through parallelism, 158–160; through periodic sentences, 161–162; through word order, 162
Encyclopedias, 421–422
Euphemism, 279
Evaluating sources, 131
Exclamation mark, 161
Expository essay, analysis, 243–246; audience for, 253; classification, 241–242; comparison and contrast, 240–241; definition, 242–243; form, 254–259, 265–266; purpose of, 266; relationship to writing process, 246–248; thesis statement, use of, 255–257

Facts, 119; as evidence, 186; compared to inferences and opinions, 119–121; evaluating worth of, 185–186; interpreting, 186–187; objective investigation of, 175–187, 196–198; perception of, 125; relation to 5 *W* lead, 139–141; relation to imagination, 183–185; relation to objectivity, 118–119; strategies for finding, 128–129, 181–182
Fallacies (*see* Logic)
Feeling, role of in objective essays, 182–183
Ferlinghetti, Lawrence, 403
Fiction, basic elements, 381
Figurative language (in poetry), 382
First drafts, 5–6; in critical analysis, 342–343; in research paper, 450–451; relation to "failure," 40–42; relation to 5 *W* lead, 139; relation to imaginative leads, 206–207; relation to scene, 95; right mental attitude, 42–43
5 *W* lead, 139–141, 143–144, 182
5 *W*'s, as perception strategy, 182; in critical reading, 378–379; in documentation, 195–196; in scholarly research, 423
Focusing statement, 255–257, 339, 443–445
Focusing the subject, 178–181; descriptive focus, 74–77; in research, 422–424; narrative focus, 77–78; through analysis, 243–246; through classification, 241–242; through comparison and contrast, 240–241; through definition, 242–243
Footnote forms, 451–453
Form, body of essay, 257–259; checklist for, 468; discovery of, 4–5; 5 *W* leads, 139–141, 143–144, 182; general to specific, 92–94; in a scene, 90–95; in formal essay, 253–257; in literary critique, 391–395; in objective report, 139–144; introductions, 254–257, 337–339; review of techniques, 445–446; specific to general, 94–95; visual designs, 210–215, 258–259
Formal analysis, conclusions, 341–342; first draft, 342–343; introductions, 337–338; objective analysis, 339–341; relation to critical reading, 321–325, 331–334; relation to critical thinking, 309–317; thesis sentence, 339
4 *C*'s, 125–128, 182; as method of organizing, 442; relation to research, 423

Gaylin, Willard, 439
Geisel, Theodore, 41
Generalizations, 17–20; writing about, 237–240

Giacometti, Alberto, 361
Grammar, 283. *See also* Usage

Hall, Donald, 111
Hardy, Thomas, 400
Hasty conclusions, 313
Havens, Jim, 392
Hayakawa, S. I., 19–20
Hemingway, Ernest, 45
Hidden assumptions, 459–460
Hinkle, David, 62
Hogarth, William, 123
Honesty, 24–28
Hooks, 270–271
Humanistic heritage, 366–367

Images, 20–21; in literature, 382
Imagination, role of in objective essays,
    183–185
Indexes, 424–425
Inference, 119–120, 187; compared to
    opinions, 121
Integrating quotations and summaries,
    150, 151
Interpretation, 185–187, 390–393
Interviewing, 128–131
Introductions, in critical analysis,
    337–339; in formal essay, 254–257; in
    literary critique, 391–392; in research
    paper, 448–450. *See also* Leads
Item analysis, 244–245
Inverted pyramid, 141–145, 211

Jackson, Bruce, 73–74
Jargon, 277–280
Jefferson, Thomas, 208
Johnson, Samuel, 21
Joyce, James, 208

Kennedy, John F., 160
Key, Diane, 395
Kline, Morris, 138
Knowles, John, 95
Kohl, Judith and Herbert, 137

Language, relation to perception, 17–19
Lawrence, D. H., 271, 385
Leads, 201–202; contrast, 202–203;
    cumulative interest, 204–205;
    descriptive, 205–206; discovery of,
    206–207; dramatic, 202; 5 *W*, 139–141;
    joined with introductions, 448–450;
    question, 203–204; relation to form,
    211–215
Lester, Julius, 64
Levertov, Denise, 402
Lewis, C. S., 321, 325
Library research (*see* Research)
Lincoln, Abraham, 155

Line, Les, 135
Listening, as editing technique, 222; in
    interviews, 130; to your own prose,
    154–163, 222
Literary critique, audience, 389–390;
    conclusions, 393–394; critical process,
    390–391; introduction, 391;
    organization, 392–393; relation to
    critical reading, 374–376, 380–383;
    relation to emotion, 383; sensory
    perception, need for, 360
Logic, appeals to emotion, 315; deductive
    reasoning, 316; emotional blocks, 314;
    false analogies, 314; hasty conclusions,
    313; hidden assumptions, 459–460;
    inferences, 119–121, 187; misleading
    statistics, 315–316; name-calling, 315;
    opinions, 120–121; overgeneralizations,
    313; oversimplifications, 312–314;
    undefined abstractions, 313;
    stereotyping, 310–311; syllogisms,
    316–317

McCullers, Carson, 67
MacDonald, Dwight, 207
Manuscript form, 295–296
May, Rollo, 9, 421
Mead, Margaret, 21
Miller, John Hawkins, 440
Modifiers, misplaced, 285

Narration, 71–78
Neihardt, John G., 77
Newman, Dorothy K., 438
Newton, Huey P., 207
Nicolle, Charles, 117–118
Note-taking, 430, 433–437
Nouns, 57

Objective report (*see* Reports)
Objectivity, 118; relation to abstraction,
    121–122; relation to feeling, 182–183;
    relation to imagination, 183–185;
    relation to perception, 117–118
Ogilvy, David, 224
Omissions, in argumentation, 458–459
Opinion, 120–121; evaluation of, 186
Orage, A. E., 175
Organization (*see* Form)
Ott, Karl, 167
Outline, of critical analysis, 342; of formal
    introductions, 257; of literary critique,
    395; of steps in critical reading, 384;
    topic, for research paper, 446–447
Overgeneralizations, 313
Oversimplifications, 312–314

Paley, Grace, 411

Paragraph, checklist for, 465; development of, 220–221; major components, 218; model, 217–219

Parallelism, in sentence structure, 158–160; to achieve coherence, 273–274

Paraphrase, 435–437. *See also* Summarizing

Passive voice (*see* Verbs)

Pastor, Donna, 473

Perception of subject, expository patterns of, 239–246; focusing perceptions, 73–78, 178–181; 4 *C* strategy, 125–128; in character sketch, 82; in factual investigation, 193–198; in personal essay, 11–14, 20–21, 24–26; in scholarly research, 421–426; interviewing, 128–131; relation to clichés, 26–28; relation to critical reading, 322–325, 374–376, 378–384, 430–431, 433–437; relation to critical thinking, 312–317; relation to emotion, 182–183, 310–312, 360; relation to imagination, 183–185; relation to language, 17–20; relation to study of arts, 360–366; relation to objectivity, 117–118; selecting of facts, 181–182

Persig, Robert, 22–23

Person consistency, 286–287

Personal essay, appropriate voice, 37; audience for, 31–32; editing, 53–59; first draft, 40–43; natural voice, 32–37; need for honesty, 24–26; rewriting for connotations, 47–50; rewriting for precision, 46–47; sensory perception, 11–14; use of concretions, 17–20; use of images, 20–21

Peterson, Arthur, 334

Picasso, Pablo, 368

Plagiarism, 435–437

Poetry, basic elements, 382

Pound, Ezra, 367

Precision (*see* Accuracy)

Process analysis, 245

Pronouns, 284–285

Proofreading, how to, 296–297; reasons for, 282–283

Punctuation, colons, 293; commas, 291; in quotations, 293–294; relation to sentence fragment, 287; semicolons, 292

Purpose, 133–134. *See also* Audience

Questioning (in interviews), 129

Quotations, correct use of, 149; editorial insertions, 293; omissions from, 293; punctuation of, 293–294

Rapoport, Roger, 230

Reading aloud, 222

Reasoning, 310. *See also* Logic

Reference librarian, 426

Reference works, 421–422, 424–426

Repetition (to achieve coherence), 271–272

Reporting, 115–116

Reports, audience for, 133–134; evaluating facts for, 131; 5 *W* lead, 139–141; formal voice, 134–135; 4 *C*'s of perception, 125–128; informal voice, 135–136; interviewing, 128–131; need for objectivity, 118–121; organization, 141–144; perception of details, 117–118; purpose, 133–134; quoting, 149–150; summarizing, 148–149; use of first person, 136–137; use of third person, 135

Research, accuracy, need for, 456–458; bibliographic forms, 454–455; bibliography cards, 431–432; card catalog, use of, 426; categorizing notes, 442–443; critical reading, 433; documentation in first draft, 450–451; first draft, 450–451; focusing subject, 422–424; footnote forms, 451–453; forming questions, 423; introduction, 448–450; note-card mechanics, 437; note-taking, 430, 433–437; organizing, 445–446; outlining, 446–447; paraphrasing, 435–437; plagiarism, 435; preliminary steps in, 419–428; thesis statement, 443–445; use of reference tools, 424–426; work schedule, 419–420; working bibliography, 426–428

Revision, 47. *See also* Rewriting

Rewriting, 6–7; for coherence, 268–274; for organization, 146–151; for paragraph development, 217–222; for strong verbs, 98–103; for word choice, 45–50

Rhythm, 155–156; in poetry, 382

Ricciuti, Edward, 135

Rilke, Rainer Maria, 249

Rossi, Alice S., 276

Sack, John, 90

Sagan, Carl, 74

Scene, as perception strategy, 182; elements of, 91–92

Schaeffer, Susan Fromberg, 370

Schultz, Charles, 54, 278, 443

Semicolons, 292

Senses, in the arts, 359–367; use of in writing, 11–14

Sentences, backward sentence, 55; balanced, 160–161; checklist for effectiveness, 464; combining, 161; editing, 54; emphasis, 162–163; fragments, 287–288; parallel, 158–160; periodic, 161–162; rearranging for effect, 221; rhythm, 155–156; variety in, 156–158

Shakespeare, William, 102, 403

Shamansky, Robert N., 334

Shuster, E. G., 353

Silko, Leslie, 404

Simplicity, need for, 277–280

Sources, evaluating worth of, 185–186; documentation of, 194–196; primary, 193–194; secondary, 194

Specific words (*see* Concretions)

Spelling, 290–291

Stafford, William, 364

Steinbeck, John, 103, 248

Stereotypes, 310–311

Subject, as it relates to context, purpose, 133–134; narrowing the subject, 74–77, 178–181, 422–424. *See also* Perception of subject

Subject-verb agreement, 283–284

Subjectivity, compared to objectivity, 118–119

Suggestiveness, in art, 363

Summarizing, 148–149. *See also* Paraphrasing

Tags, 272–273

Tense consistency, 285–286

Terminal note forms, 453

Thesis statement, 255–257; as it restricts subject, 339; examples, 444–445; in research paper, 443–445; relation to larger pattern, 258–259

Thimmesch, Nick, 350

Thomas, Lewis, 39

Thoreau, Henry, 73, 219

Thornley, Wilson R., 91

Titles, 294

Tolstoy, Leo, 146, 207

Tone, 33–34

Topic (*see* Subject)

Topic sentence, 218–221

Transitions, 268–270

Truth, evaluation and interpretation, 185–187

Unifying idea in paragraph, 218–221

Usage, 288–290

Verbs, weak and strong, 98–103

Visual design, 211–212; contrast design, 213–214, 258; dramatic design, 212–213, 259; inverted pyramid, 141–144, 211; literary design, 215, 258

Voice, active and passive, 98–103; appropriateness, 37; colloquial, 36–37; formal, 36–37, 134–135; informal, 35–37, 135–137; natural, 32–35

Walker, Tom, 135

Watergate, 177–178, 183, 186

Waterman, Philip, 223

Weinberg, Nancy, 301

Whittemore, Reed, 438

Whol, Anthony S., 440

Woodward, Bob, 177–178

Woolf, Virginia, 32

Word Choice, abstractions, 17–22; accuracy, 46–50; appropriate diction, 32–37; checklist for, 464; circumlocutions, 279; clichés, 26–28; colloquial usage, 36; connotations, 48; denotations, 46; double negatives, 288; euphemisms, 279; formal usage, 35–37, 134–135; frequently confused words, 288; informal usage, 35–37, 135–137; jargon, 277–280

Wright, James, 386, 392

Writing process, expository methods in, 246–247; mental attitudes in, 42–43; role of failure, 40–42; steps in, 1–8

Zagano, Phyllis, 234

Zweig, Paul, 434

Zwick, Debbie, 277